Windows® Home Server Bible

Greg Kettell and Jennifer Ackerman Kettell

WILEY

Wiley Publishing, Inc.

Windows® Home Server Bible

Published by
Wiley Publishing, Inc.
10475 Crosspoint Boulevard
Indianapolis, IN 46256
www.wiley.com

Copyright © 2008 by Wiley Publishing, Inc., Indianapolis, Indiana

Published by Wiley Publishing, Inc., Indianapolis, Indiana

Published simultaneously in Canada

ISBN: 978-0-470-22956-9

Manufactured in the United States of America

10 9 8 7 6 5 4 3 2 1

For general information on our other products and services or to obtain technical support, please contact our Customer Care Department within the U.S. at (800) 762-2974, outside the U.S. at (317) 572-3993 or fax (317) 572-4002.

Library of Congress Control Number: 2008921212

About the Authors

Greg Kettell is a software engineer with over 20 years experience in managing servers and programming enterprise applications, single- and multi-player games, and internet applications. He's written and contributed to books on HTML, Dreamweaver, ColdFusion, Microsoft Office, Access, and various graphics packages. Greg is a home theater enthusiast and amateur astronomer who misses the Arizona night sky since moving to upstate New York.

Jennifer Ackerman Kettell is a web designer and the author of several books on software applications, graphics, and web design. Some of her titles include *Microsoft Office 2003: The Complete Reference* and *The Absolute Beginners Guide to FrontPage 2003*. Jenn is also a fiction author and avid (some say obsessive) researcher. Greg and Jenn live with their two children, two dogs, and two cats in a house that sometimes seems to be made more of fur than wood and tile. The kids want to add to the menagerie, but shouldn't hold their breath.

This book is dedicated to our children, Zach & Mandy.

Credits

Senior Acquisitions Editor
Stephanie McComb

Project Editor
Beth Taylor

Technical Editor
James Kelly

Copy Editor
Lauren Kennedy

Editorial Manager
Robyn Siesky

Business Manager
Amy Knies

Sr. Marketing Manager
Sandy Smith

Vice President and Executive Group Publisher
Richard Swadley

Vice President and Executive Publisher
Bob Ipsen

Vice President and Publisher
Barry Pruett

Project Coordinator
Lynsey Osborn

Graphics and Production Specialists
Carrie A. Cesavice
Jennifer Mayberry
Ronald Terry

Quality Control Technicians
David Faust
Caitie Kelly
Jessica Kramer

Proofreading
Sossity R. Smith

Indexing
WordCo Indexing Services

Acknowledgments

A book on this scale is always a group effort. In the case of this particular book, we'd first like to thank our editor, Stephanie McComb, for giving us the opportunity to work together. Having your co-author working in the same room with you, taking turns shooting screenshots and cooking dinner for the kids, is a rare treat.

We'd also like to thank Stephanie for bringing us into the Wiley fold. We appreciate the efforts of Beth Taylor and Jim Kelly who worked tirelessly checking for mistakes and helping this book come to fruition. Thanks to our family and friends (and friends who are like family) — Roberta Ackerman, Harriet Levy, Robin Thomas, and Rhonda Henneberry — for their continued support. Thanks to the MAMBA Kings for the very-necessary BHRT break, and may there be many more.

Zach and Mandy deserve special thanks. They've grown up with our assorted deadlines, and they continue to be supportive even when family game night needs to be a quick round of Five Crowns instead of a lengthy Carcassonne challenge. We couldn't have written this book without them!

Contents at a Glance

Contents

Contents

Contents

Contents

Contents

Contents

Introduction

With the introduction of the Windows Home Server operating system and the hardware that has been designed around it, Microsoft and the various OEM vendors have created a system that many people have been waiting for: an easy to use home server solution that goes beyond the more typical NAS systems by leveraging the power of a full-fledged Windows Server operating system. As a complete solution for your backup needs, file sharing, media sharing and remote access, Windows Home Server is truly more than the sum of its parts. The coup de grâce is the add-in framework that promises to usher in a veritable industry of new features, enhancements and tools. These features ensure that Windows Home Server will be desirable platform for everyone from the neophyte who wants a plug-and-play user friendly system all the way to the techno-geek who wants to push it to the limit.

Windows Home Server Bible is intended to be useful for this same spectrum of users. For those looking for plug-and-play, it should provide useful information on choosing Windows Home Server hardware, building a home network, and installing and configuring the server. For advanced users, it provides information on how to take full advantage of the server features, both in the advertised ways and perhaps in a few ways that are somewhat unexpected.

About the Icons

At various points throughout the book you'll see icons interspersed through the text that offer you additional information related to the subject being discussed. It's worth taking the time to read these icons as they often will provide insight into a feature. Sometimes you may even be drawn to the icons and end up reading the text around it to learn more!

NOTE   **Notes present a little bit of additional information of interest for those reading the text. They are often used to highlight something of particular importance.**

TIP   **Tips are provided to help you solve common problems related to the subject under discussion. These are often not altogether obvious solutions, so it pays to read them.**

 **Cross references are navigational aids. They will point you to another chapter in the book that provides more information about a function or feature being discussed. Think of them as hyperlinks without the annoying clicking.**

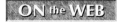 This is a pretty big book, but it can't contain everything. On the Web icons point you to Web resources that provide a wealth of information on the feature being discussed.

 Caution icons are there help keep you out of trouble. Potentially dangerous side effects, pitfalls, and other downsides to doing something are presented to you here.

How This Book Is Organized

The *Windows Home Server Bible* is organized in a way that makes it easy to find all of the chapters relating to a specific feature. Beginning users who are not well versed in building a home network or installing an operating system will find the first parts of the book invaluable. Intermediate users who want to learn how to get the most out of Windows Home Server's features will want to read the middle parts. Finally, advanced users will be able to take things to the next level

Part I: Getting Started

Part I is for those who are just getting started. The chapters in this part provide an introduction to Windows Home Server and guide you through the process of building or buying the hardware you need to create your own home server network.

Part II: Installing and Configuring

With Part II, you start digging in to the features of Windows Home Server. You will find information on how to install the server operating system and how to connect your home computers to the server. You will learn about the console and how it is designed to be the only interface to the server functions that most users will ever see. You will learn how to create user accounts for the members of your household, and how to monitor the server and your home computers for problems.

Part III: File and Printer Sharing

The chapters in Part III are where you start putting Windows Home Server to work, This part teaches you about the shared folder feature and how to make the best use of them. Creating shared folders, controlling who can access them, and accessing them from a variety of different computer types are all covered. In addition, you will learn how to turn your home server into a printer server.

Part IV: Remote Access

Part IV covers the remote access features of Windows Home Server. The ability to access your files from anywhere is an important aspect of Windows Home Server, but it doesn't end there. You also get the ability to access the server console and, in many cases, your home computers, as well.

Part V: Creating Backups

Part V is intended to provide information on a sorely neglected aspect of home computing — the task of backing up your computers. You will learn how to schedule backups for not only your Windows PCs, but for Macs as well. You will also learn how to recover from a catastrophic failure on your home computers with the Recovery CD. Finally, the subject of backing up the server is discussed for those who desire the utmost in protection.

Part VI: Building a Media Hub

Downloaded music and video, digital snapshots, and camcorder videos are a way of life in our technology-obsessed society. Part VI shows you how your Windows Home Server can be the hub of your digital entertainment system, streaming video not only to PCs, but to game systems such as the XBox 360 and the Playstation 3 as well.

Part VII: Advanced Topics

Part VII is for anyone who sees the features of Windows Home Server as a starting point instead of a final destination. In this section, you will learn how to install add-ins, how to automate your home, use webcams, and customize your Home Server website. For the truly creative, the final chapter shows you how to go about creating your own Windows Home Server add-ins.

Part I

Getting Started

Chapter 1

Introducing
Windows Home Server

In today's information technology culture, the term *server* is thrown around quite a bit. Web servers, print servers, proxy servers, file servers — all of these refer to various computer systems and applications that provide a service for others to use.

Defining a Server

The term *server* can refer to several different things. First of all, it can refer to the computer hardware used to run server applications. Unlike desktop and laptop computers that most of us see every day, servers traditionally sit in a data center somewhere with only other servers and the occasional technician to notice them. They quietly offer their applications to users over a network — whether on a corporate, local, or wide area network, or the Internet. Applications typically run on a server machine dedicated to that task. Computers that connect to the server are known as clients.

A server can also refer to a *server operating system*. A server OS usually differs from desktop operating systems in focus, if not in main functionality. While a desktop OS is concerned with providing a rich user interface, graphical abilities, and desktop applications, a server operating system tends to leave all of that stuff out to focus on performance, storage, and tools to make it easier to run server applications. Windows 2000 and 2003, Linux, and Unix are all typically used as server operating systems.

Finally, server can refer to a *server application* that accepts connections from other applications. A few common server applications (not to mention ones that are provided by Windows Home Server) are

3

- **File server:** Many times, people need to be able to share access to the same files, and although it is possible to connect directly to another computer in a peer-to-peer fashion, it is more convenient to share files in a central location that is not dependent on the client computer being constantly available. The term NAS (Network Addressable Storage) has been adopted in recent years to refer to a device used for file server purposes.

- **Web server:** At the other end of the connection your browser makes to a Web site is an application that serves pages. Web servers have become quite complex in recent years, with sophisticated application frameworks generating pages dynamically being the norm.

- **Print server:** Although "personal computer" means that everyone needs one to themselves, the same is not usually true about printers. Print servers serve as an access point for computers to connect to in order to print. Some printers today are network enabled; in essence they have a print server built in.

- **Backup server:** Performing regular backups of important files has been a recommendation since the beginning of the computer era, and unfortunately it is one that is often ignored. A backup server can access files on a client computer and store them locally or on an archival storage medium such as tape. It can be used to schedule and check the status of backups of all client computers in one location.

- **Media server:** A media server is a specialized file server that can stream video, music, and photos to client devices. The advantages, of course, are that multiple users can make use of a single copy of these files, which can be large, without having to tie up space on their local hard drives.

- **Remote access server:** In our increasingly mobile world, it's often necessary to access files and systems remotely. A remote access server, sometimes called a communication server, provides the means for users to connect to the network remotely while also securing the network from unwanted intrusion.

Bringing Home a Server

It wasn't long ago that having even one computer in the home was a rare thing. It's easy to see why — personal computers once cost a great deal more and did a lot less than the machines of today. In addition, prior to the Internet and the World Wide Web becoming household terms, there simply wasn't as much of a pressing need for a computer, and especially not for more than one. Of course, home computers were still useful: they could be used to play games, write letters, do the taxes, and connect via dialup modem to online services and bulletin board systems. Still, they were limited.

Gradually, all of this has changed. As the information technology revolution changed the way offices worked, people became much more comfortable with computers, and in fact, often needed to take their work home with them. The World Wide Web became so ubiquitous that it is now a virtual necessity to have access at home. Parents use the Web for news, shopping, and following the stock markets. They connect to the office using VPNs. Kids do research for homework, play games, and download music. And everyone, it seems, likes to gather on Internet forums and social networking sites, such as MySpace and YouTube.

The rather dizzying drop in prices for computer technology in recent years has meant that it has become practical for many families to own more than one computer. The final piece of the puzzle was affordable broadband connectivity. Now, not only can you get on the Internet without tying up your phone line, but everyone in the house can do it at the same time at speeds that make dialup seem lethargic.

It's not just personal computers, either. In recent years, other network-enabled devices have invaded our homes. Personal video recorders have not only changed the way we watch TV, but they can be controlled over the network and in some cases can even share videos with other devices in the home. Video game consoles have evolved from the single-function devices of yesterday into multipurpose set-top computers. Now they can play incredible games as well as connect to the Internet to download movies, surf the Web, and play multi-player games with others around the world. They can also be used to play video, music, and view photo slide shows.

Along with this explosion of network connectivity has come some fresh chaos. Sharing files can be painful, because connecting directly to another computer can be problematic, especially if the computers are using different operating systems or security. Music is downloaded or ripped from CDs, but then every device in the house that plays that music ends up with a copy of each song, wasting valuable storage space. Sharing files or a printer that is hooked up to one computer depends on that computer being connected to the network at the time. This is becoming a greater problem as people replace their bulky desktop computers with portable notebooks, enabling them to leave the local network behind and work far afield. Backups are rarely if ever done, leaving data vulnerable to hardware failures.

Clearly, the time has come for our homes to be as organized as our offices. When families have two, three, or more personal computers, video game consoles, a printer, PDAs, and other devices connected to the network, creating a central hub that all of these devices can share makes a lot of sense. Although almost any PC running Windows or Linux could act as a server, Microsoft envisioned going one step further by leveraging their expertise in corporate server operating systems to create an easy-to-use product for the home. The result is the newest member of the Windows operating system family, Windows Home Server. This is the Windows operating system that is designed to bring everything together (see Figure 1.1).

FIGURE 1.1

A typical Windows Home Server network

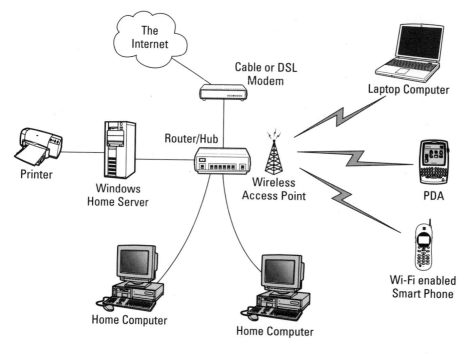

Exploring the Windows Home Server

The first edition of Windows Home Server is based on Windows Server 2003, in particular Windows Server 2003 Standard SP2 (service pack 2). It includes features to make building a server for the home simple and easy. The next section describes what this new breed of server OS can do.

As the second Windows Operating System release in 2007, the approach taken with Windows Home Server could hardy be more divergent from that of its cousin, Windows Vista. Vista was focused on improving the desktop experience with enhanced navigation, new GUI features (Aero), and utilities (the Sidebar). Like its corporate server OS brethren, however, Windows Home Server has been streamlined to provide the functions necessary to act in the role of a file, Web, and application server, while stripping away the fluff of a desktop operating system. 3D graphics, sound, and desktop gadgets have been removed or hidden away so as to not distract from the purpose of acting as a central connectivity hub for all of the computers and other devices in the home. Solitaire is nowhere to be found.

Figuring out the Windows family tree

Windows Home Server is based on the Windows Server line of operating systems. Those not familiar with this line may be interested in learning how these operating systems relate to the desktop-oriented versions of Windows. Figure 1.2 shows the lineage of the major editions of Windows.

FIGURE 1.2

The Windows OS family tree

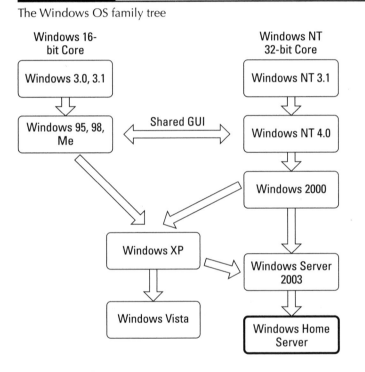

Windows started along two different branches: the 16-bit and 32-bit cores. Starting with XP, the 16-bit core was officially retired and two new product lines were created — the desktop and server lines, both now with 32-bit and 64-bit versions.

Windows desktop operating systems

The 32-bit (and 64-bit) Windows desktop operating systems include products that are familiar to both office and home users:

■ **Windows XP:** XP was designed to replace both Windows 2000 Professional and Windows 98, the long-awaited convergence of the home and business product lines. The 32-bit NT core was finally utilized for the home market, replacing the previous 16-bit

Windows core once and for all. XP Professional, on the other hand, replaced Windows 2000 Professional to become the business desktop OS of choice.

A Graphical User Interface refresh ruled the day with this release, with the new Luna theme taking over from the look introduced way back with Windows 95. Windows XP Media Center Edition is a version of XP including features to allow it to function as an entertainment system hub, with special software called Media Center for TV recording and playback, DVD playback, and photo, video, and music playback in an entertainment center.

- **Windows Vista:** Windows Vista adds a completely new user interface (called Aero), small desktop applications called gadgets, and new connectivity and media center functionality. The Premium and Ultimate versions of Vista include the Media Center functionality from XP Media Center Edition.

Windows server operating systems

In addition to the desktop operating systems, Microsoft has created server-specific versions of Windows with the power and features necessary to act as servers for everyone from large data centers to small businesses. The most common Windows servers in use are

- **Windows 2000 Server:** A hugely successful release, with many new server functions, including Active Directory (providing security and domain server capabilities), and more advanced multimedia and game capabilities, allowing it to make inroads into the home market for advanced users. Windows 2000 was offered in four different server configurations to meet the needs of a wide variety of business needs. Windows 2000 server products are still in wide use in data centers.

- **Widows Server 2003:** Because the new GUI features of XP weren't necessary for servers, the Windows 2000 Server product line was advanced along a divergent path. The classic GUI was retained and features such as themes and audio that are nonessential for a server OS were either eliminated or disabled.

The minimalist philosophy

Rather than add yet another new user interface look, Windows Home Server doesn't even incorporate the XP Luna theme (although it is available — see Chapter 5 for an advanced tip on enabling the XP theme if you really miss it). Instead, Home Server makes do with the classic Windows look it borrows from 2003 Server. The idea is that you won't really miss it. Windows 2003 is designed to be configured and maintained almost exclusively through a new Console application accessible from client PCs.

In fact, some users may never see the desktop. Purchasers of prebuilt Windows Home Server boxes are expected to be able to literally plug and play — plug it into the network, power it on, and it'll automatically configure itself to allow client PCs to connect to it. In many cases, these server boxes may never need to be connected to a monitor or even a keyboard!

However, even though at first glance Windows Home Server may seem simple, don't be fooled. Under the hood is the power of the Windows Server 2003 OS, and that power can be leveraged to extend functionality beyond what can be attained just by using the Console.

Touring the Features

Although Windows Home Server is designed to be easy to use, it is still quite capable out of the box, with a lot of complexity behind it. Later chapters go into more detail, but for now here is a look at the major features and capabilities provided by Windows Home Server.

Understanding the Windows Home Server Console

The Console is a unique application among the Windows Server products, and is the defining characteristic of Windows Home Server. All of the standard configuration and management tasks that can be accomplished with Windows Home Server can be done through this portal.

The major management tasks — configuring computers, maintaining users, setting up shared folders, and monitoring server storage and network health — are accessed with the tabs at the top of the Console. In addition, a button on the right side allows access to the server settings dialog box, where server settings can be configured.

The Console can be accessed from the desktop of the Windows Home Server computer itself. It can also be accessed remotely from any Windows XP or Vista client that you install the Connector software on, presuming the user knows the administration password for the server.

CROSS-REF The Console is discussed in more detail starting in Chapter 7. Installation of the Connector is described in Chapter 10.

Finding out about Shared folders

One of the main functions for any home server operating system is to act as a file server, and Windows Home Server is no exception. The Shared Folders tab on the console, shown in Figure 1.3, is used to view, configure, and manage folders that are being shared.

Shared folders can be set to be duplicated. What this means is that if you have more than one physical hard drive in your server, your duplicated folders are copied to another drive automatically, providing protection from the failure of any single drive.

The following shared folders are available by default:

- **Music:** A folder for sharing music.
- **Photos:** A place to share family photos and downloaded pictures.
- **Videos:** Store home movies, downloaded video, and other such media here.

- **Software:** This folder contains a copy of the Connector and Restore CD software just in case you don't have the CDs handy. It is also the location to copy add-in installation files so that they may be installed on the server.

CROSS-REF The Connector and Restore CDs should be included with Windows Home Server. For information on the Connector, see Chapter 6. For information on using the Restore CD, see Chapter 22.

- **Public:** All users have access to the Public folder by default. This is a convenient place to share documents and other files with other members of your household.

- **Personal folders:** Each user account has a folder created for it automatically. By default, that user is the only one who can access it aside from the server administrator account.

You are not limited to these default shared folders by any means. Additional shared folders can be added and maintained on this tab as well.

CROSS-REF The Shared Folder tab in the console is discussed in more detail in Chapter 7. File sharing is discussed in detail in Chapter 12 and Chapter 13.

FIGURE 1.3

Viewing shared folders in the console

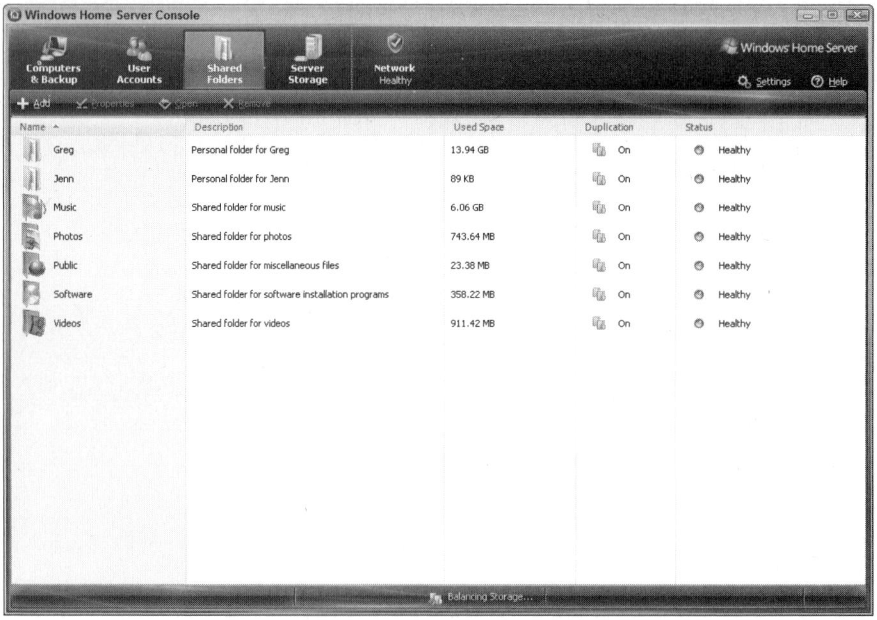

Making backups

Windows Home Server finally allows home users the ability to easily and quickly back up their computers, providing a simple way to address this often neglected task.

The console's Computers & Backup tab, shown in Figure 1.4, is the place where you can choose which folders on each Windows XP and Vista computer you want to back up. You can also see the status of each backup, enable and disable backups, and view backup history, all from the convenience of the console.

You can also use Windows Home Server to back up other operating systems, as long as they can map to a shared folder. Simply point the backup software of your Linux, Macintosh, or other computer capable of accessing Windows shared folders.

CROSS-REF You can learn about Windows Home Server backups in Part V, starting with Chapter 20.

FIGURE 1.4

The Computers & Backup tab lets you see at a glance the status of all computer backups.

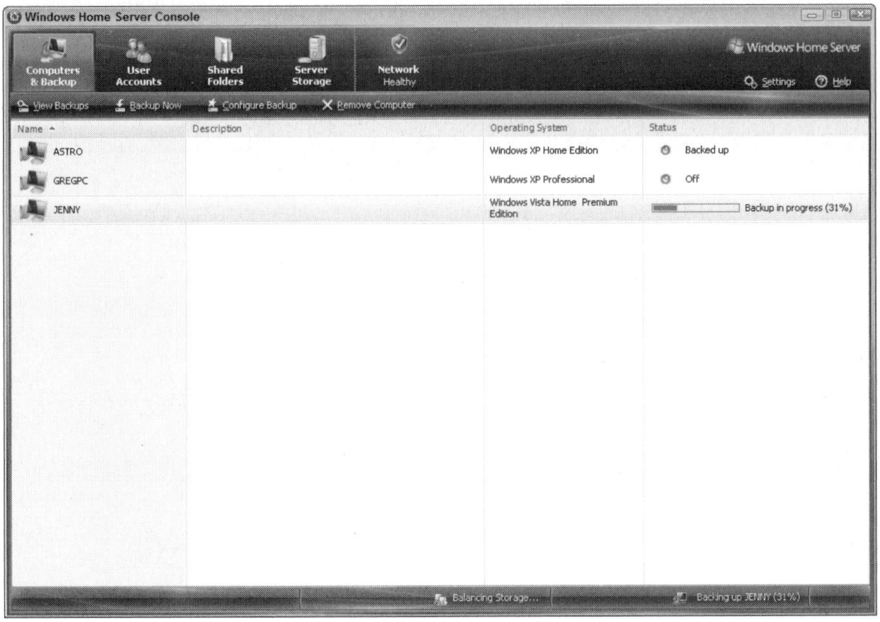

Media library sharing

Now we are getting to the fun stuff. The next feature of Windows Home Server is the ability to stream media to connected computers or other devices such as capable game consoles using Windows Media Connect. Streaming media allows you to keep one copy of your photos, video, and music on the server, and play them from any supported digital media reader (DMR) device.

Although the Shared Folders tab is used to manage the file-level access for all of the photos, music, and video folders, you can also enable streaming for each of those types of media separately, as shown in Figure 1.5.

CROSS-REF Media library sharing is covered in detail starting in Chapter 25.

FIGURE 1.5

You can specify the media folders to share in the Windows Home Server Settings dialog box.

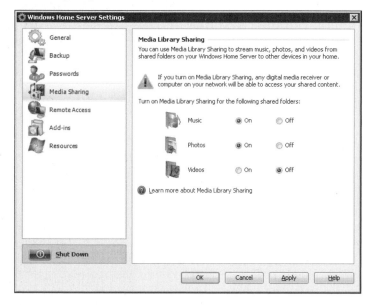

Remote access

With Windows Home Server, you are not limited to accessing your shared files or your home computers from inside your home. You can use the remote access feature to gain access to your shared files and computers from anywhere over the Internet. All you need to do is configure your server with a dynamic domain name (shown in Figure 1.6) and you can access your server's Web site, shared files, and even the desktop of some of the computers on your network. Windows Home Server can even automatically configure your router to direct all Web site access to it.

CROSS-REF   **Remote Access is the subject of Part IV, starting with Chapter 17.**

The Windows Home Server Settings dialog box allows remote access to be configured.

Add-ins

Do you want your home server to do even more? Fortunately, you are not limited to the functionality provided by Windows Home Server itself. Microsoft has included an add-in facility, as shown in Figure 1.7, which allows you to install third-party extensions that are specifically designed to work with Windows Home Server. Add-ins can be installed and uninstalled directly from the Console. The add-ins themselves are managed from the console: an add-in that requires user configuration adds a tab to the configuration utility.

Even though Windows Home Server is a new operating system, it seems to have already inspired a wave of creativity among users, and new add-ins are being created and released all the time.

CROSS-REF   **Some popular add-ins are discussed in detail in Chapter 32. If you are a programmer, you may want to develop your own add-ins. See Chapter 36 for an example.**

FIGURE 1.7

Add-ins are managed from the console.

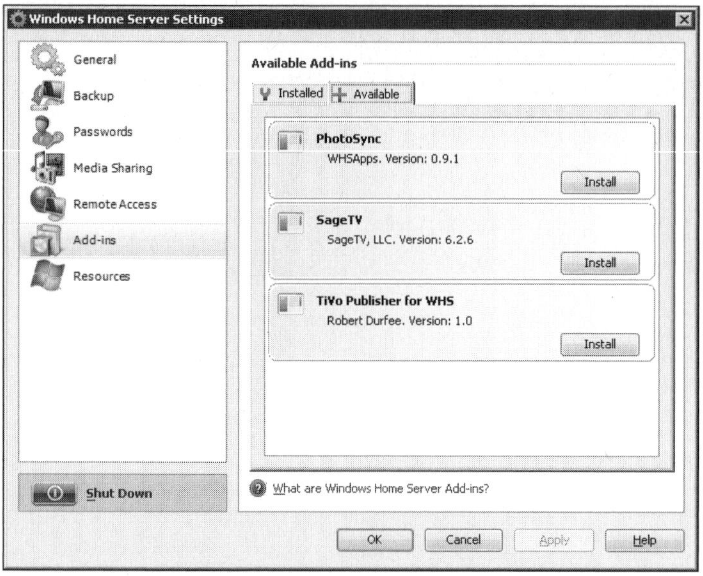

Automating storage maintenance

It's easy to expand your server when you add new devices that need to be backed up. When you add a new hard drive to the server, either internally or externally through an eSATA or USB port, Windows Home Server recognizes it when you reboot and allows you to format it automatically and add it to the total pool of storage. There is no need to worry about drive letter assignment.

CROSS-REF See Chapter 3 for information on adding storage to your server.

The Server Storage tab on the console, shown in Figure 1.8, is where you can see at a glance how much of your server's storage is allocated and for what purpose. From here you can also add, remove, and repair hard drives.

FIGURE 1.8

The console shows you at a glance how storage is allocated on the server.

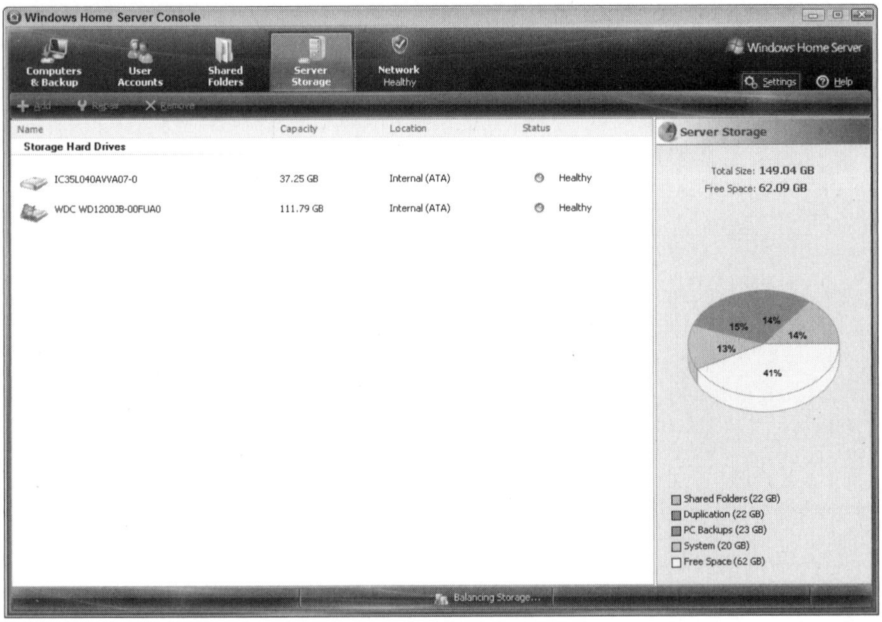

Buying or Building

By now you may be wondering how you can take advantage of Windows Home Server yourself. There are essentially two ways to go about it. One is to purchase a complete ready-to-go server with the OS preinstalled and configured, and the other is to build a computer or repurpose an existing computer for the job.

The complete solution

In keeping with the desire to make Windows Home Server the server operating system for everyone, Microsoft is teaming up with a number of ISVs (integrated software vendors) and OEM partners to build server systems with Windows Home Server preinstalled and configured. At the time of this writing the list of OEMS include such companies as HP, Gateway, Lacie, Medion, Fujitsu-Siemens, and Iomega.

The expectation is that in most cases you will be able to plug one of these devices into your network, and then simply install the Connector software onto each client on the network. The connector will automatically find the server on the network and allow it to be managed through the console. It may be a cliché, but quite literally a plug and play experience.

CROSS-REF   See Chapter 2 for information on features of turnkey Windows Home Server systems.

The DIY option

If you have an older computer or laptop lying around gathering dust, you may have the ability to run Windows Home Server already. The hardware requirements are not very stringent. Likewise, if you have built a computer from parts before, you already have the skills necessary to build a machine to act as a server.

To satisfy the do-it-yourselfer, Windows Home Server is available in a System Builder edition which will be available through many online retailers, generally the same ones that supply OEM system builder versions of Windows now.

CROSS-REF   Chapter 3 goes into detail on what you need to do in order to build your own Windows Home Server machine.

Summary

Windows Home Server is a brand-new operating system from Microsoft that can simplify and improve your digital lifestyle. With many households having more than one computer or other device capable of accessing shared files, streaming media and the Web, the time is right for a solution to address the increasing needs of a connected home in the same way that offices have done for several years.

Although there are other ways to achieve the server functionality that Windows Home Server provides, the plug and play nature of the system along with the power of Windows Server behind it is a pretty potent solution that should not only be able to meet the current needs of the majority of home users, but also grow with them in the future.

Chapter 2

Choosing Windows Home Server Hardware

IN THIS CHAPTER

Building versus buying

Understanding hardware requirements

Using an old PC

Choosing from OEM manufacturers

Are you the type of person who just wants to buy something and just have it work without too much fuss? Or are you the type who likes to build things from scratch and enjoy the satisfaction of tweaking them to make them work better? Whichever type of person you are, there's a Windows Home Server option for you. You can buy a system that has Windows Home Server preinstalled, with all of the hardware that you need to make effective use of it. Or, if you are the do-it-yourself type, you can build a computer from component parts and install Windows Home Server on it, thereby getting exactly the features you want. You can also reuse a computer that you may already have but stopped using because you thought it was obsolete. Given Windows Home Server's modest hardware requirements, older computers can have a new lease on life.

Understanding Hardware Requirements

Compared to the horsepower required to run recent desktop versions of Windows such as Vista, the hardware requirements for Windows Home Server are pretty modest. This makes it ideal for the do-it-yourself enthusiast who wants to either build a Windows Home Server system from scratch or reuse an older computer that isn't suitable for the newer desktop operating systems.

CPU requirements

The minimum CPU for Windows Home Server is a Pentium III 1 GHz (gigahertz) processor, although a Pentium 4 or AMD x64 CPU or newer is recommended. You can get away with such a modest CPU speed because a lot of the CPU-intensive tasks that a standard computer would perform (number crunching, video playback and games) are simply not done on a server.

Of course, if you are building a new computer, you should choose a faster processor, but you don't have to spring for the fastest you can find. If you would like to save money, go for a bang-for-the-buck budget CPU such as an AMD Sempron or an Intel Celeron. They provide plenty of horsepower for Windows Home Server, cost less, consume less power, and generate less heat.

Hard drive requirements

A single 80 GB (gigabyte) hard drive is the minimum requirement. If you intend to use your server for file storage, particularly for backups, music, photos, and video, you will definitely want more than this. Hard drives are very inexpensive now; at the time of this writing you can find 500 GB SATA hard drives for about $100, so this is one area where you shouldn't have to skimp. If you are purchasing new hard drives, 7200 RPM (revolutions per minute) drives or faster are recommended.

Storage isn't limited to internal drives. If your computer supports external USB 2.0, FireWire, or eSATA hard drives, you can make use of those as well, making laptops and other small footprint computers a viable choice for Windows Home Server use.

> **TIP** Whatever you decide as far as total storage, you should plan to get at least two hard drives. This will allow you to make use of the folder duplication feature of shared folders, providing protection of critical files in case one of your hard drives bites the dust.

Network requirements

In order for Windows Home Server to connect to your home network, your system will, of course, require a network connection. For the most part you will probably want to utilize the network port on your motherboard, assuming it has one. If you do, you should make sure that it's at least as fast as the other devices on your network. If you are purchasing a motherboard for Windows Home Server, it is recommended that you get one that has Gigabit Ethernet built in. Even if other devices on your network are 100 megabit or even slower, eventually you are going to want to maximize the speed of your home network. Choosing Gigabit Ethernet now means you will have one less device to update in the future.

If your motherboard doesn't have integrated Ethernet, you can purchase an internal Peripheral Component Interconnect (PCI) or PCI Express card to provide that function. If the computer you are using is a laptop or doesn't have internal PCI slots, you have the option of using a Personal Computer Memory Card International Association (PCMCIA) or Universal Serial Bus (USB) network adapter.

 While most Ethernet network adapters can be used for Windows Home Server, wireless network adapters can't. Wi-Fi is not supported with the initial release of the operating system.

Video card requirements

You don't need a fancy 3-D video card for Windows Home Server. Almost any video card that supports 1024 x 768 or higher resolution will work. If your motherboard includes integrated video, by all means use that in order to save a slot and reduce power consumption. If it doesn't, almost any PCI or Accelerated Graphics Port (AGP) video card will do the trick.

DVD ROM drive

The Windows Home Server System Builder edition is provided on a single DVD ROM drive; therefore one is generally required for installation. It is possible to use an external USB DVD ROM drive if your motherboard supports it.

CROSS-REF Chapter 3 goes into more detail regarding your hardware options when building a Windows Home Server system from components.

Choosing Windows Home Server Systems

At the time of this writing, already a large number of computer manufacturers have Windows Home Server based systems, and there are more being announced all the time. While we can't go into great detail on all of the solutions on the market, we provide an overview of some of them so that you can get some idea on the type of system that might fit your needs best.

HP MediaSmart Server

One of the biggest names in computer products is one of the first out of the gate with a Windows Home Server solution. The HP MediaSmart Server, shown in Figure 2.1, offers some features that go above and beyond the standard Windows Home Server experience. The server is fairly diminutive, at 5.5 inches wide by 9.8 inches tall by 9.2 inches deep, considering the amount of storage it can provide. The MediaSmart Server takes the Windows Home Server headless concept to heart: The system includes no monitor port whatsoever. Any maintenance you do using Remote Desktop must be done using Remote Desktop.

FIGURE 2.1

The HP MediaSmart Server packs a lot into a compact package.

Picture courtesy of Hewlett-Packard.

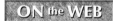 **ON the WEB**   You can find HP's product information Web site for the MediaSmart Server product at `http://h71036.www7.hp.com/hho/447351-0-0-225-121.html`.

The HP EX470 andEX475 MediaSmart Server comes in a black "micro-tower" style case with room for oodles of internal storage, along with ports for more external storage if desired. The basic specs are as follows:

- 1.8 GHz AMD Sempron 64-bit processor.
- 512 MB of installed DDR2 RAM.
- 500 GB hard drive (EX4700) or 2x500 GB hard drives (EX475). Drives are 7200 RPM. Two hard drives are required for the folder duplication feature.
- Four internal drive bays (with one or two used by the included drive) for expanding storage using SATA I or SATA II hard drives. The drive bays use slide-out trays for easy drive expansion.
- Four USB 2.0 ports (one on the front and three on the back) for additional storage or for other devices such as printers.
- 10/100/1000 MBit/second Ethernet (Gigabit).
- One eSATA port for connection to an external hard drive.

The HP MediaSmart server comes with several software additions to the Windows Home Server base operating system to enhance media sharing, including the Control Center, HP Photo Webshare, customized Remote Access, and a feature to make it easy to sync and stream iTunes music.

Control Center

The HP Control Center software, shown in Figure 2.2, runs on your home computers and provides enhanced connectivity to your media shared folders and to custom MediaSmart features such as the Webshare.

FIGURE 2.2
_____

The MediaSmart Control Center is a custom interface to your media shared folders and the HP Photo Webshare.

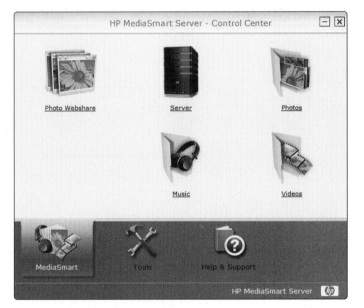

HP Photo Webshare

The HP Photo Webshare extends the Windows Home Server Web server capabilities. The software allows you to easily share your digital photos with others over the Web through your homerserver.com domain.

In addition, the HP Photo Webshare includes links to the Snapfish service where you can order prints, calendars, mouse pads, and other items with your photos on them.

ON the WEB   You can find more information on the Snapfish service at www.snapfish.com.

Tranquil PC Limited T7-HSA

Tranquil PC Limited is a UK-based manufacturer of "green PCs,, which are designed for ultra-low power consumption and unobtrusive size. This combination is ideal for a Windows Home Server platform: its small device can to fit into virtually any décor, while its low power consumption works well for 24/7 operation. The T7-HSA, shown in Figure 2.3, measures 2.2 inches wide by 9.1 inches tall by 9 inches deep and consumes 24 watts of power.

FIGURE 2.3

The Tranquil T7-HSA is a compact low-power Windows Home Server solution.

Picture courtesy of Tranquil PC Limited.

ON the WEB   Tranquil's product page for the T7-HSA is located at `www.tranquilpc-shop.co.uk/acatalog/T7-HSA.html`. The T7-HSA user's manual can be found at `http://tranquilpc.files.wordpress.com/2007/09/t7-hsa-manual2.pdf`.

Due to its diminutive size, the T7-HSA server can only support one internal hard drive. It is recommended that an external hard drive be used with this system to allow for folder duplication. It offers expandability in the form of external USB ports. This device is a headless unit with no monitor port. The system specs are

- 1.5 GHz via CPU consuming 12W
- 512 MB RAM
- 500 GB SATA hard drive or 1 terabyte (TB) Western Digital GreenPower drive

- Four USB 2.0 ports for external hard drive connectivity
- Fanless operation due to a TranCool cooling system
- 12V DC power
- 10/100/1000 MBit/sec Ethernet (Gigabit)

Medion MD 90110

Medion's MD 90110 Home Server, shown in Figure 2.4, is actually a range of systems with varying CPU and storage capabilities. Like the HP MediaSmart Server, the Medion MD 90110 servers are in a micro-tower configuration with four internal drive bays.

Medion promises to include additional PacketVideo Connect software to allow media sharing on portable devices such as mobile phones.

FIGURE 2.4

The Medion MD 90110 comes in a micro-tower configuration.

Picture courtesy of Medion.

 Medion's worldwide Web site is www.medion.com. Their USA site is at www.medionusa.com.

Specifications for this system are

- AMD Sempron 1200LE 1.9 GHz, or AMD X2 BE 2300, or Intel Mobile Celeron
- 1 GB DDR2 SDRAM
- 2x250 GB (basic) or 2x500 GB (premium) SATA hard drive storage
- Screwless slide-out internal drive trays for easy expansion
- Four internal drive bays (two available)
- Four USB 2.0 ports on the rear
- One eSATA port on the rear for external hard drive expansion
- 10/100/1000 MBit/sec Ethernet (Gigabit)

Velocity Micro

A stylish entrant into the Windows Home Server hardware race is Velocity Micro. This server, shown in Figure 2.5, uses an Intel Conroe based processor, and has all of the standard goodies such as SATA II, eSATA for external storage, and Gigabit Internet. An optional drive expansion box is also available. Detailed specifications are not available at the time of this writing.

FIGURE 2.5

Velocity Micro's Windows Home Server device comes in a stylish case that can be oriented horizontally or vertically.

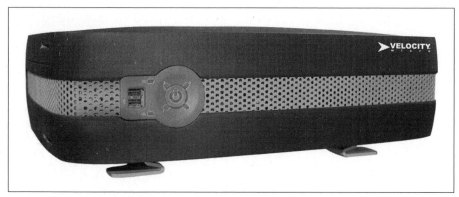

Picture courtesy of Velocity Micro

Others

Several other manufacturers have entered the fray as well, promising systems based around Windows Home Server. Among these are such stalwart brands as Fujitsu-Siemens, Gateway, Iomega, and LaCie. While details on their Windows Home Server based products are sparse at the time of this writing, it is clear that there is no shortage of options for those who wish to purchase a complete Windows Home Server solution.

Summary

Whether you prefer to build your own or purchase ready-to-go Original Equipment Manufacturer (OEM) systems, there is a Windows Home Server option that is right for you. Microsoft has recognized that many of you will want to take advantage of reusing old hardware or building a system from scratch. The System Builder edition of Windows Home Server allows for this, as well as for custom PC builder shops to create systems to your specifications, which means that you aren't just limited to what the OEM manufactures decide you need.

On the other hand, the plethora of OEM solutions for Windows Home Server makes that an attractive option as well. Windows Home Server systems are and will be available in a large number of form factors to fit your décor and storage space. As systems designed for server duties, they are oriented around the features that matter most in that regard — storage and storage expandability, compact size, and reduced power requirements for 24/7 operation.

If you choose to go the system builder route, the next chapter will give you ideas on options for the computer components you can choose from in order build the perfect server for your needs.

Chapter 3

Building a Windows Home Server

You're handy with a screwdriver. You've installed new hard drives and video cards into your PCs before. Maybe you've even put together PCs from parts. You're not alone — self-assembled computers are quite popular, and building your own is a surefire way of knowing exactly what components are going into it.

The build-your-own option is terrific for creating a Windows Home Server machine. While it is not always as economical as buying a complete system, you do have the opportunity to choose exactly the hardware you want, with the features you need.

Perhaps you even have an old desktop or laptop computer stashed away in the basement or in a closet, with specs that meet or almost meet Windows Home Server's fairly modest requirements. Why not reuse it as your Home Server machine? Sure, it may not have the cool, updated looks and sleek design of some of the dedicated Windows Home Server systems available, but for only the price of the operating system itself and perhaps a hard drive or two, you can have a machine that is just as capable as its flashier commercial brethren.

Choosing Components

Building a server from component parts lets you choose exactly what you want. Do you want a compact server that you can hide away somewhere? Or do you want a large tower machine that you can cram full of hard drives? Perhaps you would be happy with something in between. Either way, you are likely to find an option to suit you.

The heart of your computer is the Central Processing Unit (CPU) and motherboard. In essence, this is the computer itself. There are an almost unlimited number of options in terms of computer motherboard and CPU combinations to choose from, and with Windows Home Server, the form factor is probably one of the most important things to consider.

The following motherboard form factors are commonplace:

- **ATX:** The Advanced Technology Extended (ATX) specification has been in wide use since the mid 1990s. This standard replaced the original AT specification developed by IBM and incorporates a number of enhancements, most notably a standardized back panel to contain common ports and jacks. There are ATX motherboards available that support Intel and AMD processors. Figure 3.1 shows a typical AMD based ATX motherboard.

- **Micro ATX:** This is a smaller form factor than ATX, designed for more compact systems. The main limitation as compared to full-size ATX motherboards is a reduced number of expansion slots (typically only 2 or 3). This can be an ideal form factor for Windows Home Server, however, as expansion slots are not as necessary given the proliferation of Universal Serial Bus (USB) and Serial Advanced Technology Attachment (SATA) connectors for hard drive and peripheral connections.

- **BTX:** This was developed by Intel as a replacement for the ATX standard, and offers a number of improvements, such as better airflow. While this standard has gained some support among prebuilt system manufacturers, it hasn't caught on with do-it-yourselfers.

- **Mini ITX:** This ultra-small form factor (17 cm by 17 cm) was created by Via technologies for ultra-compact applications, and Intel and AMD have gotten into the act as well. Although too small to contain standard PCI expansion slots, these boards are usually loaded with enough SATA and USB ports that expandability is not a great concern. These are an intriguing option for those looking to create a diminutive box. These boards usually have an embedded CPU that cannot be replaced.

ON the WEB You can find a good information resource concerning motherboard form factors and how to choose one at www.formfactors.org.

Many motherboards come complete with integrated components that provide video, networking, audio, and other functions. Integrated video and networking are especially nice to have for server use, as it means you won't have to purchase additional add-in cards for these functions.

The choice of CPU is surprisingly not as critical, as Windows Home Server will run well on anything from a Pentium 3 on up. A top-of-the-line CPU may sound intriguing, but you are not likely to notice much of a difference in performance on your server. Our recommendation is that you shop mainly based on cost and power considerations. A processor that is designed for mobile applications will use less power and generate less heat, so you can put them in smaller enclosures with smaller power supplies and less strict cooling factors.

Intel and AMD are the two main vendors of the type of x86 compatible CPUs that Windows Home Server, like all versions of Windows, runs on.

Intel CPUs such as the Pentium 4, Core, Core 2, Core 2 Duo, and Celeron processors (other than the original Pentium 2 based versions) are all good choices to use. The Core architecture CPUs are more powerful than the older Pentium 4, however in terms of price you can find good deals on the older processors and so you shouldn't rule them out. Celeron processors are the budget CPU line, and can also work well for Windows Home Server use.

AMD CPUs include the Athlon (Athlon XP, Athlon 64, and Athlon 64 X2), designed to compete with the Pentium line from Intel; the Sempron line, designed to compete with the Celeron; and the Turion line, which competes with Intel's Core series. As with Intel processors, the budget CPU line (Sempron) is a reasonable choice for Windows Home Server use.

FIGURE 3.1

A typical microATX motherboard with Pentium 4 CPU

Putting It Together

In addition to a CPU and motherboard, you will need some additional components in order to assemble a computer. The following list should give you some idea:

- **RAM:** You will need at least 512 MB of RAM for Windows Home Server. More can enhance performance in some respects. We recommend that you install at least 1 GB (gigabyte) of RAM in your server. Purchase the type recommended in your motherboard manual.

- **CPU fan:** If you purchase an Original Equipment Manufacturer (OEM) version of a CPU, you will typically need to get a CPU fan to go with it. Retail editions of CPUs, as well as motherboard/CPU combo deals, tend to include the fan.

- **Network card:** If your motherboard doesn't have integrated networking, or it is slower than you would like, you will need a network interface card (NIC). While 100 megabit network cards are commonplace these days, gigabit Ethernet is starting to take over for new installations. Plan for the future and get a gigabit-capable card or motherboard.

- **Video card:** Fortunately, you don't need a super fast 3-D accelerated video for server use. Windows Home Server is designed to be used remotely, so chances are good that you will rarely see the server's desktop anyway. This is one area where you can skimp. We strongly suggest that you choose a motherboard with integrated video.

- **Case and power supply:** Your choice of a case is largely dependent on the motherboard form factor you choose (or vice versa), and the internal expansion you desire. If you want a tiny compact server, look into micro ITX-based cases and designs. Micro ATX cases are another good choice for fairly compact systems. Choose a power supply depending on the recommendations from your CPU manufacturer. Go beefier than recommended if you plan to add more than a couple hard drives.

- **Monitor, keyboard, and mouse:** Although Windows Home Server is designed to run headless, without a monitor, keyboard, and mouse, they are necessary for installing the OS itself. Unless you want to dedicate these components to the server, you can just temporarily borrow them from another computer while you install the OS. If you do decide to purchase these components specifically for the server, this is another area where you can skimp, as you won't be using them often.

- **Floppy drive:** These are not as useful as they once were, thanks to USB flash drives. Don't bother unless you happen to have one lying around or you know you'll need drivers during installation.

- **DVD-ROM drive:** Windows Home Server's installation disk is a DVD-ROM, so you can't really get away from this requirement. It's not strictly necessary to keep the drive connected permanently once the OS is installed, though.

- **Windows Home Server Operating System:** You'll need to purchase the OS. The best source is your favorite online computer vendor.

Building a computer is not difficult, but there are some tips to keep in mind as you assemble the system:

- **Watch out for static electricity.** You can easily fry sensitive computer components when you touch them if they're not properly grounded. Touch the metal case before handling any components, or better yet use a grounding strap. Stay away from carpeting if at all possible!

- **Read the installation instructions all the way through.** Yes, sometimes these are badly translated and hard to understand, but it's better than guessing.

- **Work slowly and deliberately.**

ON the WEB Complete information on how to assemble a computer is beyond the scope of what this book can provide. However, there are many Web and book resources that can help. `www.diylife.com/2007/08/10/introduction-building-a-computer-from-scratch` provides one such recent tutorial. If you are looking for a book, take a look at *Building a PC For Dummies* by Mark L. Chambers (Wiley, 2005).

Managing Storage

Perhaps the most important consideration for Windows Home Server is storage. Many of the features of Windows Home Server — file server, media streaming, and backups — revolve around providing a large central storage repository.

While there are several standard interfaces for hard-drive connectivity in desktop computers, these three are most common:

- **Parallel ATA (PATA):** ATA, or Advanced Technology Attachment, was the most popular method for interfacing with a hard drive from the 1990s through the mid-2000s. This interface, also known as IDE (Integrated Device Electronics), is still widely available. It became known as Parallel ATA as a way to distinguish it from the newer Serial ATA standard. This system uses a wide, flat ribbon cable to connect one or two hard drives or optical drives per controller.

- **Serial ATA (SATA):** This is a newer standard that has a number of benefits over the older parallel ATA (PATA) interface. Chief among them are thinner cables, faster transfer speeds, and hot swap capability. For new systems, this is the recommended hard drive standard to use. An external version, called eSATA, is also available. Figure 3.2 shows a 3.5 inch SATA hard drive and cable.

- **SCSI:** The Small Computer System Interface (SCSI), often pronounced as *skuzzy*, is another popular peripheral interface. While popular in server-class machines, it never really took off for the desktop computer market as ATA provides a less expensive option.

CAUTION While PATA and SATA drives are supported natively, SCSI installation can be a bit trickier. While SCSI hard drives are popular in server computers and will work with Windows Home Server in many cases, they usually require a controller card with custom drivers. In Chapter 5, you learn how to install Windows Home Server when third-party storage drivers are required.

The 3.5 inch SATA hard drives give you the best bang for the buck for increasing storage.

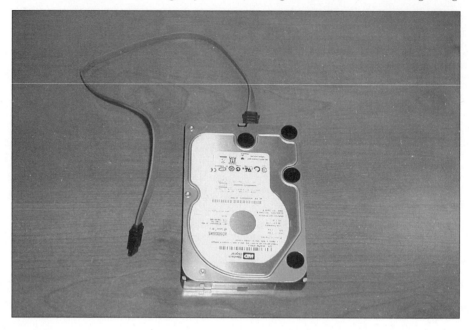

Sizing up your needs

Hard drives have dropped in price significantly in recent years. At the time of this writing, you can find 500 GB SATA hard drives for around $100. For a mere $200 or so, you can obtain a full terabyte of storage! At these prices, storage is definitely not an area that you should skimp on.

Windows Home Server works best with multiple hard drives. This is due to a feature called *folder duplication*, which ensures that files in shared folders are duplicated on another hard drive in order to ensure full recoverability in the event that one of the drives fails. It is strongly recommended that you take advantage of this capability and purchase two hard drives for your server.

Adding additional storage

One of the ways in which Windows Home Server makes your life easier is in dealing with server storage. All hard drives that are installed on the server are automatically combined into one large storage pool, with only 20 GB reserved for the system partition. It's also easy to add storage later. Once a drive is installed, it can be added in the Server Storage tab, as shown in Figure 3.3.

FIGURE 3.3

Server storage is easy to manage in the Console.

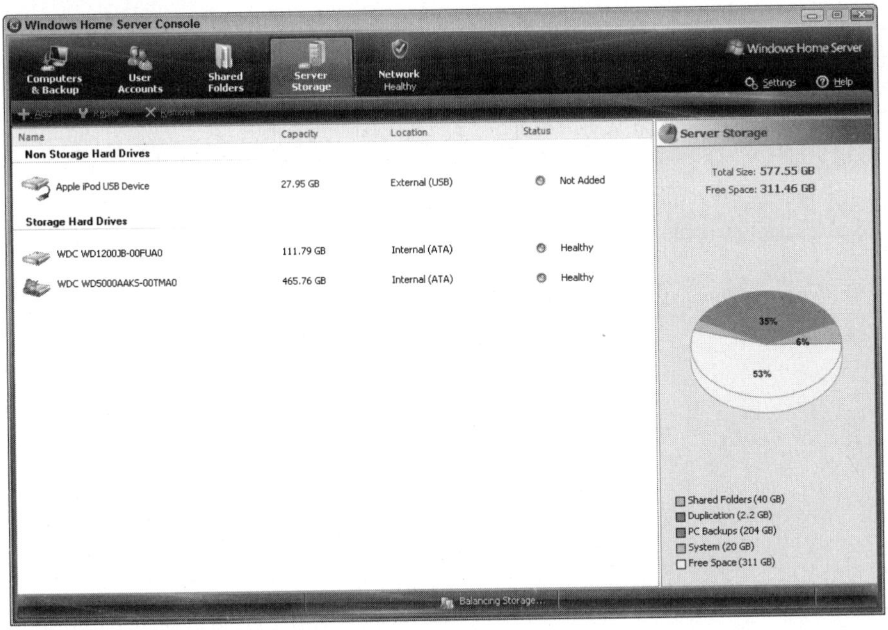

Follow these steps to configure a new hard drive in the Console:

1. **Install the drive.** This can be either an internal (SATA, PATA or SCSI) or external (IEEE 1394, USB 2.0 or eSATA) drive. External drives can be installed with the server powered on (hot swap).

2. **Power up Windows Home Server.**

3. **Launch the Console from either the server's desktop, or from a connected computer.**

4. **Click the Server Storage tab.** A page showing all of the drives attached to the computer and their current status is shown as in Figure 3.4.

5. **Your newly added hard drive is shown with a status of Not Added.** Select it by clicking it.

6. **Click the Add button on the toolbar to launch the Add a Hard Drive Wizard, shown in Figure 3.4.**

7. **Click Next.**

8. **You are given a warning indicating that all existing files on the drive will be lost.** Click Finish to complete adding the drive.

 **CAUTION**   While hard drives are easy to add using an external interface, do not just unplug the drive to remove it. You must first remove the drive from the storage pool in the Console.

FIGURE 3.4

Use the Add a Hard Drive Wizard to add to your server's storage pool.

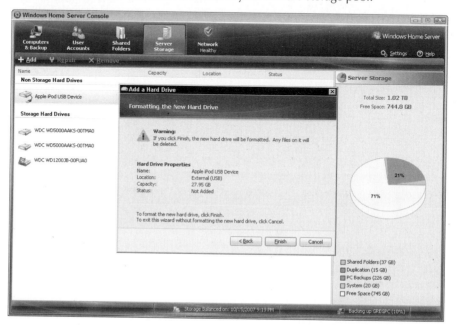

Removing a hard drive

You can remove hard drives from the storage pool almost as easily as you can add them. The biggest concern when removing a drive is that any files stored on it be safely moved to another drive first. This requires two things. First, the other drives must contain enough free space to hold all of the files. And second, the Remove a Hard Drive Wizard needs to be run before you physically remove the drive. Follow these steps to safely remove a drive:

1. Log on to the Console.
2. Click the Server Storage tab.
3. Select the drive you wish to remove.
4. **Click the Remove button on the toolbar.** This launches the Remove a Hard Drive Wizard.
5. Click Next.
6. **If there are any files open in the shared folders, you are given a warning to close them first.** Make sure all shared folder access has ceased before clicking Next.

7. **You'll be warned of any files that will be lost with the removal.** This can include folders that are not marked for folder duplication as well as backups that another drive doesn't have room for, as shown in Figure 3.5.

> **TIP** If you're removing a hard drive in order to install a larger one, add the new one to the storage pool first. This allows the Remove a Hard Drive Wizard to safely copy files from the drive to be removed.

8. **Click Finish to complete the wizard.** The drive removal can take a while if there are a lot of files to be moved.

9. **Once the status shows in the Console as Not Added, you can safely remove the drive.** Power the computer down before removing an internal hard drive.

FIGURE 3.5

The Remove a Hard Drive Wizard moves files off of a drive so that it can be safely removed.

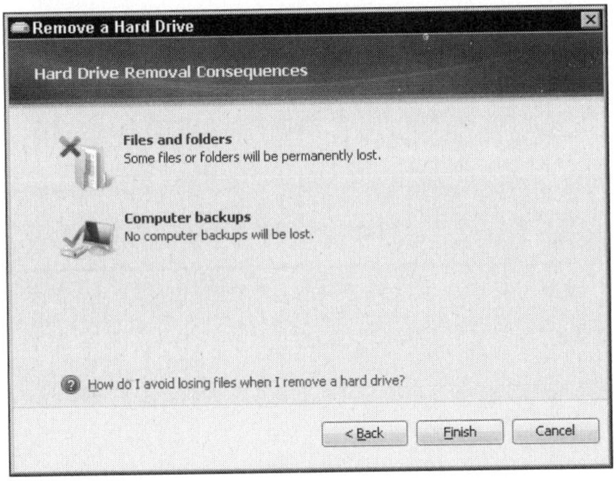

> **CROSS-REF** This is just a taste of what you can easily accomplish in the Console. To learn your way around the Console and see all of its features, see Chapter 7.

Upgrading an Old Computer

If you're anything like us, you have lots of old computer parts and perhaps a complete computer that is for the most part obsolete, and has depreciated in value to the point that it's just not worth selling. This is a fact of life for anyone who has been at this for a while — computers become obsolete quickly, and although you can keep upgrading them, eventually it gets to the point that purchasing a new computer would be more cost-effective than continuing to fight the aging process.

Reusing a desktop

It can make sense to use an old desktop computer, such as the one shown in Figure 3.6, for your Windows Home Server platform. Many of them come in a tower or mini tower configuration, which allows for the addition of a number of internal hard drives and optical drives. Some things to keep in mind when deciding whether or not to reuse a desktop include:

■ **CPU:** It must be a Pentium III class or newer CPU. Pentium 4 class or newer is recommended.

■ **RAM:** 512 MB is required, but most compatible computers can be expanded to this much or more.

■ **Hard drives:** Storage capabilities have skyrocketed recently, so much so that computers from just a couple years ago have perhaps a quarter of the typical amount of storage as newer computers. This is one area where you might consider upgrading.

■ **Video:** If this computer has a fancy 3D-accelerated video card, pull it out! That is, if the motherboard has integrated video that you can use instead. Video capabilities are generally wasted on a server, it's better to have fewer things that can break.

FIGURE 3.6

That old beige box can have a new life as your server. Here's one of ours.

Reusing a laptop

At first thought, you might not think an old laptop would make a good Windows Home Server platform. In reality, it can be a great choice for several reasons:

- **Energy efficiency:** Laptops tend to use much less power than typical desktop computers, often one-third as much power or less.

- **Compact size:** If you want to stash your Windows Home Server out of the way, the smaller form factor of a laptop will give you more options.

- **Built-in monitor and keyboard:** Windows Home Server is designed to work in a "headless" mode, without a monitor, keyboard, or mouse. However, sometimes it is nice to be able to check on a computer's status directly, especially if network problems are preventing it from being seen or accessed remotely.

Figure 3.7 shows Windows Home Server in the process of being installed on a laptop computer.

FIGURE 3.7

An older laptop can make a very nice Windows Home Server platform.

There are some downsides, of course. As closed systems, laptops don't have the expansion and upgrade capabilities of a desktop. Although in many cases, you can upgrade the hard drive, you can't yet find 2.5 inch drives with the capacity that is now available in 3.5 inch sizes that desktops use, and the price per GB is higher.

That's not to say that laptops aren't expandable — with expansion options including USB, IEEE 1394, and PC Cards, you can configure a laptop-based Windows Home Server that is just as capable as bigger desktops.

TIP Remove the battery! Your laptop should run fine connected to AC power only. Removing the battery will improve power efficiency by not having to keep the battery topped off all of the time. It may seem obvious, but your server is going to stay put, right?

Upgrading storage

If your laptop's hard drive is less than the required 80 GB, you will want to upgrade it. The standard laptop hard drive size is 2.5 inches, and as with desktop drives, they come in both parallel ATA (PATA) and serial ATA (SATA) versions. Be sure to check before you buy a replacement drive! Most Windows Home Server capable laptops will have one or the other, and upgrading is usually as easy as removing a screw or two and sliding the drive out, as shown in Figure 3.8.

FIGURE 3.8

Expanding a laptop hard drive can be as easy as just sliding it into place.

Because the process of installing Windows Home Server wipes out any data that is on a hard drive anyway, you don't have to worry about saving any data off of the old hard drive. Just plug in the new one and install.

> **TIP** Are you wondering what to do with that old laptop hard drive? Simply purchase an inexpensive USB enclosure for it, and you'll have portable storage that you can take anywhere. You can even add it to Windows Home Server's storage pool.

If you are looking for more storage than a 2.5 inch hard drive can give you, you're not limited to the internal disk. Many laptops offer USB or IEEE 1394 (aka FireWire) ports that you can use to attach to an external hard drive, demonstrated in Figure 3.9.

If you are planning to use a USB drive, make sure that the computer supports the USB 2.0 specification. Many laptops that are more than a few years old will only support the 1.0 or 1.1 USB specs, and are, therefore, not suitable to use with external hard drives.

If your laptop has a PC Card (formerly known as PCMCIA) slot, you have the best options for expandability. You can buy PC Cards that adapt USB, IEEE 1394, and even eSATA (external SATA) connectors, which will allow you to use of just about any external hard drive enclosure.

FIGURE 3.9

An external USB enclosure allows a laptop to support additional storage.

Networking options

Laptops are designed to be connected to networks — most modern laptops contain all that you need to connect to the network to serve as your Windows Home Server.

Many laptops have built-in Ethernet connections; however, in some cases (especially for older systems), these are limited to 10 BASE-T 100 BASE-T speeds. While 100 Mbps is often fast enough, if you are installing a new network and using Gigabit speed network hardware in the rest of your house, you may want to look into adding a Gigabit-speed PCMCIA card in order to get the most out of your laptop's network connection.

If you decide to go this route, you should make sure that the PCMCIA network adapter you choose is compatible. If it specifies compatibility with Windows 2003 Server or even Windows 2000, it is likely to work with Windows Home Server as well.

> **TIP** If you are adding both a PC Card USB adapter and a PC Card network adapter, be sure that the cards will fit. Some laptops have dual PC Card slots right above one another, but the large connector ends of these cards can often make installing multiple cards problematic.

Summary

Whether you want to assemble your own computer, or reuse an old desktop computer or even laptop, building your own Windows Home Server machine can save you some money over buying a packaged system. With the reuse option, you get the satisfaction of knowing that your formerly obsolete computer will stay out of the landfill for a while longer.

Computer hardware is a commodity market these days, and you can purchase high-quality products for low prices. You can assemble a computer from component parts, and while the total cost may not save you much if anything over buying a comparable packaged system, you can be assured of getting exactly the components and features you like.

Reusing a computer can provide substantial economic savings. Many older computers will simply need to be outfitted with larger hard drives to serve as formidable Windows Home Server systems. Laptops are another option, with a number of advantages. Low power consumption, small form factor, and a built-in keyboard and monitor means that your laptop can fit in where a desktop may not.

Now that we've covered the hardware you need for Windows Home Server, in the next chapter we'll show you what you need in order to create a complete home network, so that all of the computers in your house can make use of your broadband Internet connection as well as your Windows Home Server.

Chapter 4

Creating a Home Network

Windows Home Server can serve as the nerve center of your household computer system, but a hub needs spokes. Your home's network, from the cables, to the router, to your broadband modem, serves that purpose. It is what connects all of your computers and other devices to each other, to the Windows Home Server, and to the Internet.

Perhaps you already have a network. If you have multiple computers that are connected to the Internet, then this is likely the case. If not, this chapter will help you explore your networking options to not only help you connect all of your computers to your server, but also the Internet.

There are quite a few options when it comes to household networks today. You could have a completely hard-wired network, using physical cables run to each computer. Or, you may decide to have all or part of your network be wireless, allowing computers and other devices access to network resources from anywhere in the house. You could even have a combination of both—with reliable, fast wired connects for your server and stationary desktop computers, and a wireless network for laptops and other portable electronics such as personal data assistants (PDAs) and smart phones. This option, in fact, is ideal for a network built around Windows Home Server.

Networking Options

There are more options than ever for building a home network, at different price points for different levels of functionality. Further, even many of the technologies that used to be quite expensive, such as Gigabit Ethernet, have come way down in price and are accessible to those on almost any budget.

Wireless, too, has become much more affordable in the last several years: the formerly high-end 54 Megabit per second (Mbps) has become the standard, with newer technologies supplanting it on the high end.

The network diagram shown in Figure 4.1 should give you an idea of the different ways that devices can be connected to your Windows Home Server, to each other, and to the Internet.

FIGURE 4.1

Windows Home Server serves as the heart of your home network.

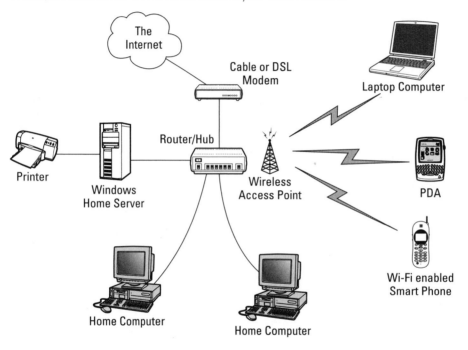

Although there are many ways to organize a home network, most are based around the following items:

- **You have a broadband Internet connection.** It can be cable, Digital Subscriber Line (DSL), satellite, fiber — the choices here getting more diverse all the time. While a broadband Internet connection is not a strict requirement of a home network, the always-on nature of such a connection makes it a practical necessity if you need to give multiple computers and other devices access to the Internet simultaneously.

- **All of your computers connect through a central point to your broadband access device (such as a cable or DSL modem, or a satellite receiver).** This is typically done through a device called a *router*. A router does what its name implies: it routes all network traffic intended for the Internet to the broadband device, and all network traffic intended for computers inside your network to those devices. All devices that need to access the Internet or other computers such as your Windows Home Server machine need to connect to the router.

■ **Wireless devices need a Wireless Access Point (WAP).** This is typically, although not always, built into the router. A WAP provides the means for wireless devices to communicate with your network as if they were physically connected. The WAP is configured with the wireless security settings, an identifying name for the connection, and a channel number to use.

The way you decide to create your network depends on a lot of factors that only you can decide on. We discuss some of these options in the next few sections, and then give you some information on configuring Windows Home Server for network use.

Building a wired network

Wired networks are tried and true, and are your most inexpensive and reliable choice for networking if your computers stay put. The current standard for a local area network (LAN) is known as *Ethernet*. Ethernet was developed in the 1970s at Xerox Palo Alto Research Center (PARC), and over the course of the next two decades won out over competing networks and evolved into the standard we enjoy today.

Ethernet standards

There are currently several widely supported standards in common use in the home. They are named according to the speed of transmission, and are as follows:

■ **10BASE-2:** Before today's hub- and switch-based Ethernet standards, there was 10BASE-2. This standard utilized coaxial cables, which had to be fitted with terminators. Computers are connected together in a series, with the cable from one computer feeding into the next, and so on. This standard is now pretty much obsolete, but may exist in some homes that had networks set up before 10BASE-T became popular. If you have this standard, you should probably consider upgrading as newer solutions are faster, and it is harder to find compatible devices today.

■ **10BASE-T:** Providing up to 10 Mbps speed, 10BASE-T quickly surpassed 10BASE-2. 10BASE-T (10 is for the speed, BASE for the baseband signaling employed by the technology, and T for the twisted pair cabling that is used) cables use an RJ-45 connector, which is similar to a standard modular phone jack but somewhat larger (see Figure 4.2).

■ **100BASE-T:** Ten times faster speed is offered by the 100BASE-T standard. While you can use 10BASE-T to connect to shared drives and folders, it can bog down quickly when transferring large or many files. At 100 Mbps speeds, it is a much more practical option. We recommend a 100 Mbps network as the minimum for Windows Home Server use.

■ **1000BASE-T:** Gigabit Ethernet has been popular in corporate networks and data centers due to the large number of computers that must share network bandwidth. This technology is now filtering down to the home — and is highly recommended as the choice for new networks as well as for upgrades to existing networks as the cost is not much of a premium. This speed is often written as either 1000 Mbps or 1 Gbps (Gigabit per second).

FIGURE 4.2

The RJ45 connector is the standard for nBASE-T Ethernet based networks. You can use a crimping tool to attach them to the end of a cable.

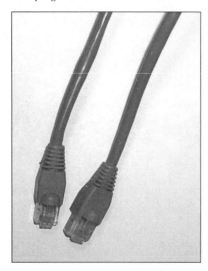

In order to build a wired network, you will need to run Category 5 enhanced (better known as Cat 5e) or Cat 6 Ethernet cable from your router to each location that needs access to the network. This can include the family room to hook up a game console, bedrooms to hook up the kid's computers, the basement to hook up a home theater system. You can see that it is important to plan where you want your router to be located in order to minimize the amount of cable that is run through the house.

NOTE   In a pinch, you can use regular Category 5 (as opposed to Cat 5e) cable; however, Cat 5e is recommended for gigabit speeds. For gigabit speeds, you need to make sure that the cable you choose includes eight wires (four twisted pairs); otherwise you will be limited to 100 Mbps speeds.

You can purchase Cat 5e cable from a number of different places; the most convenient may be your local big box home improvement store, where you should also be able to find the RJ-45 connectors, crimping tools, and wall plates you need in order to make a clean installation.

Network interface cards

With a router at one end of the cable, your computer needs to be able to connect to the other end. The device that allows this is traditionally referred to as a NIC (network interface card), like the example in Figure 4.3. Nowadays there are many more choices, from Universal Serial Bus (USB) and PC Card adapters for laptops, to built-in network jacks on computer motherboards and newer laptops. It is rare to find a computer sold today that doesn't already include an RJ-45 connector to plug in an Ethernet cable — although you can still purchase a real NIC expansion card for computers that don't offer one, or only offer slower speeds.

FIGURE 4.3

A Network Interface Card allows older computers without built-in networking hardware to connect.

Photo courtesy of Netgear

Handling unique situations

If you have several devices located in one spot in your house (such as several game consoles that utilize network connections in your family room), you don't need to run a cable from the router to each device. You can, instead, run a single wire and then employ a device called a *hub*, shown in Figure 4.4. A hub will allow you to branch a single connection into many, allowing a short cable to then be run from the hub to each device.

A similar device, known as a *switch*, is more expensive but can often provide higher performance than a hub. A hub will send any message packet it receives out to all devices that are attached to it without any regard as to which device it is actually intended for. A switch is smarter, and will identify the intended device and only route a message to that device, freeing up other connections up for other devices to use.

TIP   **If you need to mix network hardware of differing speeds, it is a good idea to isolate slower equipment from the faster equipment using a switch. With a standard hub where all devices are listening to the same messages, you can only transmit at the speed of the slowest attached device. A switch allows the slower speed devices to work independently.**

FIGURE 4.4

A hub or a switch allows you to connect many devices to the same cable run.

Photo courtesy of Netgear

ON the WEB   **Teaching you how to install wall plates and fish cables through walls is beyond the scope of this book. You can find a number of useful tips for these and all other aspects of home network construction at Small Net Builder (www.smallnetbuilder.com).**

Building a wireless network

As computers have become more mobile, networks have had to follow — and thus wireless networks have proliferated. It's easy to see why, even for computers that don't go anywhere. Wireless networks require you to set up a single WAP, which can then be accessed by any compatible device within range of the receiver. This convenience can trump the reliability and speed of a wired network in many cases, especially in older homes where it may be difficult at best to run Ethernet cable.

Fortunately, most wireless networking equipment conforms to the various 802.11 standards. This adherence makes it easy to find compatible wireless networking hardware even if from different manufacturers.

NOTE   **802.11 is a standard promoted by the Institution of Electrical and Electronics Engineers, better known as IEEE or I-Triple-E. The 802 group of standards specifically refer to those used local area networks. Different subgroups refer to different LAN technology standards. For instance, Ethernet is defined by the 802.3 standard.**

Wireless standards

As with wired Ethernet, wireless standards have improved over the years. Newer devices tend to be compatible with older ones. The 802.11 wireless standards are described as follows:

- **802.11a:** Although this standard was developed first, it didn't take off as quickly as the later 802.11b standard, as it was significantly more expensive. 802.11a devices operate in the 5 gigahertz (GHz) band. The standard supports data transfer rates of up to 54 Mbps.

- **802.11b:** This is the first widely used standard, even though the speed caps out at 11 Mbps. 802.11b devices operate in the crowded 2.4 GHz band, which is also used by cordless phones, baby monitors, Bluetooth devices and more. This can often lead to interference problems between devices.

- **802.11g:** Also operating in the 2.4 GHz band, 802.11g raises the maximum throughput to 54 Mbps. This is the most common, cost effective, and fully ratified wireless standard in use today.

- **Super G:** Super G is a proprietary extension to the 802.11g standard that supports several optimizations, but its most important characteristic is the ability to combine two 802.11g channels to potentially double the maximum throughput to 108 Mbps. Although not part of the 802.11 standard, it has enjoyed support from a number of manufacturers.

- **802.11n:** This proposed standard hasn't yet been finalized, and isn't expected to be until September 2008. However there are many devices on the market that make use of the Draft N standards. 802.11n devices can reach speeds of 248 Mbps.

Actual attainable speeds from any of these devices can vary due to a number of factors, including distance from the access point, the obstacles such as walls or floors in the way, and interference from other devices in the same band, such as other wireless networks to cordless phones and other devices.

> **TIP** Hide your SSID (Service Set Identifier). Keep in mind that when you can see your neighbor's wireless networks, they can see yours as well if your SSID isn't hidden. See the information presented later in this chapter for details on setting up your wireless security.

Extending your reach

Wireless networks can have a limited range, and may not necessarily be useable by all devices that you need to connect. TV set top boxes, including game consoles, HD DVD players, and satellite TV receivers, often don't include Wi-Fi capabilities in order to keep costs down. They do, however, provide Ethernet ports, and it is often desirable to connect them to your network wirelessly. A device called a *wireless bridge*, shown in Figure 4.5, can be used to do this. These devices are often sold as "game adapters," denoting their common usage as a way to enable game consoles to connect to the network, though they can be used for other devices as well. In order to use a wireless bridge, you must configure it using a PC to match it to your wireless access point. A device (or multiple devices) can then be connected into it and communicate over your wireless network transparently, without even knowing that it is there.

FIGURE 4.5

A game adapter or wireless bridge can be used to extend the reach of your network.

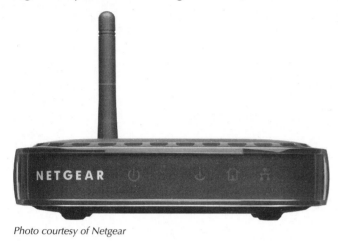

Photo courtesy of Netgear

Another device that can extend the reach of your wireless network is a *wireless range extender*. A range extender acts as a relay, sitting between your router and the devices that need to connect to it.

Wireless adapters

Almost all new laptops sold today include built-in Wi-Fi access capabilities, and most are 802.11g or 802.11n. It is simple to add to computers that don't have it built in, such as older laptops or desktop systems. All you need to do is to make use of a special wireless NIC or adapter. They are available as USB, PC Card, and internal Peripheral Component Interconnect (PCI) and PCI Express cards for desktop systems.

Alternative network connectivity

If you have an area in your house that is tricky to run Ethernet wire to, and can't get a good wireless signal, there is a third alternative: the powerline adapter. A powerline adapter, shown in Figure 4.6, plugs into a standard electrical outlet and makes use of your household wiring as a transmission medium. While powerline adapters can be a convenient option (simply plug them in at each end of the network connection), they suffer some limitations compared to Ethernet. Performance, especially, can be highly variable and can't match the speeds provided by 100BASE-T or faster Ethernet.

FIGURE 4.6

Powerline adapters can solve tricky wiring problems.

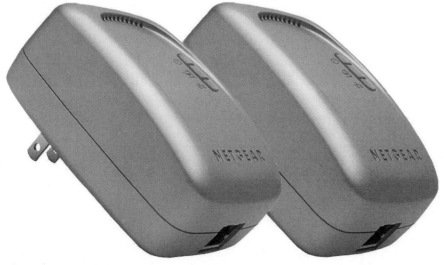

Photo courtesy NETGEAR

Choosing and Configuring a Router

Hopefully, you've made a decision as to which network technologies you need to support in your home based on the devices you need to connect to it and their location in the house. You will need to choose a router to serve as the device to tie everything in your network together. Here are some tips:

- **Get a router that supports the technologies you already have.** If you already own a laptop that supports 802.11n, for instance, you may want to consider an 802.11n capable router to take advantage of it. If you have no wireless devices, you could save some money by getting a wired-only router.

- **Make sure the router supports Universal Plug and Play.** See the section on Universal Plug and Play (UPnP) in this chapter to see why.

- **Make sure you have enough ports.** Many routers for home use are limited to the use of four ports, and one of those ports is often reserved for connecting to the broadband device. Make sure it will support the number of cables you wish to run; otherwise you will need to extend the network using a hub or a switch.

In reality, most current name brand commercial routers will do the job and will have similar specs. You can decide if you want extra features, such as more LAN ports or a printer port, or choose on price. Table 4.1 shows some popular router models you might want to consider.

TABLE 4.1

Popular Router Models

Manufacturer/Model	Features
Apple AirPort Extreme	802.11a/b/g wireless, 3 port Ethernet switch (100 Mbps).
Apple AirPort Extreme (802.11 draft-n)	The newer version of the AirPort Extreme router includes a 3 gigabit Ethernet port switch for wired connections, 802.11a/b/g and draft-n wireless standards, and a USB port for adding a printer or a USB hard drive.
D-link RangeBooster N 650	802.11b/g/n draft, 4 port Ethernet switch (100 Mbps).
Netgear WGT624	802.11b/g + Super G with 4 port Ethernet switch (100 Mbps).
Netgear WNR854T RangeMax NEXT	802.11b/g/n draft, with 4 port gigabit switch.
Linksys WRT54G	A popular 802.11 b/g router with 4 Ethernet port switch (100 Mbps). Some variants with additional features, such as the WRTSL54GS with a USB 2.0 port for attaching storage.
Linksys WRT350N	802.11b/g/draft-n, with a 4 port gigabit switch.

Most modern routers include a small Web server, to allow for management and configuration via a browser, as shown in Figure 4.7. The management tool will typically include a way to define the connection to your broadband Internet device, a way to configure standard network settings so that devices can connect to it, and, finally, a way to configure wireless settings in the case of a Wi-Fi router. Figure 4.7 shows the management console for a popular home router, the Netgear WGT624 802.11g router. Other routers have similar settings; however, they may be in different locations in their management interfaces or named somewhat differently.

The following are some of the typical configuration settings possible on a typical wireless router:

- **WAN Port:** The WAN (wide area network) port is the port on the router that connects to your broadband access device, such as a cable modem. Your ISP should provide you with any special settings that need to be made.

- **LAN Settings:** The router determines your local network's subnet settings; the LAN settings allow you to configure the IP address, subnet mask and gateway address.

- **DHCP Server:** Most routers can act as a DHCP (Dynamic Host Configuration Protocol) server, which allows client computers to ask the router to provide their network parameters, including the IP address, default gateway, subnet mask, and DNS server settings. DHCP is recommended for most systems as in makes configuration simple; however, there are some devices you might want to configure with static IP addresses.

  If you have other networking devices to install (such as a wireless bridge or a network printer), they can be easier to maintain if you assign them a static IP address. The router should allow you to specify the range of addresses to use for DHCP. Reserve about 20 or so addresses at the start of the IP range to be able to accommodate any potential static devices.

FIGURE 4.7

A router is typically configured using a Web-based management console.

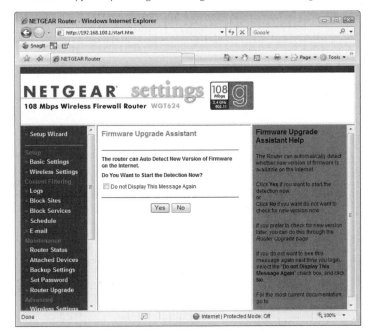

- **Port forwarding or Network Address Translation (NAT):** Port forwarding allows you to direct incoming requests to your network to specific computers. For example, if you have a computer acting as an FTP server, you would configure the router to forward requests on port 21 to that computer. Most routers include a listing of common port numbers to help in this, as Figure 4.8 shows.

  Windows Home Server utilizes port forwarding when you configure the Remote Access feature.

- **Site and service blocking:** Site blocking lets you block Web sites based on keyword or domain name matching. Service blocking prevents the router from being used for certain services such as peer to peer file sharing by blocking the ports those services use.

This by no means covers all of the settings of a typical router, but it should give you an idea of the types of services provided.

FIGURE 4.8

You can use port forwarding to direct outside requests to the proper server IP address.

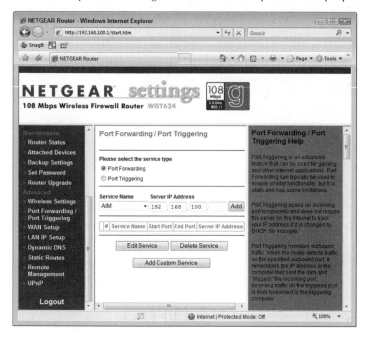

Many current routers support Universal Plug and Play, or UPnP, shown in Figure 4.9. UPnP provides a standard way for software to automatically configure a router for its requirements. Windows Home Server makes use of UPnP in order to configure the Remote Access feature. Using UPnP, Windows Home Server can automatically set up port forwarding on your router so that Web requests coming from the Internet are automatically forwarded to the server.

CROSS-REF   See Chapter 17 for information on using UPnP to configure Remote Access.

FIGURE 4.9

Enable UPnP to allow Windows Home Server to automatically configure port forwarding.

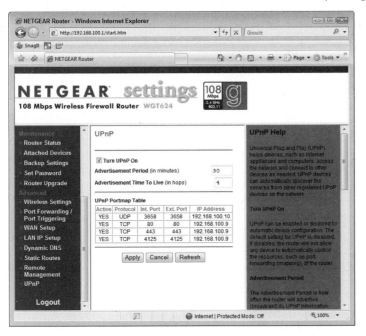

Configuring Wireless Security

If you choose to add a wireless component to your network, you should be mindful of wireless security. A wide open wireless network is an open invitation for your neighbors or even people driving by to eavesdrop on your network. They'll have just as much access as if they walked into your home and plugged their computer directly into your router!

Clearly, configuring security is not an option, it's a necessity. However, with all of the wireless security settings available, which should you choose, and how much security is enough?

Exploring Wi-Fi security

There are several standards for wireless network security, along with variations of them. The first is the WEP (Wireless Encryption Protocol, or Wired Equivalent Privacy), along with its variant WEP2, among others. The second, more up-to-date standard is WPA (Wi-Fi Protected Access), along with its newer variant WPA2. Which should you choose? Read on to find out.

Wired Equivalent Privacy (WEP)

The WEP standard is so named because when it was created, it was intended to secure wireless networks to the same extent that wired networks are naturally protected. However, since its introduction a number of glaring weaknesses have been found, and tools created to exploit them.

WEP requires the assignment of a 64-bit or 128-bit encryption key. The first 24 bits of this key are reserved for use as an initialization vector, and the remaining 40 or 104 bits are used to hold the key. You must enter the key itself on the router and on the client machines that require access. Typically you use a string of ten or 26 hexadecimal digits, although you can use a *passphrase* to generate the key as well, as shown in Figure 4.10.

NOTE Some routers allow for keys longer than 128 bits; however these schemes are proprietary and in general require NICs from the same manufacturer.

FIGURE 4.10

A WEP key can be entered as a string of hexadecimal digits or as a passphrase.

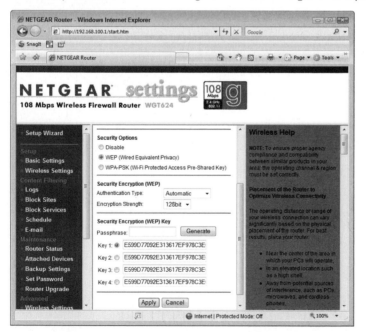

WEP can be configured with two different modes of authentication. They are as follows:

- **Shared Key Authentication:** This method requires a four-step handshake process where the client system first requests access, followed by the access point returning a clear text challenge string. This string is encrypted using the key and sent back to the access point. The access point can then decrypt it and matches it to the original challenge string. The access point then sends an accept or reject response back to the client. If the access point accepts the response, communication can commence using the WEP key for encrypting data.

- **Open System Authentication:** With this method, the four-step authentication step is skipped. The access point essentially allows any client to connect to the network; however, all data transmitted from the server must be encrypted using the WEP key.

The Shared Key method of authentication has a weakness in that it is susceptible to eavesdropping. The handshake process can be intercepted and studied to learn the key. If you are going to use WEP authentication, you are better off using the Open System Authentication method.

As we've mentioned, WEP has some significant flaws in its approach to security that make it susceptible to attacks. There are a number of tools out there that allow users to sniff and ultimately crack WEP-encrypted wireless networks. While we don't recommend that you use them to invade other networks, using them on your own to discover just how weakly it is protected can be an eye-opening experience.

WEP2 is a somewhat enhanced version of WEP. It requires 128-bit keys and allows for a longer initialization vector, which can prevent some common attacks. It is still fairly week, however, and you should use WPA instead whenever possible.

Wi-Fi Protected Access (WPA)

The successor to WEP is the WPA, which implements most of the standards specified by the 802.11i. WPA was created in response to the weaknesses discovered in the WEP protocol. WPA settings are shown in Figure 4.11.

WPA improves upon the encryption of WEP by introducing the concept of changing keys over time, a process called the Temporal Key Integrity Program (TKIP). A master key is known to both the client and the server; however, the actual working key used in transmission is changed over time to prevent attacks based on recording and playing back messages to gain access to a server.

WPA includes a 48-bit initialization vector, an improvement over the 24-bit IV (Initialization Vector) used by WEP. This reduces the number of packets that can share the same IV, making them harder to decrypt.

WPA2 is a further enhancement of the WPA standard that implements all of the mandatory portions of the 802.11i standard. WPA2 is now required for all new devices seeking to be Wi-Fi certified.

ON the WEB   There are a number of articles on the Web that go into more detail regarding wireless security and how it is implemented. A good starting point is in this column on Microsoft TechNet: www.microsoft.com/technet/community/columns/cableguy/cg0505.mspx.

FIGURE 4.11

Use WPA or WPA2 security instead of WEP whenever possible.

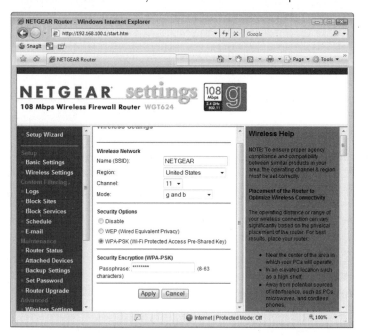

Choosing a security standard

In case we didn't make it obvious, the WPA, and especially the WPA2 standards, are the ones to choose for your wireless network. The only case in which you should resort to using WEP is when you have no other options. Your network is only as secure as the weakest device on it. If you have an older computer or device that only supports WEP, you will be stuck using that unless you retire or replace that device.

Our recommendation is that you choose WPA2 whenever possible. All newer wireless devices must support it, so you can be assured that any new hardware that comes out will be WPA2 compatible. There are still plenty of devices on the market now, particularly routers, that only implement WPA. However, WPA is a vast improvement over WEP.

There are other things you can do to enhance your network security that most wireless routers will support:

- **Disable SSID broadcasting:** When you are looking for network connections, and you see your neighbors connections listed, it is because they are broadcasting the SSID. If the SSID is not broadcast, clients must know it in advance in order to connect to it.

- **Turn off remote management:** Most routers allow their Web interfaces to be accessed from the WAN side of the connection, in essence the Internet. This means that someone simply needs to guess your router's administrator password to gain access to it.

- **Enable MAC filtering:** A MAC (Media Access Control) address is a unique identifier assigned to all networking devices. MAC addresses are typically represented as a string of six hexadecimal (base 16) numbers separated by a color or a hyphen; for example, 00:11:22:33:44:AB:CD.

MAC filtering lets you set up an authorized list of MAC addresses that can access your network. Your router will mostly likely have a screen that lists the devices attached to your network along with their MAC addresses, which you can use as the basis for deciding what to allow. Figure 4.12 shows MAC filtering at work.

FIGURE 4.12

You can enhance network security by preventing SSID broadcasting and enabling MAC filtering.

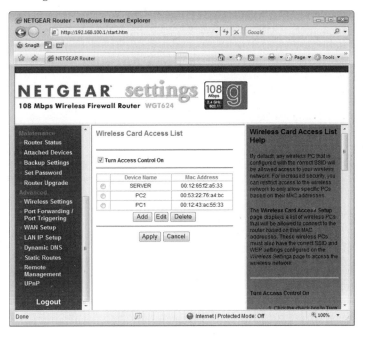

Configuring Windows Home Server

Any Windows Home Server installation will have at least one wired connection to the router—that of the server itself. Due to the fact that Windows Home Server is intended to be used in headless installations, without a monitor or keyboard, Microsoft decided to leave wireless capabilities out of the initial release. Instead, you will need to be able to connect the server to your router using a Cat 5 cable. This means that you will have to locate the server within close proximity to the router or run a cable to your desired location.

TIP   **If you really need to connect the server wirelessly, you can use a wireless bridge of the type described in that section. Configure and test the bridge, and then simply connect the server to the bridge using an Ethernet cable. In many cases this will work fine; however, keep in mind that when transferring files from the server to the computer and vice versa, speed is reduced because the available bandwidth is used up by both wireless connections sharing the same channel.**

When installed, Windows Home Server is configured to use DHCP in order to provide the highest level of compatibility as possible. With DHCP, Windows Home Server will look for a DHCP server, typically your router, to issue an IP address and configure gateway and subnet information.

DHCP has a potential downside, though. Because your IP address is assigned by the router, it is only guaranteed to be active for a specific period of time, called a *lease*. After the lease expires, your router may or may not assign a different IP address.

For most Windows Home Server installations, this is acceptable. Your client computers will have no problems finding the server by name for backups, shared folders, and media streaming. If you plan to install other software on the server, however, such as a game server or some other network enabled application, it may be beneficial to assign a static IP address to the server. A static IP address will never change, meaning that no matter what you should be able to reach the server over the network. It may just come down to personal preference as to which you use. Another perhaps safer option is to configure your router to always assign the same DHCP address to the server. We discuss both options here.

CAUTION   **Be very careful when changing network settings on a headless server (one with no monitor or keyboard). Because the only way you can connect to the server is through remote desktop, you may end up misconfiguring the system to the point that it may be difficult to impossible to find on the network, at which point you will likely have to resort to your system recovery process.**

Configuring a static IP address

You can configure the network connection for Windows Home Server in exactly the same way as you can with other Windows operating systems. As a result, it is simple to give your server a static Internet Protocol (IP) address if you so choose by using the Network Connections control panel.

Before you can assign a static IP address, you need to remove the address you wish to use from the range used by the router for DHCP. See the section on router configuration for more information. Figure 4.13 shows an example of setting the DHCP range for a NETGEAR router.

FIGURE 4.13

You must exclude the IP addresses you wish to use for static addresses from the DHCP pool.

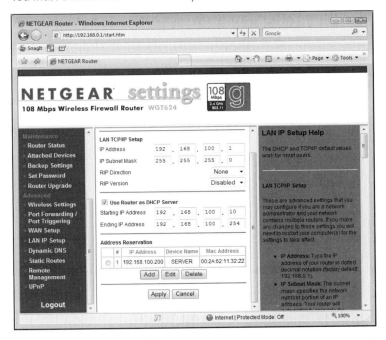

Once you have successfully configured the router, follow these steps to assign a static IP address on the server:

1. **Using a monitor and keyboard, log onto the server's desktop.** (This is preferable to using Remote Desktop, as the Remote Desktop connection will be lost as soon as you change the network settings.)

2. **Open the Network Connections control panel.** Choose Start ➪ Control Panel ➪ Network Connections. This panel is shown in Figure 4.14.

3. **Right-click on the item labeled Local Area Connection, and choose Properties.**

4. **In the Local Area Connection Properties window, select Internet Protocol (TCP/IP), and click Properties.**

5. **In the Internet Protocol (TCP/IP) window, shown in Figure 4.15, select the Use the following IP address radio button.**

6. **Enter the IP address of your choice.** This IP address should be on the same subnet as your router. If your router is configured with an IP address of 192.168.1.1, give the server an address of 192.168.1.2 or something similar.

7. **Enter a subnet mask.** This should be the same subnet mask that your router uses. For home networks, it is typically 255.255.255.0.

8. **Enter a default gateway.** This will be the IP address of your router.

FIGURE 4.14

Change network settings in the Network Connections control panel.

FIGURE 4.15

Choose a static address that is on the same subnet as your router.

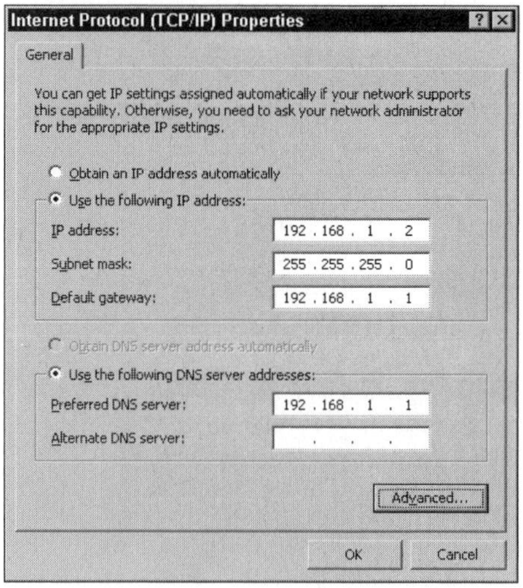

9. **You must enter a DNS server address, as well.** You can enter your router's IP address here as well. If your ISP gives you an IP address of a DNS server, you can enter that as well. If you have two DNS server addresses, enter one as the primary and the other as the secondary. Otherwise leave the secondary DNS server address blank.

10. **Click OK.**

11. **Click Close.** When prompted with a warning to acknowledge that your network connection will change immediately, click Yes.

If all went well, your server will now have a static IP address, which can always be used to reach the server.

Reserving a DHCP address

If you have a headless Windows Home Server system, or you are uncomfortable with configuring network settings as we've described, you may have another option. Many routers allow a DHCP address to be permanently assigned to a machine. This prevents the router from assigning the IP address to any other computer, even if the server is not connected to the network. Meanwhile, the computer continues to obtain its IP address and other network settings from the router.

In many cases, as Figure 4.16 shows, the router will let you choose the computer to use based on its MAC address, in much the same way as MAC filtering for enabling access described earlier.

FIGURE 4.16

Reserving a DHCP address for your server will prevent it from being assigned to any other device.

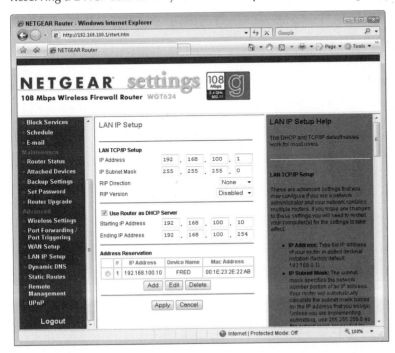

Summary

There are several options for home networking, and no single choice is going to be right for everybody. Whether you choose the reliability and performance of wired, the flexibility of wireless, or a mix between the two, there are more options than ever for building a home network. Whatever you choose or may already have installed, Windows Home Server will fit in nicely. In most cases, a network consisting of both wired and wireless devices will fit the needs of most households.

When choosing network devices, you have a number of choices to make in terms of both wired and wireless connections. Wired networks can range from 10 Mbps to 1000 Mbps devices, while wireless ones range from 11 Mbps with 802.11b to 248 Mbps with 802.11n; and while the affordable standards of yesterday are approaching obsolescence, it's not always practical to replace all of your existing network devices.

Wireless security is another important aspect to consider. If you have the choice, make sure you choose WPA or WPA2 security with a long passphrase to provide the best security for your network. WEP encryption, while it will not provide strong security, will still keep casual eavesdroppers off of your network. Under no circumstances should you disable security entirely unless you feel like sharing your Internet connection, as well as access to all of the computers in your house, with the whole neighborhood.

Now that we've explored how to build or choose a Windows Home Server computer, and how to integrate it into your home network, it's time to explore the Windows Home Server features in depth. In the next part of this book, we discuss the installation of Windows Home Server and show you how to configure it and add users and computers in your household to it.

Part II

Installing and Configuring

Chapter 5

Installing
Windows Home Server

Previous chapters presented you with the choice to build a server from scratch or buy a complete server solution from an OEM vendor. The assumption in this chapter is that you have chosen to either build a new server or reuse an older PC as a server. This means that you need to obtain and install the System Builder edition of Windows Home Server. If you're going the OEM route and buying a machine with Windows Home Server preinstalled, you can probably skip to Chapter 7 to learn more about the Windows Home Server Console (unless you're still curious).

If you are already familiar with the installation of other versions of Windows, such as XP or 2003 Server, you'll find that the process of installing Windows Home Server is not all that different. However, there are some unique choices to be made. This chapter will guide you through them.

Preparing for Installation

Before you can install Windows Home Server, you need to make sure that the server is ready for it. Although Windows Home Server is designed to operate in a headless capacity in day-to-day usage (without a monitor, mouse, or keyboard attached), you need at least a keyboard and a monitor to complete the installation. A mouse is also helpful but not strictly necessary.

Making sure the boot order is correct

In order to install the Windows Home Server DVD, your computer needs to be able to boot from the DVD-ROM drive. If you've built your computer from scratch, or if you're reusing an older PC or laptop, it may not have been configured to boot from the DVD drive. In other cases, the hard drive may have boot order priority.

CROSS-REF   See Chapter 3 for more information on building a server computer.

To figure out if this will be the case with your server, simply try to boot the installation DVD. If it doesn't start the Windows Home Server setup, either by giving you an error or booting into an operating system that is already on the hard drive, you need to change the configuration in the computer's BIOS (Basic Input/Output System, the ROM-based program that controls what your computer does at startup). Figure 5.1 shows a typical PC BIOS configuration screen for setting boot order.

FIGURE 5.1

A typical BIOS screen for configuring boot devices

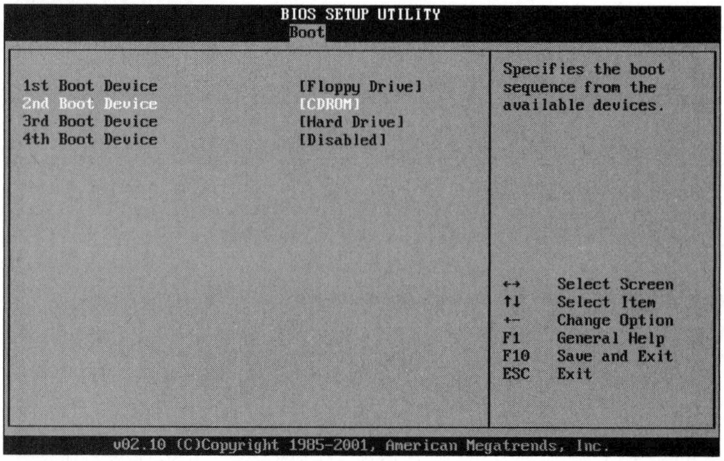

```
                         BIOS SETUP UTILITY
                              Boot

  1st Boot Device          [Floppy Drive]    Specifies the boot
  2nd Boot Device          [CDROM]           sequence from the
  3rd Boot Device          [Hard Drive]      available devices.
  4th Boot Device          [Disabled]




                                             ↔    Select Screen
                                             ↑↓   Select Item
                                             ←    Change Option
                                             F1   General Help
                                             F10  Save and Exit
                                             ESC  Exit


       v02.10 (C)Copyright 1985-2001, American Megatrends, Inc.
```

You should be able to determine which BIOS you have by the text displayed at startup. Although there are many different PC BIOS variations on the market, there are a few popular ones. Here are instructions for three of them.

Phoenix BIOS

To configure many computers with the Phoenix BIOS, try the following:

1. **At the startup screen, press F2 to enter the BIOS setup utility.**

2. **Use the Right Arrow key to select the Boot menu on the top menu bar.**

3. **Look over the list of boot devices.** CD-ROM (or similar) should be one of the options. If it is not at the top of the boot order, or at least above the hard drive, continue with Step 4.

4. Using the Down Arrow key, highlight CD-ROM.

5. Use the F6 key to move the highlighted CD-ROM item to the top of the boot menu. Note that some versions of the Phoenix BIOS use the numeric keypad's + and - keys instead.

6. Press F10 and then choose Yes to save the configuration changes and reboot.

AMI BIOS

If your computer uses the AMI (American Megatrends, Inc.) BIOS, follow these steps:

1. On the startup screen, press the Delete key to access the BIOS setup utility.

2. Use the Right Arrow key to select the Boot menu on the top menu bar.

3. Use the Down Arrow key to select the Boot Device Priority item.

4. Press Enter.

5. Look over the list of boot devices: CD-ROM (or similar) should be one of the options. If it is not at the top of the boot order, or at least above the hard drive, continue with Step 6.

6. Use the Down Arrow key to highlight the 1st Boot Device item, and press Enter.

7. Use the arrow keys to select the CD-ROM from the boot list options and press Enter.

8. Configure the other boot devices. At least one of them should be configured to boot the hard drive.

9. Press F10 and then choose OK to save the configuration changes and reboot.

Award BIOS

If you have the Award BIOS or the Phoenix - Award BIOS, try the following steps:

1. At the startup screen, press the Delete key to access the BIOS setup utility.

2. Use the Down Arrow key to select the Advanced BIOS Features item. Press Enter.

3. If your screen has a separate menu item labeled Boot Seq & Floppy Setup, use the arrow keys to select it and press Enter. Otherwise skip to Step 4.

4. Highlight the First Boot Device option using the arrow keys and press Enter.

5. Choose CD-ROM or an equivalent choice from the list of devices.

6. Configure the other boot devices. One of them should be the hard drive.

7. Press F10 and then click Y when prompted to save the configuration and reboot.

There are many different BIOSes from different manufacturers, and even the same brand of BIOS as one of the above could use different means for configuring the boot order. An extensive guide on this subject is beyond the scope of this book. If one of the above sequences doesn't work for you, your best bet is to consult the owner's manual for the computer or motherboard you're using. It should include step-by-step instructions along with screenshots for your specific BIOS version.

Booting from the installation DVD

Hopefully at this point your server will successfully boot from the DVD drive. Insert the installation DVD and power on the computer. It should either automatically boot from the DVD, or at least detect the bootable disc and prompt you to press a key to boot from it.

If you are successful, you should be rewarded with the simple text screen with a progress bar, followed by the screen shown in Figure 5.2.

FIGURE 5.2

The installation process has begun.

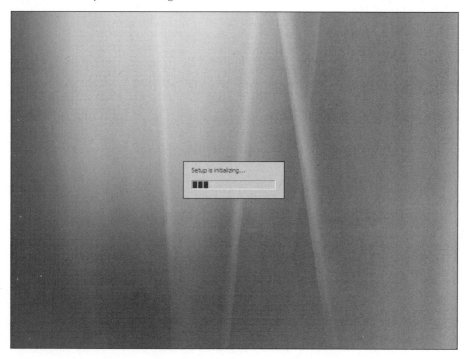

Gathering information

The next few steps should be familiar to anyone who has installed a Windows OS in the past. These steps are where user information is collected for your server's initial settings. The Windows Home Server Setup Wizard, shown in Figure 5.3, pauses at this step to wait for you to be ready to continue. Click Next or press Alt+N to continue.

FIGURE 5.3

Starting the setup process

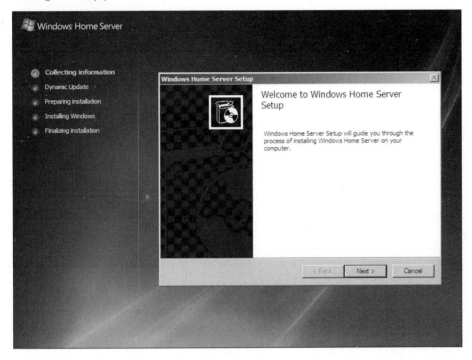

Configuring hard drives

In some cases, your computer requires a special driver for your hard drive. This could be the case if you are using SCSI, USB, or other types of drives. Plain vanilla IDE and SATA drives generally don't require a driver. The next step in the installation process is the Load Additional Storage Drivers screen, shown in Figure 5.4. If you don't need a driver for your hard drive, you can simply click Next or press Alt+N to skip it.

NOTE   Because Windows Home Server is based on Windows Server 2003, you can generally expect the same drive controller compatibility. If your hard drive controller requires a special driver for Windows Sever 2003, it will most likely be needed for Home Server as well. Consult the documentation for your motherboard or hard drive controller for more information.

If you do need to install a special driver for your hard drive, click the Load Drivers button. If you don't have a mouse attached, you need to tab to this button and press Enter. This opens a file selection dialog box that you can browse to the folder where the driver is located. There is a special file called an INF file (with a .inf extension) on the driver disk that tells Windows about the driver.

FIGURE 5.4

Any special storage drivers can be installed at this step.

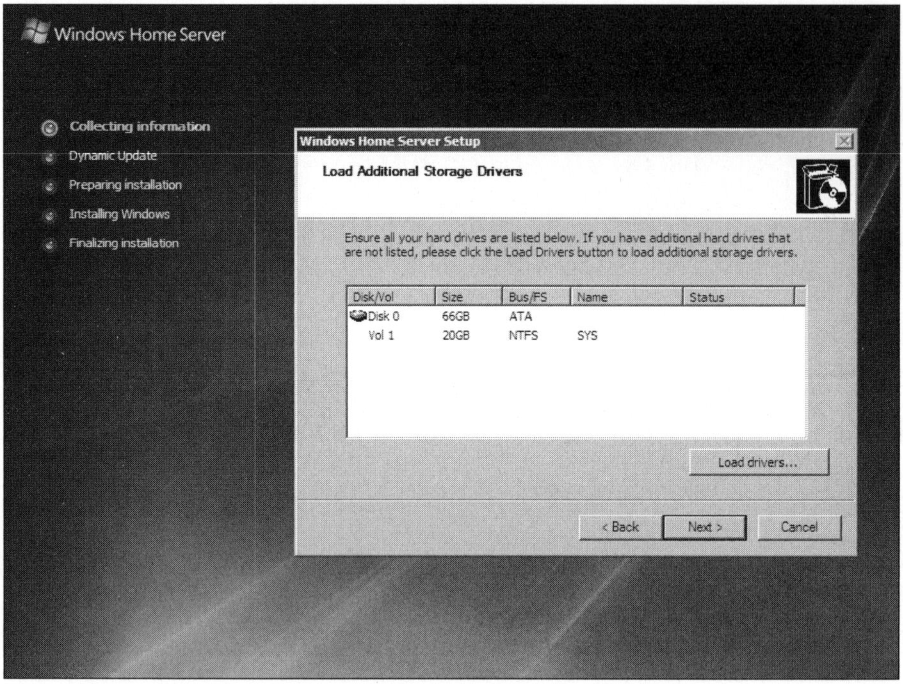

CAUTION The installation process in the prerelease version of Windows Home Server doesn't recognize a driver CD inserted in the drive during the installation. We recommend using a floppy drive or a USB drive if you need to install special drivers.

After you've managed to locate and install the INF file for your driver, click Next or press Alt+N.

Choosing an installation type

If the hard drive on which you're installing Windows Home Server already has an installation of Home Server on it, the next step gives you the option to either do a new installation or to reinstall. If you are reinstalling, see the Reinstalling section later in this chapter. Otherwise, choose New Installation as shown in Figure 5.5, and click Next or press Alt+N.

FIGURE 5.5

Choose New Installation if you are building a new server.

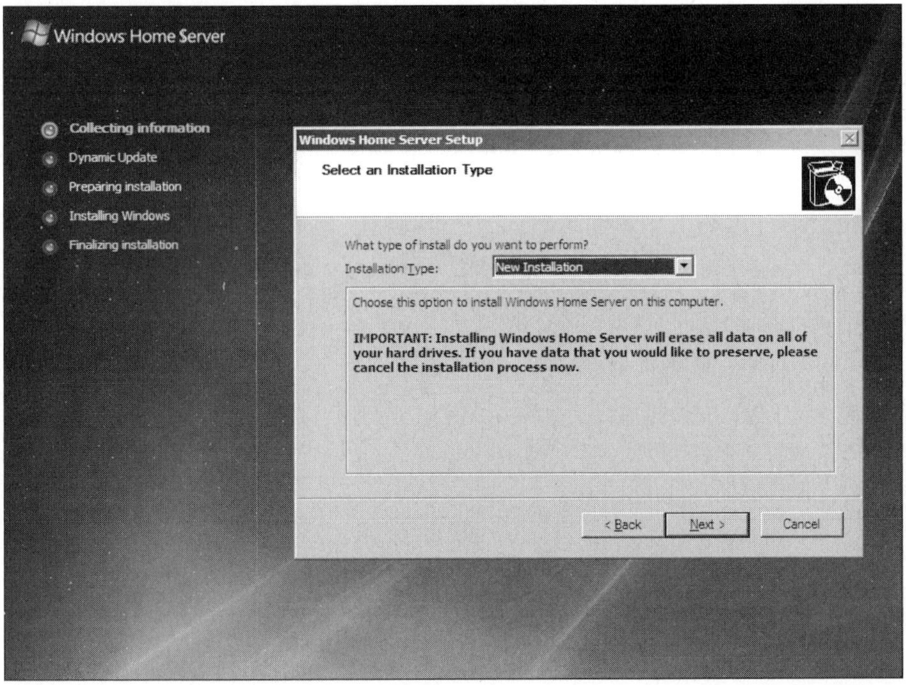

> **CAUTION** The New Installation choice is absolute. When you install, all existing data on your hard drive is erased. Pay heed to the warning given by the installation wizard to cancel the installation at this point if you have any data you want to keep on the hard drive.

Choosing localization settings

If you want to set localization settings other than the defaults specified for the US, you have that option on the next page of the wizard, the Select your Regional and Keyboard Settings page, shown in Figure 5.6. Here you can choose your time and currency format as well as your keyboard type. Make your choice and click Next or press Alt+N.

FIGURE 5.6

Customizing Home Server for your locale

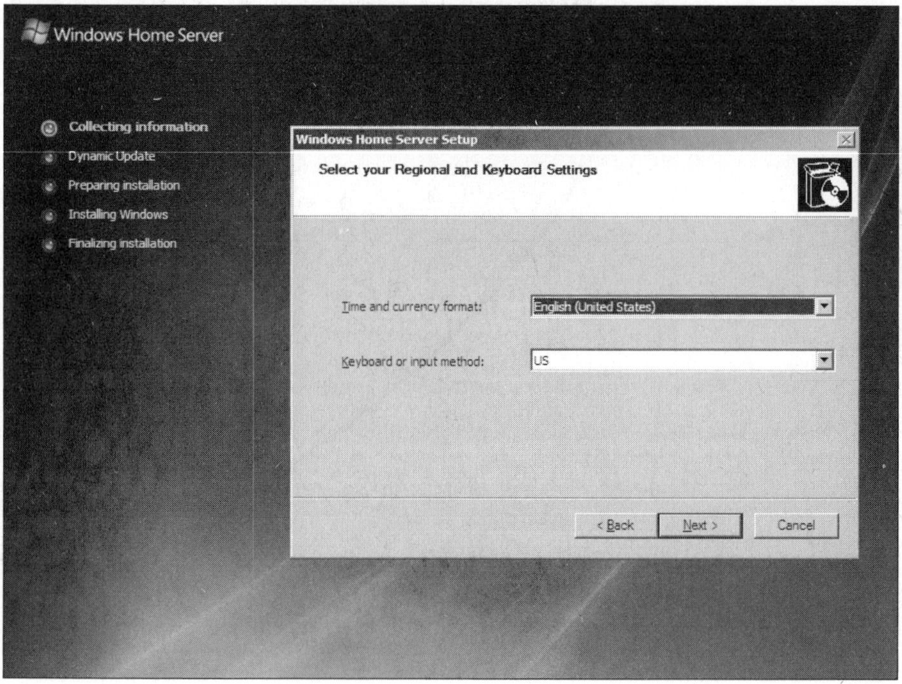

Installation agreement

The next page contains the End User License Agreement (EULA). Click the radio button (or tab to it and press the Spacebar) to accept the agreement to proceed. If you don't agree, you won't be able to complete the installation. Click Next to continue.

The next step, familiar to all Windows OS installer veterans, is to enter the 25-alphanumeric-character product activation code, shown in Figure 5.7. This key was provided with your Home Server DVD. If you purchased a computer with Home Server preinstalled, there should be a sticker on the box with the activation code on it. When complete, click Next.

CAUTION If you're reusing an older Windows computer, it may have a product key sticker on it from a different Windows OS. You cannot use this product key to activate Home Server. Be sure to use only the product key provided on the Home Server DVD.

FIGURE 5.7

The product key allows you to activate Home Server.

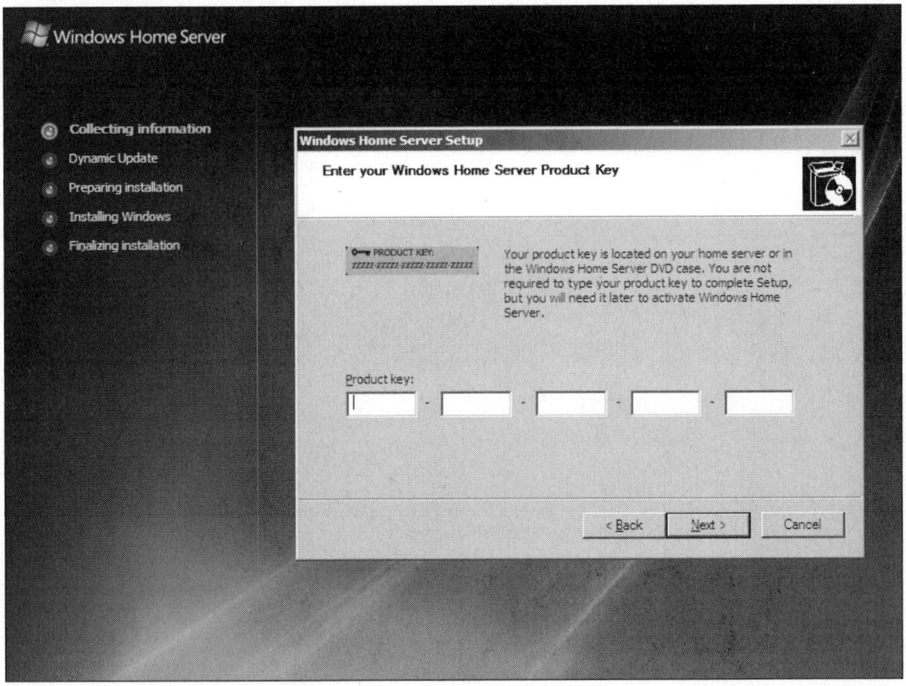

Name your server

The next steps are where you customize your Home Server. First, you need to choose a name for your server as Figure 5.8 shows. This name is used to find the server on the network by everyone that needs to connect to a file share, media share, or the console. The name must be 15 characters or less, using letters numbers or hyphens. No spaces are allowed. "FamilyServer" or "HomeServer" are good choices, or you could give your server a funny nickname or name it after your favorite superhero. The choice is yours. You can even leave it the default setting, "SERVER," if you so desire. Enter your server name and click Next or press Alt+N.

FIGURE 5.8

FIGURE 5.8

Give your server a name to uniquely identify it over the network.

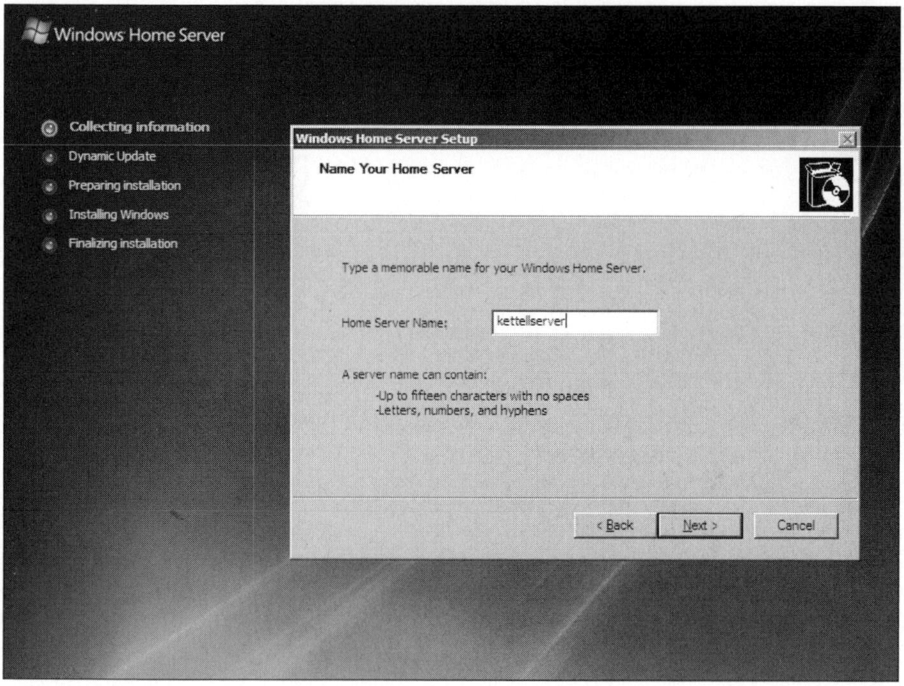

Formatting the hard drives

Your next task is to review the hard drives that Home Server has identified and agree to allow them to be reformatted. You really don't have any other choice at this point, because Home Server needs to automatically format your hard drives to add them to the combined storage pool. Your only choice on this screen, shown in Figure 5.9, is to accept the choices or cancel the installation to make any desired changes to your attached drives. Click the acknowledge check box or press Alt+A. Click Next or press Alt+N to continue. Just to hammer home the point that the drives will be erased, you are presented with a warning message to confirm that you understand this. Click Yes or press Alt+Y to acknowledge.

> **TIP**   Because any hard drive installed on the computer automatically becomes reformatted for inclusion in the storage pool, if you want to add a hard drive on your server that isn't part of this pool, you should remove it from the computer or disable it in the BIOS during installation. Only the most advanced users will require this, because in most cases, you'll want all of your hard drives to become part of the storage pool.

FIGURE 5.9

You must agree to reformat all of the drives found to proceed.

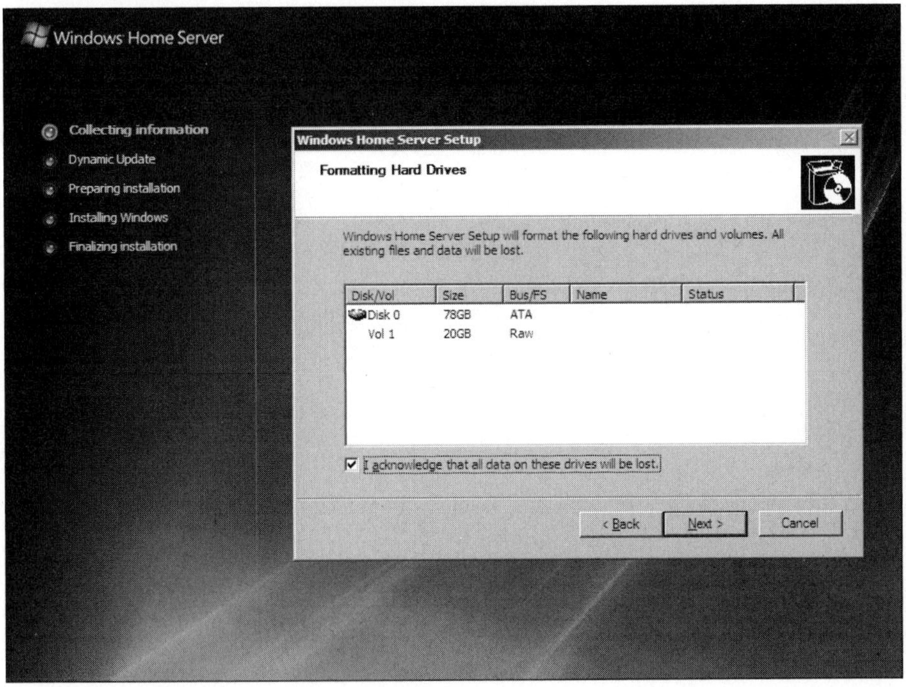

Starting the installation

At this point, Home Server has gathered enough information to continue with the installation. Click the Start button (or just press Enter) to continue. The server automatically goes through the steps necessary to install, including formatting the hard drives, copying installation files and OS files, and installing programs and drivers. The screen shows the current step and the approximate time left for installation on the left, and presents you with a series of informational blurbs explaining various features of Windows Home Server. This is shown in Figure 5.10.

FIGURE 5.10

The installation continues unattended.

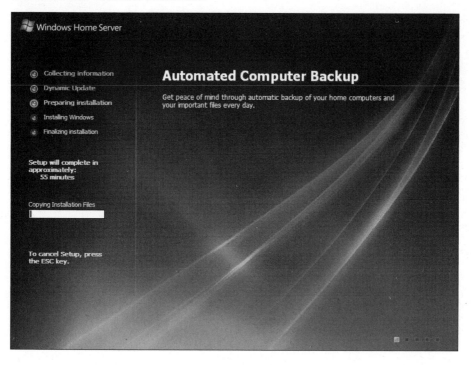

At some point, the server automatically reboots and continues the installation in the text mode installation screen that is common to server versions of Windows. Once files are copied at this screen the server again automatically reboots back to the graphical installation program. There are a couple additional reboots required — Home Server's installation process isn't as refined as more consumer-oriented versions of Windows. However, there aren't any more prompts for information, and the process essentially takes care of itself. The installation should complete and then boot into the Home Server OS.

NOTE Don't be alarmed if you see a screen saying that Windows 2003 Small Business Server is being installed; it isn't. This screen simply belies the 2003 Server roots of Home Server.

Completing the Installation

Eventually the installation completes, and the server reboots for the last time. When it comes back up, the Welcome screen shown in Figure 5.11 appears. Don't worry, there are only a few steps left in the installation process. Click the Welcome button or press Enter to continue.

FIGURE 5.11

Welcome to Windows Home Server.

Choosing a password

Before you can use your server, you must choose a password. Although the screens say that you are choosing a password for Windows Home Server, what you are actually doing is choosing a password for a special Administrator user account.

Your home server will likely be the repository of a lot of your most treasured items. It will house your family photos, your home videos, and your valuable documents. Because it's going to store such important files, it needs to be protected — and Home Server's strong password protection is a great start. Although there are different options for user accounts you create later, the Administrator password must be a strong password. This means that it must conform to the following:

- It must be at least seven characters long
- It must have at least three of the following categories of characters: uppercase letters, lowercase letters, numbers, and symbols.

CROSS-REF See Chapter 8 for more information on strong passwords and Home Server's password options.

When prompted as shown in Figure 5.12, enter a password and confirm it in the next text box. If you don't have a mouse, you can tab to the text boxes. Finally, enter a hint for the password, but keep in mind that this hint can be obtained by anyone on your network who attempts to connect to the Console, so you shouldn't make it too obvious. The hint cannot be the same as the password itself. When you are done, click the Right Arrow button to move forward, or press Alt+N.

Automatic updates

Next, choose whether or not you want Windows Home Server to install updates automatically. Microsoft recommends that you choose the automatic update option. My recommendation is that you do this as well, especially if you plan to leave your server mostly unattended. If you choose not to perform automatic updates, you will have to check for updates and install them manually, and it's easy to forget to do this regularly. Click the appropriate radio button or press Alt+O to choose automatic updates, or Alt+F to choose not to. Right-click or press Alt+N to move to the next step.

FIGURE 5.12

Choose an administrative password for Home Server.

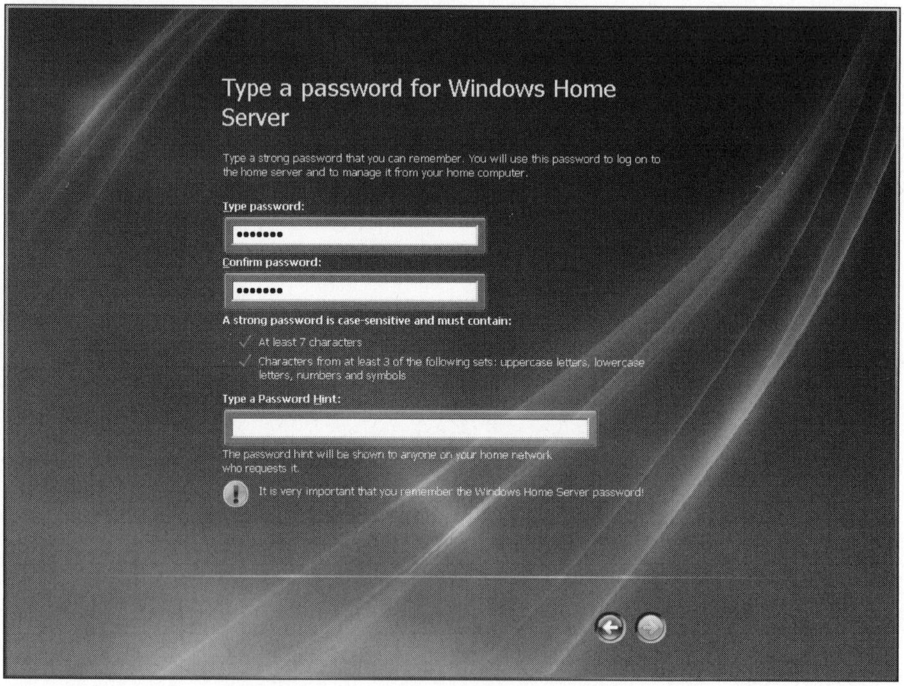

Customer Experience Improvement Program

You are now asked whether or not you want to participate in the Microsoft Customer Experience Improvement program. This program gathers information about your server and submits it to Microsoft so that they can use it to improve their products. Anecdotal research has shown that most participants in the Customer Experience Improvement Program are new users; experienced and advanced users tend to disable this feature because of privacy and speed concerns. Keep in mind, however, that if the only feedback Microsoft receives comes from new users, they're less likely to know or consider the needs of advanced users when designing future features and versions of the OS. Choose Yes (or press Alt+N) to participate or No (press Alt+O) to opt out. Then click the Right Arrow button or press Alt+N.

ON the WEB For more information about the Customer Experience Improvement Program, visit `http://www.microsoft.com/products/ceip/en-us/default.mspx`.

Windows Error Reporting Program

Another program for automatically collecting information and providing it to Microsoft is the Windows Error Reporting program. This program automatically reports errors that your server encounters for analysis. Again, this program is completely optional. Choose Yes (or press Alt+N) or No (press Alt+O), and then click the Right Arrow button or press Alt+N.

Your installation is now complete. That was rather painless, wasn't it? When you finish, you are greeted with a screen that warns you about being logged into the desktop, shown in Figure 5.13. This screen (which is really just an HTML page stored locally on the server) appears any time you log into the desktop, either on the server itself or remotely. You need to be cautious about working directly on the server, because many of the utilities provided for maintaining Windows 2003 Server can break functions of Home Server. Fortunately, you shouldn't have to access the server's desktop very often. As you'll soon see, most Home Server tasks can be performed on the Console.

CROSS-REF See Chapter 7 for more information on working with the Windows Home Server Console.

Activating Windows Home Server

In order to continue to use your Home Server, you must activate it. Until you do, the Console and the server's desktop give you periodic warnings showing the time remaining. You can access the activation dialog box either from the console or from the Home Server desktop.

- To activate from the console, click the Network tab and click the Activate button. If there is no Activate button visible, you have to activate from the server's desktop.
- To activate from the desktop, click Start ➪ All Programs ➪ Activate Windows.

FIGURE 5.13

This screen warns you to be careful in the server's desktop environment.

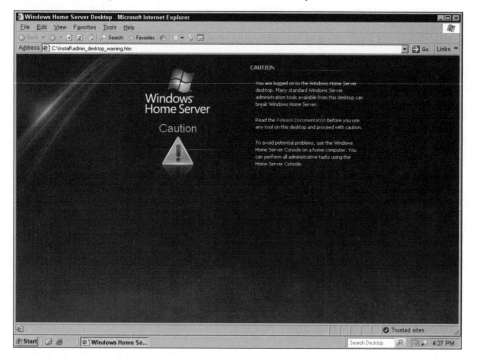

CAUTION   If you neglect the activation, your server will become inoperable past the 30-day grace period.

Once in the activation dialog box, shown in Figure 5.14, you will notice that there are two ways to activate: over the Internet, and by telephone.

To activate over the Internet, follow these steps:

1. **Select the Yes, let's activate Windows over the Internet now radio button.** You can press Alt+Y, and then click Next or press Alt+N.

2. **Choose whether to register your software with Microsoft.** If this is your first time installing, you should select this option. Select Yes or press Alt+Y, and then click Next.

3. **If you chose to register, enter your registration information in the appropriate input fields of the registration page, shown in Figure 5.15.** Click Next or press Alt+N. Assuming you have Internet connectivity, Home Server contacts Microsoft and activates.

4. **If the server is unable to make a connection to register, or if it reports that you need to register over the phone, follow the telephone activation steps.**

FIGURE 5.14

You must activate Windows Home Server within 30 days of installing.

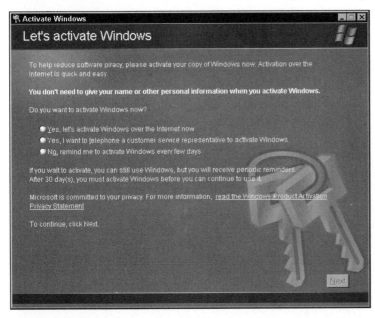

FIGURE 5.15

When you activate over the Internet, you can register at the same time.

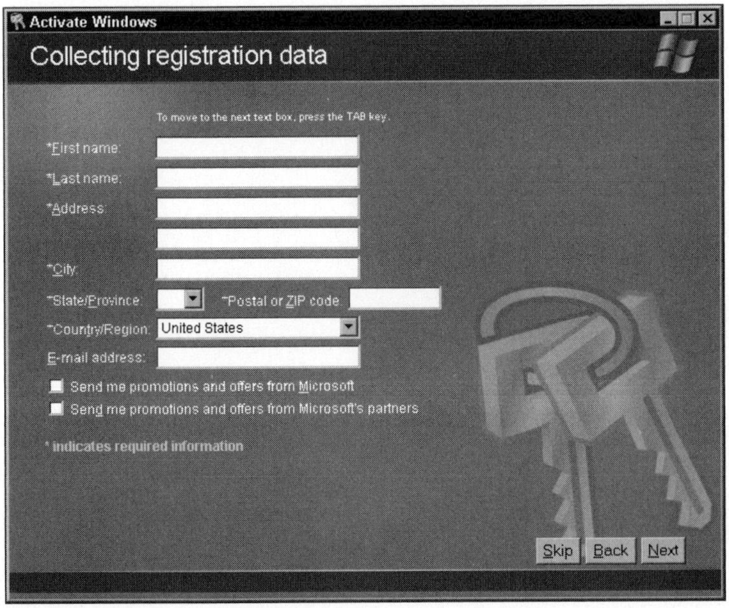

To activate over the phone, do the following:

1. **Select the Yes, I want to telephone a customer server representative to activate Windows, or press Alt+T.** Click Next or press Alt+N. You see the page shown in Figure 5.16.

2. **Choose your location from the drop-down box.**

3. **Call one of the telephone numbers provided.**

4. **You will speak with a customer service representative who will ask you to recite the installation ID numbers shown on the screen.**

5. **The customer service representative will recite numbers back to you; enter them in the seven fields provided.**

6. **When the numbers are entered correctly, the Next button activates. Click it or press Alt+N to complete the activation.**

FIGURE 5.16

You may activate over the phone if you don't have an Internet connection.

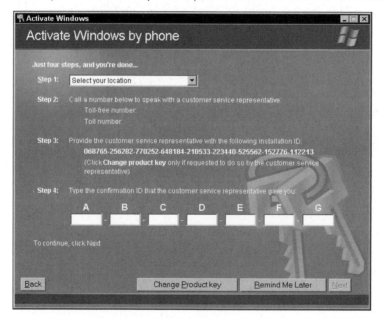

Reinstalling Windows Home Server

There are certain instances when you may need to reinstall Home Server. If you forget your administrator password, for example, your only recourse is to reinstall. Likewise, if something occurs that corrupts the system partition, a reinstall may be necessary. Fortunately, it is an easy process.

If you purchased a Windows Home Server system with the OS preinstalled, it is recommended that you consult the documentation that came with it for the reinstallation procedure. However, if you installed Home Server yourself using the instructions in this chapter, follow this procedure for reinstallation:

1. **Restart the server with the Windows Home Server installation DVD in the DVD drive.**

2. **Follow the installation procedure as described in this chapter.**

3. **When you reach the Select an Installation Type page, choose Server Reinstallation instead of New Installation, as shown in Figure 5.17.**

4. **Follow the on-screen prompts to complete installation.**

CAUTION You will need to reinstall any add-ins or other applications you may have had on your server, recreate user accounts, and change any settings that you may have altered from the default.

FIGURE 5.17

Resetting the server is as easy as changing the installation type.

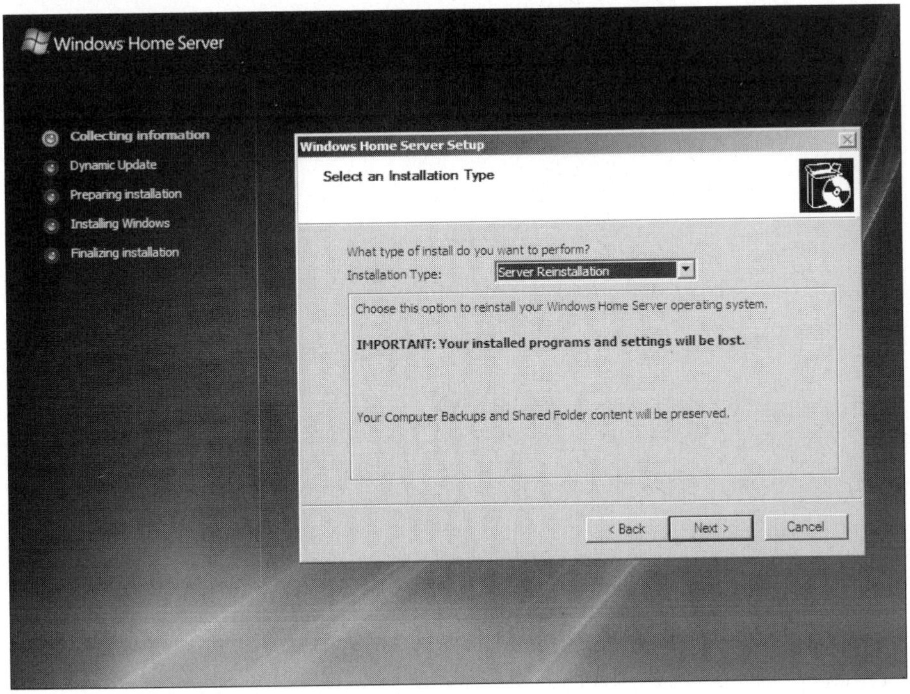

Summary

Windows Home Server's installation process is not as refined as other versions of Windows. Although it incorporates some of the look and feel of XP when entering installation information, it has to reboot often and at times resembles the Windows Server 2003 installation. I suspect this process will be improved in future versions of the software, because the focus for this release was to create a product suitable for OEM vendors to preinstall on their machines.

Even though the installation is not as refined as it could be, it still works very well. I have installed it on several machines and it has gone smoothly each time. Install with confidence!

Chapter 6

Installing the Connector

Y ou've networked all of your computers with a wired or a wireless network. You've purchased or built a Windows Home Server computer and installed the operating system. Now you need to take the final step in completing the construction of your home server — you need to connect all of your Windows computers to it. The piece of software you need to use for this task is called, appropriately enough, the Connector.

Installing the Connector accomplishes several things. For one, it tells the server about each of the Windows computers on your network and allows it to monitor their health and perform backups, and it allows the computers to be remote controlled.

The Connector also allows you to monitor and control the server from each of the Windows computers you install it on. The Connector installs as a system tray icon that can be used to launch the console application, view shared drives on the server, and monitor the server and its status reports on the health of the network without having to log onto the server desktop.

There are two options for installing the Connector. The simplest option is to install from the Connector installation CD that came with your Home Server system or with your System Builder package. Alternatively, you can install it directly from a shared folder on the server. The next sections walk you through both methods.

IN THIS CHAPTER

About the Connector

Installing from the CD

Installing from the server

Using the system tray icon

Reinstalling the Connector

Installing from the CD

Probably the simplest way to install the Connector is to use the installation CD that was provided with Windows Home Server. Follow these steps to install from the CD.

1. **Insert the CD into your computer's CD or DVD-ROM drive.** If you have AutoPlay enabled on your computer, the setup program should start automatically and you can proceed to Step 5. If the setup program does not start automatically you must run it manually.

2. **Open Windows Explorer (Figure 6.1).** The easiest way to do this is to use the keyboard shortcut Windows+E.

Locating the Connector setup program in Windows Explorer

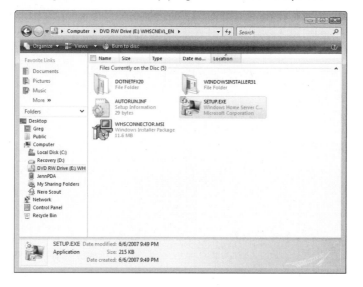

3. **In the folder tree on the left, find your CD-ROM drive.** You may need to expand the My Computer folder to see the list of drives. Click the CD-ROM drive letter.

4. **Double-click SETUP.EXE from the list of files on the CD on the right.**

5. **The Windows Home Server setup program (Figure 6.2) runs.**

6. **Click Next on the setup screen.**

7. **Review the terms of the license agreement and choose the Accept radio button.** Click Next again.

FIGURE 6.2

Running the Windows Home Server setup program

8. **The setup program then copies the necessary files to your computer.**

9. **Setup prompts you to enter your Windows Home Server password (Figure 6.3).**
   Enter the password that you chose at installation or that was provided with your server.

   If you don't remember your password, you can choose to view the hint that you provided.

FIGURE 6.3

Enter the Windows Home Server password to enable your computer to connect to the server.

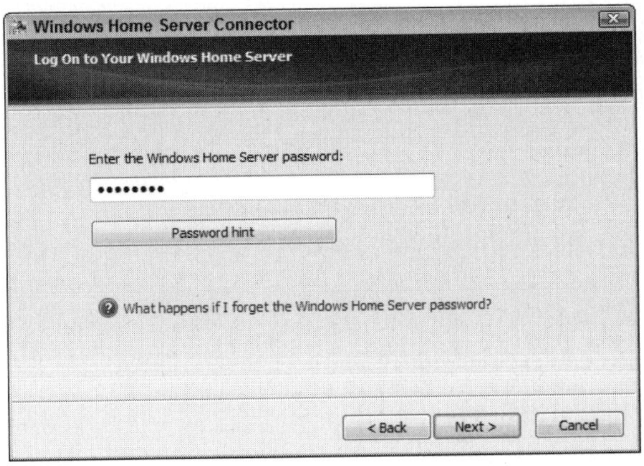

10. Setup now joins your computer to the server and sets up the initial backup settings, as shown in Figure 6.4.

FIGURE 6.4

Setup links your computer to the server.

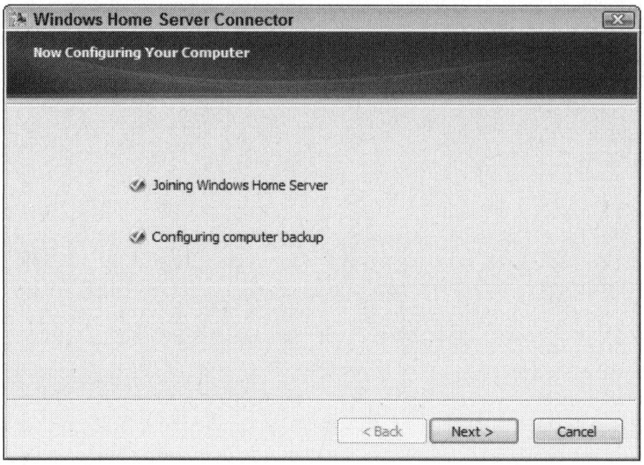

11. **Click Next to finalize the installation.** The final page of the setup, shown in Figure 6.5, shows you your initial backup settings for this computer. Click Finish to end the setup.

FIGURE 6.5

The Connector installation is complete.

Installing from the Server

If you have misplaced your Connector CD, or if you just don't happen to have it handy, there is another way to install the Connector. You can install it directly from Home Server because Microsoft had the foresight to create a Software shared folder that contains the programs that your client computers need.

Finding the Software shared folder

Because you don't have the Connector already installed, you may wonder how you can get to the shared folder. Fortunately, you can find it easily using Windows Explorer.

Follow these steps to find the Software share on your home server if you have Windows Vista:

1. **Click the Start button and then click the Network button.** The computers on your network are shown in the pane on the right in Explorer. One of them should be your server.

2. **Double-click the server's icon.** If you are prompted for a user name and password, enter **Administrator** for the user name along with the administrative password of your server.

3. **Double-click the Software folder to open it.**

4. **Open the Home Server Connector Software folder, shown in Figure 6.6.**

5. **Double-click SETUP.EXE to launch the Connector setup.** Continue the setup from Step 5 of the CD installation instructions from earlier in this chapter.

FIGURE 6.6

Browsing to the Connector folder using Vista

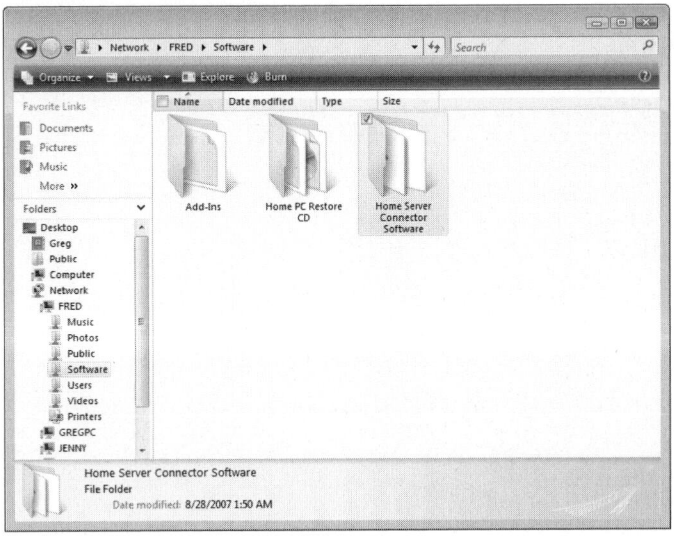

Follow these steps to find the Software share on your home server if you have Windows XP:

1. **Open Windows Explorer (press Windows+E, or find it under Start ⇨ All Programs ⇨ Accessories ⇨ Windows Explorer).**

2. **Click My Network Places in the tree on the left.**

3. **Click Entire Network.**

4. **Click Microsoft Windows Network.**

5. **Click the workgroup name that your server is on.** By default, it's in Workgroup.

6. **Double-click the server name, and open the Software folder.** If you are prompted for a username and password, enter **Administrator** for a password and your server's administrative password.

7. **Open the Home Server Connector Software folder, shown in Figure 6.7.**

8. **Double-click SETUP.EXE to launch the Connector setup.** Continue the setup from Step 5 of the CD installation instructions from earlier in this chapter.

FIGURE 6.7

Browsing to the Connector folder using Windows XP.

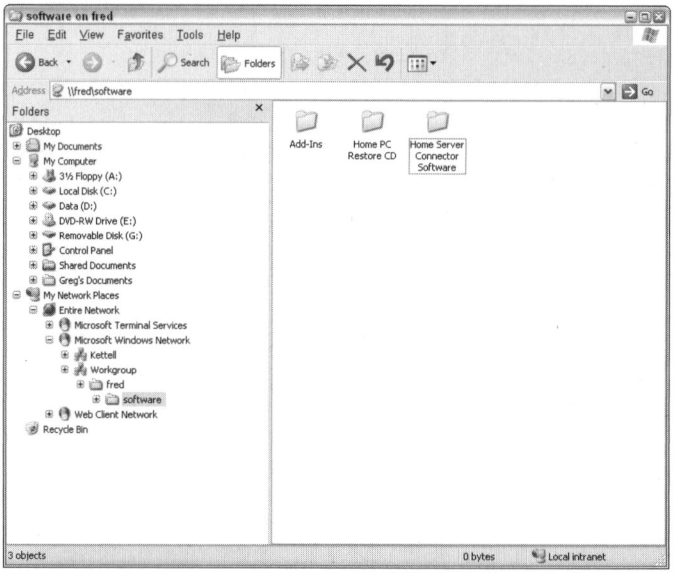

Accessing the Software shared folder directly

Occasionally, your server will not be visible in Explorer in the network section. Fortunately, you can enter the server name directly in the address bar in Explorer in both XP and Vista.

NOTE   If the address bar isn't visible in Explorer on XP, choose View ↪ Toolbars and make sure Address Bar is checked. Sometimes you have to drag it into view—right-click the toolbar and choose Unlock Toolbar if you are unable to drag the Address Bar.

To go directly to the server, enter two backslashes followed by the server name in the address bar. For example, if your server was named Fred, you would enter **\\fred** (case is not important) in the address bar, as shown in Figure 6.8.

FIGURE 6.8

Use Explorer to browse to the Connector setup folder on your server.

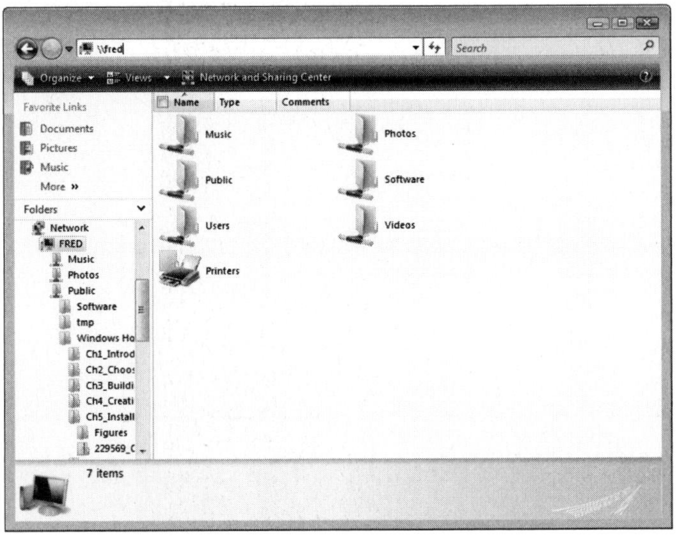

Using the Tray Icon

When you install the Connector, an icon is added to the system task tray (Figure 6.9). This icon is your main link to the server. You can use it to launch the Console, view your shared folders, and monitor the health of your server and computers on your network.

FIGURE 6.9

The system tray icon is your gateway to Windows Home Server.

System Tray icon

Exploring the tray icon status indicators

The tray icon's color and appearance change to indicate the status of your server and your computer's connection to it. The possible status indicators are as follows:

Healthy

A green icon shows that your server and all of the Windows computers connected to it are healthy. You can access the Console by double-clicking the icon in this state.

Offline

A gray icon indicates that your computer is unable to connect to your Windows Home Sever. If you see this icon, make sure that your computer is connected to the network and that the server is powered on and also connected to the network.

NOTE If your portable computer is taken off-site to a remote location, this status is normal.

Backing up

A blue icon is shown when the server is in the process of backing up your computer. If you see this icon, you shouldn't power off your computer until the icon changes again to ensure that your backup completes. You can check the status of the backup by double-clicking the tray icon.

At risk

A yellow icon is a warning that your computer or your server is at risk. You should connect to the Windows Home Server Console and click the Network Health button to learn what the problem is.

CROSS-REF For more information on accessing and using the Console, see Chapter 7.

Critical

A red icon indicates a critical state. You should connect to the Windows Home Server Console immediately and click the Network Health button to learn about the problem.

CROSS-REF For more information on monitoring your network health, see Chapter 11.

The tray icon menu

You can right click on the tray icon (Figure 6.10) to bring up a menu containing several common Home Server tasks:

- **Windows Home Server Console:** This item launches the console. This can also be accomplished in most cases by double-clicking the icon.

- **Backup now:** You can start a manual backup with this command.

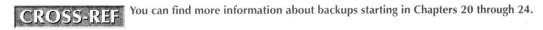

CROSS-REF You can find more information about backups starting in Chapters 20 through 24.

- **View Backup Status:** This item is enabled only if a backup is in progress (and the tray icon is blue). You can use it to view the current status of your backup.
- **Update Password:** Use this to change the password of this computer's user account.

CROSS-REF See Chapter 9 for more information about creating and managing user accounts.

- **Shared Folders:** This item opens a Windows Explorer window giving you access to the shared folders on your Home Server.
- **Display Network Health Notifications:** If this item is checked, this computer will receive health notifications from the server. This is the default setting. Uncheck this item if you don't want this particular computer to receive these notifications.
- **Help:** Accesses the Windows Home Server help file.
- **Exit:** Shuts down the tray icon. If you shut it down accidentally, you can restart it by clicking Start ⇨ All Programs ⇨ Startup ⇨ Windows Home Server.

FIGURE 6.10

Right-clicking the tray icon gives you access to common server tasks.

Windows Home Server Console
Backup Now...
View Backup Status
Update Password...
Shared Folders
Display Network Health Notifications
Help
Exit

Reinstalling the Connector

When you install the Connector, your computer is registered on the Home Server. The Connector knows about the server as well. If you need to replace your server for any reason, such as if you need to replace a piece of hardware, or if you need to reinstall the operating system, that link will be broken and you must reinstall the Connector on each of your computers.

Fortunately, the Connector setup program is smart enough to detect that you already have an instance of the Connector installed, and it prompts you to uninstall it before it reinstalls (Figure 6.11).

FIGURE 6.11

If you need to reinstall the Connector, the previous instance will automatically be uninstalled for you.

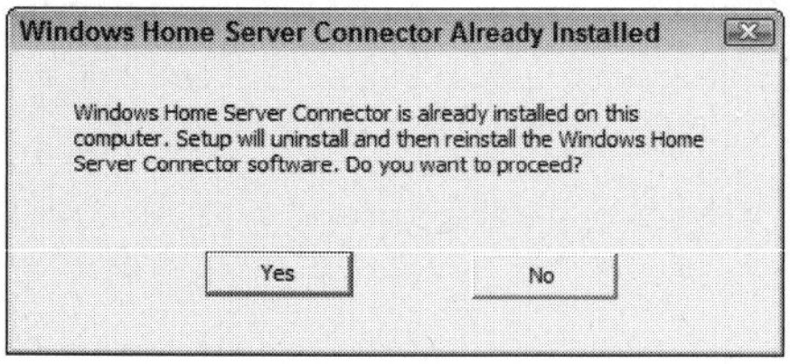

Summary

Now that you've installed the Connector on each of your Windows computers, your Windows Home Server installation is complete. Your server now knows about your computers, and you can access and manage the server from whichever computer you choose.

Now comes the fun part — configuring the server to make it do what you want it to do. The next few chapters explain how to configure computer backup, set up shared folders, stream media, and access everything remotely. It's time to put Windows Home Server to work!

Chapter 7

Touring the Console

Y ou may not think of servers as user friendly. In fact, if you think of them at all you probably think of them as those computers hidden away in your company's data center, and maintained by IT techs specially trained in the arcane knowledge of the commands necessary to keep them running smoothly.

In developing a Home Server product, Microsoft has sought to change all of that. They knew that the key to creating a successful Home Server product was to make it easy enough for anybody to use. The most visible aspect of this decision is the program they created to easily manage all aspects of the server. This program is the Windows Home Server Console.

The console is accessible from any Windows computer connected to your network, or directly from the server's desktop. You can even access it from anywhere over the Internet if you so desire. The goal of this chapter is to give you an overview of the Console, while touching on some of the major features of Windows Home Server that can be managed from it. Later chapters go into more detail concerning these Home Server features.

Launching the Console

You can launch the Console from the server's desktop, but more often than not you will probably launch it from one of the computers on which you've installed the Connector. When you install the Connector, it installs an icon in your system tray that is your launching point for various Home Server items.

NOTE The Console is not resizable and really needs a screen resolution of 1024 x 768 or higher to be useful. If your computer is running at a resolution of 800 x 600, you should look into changing the display settings in the Control Panel if you want to run the Console on that computer.

To access the Console, double-click the Windows Home Server icon in the system tray. When it launches, the Home Server login screen (Figure 7.1) appears. If you have chosen to have the Console remember your password, the login screen will already be filled in, and all you have to do is click the arrow button or press Enter to access the Console.

NOTE If you are unable to connect to the server, verify that you are connected to the network and that the server is as well. If you are using a wireless connection, make sure that your connection settings are correct.

FIGURE 7.1

Logging into the Console

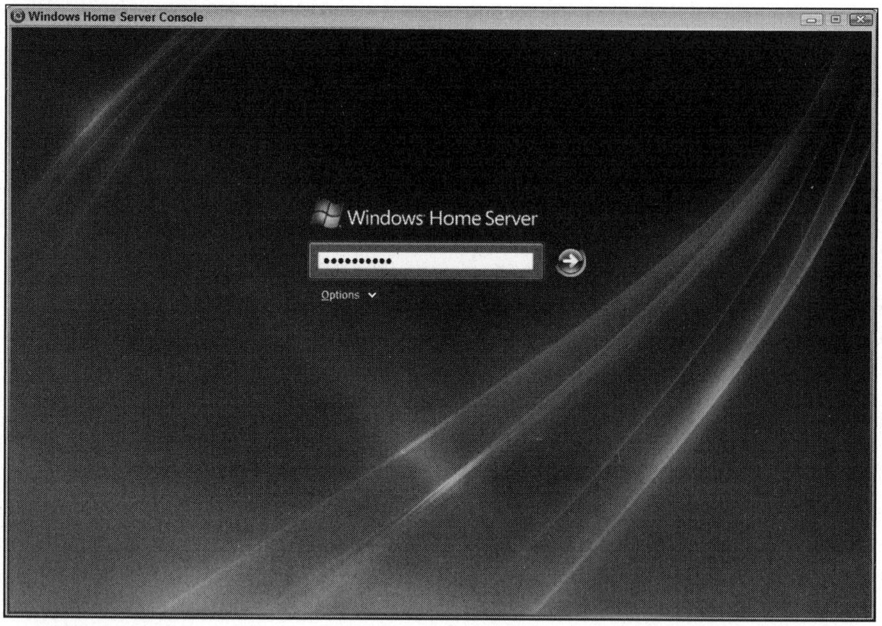

Before you sign in, you may notice that there are a few other options available on the login screen. Click the Options drop-down list to access them, as shown in Figure 7.2. The additional options are the following.

- **Remember the Windows Home Server password:** Check this option if you want this computer user to continue to keep track of the Home Server's administrator password. Uncheck it if you want to require this user to enter the password. This is useful if you want to prevent children from accessing this server, for example.

- **Password hint:** This item displays the password hint that you provided when you first entered your Home Server password.

- **Reset the Windows Home Server Console:** If the Console appears unresponsive and you are unable to log into it, choose this item to reset it on the server.

FIGURE 7.2

The Options drop-down menu gives you control over your connection.

Exploring the Console Interface

In keeping with the goal for Home Server to be the server OS for nontechnical folks, the Console interface has been kept quite simple. Most of the major functions that Home Server provides are accessible via large tabs at the top of the Console window. Underneath the tabs is a toolbar with buttons that are specific to the function of the currently selected tab.

All of the space below the toolbar is used to provide the information specific to that function in an uncluttered, easy-to-read manner. These details of the Console window are shown in Figure 7.3.

The following sections explore each of the tabs on the Console and describe their function. When appropriate, you'll be directed to the chapters in which specific features are discussed in more detail.

FIGURE 7.3

The major components of the Console interface

Computers & Backup tab

Selecting the Computers & Backup tab shows you a list of all of the Windows XP and Vista computers that your server knows about, which is to say all of the computers that have had the Connector installed on them. Computers that are not currently connected to the server are grayed out.

Although you can use this tab to see the computers on your network, its main purpose is for backups. From this tab, shown in Figure 7.4, you can view backups, start manual backups, or use the Configure Backups button to launch the Backup Wizard, which lets you customize each computer's backup settings.

If you retire one of your home computers, this is the place you go to remove the computer from the server's list. Simply click the Remove Computer button and accept the acknowledgement, then click Remove. You will need to uninstall the Connector on the computer itself, through the Control Panel's Add & Remove Programs applet.

FIGURE 7.4

The Computers & Backup tab is used to manage and monitor backups for your Windows computers.

NOTE Windows Home Server allows for a maximum of ten computers to be connected to it and managed through this tab. If you already have ten computers listed on the Computers & Backup tab, you must remove an existing one to add any more.

Fortunately, this ten-computer limitation does not apply to accessing file shares or other server functions of Windows Home Server. It limits only the number of computers that can have the Connector installed and be backed up to the server.

CROSS-REF Backups are an important feature of Windows Home Server. For extensive information on backing up and restoring the computers on your network, see Chapters 20 through 24.

User Accounts tab

The User Accounts tab, shown in Figure 7.5, is used to keep "tabs" on the users of your network (that is, you and your family). On this tab you can add, remove, and decide which shared folders a user should be able to access.

Every person in your household who needs access to the server should have his or her own user account. This account allows access to shared folders that are available to anyone, as well as to shared folders that only that user can access (one of which is created automatically when you create the user account). A single user account can be used to access the server from any number of computers; however, user accounts should normally match the user name used on the computer they are connecting from.

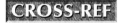

CROSS-REF **More information about adding and maintaining user accounts can be found in Chapter 9.**

FIGURE 7.5

Keep track of users on the User Accounts tab.

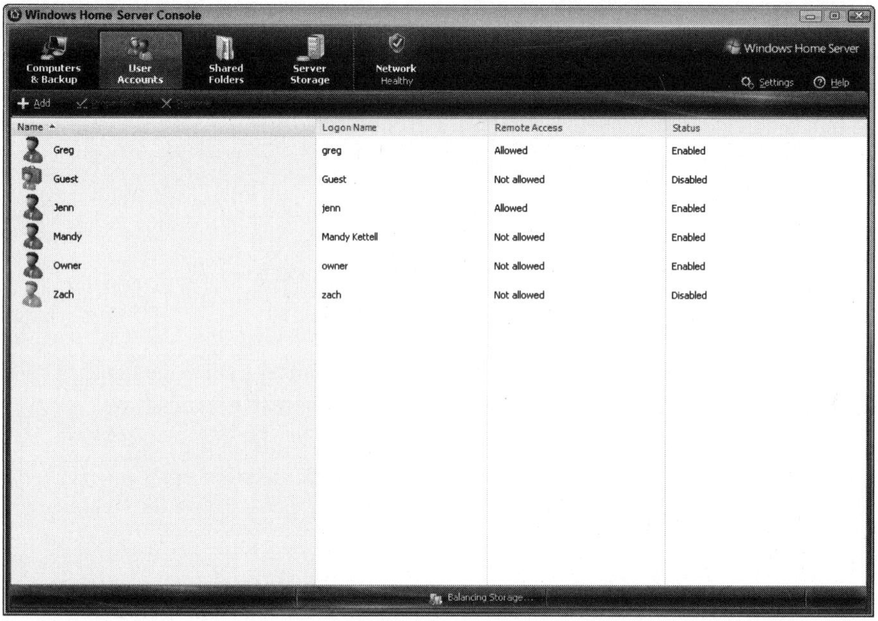

Windows Home Server Console
Computers & Backup
User Accounts
Shared Folders
Server Storage
Network Healthy
Windows Home Server
Settings
Help
Add
Name
Logon Name
Remote Access
Status
Greg
greg
Allowed
Enabled
Guest
Guest
Not allowed
Disabled
Jenn
jenn
Allowed
Enabled
Mandy
Mandy Kettell
Not allowed
Enabled
Owner
owner
Not allowed
Enabled
Zach
zach
Not allowed
Disabled
Balancing Storage...

Shared Folders tab

The third tab in the Console is the Shared Folders tab (shown in Figure 7.6). The Shared Folders tab allows you to add, remove, and configure the shared folders on your server. You can also control user access to the shared folders here.

Windows Home Server creates several shared folders that cannot be removed. They are the Public, Music, Photos, Software, and Videos folders.

In addition to these folders, a shared folder is automatically created for each user account. Additional folders can be added manually.

CROSS-REF   See Chapter 12 for more information about sharing folders.

FIGURE 7.6

Use the Shared Folders tab to create and manage folders that are accessible to connected computers.

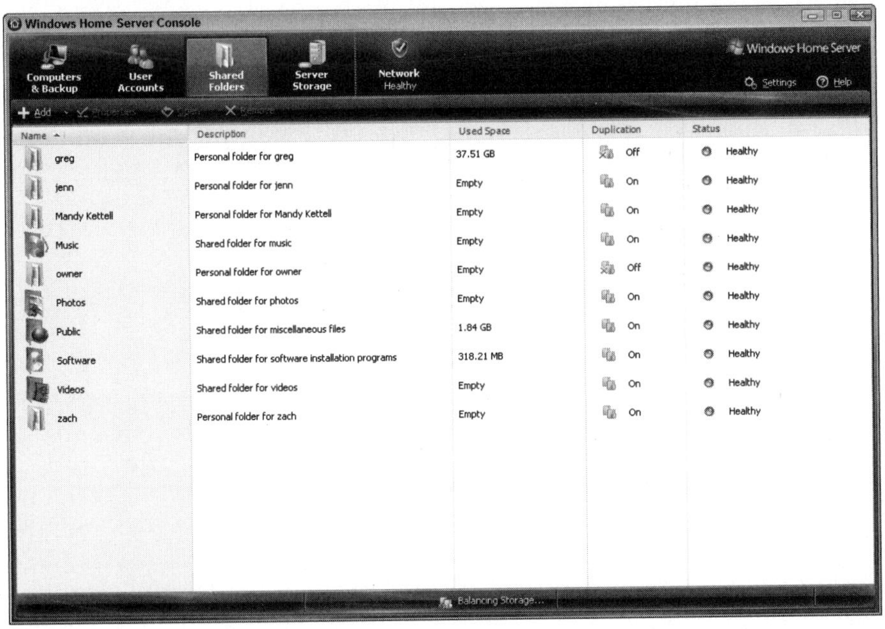

Server Storage tab

With all of the backups you are doing and files you are sharing on the server, you need to be able to tell just how full your server's hard drives are getting. The Server Storage tab, shown in Figure 7.7, is just the place for that.

This tab shows you all of the hard drives on your server along with their status. On the right side of the window is a pie chart that shows you at a glance just how much of your storage has been used, and what it has been used for. It's easy to tell of your storage is being used for backups, shared files, and folder duplication.

CROSS-REF   Find out more about adding hard drives to your server in Chapter 3.

The drives on your server are grouped into two categories: Server Storage and Non Storage. Drives in the Server Storage category are used for the storage pool, which is the storage available for shared folders and backups. Drives that you have connected to the server but not added to the storage pool are listed in the Non Server Storage category.

> **FIGURE 7.7**

The Server Storage tab lets you manage the hard drives in your server.

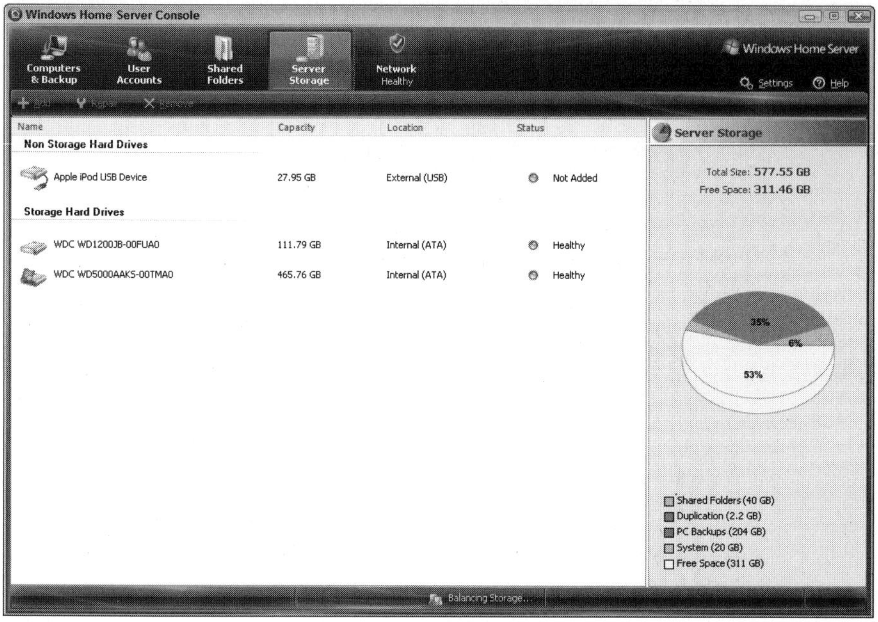

> **NOTE** You may have drives that you don't want to include in the storage pool, say for a server application that needs its own server. It is perfectly reasonable not to add a drive to the Server Storage category and instead format it on the Server for such use. Just be sure that you don't add it to the Server Storage later because it will format the hard drive, erasing all content on it.

The drive list shows you the following information for each of the hard drives on your server:

- **Name:** This is the manufacturer's identification for the drive, pulled from the drive's ROM. This is the same identification that you would see in your server's BIOS.

- **Capacity:** Tells you the amount of storage provided by the drive, in gigabytes.

> **NOTE** You may have noticed that the reported drive capacity is less than you may expect it to be based on the hard drive's specs. The answer is that the capacity shown by Windows is measured in true gigabytes, where one gigabyte is equal to 1,073,741,824 (or 1024^3) bytes. Hard drive manufacturers typically measure their hard drive with one gigabyte equal to 1,000,000,000 (or 1000^3) bytes.

- **Location:** This tells you whether a drive is internal or external, as well as the type of drive that it is (ATA, USB, SCSI).

- **Status:** Shows you the current status and health of the hard drive.

Network Health button

Being able to see the status of your networked computers at a glance is a tremendous help in staying on top of potential problems. Click the Network Health button (because it launches a dialog box instead of displaying information in the window below, it's not really a tab) to view color-coded status messages from your server and connected computers, shown in Figure 7.8.

CROSS-REF For more information on monitoring the health of computers on your network, see Chapter 11.

FIGURE 7.8

The Network Health tab is where you monitor the health of your server and the computers connected to it.

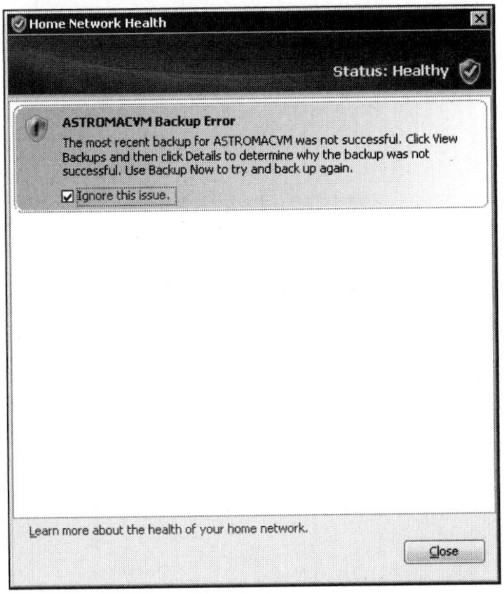

NOTE Health status notifications are available only for computers running Windows Vista.

Discovering Additional Console Features

Although the tabs are the most obvious features of the Console, there are a few other key features of the Console to discuss as well, including the Settings dialog box, the status bar, and the help system.

Settings

Although they didn't see fit to put it on a tab, the Settings dialog box, shown in Figure 7.9, is one of the most important features of the server. Here is where you can make changes to the overall settings that affect your server.

The Settings dialog box is used for most Home Server configuration tasks.

To access the Settings dialog box, click the Settings button on the upper-right portion of the Console. The following items can be configured from this dialog box:

- **General:** These are the settings that didn't fit under the other categories. These include the Date & Time, Region, Windows Update settings, and whether or not you want to report errors or participate in the Windows Customer Experience Improvement program.

- **Backup:** Here you can configure global backup settings, such as the time of day to back up your computers, and the length of time to keep backups. You can also elect to purge old backups from here.

- **Passwords:** Set the user account password policy, and change your Administrator password here.

- **Media Sharing:** Control the media library sharing for the Photo, Video, and Music shared folders.

■ **Remote Access:** Configure the remote access settings for your server, including the domain name to use to reach your server as well as configuration settings for the Web site hosted on your server.

■ **Add-ins:** Install and remove add-ins that have been created for adding functionality to your server.

■ **Resources:** Activate Windows and view server software versions. There are also some useful links to sites with information on Windows Home Server.

NOTE These buttons are those that Windows Home Server provides. It is possible that your server's manufacturer or an add-in you installed added another item to the settings window. Please consult the documentation for these products to learn more about them.

CROSS-REF The Settings dialog box is discussed in Chapter 8.

Shutdown

In the lower left of the Settings dialog box is the Shut Down button. This button allows you to shut down or restart the server. Clicking this button displays the shutdown options as shown in Figure 7.10. Simply click the option you want.

NOTE If you choose to shut down the server rather than restart it, you must physically turn the computer back on to restart it later.

FIGURE 7.10

The Shut Down button lets you restart the server remotely.

The Console status bar

The status bar at the bottom of the Console window, shown in Figure 7.11, shows three different status indicators for the server. They are as follows:

■ **Remote Access status:** The left side of the status bar shows any user that is accessing the server remotely through the Web interface.

- **Drive Extender status:** Drive extender is the technology that allows Windows Home Server to combine various hard drives into one storage pool. This status indicates whether the drives are balanced, meaning any folders marked for duplication have been copied to their backup folder, or if they are balancing.

- **Backup status:** On the right side of the status bar, the name of any computer that is currently being backed up along with the percentage complete is shown. Backups of multiple computers happen sequentially.

FIGURE 7.11

The status bar shows activities that are currently in progress.

| Remote access: greg | Balancing Storage... | Backing up JENNY (6%) |

Help

The Help button is next to the Settings button on the upper right side of the Console window. Clicking this button activates the Help system, shown in Figure 7.12. To make it easier to find information on your current activity, the Help system automatically goes to the section specific to the tab or dialog box that you happen to be on.

FIGURE 7.12

Activating the Help screen

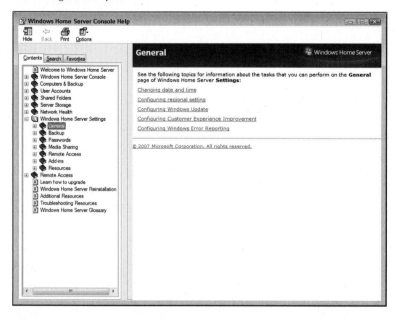

Summary

The Console is the face of Windows Home Server. For many users, it will be all they ever see, because Microsoft designed it to be the one place where all Windows Home Server functions are managed in as simple a way as possible. The same Console look and feel is available on the server's desktop, on a client computer, or even remotely over the Internet. Only one user may be connected to the Console at a time.

This chapter has presented a quick overview of the features and use of the Console. The next chapter goes into more detail on configuring the server settings.

Chapter 8

Configuring Windows Home Server

Your Home Server is now operational and you've installed the Connector on each of your Windows computers. In the last chapter, you toured the Console so that you could become familiar with the features of Windows Home Server and how they are managed. This chapter digs deeper into the server configuration.

Configuring General Settings

General   The General Settings page, shown in Figure 8.1, is used to configure global settings for the server itself, instead of settings for any one particular feature. These are settings that you may have entered when you first installed Windows Home Server, and to change them in most versions of Windows you would typically have to go to the Control Panel. You can do this on Windows Home Server, as well, but putting them in the Settings dialog box, however, reduces the need to ever visit the server's desktop, which is in keeping with the headless server philosophy.

CROSS-REF Installing Windows Home Server, including the initial server settings, is discussed in Chapter 5.

Here is a look at the settings that you can change on the Settings page.

IN THIS CHAPTER

Configuring General settings

Scheduling backups

Establishing a password policy

Sharing media

Enabling remote access

Installing add-ins

Accessing resources

FIGURE 8.1

The General Settings page is used to configure server settings.

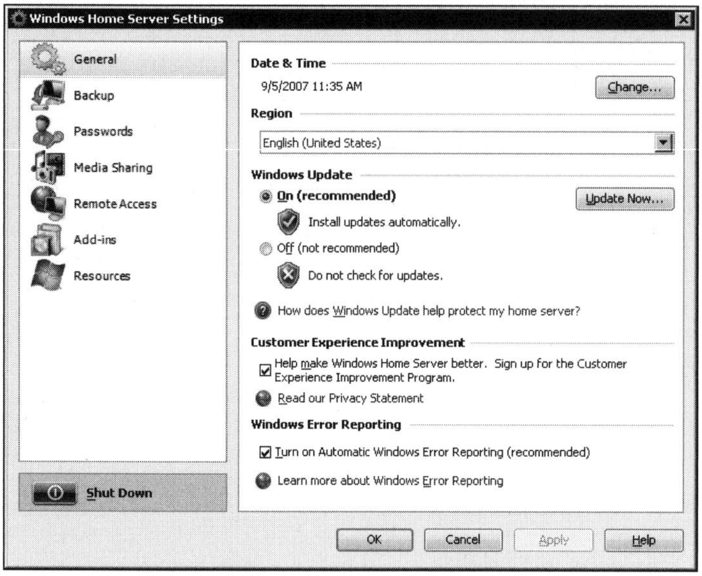

Setting the date and time

If you didn't install Windows Home Server yourself, you never had the opportunity to set the initial date and time settings. The Settings dialog box gives you the opportunity to do so at any time without having to visit the server's control panel.

To set the date and time, click Change. A standard Windows Date and Time Properties dialog box, as shown in Figure 8.2, lets you set the clock, the date, and choose a time zone. Click the Internet Time tab to configure automatic time synchronization with a number of time servers.

NOTE Time synchronization is the default setting, and it requires that your server is connected to the Internet at the scheduled update time.

Choosing a region

If your region differs from the default setting (typically English United States), you can change it in this section. Choose your correct region from the drop-down list to ensure that the server is configured correctly for your country or region. This setting affects the display of information such as dates, times, currency units, and measurement units. For example, European users would likely prefer that currency be displayed in Euros instead of dollars, measurements in metric rather than English, and dates formatted as DD/MM/YY instead of the U.S. standard format of MM//DD/YY. As Figure 8.3 shows, you can see the immediate effect of this setting by looking in the formatting of the Date & Time display.

FIGURE 8.2

You can choose to automatically synchronize your server's clock via an Internet time server.

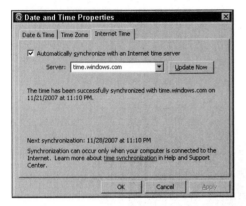

FIGURE 8.3

The effect of the regional settings is immediately apparent in the Date & Time settings.

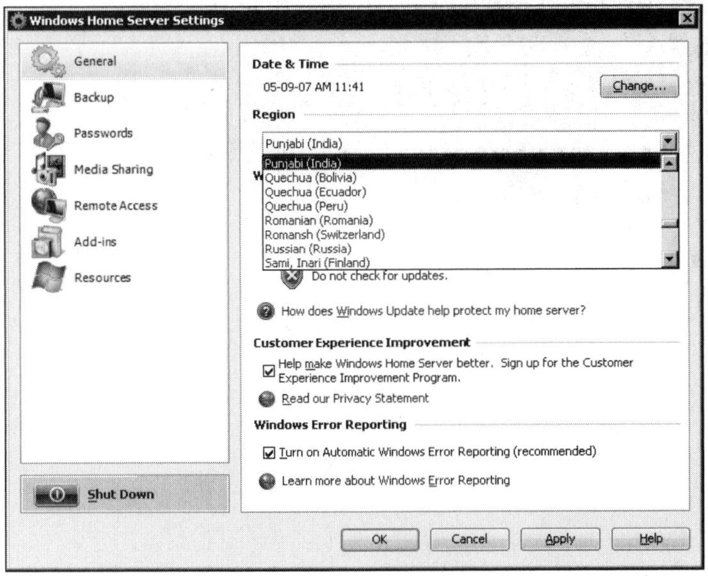

Running Windows Update

Windows Update is familiar to most Windows users, and it's the same concept with Windows Home Server. You can choose to have updates install automatically (the default setting), or you can choose to not perform updates. I recommend that you choose to install them automatically. If you choose automatic installation, you are notified whenever updates are ready to be installed in the Console in the Network Health area.

No matter what setting you choose, you can click Update Now to check for updates to be installed. If there are updates, you are given the option of installing them. If not, you are given the all clear, as shown in Figure 8.4.

FIGURE 8.4

Windows Update helps to keep your server secure.

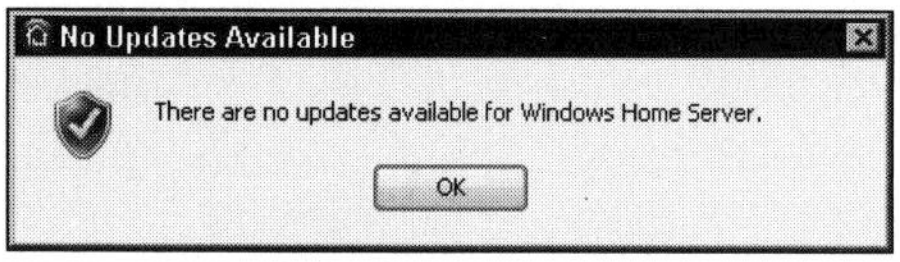

Customer Experience Improvement Program

The Customer Experience Improvement Program was described in Chapter 5, but if you bought a Windows Home Server box and didn't install the OS yourself, you may have missed it. The CEIP gathers information and statistics about your server such as the features you use the most as well as the way that you access them. This information is collected anonymously so that Microsoft can use it to improve its products. Many of the design changes that Microsoft has made to its core products in recent years have been a result of the feedback obtained from this program.

To enable participation in the CEIP, select the check box to sign up. You can click the Read our Privacy Statement link to be directed to a Microsoft Web site with the CEIP privacy policy.

ON the WEB For more information about the Customer Experience Improvement Program, visit `www.microsoft.com/products/ceip/en-us/default.mspx`.

Windows Error Reporting

The Windows Error Reporting Program is another program that has been provided in order to gather information about Microsoft products in order to improve them. When an error occurs, this program automatically reports it to Microsoft for analysis. According to Microsoft, the information that is collected includes the following:

- Whether the problem was caused by hardware or software
- The severity of the problem, and the type of error reported
- System files that can help diagnose the problem, typically containing information about the behavior of the system before or after the error occurred
- Software and hardware configuration information such as the OS version, hardware manufacturers and product models, memory and hard drive size

When an error occurs on a typical Windows computer, it often asks you whether you want to submit information about the error to Microsoft. Due to the headless nature of Windows Home Server, you may never see such an error if you aren't looking at the server's desktop. For this reason, you have the option of submitting errors to Microsoft automatically. Select the check box in this section if you want to participate. You can also click the Learn more about Windows Error Reporting link to get more information about this program.

Modifying Backup Settings

🖥️ Backup   Backups are one of the major features of Windows Home Server, and they are covered extensively in Part V of this book. For completeness, the Backup settings available in the Settings dialog box, shown in Figure 8.5, are covered.

FIGURE 8.5

Configuring the server backup settings

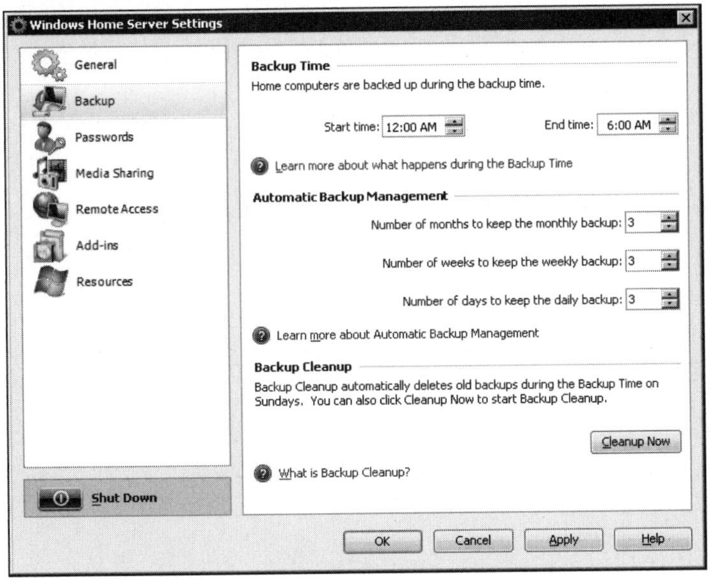

Setting backup time

The Backup Time settings allow you to set the start and end times for backups on your network. The default setting for this feature is to have backups start between 12:00 AM and 6:00 AM. No backups will start after the end time has passed, but a backup that is already in progress will continue to completion. Additionally, you cannot schedule the start and end times for a backup less than 60 minutes apart from each other.

> **TIP** You may want to change this setting to sometime during the day if your computers aren't always on. There typically won't be much of a performance hit when backing up, and you can always cancel a backup in progress if you find it is impacting performance.

The following things happen during the backup time period:

- Computers with backups enabled are backed up sequentially. This means that only one computer will be running a backup at any one time.
- Any pending automatic Windows updates are installed during the backup time. The server will reboot itself if necessary.
- Backup cleanup will run on Sundays. This will delete old backups in accordance with your backup management settings.

Managing automatic backups

With automatic backups, your computer is backed up every day.

There are three configuration settings for managing automated backups:

- **Number of months to keep the monthly backup:** This value specifies the number of months to keep the first backup of the month. The default is 3 months.
- **Number of weeks to keep the weekly backup:** This value specifies the number of weeks to keep the first backup of each week. The default is 3 weeks.
- **Number of days to keep the daily backup:** This value sets the number of days to keep daily backups. The default value for this is 3 days.

> **NOTE** If you have a notebook computer that isn't always able to connect to the network for backups, or a computer that you don't leave on all the time, don't worry about your backups being deleted after the management setting time has passed. Windows Home Server will keep the previous backups up to the number of days, weeks, or months specified.

Running Backup Cleanup

The final item on the backup page is the Backup Cleanup. This isn't really a configuration setting, as backup cleanups normally occur each Sunday during the backup time. Instead, there is a Cleanup Now button that can be used to force a backup cleanup. You can do this if you know that a computer won't be connected to the network during the normal Sunday backup cycle.

When you click this button, a warning appears telling you that the cleanup process may take a long time, as shown in Figure 8.6. You may not think deleting a backup file should take a tremendous amount of time; however, Windows Home Server's backup process is designed to conserve storage by only storing one copy of a file that is shared across multiple backups. This means that the cleanup must iterate over all of the files in the backup and verify that it is the only backup referencing that file before it is actually deleted.

> **TIP** Manually cleaning up backups may seem like a good way of reclaiming server space, but in reality it may not do much. The backup process is very efficient, and if a computer has a lot of files in common with another computer on the network, or with other backups of the same computer, there won't be a lot of files deleted with each cleanup.

FIGURE 8.6

A manual backup cleanup will remove old backups for you, but it may take a while.

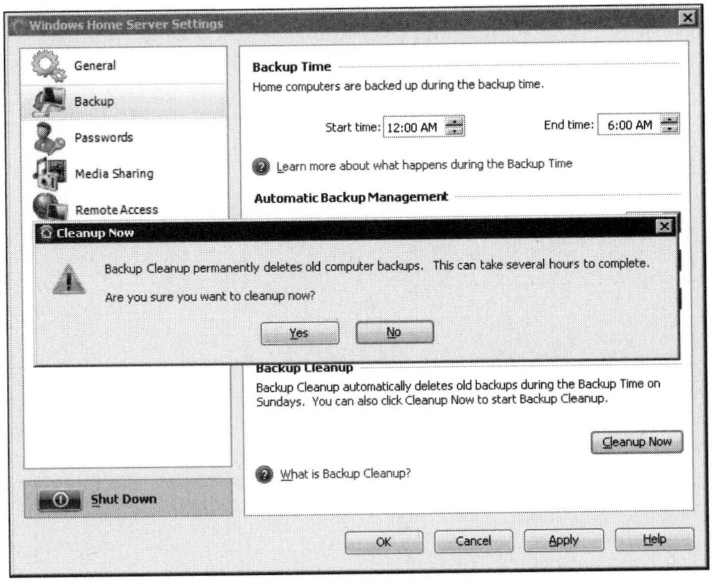

Setting and Changing Passwords

Passwords are the front line of security for your server, so it is important to maintain them. The Passwords page of the Settings dialog box, shown in Figure 8.7, allows you to change your administrative password as well as set the password policy for user accounts.

FIGURE 8.7

Setting the server's password policy

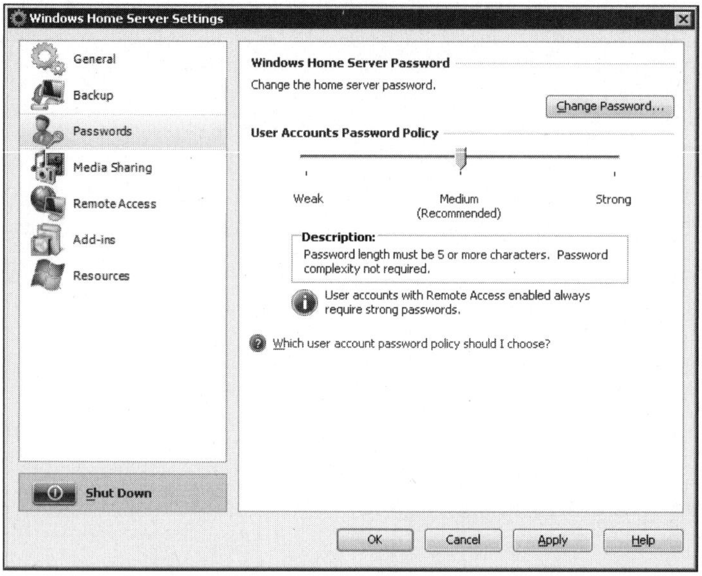

Changing the administrator password

The administrator password, also known as the Windows Home Server password, is the most important password on your server. Knowledge of this password can enable anyone to gain access to your server and all of the files on it. Therefore, it is a good idea to change it regularly and limit the number of people with whom you share it.

To change the password, click Change Password to display the Windows Home Server Password Change dialog box, as shown in Figure 8.8. Type the new password, a confirmation of that password, and a password hint.

> **CAUTION** Password hints are viewable to anyone on the server. If you make it too obvious, someone else may be able to figure out the password without much difficulty.

The administrator password must conform to the strong password requirements, which are discussed in the next section.

> **CAUTION** While you don't want to make the password too easy to guess, don't make it so difficult that you could forget it as well. If you forget this password, you will not be able to access the server and you'll have to reinstall Windows Home Server.

FIGURE 8.8

Changing the Windows Home Server password

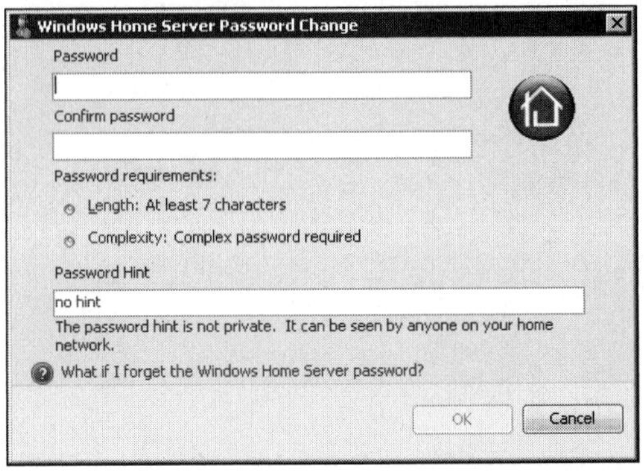

Choosing a password policy

The User Accounts Password Policy slider lets you set the password policy to one of three different values. They are as follows:

- **Weak:** This setting allows passwords that are of any length with no restrictions whatsoever. You can even have user accounts with no password at all if you desire. This setting is not recommended, as it can reduce the security of your network.

- **Medium:** This setting requires all users to have a minimum password length of five characters. No other complexity is required. This is the default setting.

- **Strong:** This setting requires all passwords to be strong. Strong passwords must be at least seven characters and meet the complex password requirements. A complex password must contain at least three of these four categories of characters:

  - Uppercase letters
  - Lowercase letters
  - Numbers
  - Symbols

The following password would be considered complex:

```
Lkj#01fT
```

This password contains upper- and lowercase letters, symbols, and numbers and is eight characters long, therefore it exceeds the minimum requirements. Now take a look at another password:

```
port0123
```

This password is not complex because it only contains two of the three character categories — lowercase letters and numbers.

> **NOTE** No matter what setting you choose for password complexity, the administrator and user accounts that you want to be able to access remotely need to have strong passwords.

Configuring Media Sharing

Media file sharing is another major feature of Windows Home Server, and is described extensively in Part IV. The settings that can be configured on the Media Sharing page of the Settings dialog box, as shown in Figure 8.9, will be described in full.

FIGURE 8.9

Configuring media sharing

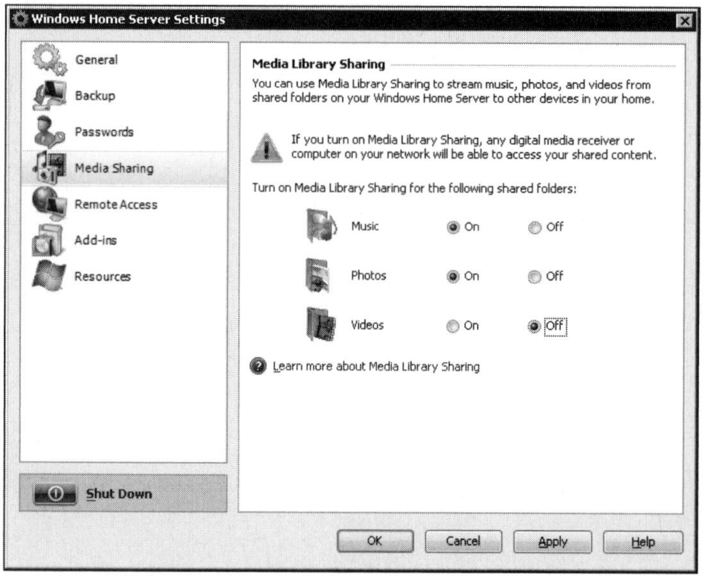

There are three categories of files that can be shared: music, photos, and video. When sharing is enabled, these files can be shared to any digital media receiver (DMR) connected to your network such as another PC, an Xbox 360, or a dedicated streaming media playback device.

To allow media streaming for a particular type of media, select the On radio button for that type. To disable streaming, select the Off radio button.

Media files are actually stored in shared folders named Music, Photos and Videos. These shared folders are created automatically when Windows Home Server is installed, and cannot be removed. When you enable one of the categories of media on the Media Sharing tab, all media files in the corresponding shared folder will be accessible via streaming.

CAUTION Media file sharing security is rudimentary at best, and works regardless of the settings for the shared folders. If you enable sharing for the Music folder, for example, but have the folder itself configured so that users don't have access, they will still be able to stream the files in your music folder.

CROSS-REF See Chapter 12 for more information about these and other shared folders.

Setting Remote Access

 Remote Access

The Remote Access page on the Settings dialog box, shown in Figure 8.10, is used to configure remote access to the server as well as the server's Web site settings. Because remote access is the subject of Part IV of this book, I won't go into great detail here but will discuss the configuration settings available on this page.

FIGURE 8.10

Configuring remote access settings

Windows Home Server Settings

General	**Web Site Connectivity**
Backup	Web sites are on. [Turn Off]
Passwords	
Media Sharing	**Router**
Remote Access	Status: Working
Add-ins	[Details...] [Unconfigure]
Resources	**Domain Name**
	Status: Working
	Name: https://gregk.homeserver.com
	[Details...] [Change...] [Unconfigure]
	Web Site Settings
	Web Site Home Page
	Windows Home Server Home Page
	Web Site Headline
	Windows Home Server Web Site
[Shut Down]	[OK] [Cancel] [Apply] [Help]

Enabling Web site connectivity

The Web Site Connectivity button is a simple toggle that enables or disables the Web site hosted by your Windows Home Server. The Web site is used both for remote access to files and computers on your network and for any custom Web sites you may add to the server. Turn this feature off if you don't want to enable remote access of any sort, or if you just want to turn it off for a period of time.

> **TIP** If you plan to remotely access your server regularly, you probably don't want to turn this off, as it's easy to forget that you disabled it. When you are out of town on a business trip and you need access to a file that you have forgotten is not a good time to remember that you forgot to enable your Web site connectivity.

Configuring the router

In order to be able to access your server over the Internet, your router must be configured to forward HTTP Web requests to the server. This is accomplished behind the scenes via an arcane protocol known as Network Address Translation (NAT). Fortunately, if you have a router that supports Universal Plug & Play (UPnP) configuration, Windows Home Server should be able to automatically configure this for you.

To attempt to automatically configure your router, click Setup. (If this button is not visible, your router is already configured for port forwarding or it cannot be.) The Router Status indicator will display one of the following values as it attempts to configure your router:

- **Not configured:** Your router has not been configured yet, or you have turned off your Web site connectivity.

- **Configuring:** Windows Home Server is currently in the process of configuring your router.

- **Testing:** Configuration is complete, and Windows Home Server is attempting to connect to itself via the Web domain.

- **Working:** Configuration and testing completed successfully.

- **Unknown:** Configuration completed successfully, but the server was unable to test the connection.

- **Disabled:** The connectivity to your Web site is disabled for some reason.

While your router is being configured, and afterward, you can click Details to see the current status of the configuration. The Router Configuration Details dialog box is shown in Figure 8.11.

FIGURE 8.11

The router configuration status display

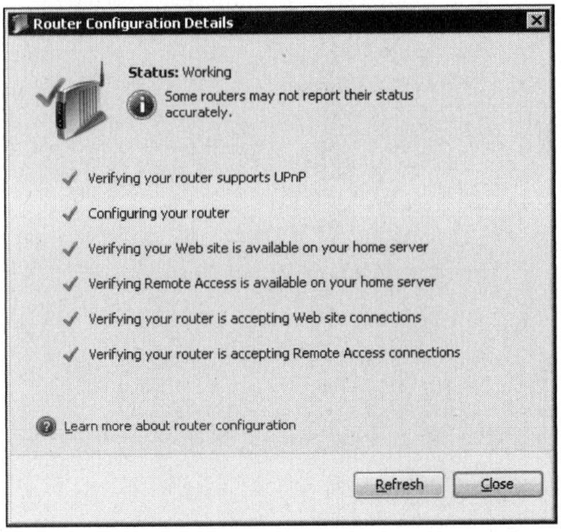

Setting up a domain name

In order to access your home network over the Web, you need to set up a *domain name*. A domain name is an address that that can be used to route a Web request to the proper server. www.microsoft.com and www.google.com are examples of common domain names. When you type the name into your browser, your computer accesses a *domain name system server* that translates the domain name into the IP address of the server.

Your purchase of Windows Home Server gives you the ability to create a domain for your server on the homeserver.com subdomain. As long as the name isn't taken, you can claim it.

CROSS-REF You can find more information about creating your own domain name using the Domain Name Setup Wizard in Chapter 17.

Configuring Web site settings

Two additional settings on the Remote Access page allow you to set some of the parameters of Windows Home Server's Web server — the Web Site Home Page and the Web Site Headline.

Web Site Home Page

The Web server creates two sites by default: One is your Windows Home Server home page, and the other is the Windows Home Server Remote Access page. This setting lets you choose which one you want to have as the default.

If you choose to have the Home Server home page as the default, you can still access the Remote Access page in two ways.

- On the default Home Server home page, there is a Log On button on the upper right of the page, as shown in Figure 8.12.

- If you type your Home Server address into your browser with an "https" prefix, it automatically goes to the Remote Access page regardless of this setting. Figure 8.13 shows the Remote Access login page.

Web Site Headline

The Web Site Headline is displayed on your home page. You can see an example of the default headline in Figure 8.12.

FIGURE 8.12

The default Windows Home Server home page

FIGURE 8.13

The Remote Access login page

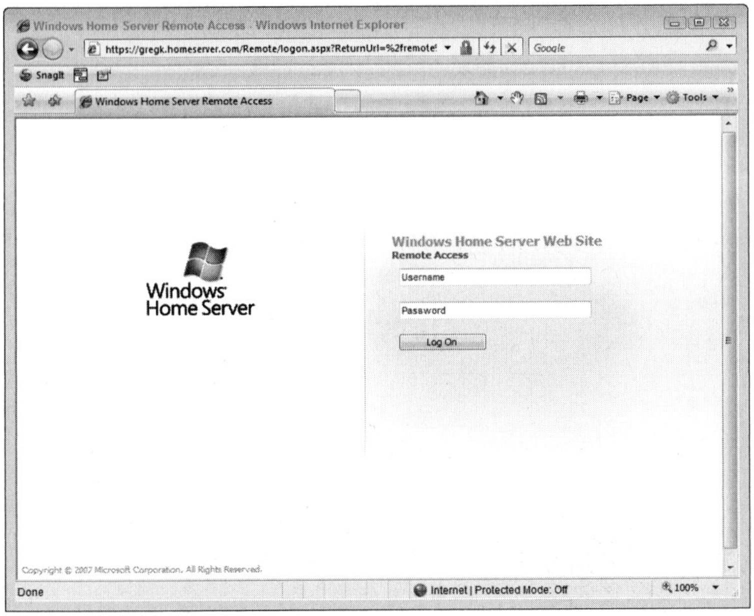

Using Add-ins

Add-ins Add-ins are an important concept for Windows Home Server. As great as the built-in functionality is, the real power with the OS is the endless amount of expandability that it offers through the use of add-ins. The Add-ins page, shown in Figure 8.14, shows two tabs. The function of these two tabs is as follows:

■ **Installed:** These tabs can be used to see the add-ins that are installed on the server.

■ **Available:** Here you can see add-ins that haven't been installed yet.

CROSS-REF Some popular add-ins are discussed in detail in Chapter 32. If you are a programmer, you may want to develop your own add-ins. See Chapter 36 for an example.

FIGURE 8.14

Configuring add-ins

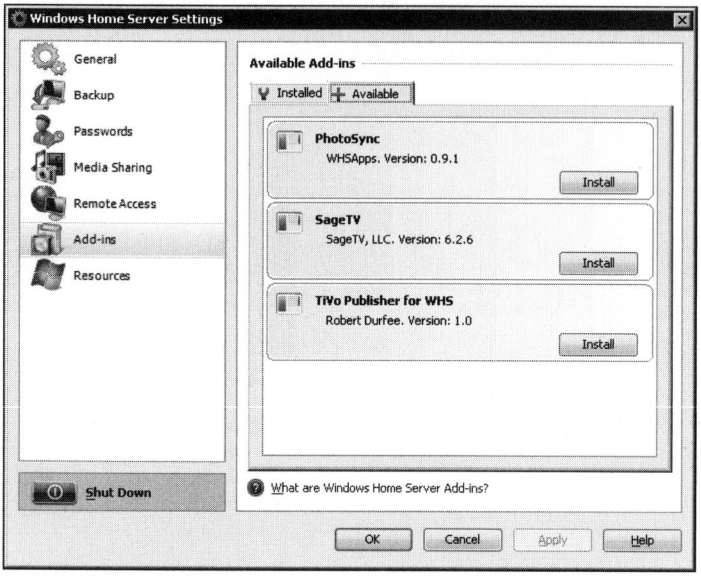

Finding Helpful Resources

Resources   The final page of the Settings dialog box is the Resources page, as shown in Figure 8.15. This page provides useful information and links regarding Windows Home Server and the machine you are running it on. This information is required if you ever need to contact Product Support for assistance.

The following information is available:

- **Microsoft Windows:** The Windows information presented includes copyright, version, and product ID for the version of Home Server you are running. If you are running an evaluation version, the expiration date is displayed. If you have not yet activated your copy of Windows Home Server, you can click Activate Windows to do so.

CROSS-REF   Chapter 5 has a section describing the activation process for Windows Home Server.

- **Home Server:** This section gives you information about the hardware your server is running on. Included are the motherboard model number, the CPU, and the amount of RAM on your system.

- **Version Information:** This section provides the version number for the software components that make up your Windows Home Server installation, including the Console, Backup & Restore, Drive Extender, Remote Access, and the Storage Manager.

- **Learn More:** This includes links to Microsoft product information Web sites where you can learn more about Windows Home Server. There is also a link to the Windows Home Server Community, a Web forum where users of Windows Home Server can exchange information and tips on how to use it more effectively and so on.

- **Support:** This link takes you to the Windows Home Server Product Support page.

FIGURE 8.15

Viewing Windows Home Server resources

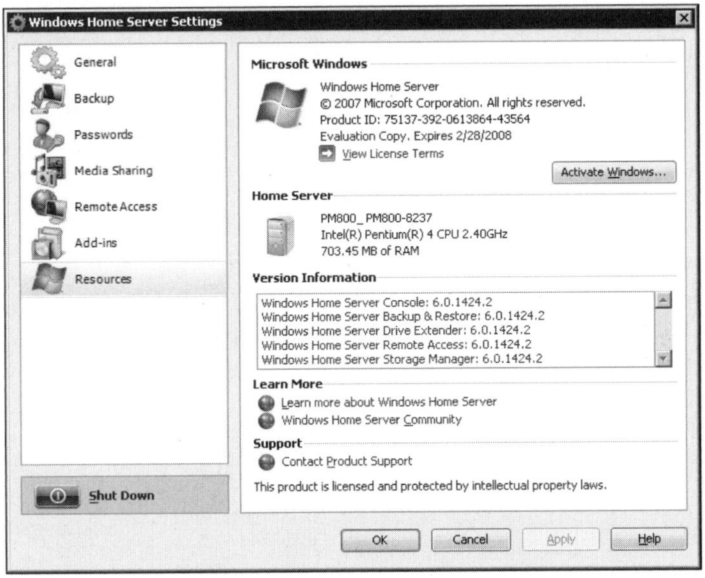

Summary

As has no doubt been hammered home by now, Windows Home Server is designed for ease of use, and the Console designed to be the single interface necessary to manage almost all of Windows Home Server's features. As you have seen in this chapter, the Settings dialog box is where you go to configure most of the server-specific settings. Here you configure the server's general settings, backup parameters, password policy, media sharing, remote access, and add-ins. You can get access to resources and activate your copy of Windows Home Server as well.

In the next chapter, you will learn how to add, remove, and manage user accounts.

Chapter 9

Managing Users

Because you are building a home server, you likely have a household full of people waiting to use it. Well, at the very least you have yourself. Every individual in your household should have his or her own user account in order to access shared folders, particularly the shared folder created just for him or her.

Even if you are the only user on the network, you should still create a user account. Certain home server functions, such as remote access to files or control of other computers on the network cannot be done with the administrator account and must, instead be performed with a user account.

Windows Home Server allows you to create up to ten user accounts, which can be used to customize access to server resources for each member of you household. Users accounts permissions are used to customize access to shared folders, so you can give each person a space just for his or her own use as well as access to public shared folders that everyone can access. You can even control which user accounts are allowed to access the server using remote access.

Adding a New User Account

As mentioned in Chapter 7 when you toured the Console, Windows Home Server allows you to create and manage user accounts without having to touch the server by using the Console's User Accounts tab, as shown in Figure 9.1.

To access the User Accounts tab, do the following:

1. **Launch the Console from any computer that has the Connector installed by double-clicking the tray icon.**

2. **Log in to the server using the administrator password.**

3. **Click the User Accounts tab.**

FIGURE 9.1

The User Accounts tab

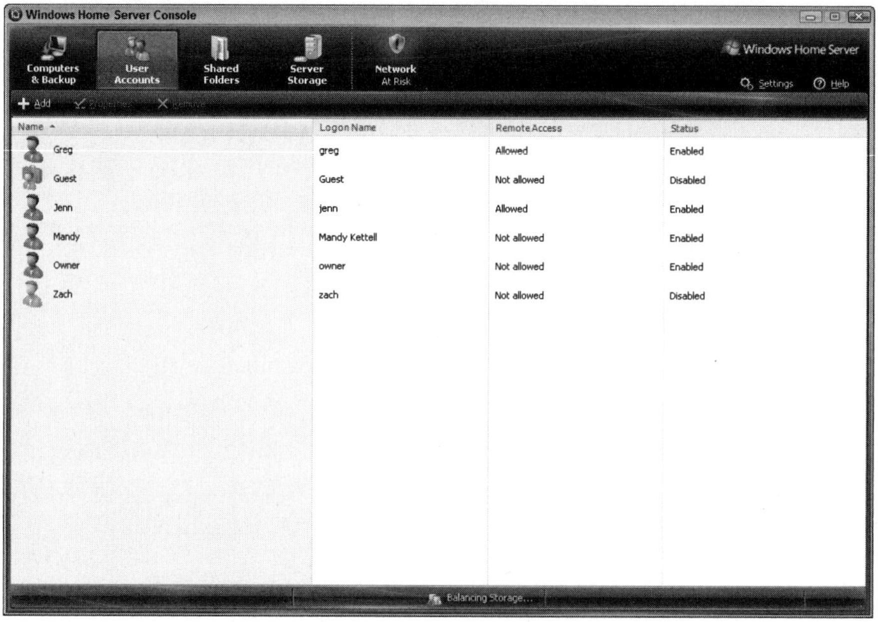

To add a new user account, click the Add button on the User Account toolbar. Doing this starts the Add User Account Wizard, as shown in Figure 9.2.

To add a user with the wizard, follow these steps:

1. **Type a first name, last name, and a logon name for this user.** The last name is optional, and you don't need to add it if you don't want to.

2. **Choose whether or not this user should have Remote Access enabled.** If so, select the Enable Remote Access for this user check box. Click Next.

3. **Type a password for this user, and then type it again to confirm it.** This password must conform to the user account password policy set for the server. If you selected the Enable Remote Access for this user option, the password must meet the strong password criteria. Click Next.

CROSS-REF   See Chapter 8 for information on setting a password policy for your server.

4. **Choose the shared folders to which you want this user to have access.** By default, users have full access to all shared folders other than the personal shared folders of other users. Although the new user's folder isn't listed here, it will be automatically created and this new user will receive full access.

5. **Click Finish to complete the account creation.**

FIGURE 9.2

The Add User Account Wizard

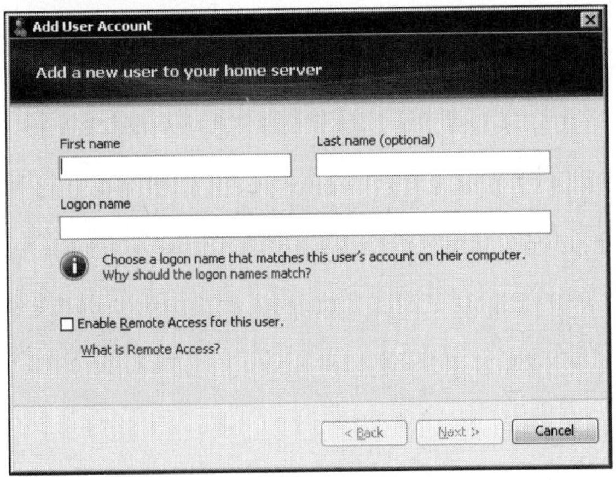

Matching account names

When you create a user account, you need to choose a logon name for that account. Choose a name that matches the name used to log on to the connected computer. You should also choose the same password. If you don't do this, the user will be required to type his or her server account credentials on every attempt to access a shared folder.

When you connect to the server by running the Connector on a client computer, Windows Home Server attempts to match the user's current credentials with a user account on the server. If one doesn't exist, a warning message appears over the tray icon. Clicking on the warning will show you the message box shown in Figure 9.3. You have several options to resolve this situation:

- Create a user account on your server that matches the user name used on the client computer. This is probably the simplest option.

- Create a user account on the client computer that matches an account on the server. This option is best when a user may need to access the shared folder using multiple computers. However, the user will lose any custom settings or programs that are only available to the original user account.

- Rename the user name on the client computer. This option allows the user to keep his or her files, settings, and programs. The procedure for renaming a user account varies depending on the version of Windows you are using. If you are using Vista, try the following:

    1. Log on to the computer with an account with administrator access.

    2. Click the Start button, and choose Control Panel.

    3. Double-click the User Accounts icon.

    4. Click Change an Account.

    5. Click the user account to modify.

    6. Click Change my Name.

    7. Type a new name, and click Change Name.

    8. Log out of the user account and then log on again to force the change.

Windows Home Server should now recognize the user account.

FIGURE 9.3

If your computer's user name doesn't match an account on the server, this notice appears.

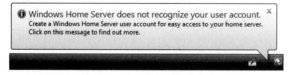

Matching passwords

If your client computer's user account matches a user account on the server, but the passwords don't match, a warning also appears over the tray icon. However, in this situation you have more options. Clicking on the warning displays the Update Password dialog box, as shown in Figure 9.4.

The Update Password dialog box lets you modify your password on your client computer or on the server to match. To use this dialog box, follow these steps:

1. Choose whether to keep the password on the server or on this computer by selecting the appropriate radio button.

2. Confirm your passwords by typing the current passwords for both this computer and for the server.

3. Click OK to change the password.

FIGURE 9.4

Windows Home Server gives you the option to change one of your passwords in order to make them match.

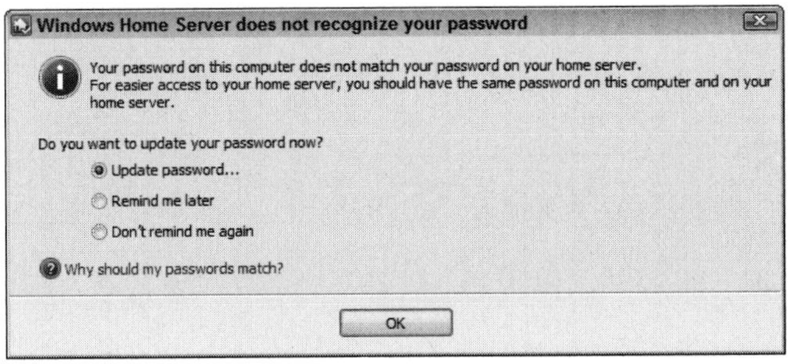

Setting User Properties

After a user account is created, you can modify the user's settings by selecting the user and clicking Properties. Alternatively, you can simply double-click on the user in the Console. This opens the Properties window (see Figure 9.5), which is where you can modify the settings for this user.

The Properties window contains two tabs: the General tab and the Shared Folder Access tab. The General tab is used to set the following account properties:

- **First name:** This is a required field and can be up to 31 characters in length.

- **Last name:** This is an optional field and can be up to 31 characters in length.

- **Logon name:** You can change the logon name for a user. For example, you may need to do this to match the logon name to the user's account on another computer.

- **Enable remote access for this user:** Toggle remote access on or off for a user.

- **Change Password:** This button allows you to change the user's password.

■ **Enable/Disable Account:** If you want to prevent an account from accessing the server, but don't want to remove the account entirely, you can disable it by clicking Disable Account. The button turns into an Enable Account button, allowing you to reenable the account when you desire. The user's current account status will be displayed above this button as well as on the main Console screen.

FIGURE 9.5

The user Properties window is where you change settings for existing users.

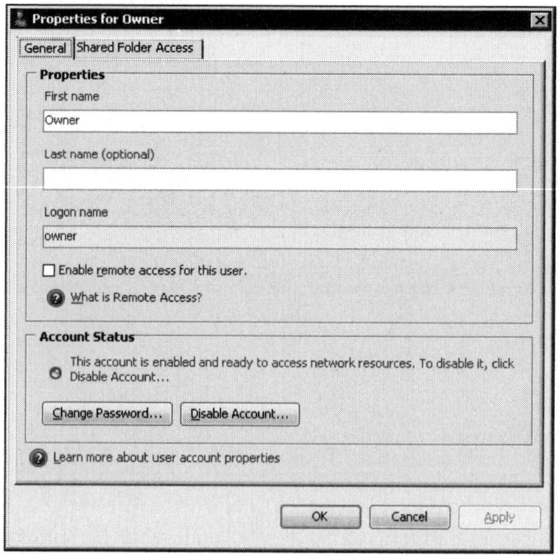

The Shared Folder Access tab, shown in Figure 9.6, is used to see at a glance which folders a user has access to as well as give you the opportunity to change them.

Click the tab and choose the level of access you want this user to have for each folder. The choices are as follows:

■ **Full:** The user will have complete access to the folder, with the ability to read, write to, and delete files.

■ **Read:** The user will have read-only access to this folder. He or she will be unable to create, modify, or delete files.

■ **None:** The user will be able to see the folder, but will be unable to access it or even see the files that are in it.

FIGURE 9.6

FIGURE 9.6

The Shared Folder Access tab is used to view and modify a user's access to shared folders.

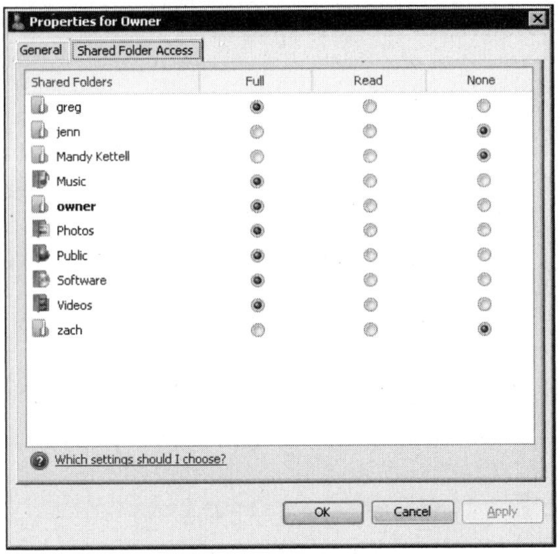

Removing a User

✗ Remove There are times, even on a home server, when you may want to remove a user account. If you need to remove a user, you can do so by selecting the user and clicking Remove. This activates the Remove a User Account Wizard, as shown in Figure 9.7. You are presented with following options:

1. **First, choose whether or not you want to keep or remove the user's shared folder. After making the choice and click Next.**

2. **If you chose to keep the user's shared folder, decide who will have access to it.** You can choose a user account to give access to it, or select the option to not give any user access to the folder. Make the choice and click Next.

NOTE If you decide to keep the folder, you can always change access to the shared folder in the User Accounts tab or the Shared Folders tab of the Console.

3. **Click Finish to complete removal of the user account.**

FIGURE 9.7

The Remove User Wizard allows you to remove a user and the user's shared folder.

Enabling the Guest Account

You may have noticed an account called Guest that Windows Home Server automatically creates. This is a special account that you can use to give access to shared folders for users that don't have their own user account.

When you view the properties for the guest account, you may notice that you cannot edit the first name, last name, or logon name. You cannot enable remote access for this user, either — the guest account cannot be accessed remotely.

The guess account is disabled by default. To enable it, double-click it and click Enable Account as you would for any other disabled account. When you do, the Guest Account Wizard, shown in Figure 9.8, appears.

FIGURE 9.8

The Guest Account Wizard is used to set access properties for users without their own accounts.

Follow these steps to use the wizard to enable the guest account:

1. **Activate the wizard by choosing Enable Account in the guest account's Properties window. Click Next.**

2. **Choose whether to require a password for the guest account. No matter what the password policy is for other user accounts, you do not need to create a password for the guest account if you don't want to.** This choice will have the following ramifications:

   - **No Guest Password:** Users are able to access shared folders enabled for Full or Read access for the guest account without typing a username or password.

   - **Create a Guest Password:** This option gives enhanced security by requiring guest users that access shared folders to type a username of Guest along with the password.

     Make your choice and click Next to continue.

3. **Set the guest account's access to shared folders.** By default, the guest user has Read access to the default shared folders including Music, Photos, Public, Software, and Videos.

4. **Click Finish to complete configuration of the guest account.**

Summary

User accounts are useful for assigning varying levels of access to each member of your household, and each user needs to have one. The user account should match the username that the user uses on the client computer — if necessary, the server will give you the option to change either the username on the home computer or on the server.

You can customize access to shared folders and remote access by setting the user account's properties on the User Accounts tab of the console. User accounts are created with a shared folder that only they have access to by default.

Those without an account of their own can access shared folders using the guest account, if it is enabled. This account cannot be removed or modified, but can be granted the same levels of access to shared folders as other user accounts Use this account with caution.

In the next chapter, you learn various ways of accessing the server from a connected computer.

Chapter 10

Managing the Server with Remote Desktop

"The best-laid plans o' mice and men oft go a'gley," Robert Burns wrote some time ago. Someone else more recently came up with "stuff happens." Either way, the message is clear: Sometimes things don't always go as planned. Microsoft designed Windows Home Server to be easy to manage from the Console, and for the most part that is true. However, there are times when you may need to actually log on to the server's desktop to investigate problems or to install an application.

Because Windows Home Server is based on Windows Server 2003, it was designed from the beginning with remote access in mind. In this chapter we show you how to use Remote Desktop to access the server and perform a variety of tasks that you simply cannot do from the Console.

Remote Desktop (also known as Terminal Services) is a technology that has existed since Windows NT 4.0 days, but hasn't been commonly used in the home versions of Windows. It has been widely used on the server operating systems because it allows technicians to access the server's desktop remotely, a handy feature to have when the server could be in a data center on the other side of the world.

IN THIS CHAPTER

Accessing Remote Desktop

Establishing a Remote Desktop Connection

Connecting from Windows

Connecting from a Mac

Finding the server's IP address

> **NOTE** You may be interested to know that whenever you access the Console from a connected client computer, the client application is actually accessing the Console running on the server itself via Remote Desktop. It is simply the Console executable HomeServerConsole.exe running instead of the normal Windows shell, Explorer.exe, so it appears seamlessly on your desktop. Pretty cool, huh?

Using Remote Desktop

Most versions of Windows XP and Vista have the Remote Desktop Connection (RDC) client already installed. You can find it in the following locations:

- **Windows XP:** Click Start, and then choose All Programs ➪ Accessories ➪ Communications ➪ Remote Desktop Connection.
- **Windows Vista:** Click Start and then choose Programs ➪ Accessories ➪ Remote Desktop Connection.

The RDC client window is shown in Figure 10.1.

FIGURE 10.1

The Remote Desktop Connection client is used to access computers remotely.

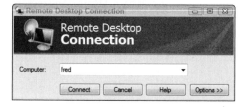

Downloading Remote Desktop Connection

If you have XP SP2 and would like to upgrade to the newest version of the Remote Desktop Connection client, version 6.0, you can find it here:

```
www.microsoft.com/downloads/details.aspx?FamilyID=26f11f0c-
    0d18-4306-abcf-d4f18c8f5df9&DisplayLang=en
```

If you have an older Windows computer (say, a Windows 98 computer, or XP SP1) that doesn't already have a Remote Desktop client installed on it, you can download it from the following URL:

```
www.microsoft.com/downloads/details.aspx?FamilyID=80111f21-d48d-
    426e-96c2-08aa2bd23a49&displaylang=en
```

> **TIP** These URLs are rather long and unwieldy, so you might find it easier to just surf to www.microsoft.com, and search for Remote Desktop Client.

Customizing Remote Desktop settings

Run the RDC client using the steps shown previously. Before you connect to the server, you have the option of customizing some of the settings for the connection. Click the Options button to expand the client to show the settings tabs, shown in Figure 10.2. You can use the tabs to set some of these options.

FIGURE 10.2

Customize the Remote Desktop Connection settings.

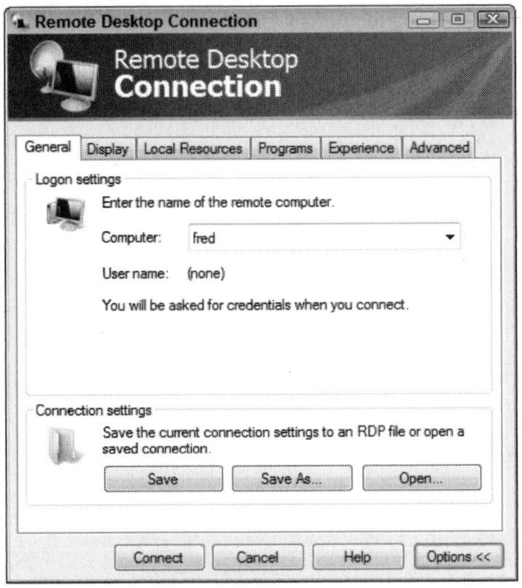

General tab

This tab contains a field where you can enter the computer name to connect to. For this discussion, you enter the name of your Home Server. There is a checkbox to force RDC to always ask for your credentials when you connect.

You also have the option of saving and opening your connection settings on this tab, which can be useful if you will use it to connect to computers that require different settings.

Display tab

The Display tab lets you set the size of the desktop window to open. If you intend to run the Console on the Home Server desktop, you should choose a size of 1024× 768 pixels or larger. However for most other tasks, you can get away with 800×600 pixels.

You also have the ability to set the color depth. Choose a lower setting for higher performance, and a higher setting if you need color fidelity, such as for viewing images or Web browsing on the server.

There is a checkbox that allows you to display the connection bar when in full screen mode. We recommend you check it, as it is a constant reminder that you are using Remote Desktop.

Local Resources tab

On the Local Resources tab, you can set sound, keyboard, and local device settings. Sound settings aren't very important while working on a server; however, if you want to hear sounds from the remote computer, you can choose to bring them to this computer.

The keyboard settings control how certain key combinations, such as Alt+Tab, are handled when the RDC window has the focus. You can choose to have them handled by the local computer, the remote computer, or only when in full screen mode.

The local devices section lets you share devices that are connected to your local computer to the server for temporary use. You can choose printers and the clipboard. Click the More button to share drives and supported plug and play devices as well.

Programs tab

The Programs tab lets you set a custom program to run on the server when you connect. For the most part you should leave this empty when accessing Windows Home Server.

Experience tab

You use the Experience tab to set your connection speed so that RDC optimizes the settings for your local network. For most home networks you should choose LAN (10 Mbps or higher).

If you like, customize the desktop settings further.

If you are connecting over a wireless network, I recommend checking the Reconnect if connection is dropped box. This way if you have a temporary disconnection, the RDC will automatically reconnect when the connection is restored.

Advanced tab

You will not need the Advanced tab settings for most Windows Home Server installations. Leave these values at the default settings.

Connecting to Windows Home Server

Now that you've made all of your setting changes for the Remote Desktop Connection, you are ready to access the server. Enter the name of your server in the Computer text box and click the Connect button.

If this is your first time connecting, you will be prompted for your credentials. Enter Administrator for the username, along with your Windows Home Server password. If you'd prefer to not have to enter your password each time you use RDC, you can check the Remember my Password box. Just remember that anyone who has access to your computer will also be able to access the server.

The Remote Desktop window, shown in Figure 10.3, should open, providing you with a view of the Windows Home Server desktop.

FIGURE 10.3

Access the Windows Home Server desktop from the Remote Desktop Connection client.

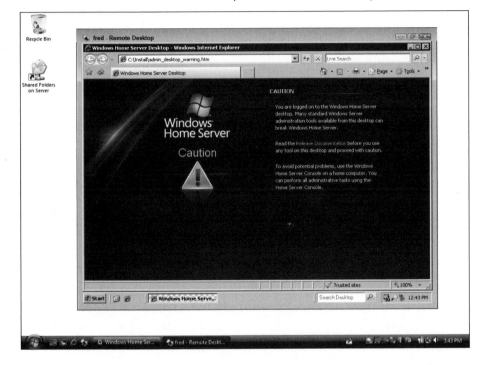

From the remote desktop, you can do typical Windows maintenance tasks including:

■ Configure a printer

■ Install a server application

■ Troubleshoot the server

■ Examine files in Explorer

■ Access the Control Panel

■ Troubleshoot using the Event Viewer

■ Access the Registry

CAUTION It is possible to severely damage Windows Home Server functions from the desktop by running some Windows Server 2003 tools. You should be cautious, especially with any utility or application that can make changes to the file system.

When you are done working with the server, you can simply close the Remote Desktop window. This will leave you logged on to the server with any applications you had open still running, and when you reconnect they will still be there. This can be useful in some cases, but if you would prefer to log off cleanly, you can do it from the Start menu as normal.

Accessing Remote Desktop from a Mac

If you want to access your server from a Mac and feel that you are out of luck because there isn't a version of the Connector for it, don't worry. You can access the desktop of your server with the Remote Desktop Connection Client for OS X , and run the Console from the server's desktop!

The RDC Client for Mac 2.0 is available as a beta download as of this writing, but in our testing it has worked rather well.

Installing the RDC Client for Mac

To install the RDC Client for Mac, follow these instructions.

1. **Go to Microsoft's Mactopia page for RDC Client for Mac at this URL:**

   ```
   www.microsoft.com/mac/otherproducts/otherproducts.aspx?pid=
       remotedesktopclient
   ```

   This page is shown in Figure 10.4.

FIGURE 10.4

A version of the Remote Desktop Connection Client is available for your OSX Mac.

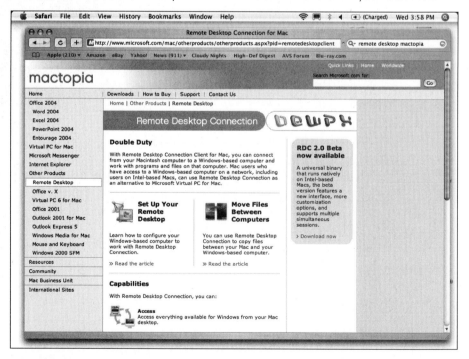

2. Click the Download now link for the RDC.

3. On the download page, review the system requirements to make sure that your Mac meets them.

4. Click the English (.dmg) link to download the file.

5. If the installation starts automatically for you, skip to Step 8.

6. Find the file in your download location folder. If you are using Safari or Internet Explorer, the default location is on the desktop.

7. Click the Install Remote Desktop Connection.pkg application in the Remote Desktop Connection volume to begin installation.

8. Click Continue to proceed through the application process.

9. **When you are prompted, choose the destination volume to install the software, and the folder you want to install to.** This step is shown in Figure 10.5. Then click Continue again.

FIGURE 10.5

Choosing a location for the Remote Desktop Connection application.

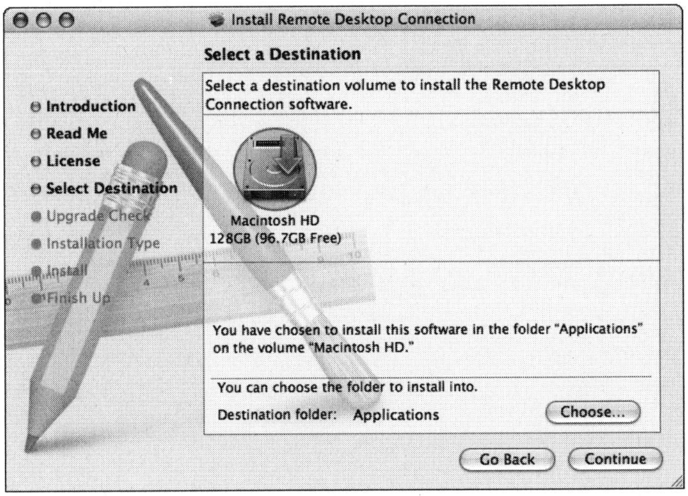

---

10. **Click Install to start the installation.** Enter your user password if you are prompted for it.

11. **When the installation is complete, click Close.**

Running the RDC Client for Mac

Now that you have the RDC Client installed, you can configure it to connect to your server. Follow these steps:

1. **Navigate to the folder that you installed the client.** By default this is your Applications folder. (From the Finder, choose Go ➪ Applications.)

2. **Double-click the Remote Desktop Connection icon to run it.**

3. **Choose RDC ➪ Preferences from the menu to open the Preferences window.**

4. **Click the Display tab and choose a screen resolution of at least 1024×768 pixels.**

5. **If you desire, you can enter your username and password information on the Logon tab.** The username will be Administrator, and the password will be your Windows Home Server password. Leave the Domain blank.

6. **Close the preferences window.**

7. **Enter the Computer name in the Remote Desktop Connection window and click Connect.** Congratulations! You are now connected to server from your Mac. If it can't find your server, you may need to use the IP address. See the Finding your Server's IP Address section to learn how.

8. **To run the Console, click Start and choose Windows Home Server Console.** Now you can perform any console tasks. Figure 10.6 shows the Console running under Remote Desktop on the Mac.

FIGURE 10.6

Using Remote Desktop Connection, you can access the Console from your Mac.

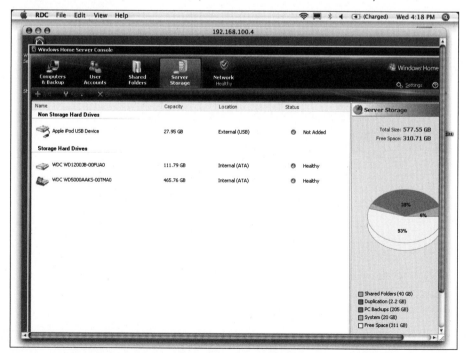

Finding the server's IP address

Sometimes the RDC client can't find the server using the name. If you find that it can't, you will have to enter the IP address instead. You can find the IP address of the server several ways.

- **From a Windows based computer, open a command prompt window.** Type **ping servername** and press Enter, with the name of your server in place of servername. The IP address will be displayed as four numbers separated by dots; for example, 192.168.100.6. This is shown in Figure 10.7.

- **On the server's desktop, open a command prompt window by clicking Start and choosing Command Prompt.** Type **ipconfig -all** and press Enter. The IP Address will be listed under the Local Area Connection, as shown in Figure 10.8.

FIGURE 10.7

Pinging the server to learn its IP address

You can use the IP address of the server in place of the server name in the Remote Desktop Connection client.

Finding the IP address of your server using the ipconfig utility

Summary

Although you can manage Windows Home Server primarily from the desktop, there are times when you may need to log on to the server itself. Fortunately, there are ways to do so even if you have the server stuck in a closet or in the basement — you can connect to it using Remote Desktop and access the server as if you were sitting at it.

The Remote Desktop Connection client program is installed by default in most versions of Windows since XP Service Pack 1; however you can download it if you do not have it. There is even a Mac version.

One exciting aspect of Remote Desktop is that you can use it to access other computers on your network as well, assuming they are running a supported version of Windows. We cover this in detail in Chapter 19.

Chapter 11

Monitoring Your Network Health

I f you have a household full of computers, and you are reading this book, you are probably the one tasked with maintaining them. If so, you understand how hard it can be to keep up with all of the routine and nonroutine maintenance that goes along with the job of household IT guru. You need to make sure all of the computers have the latest updates, you need to keep virus and spyware programs up to date, and you need to make sure none of the computer are running out of disk space or suffering from other anomalies.

Now that you've added a Windows Home Server computer to the mix, you may be thinking that it's just going to add to the burden and be one more computer to maintain. Well, you are right. It is going to be one more computer to maintain. The bright side, however, is that Windows Home Server not only makes it easy to monitor notable events on the server, but it also lets you see what's going on with other computers on your network.

The Windows Home Server feature that brings you all of this is called Network Health, and it can tell you a lot. This chapter goes into detail on how to use it. You also learn how to interpret the notification messages that you will be receiving both from the server and from your other computers.

Viewing Network Health on the Console

The Console provides two levels of information regarding your network health status. The first level, on the Console window, is the Network Health button, shown in Figure 11.1. This button's color and look changes to show

147

you the status of the most critical health notifications. You can't get any detailed information about the actual event just by looking at this button, however. Its job is to get you to click on it.

FIGURE 11.1

The Network Health button shows the most critical server events at a glance.

When you click the Network Health button, the Console brings up the Home Network Health dialog box, which provides you with the most detailed list of network health events on the server and other computers. The dialog box is shown in Figure 11.2.

Understanding notification levels

Some notifications are more important that others. Like a traffic light, there are three levels of notification states — Healthy (green), At Risk (yellow), and Critical (red). These three status levels for this button are shown in Figure 11.3.

FIGURE 11.2

The Network Health dialog box shows detailed information about all active server notifications.

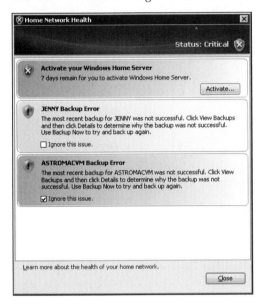

FIGURE 11.3

The Network Health button changes to indicate the current notification status.

Healthy status

A Healthy network status is what you want to see. This status means that you have no new notifications that you haven't seen.

A green status doesn't always mean you don't have events that need your attention. You can ignore some notifications, such as backup failures, by checking the Ignore this issue checkbox inside the Network Health dialog box. These events haven't gone away, but they will no longer alert you via the Console button or the tray icon.

At Risk status

At Risk warnings are those that you should address as soon as possible, but don't indicate a critical failure.

Critical status

Critical notifications are the highest level of notification alerts, and you should attend to them as soon as you see them. Critical alerts can be generated due to a hardware failure such as a storage pool hard drive no longer being available. They can also indicate a software failure, or that a Windows Update needs your approval before it is installed.

Receiving notifications in the task tray

The Console isn't the only place where you can get notifications. You can also see the status reflected in the system tray icon on connected computers. The tray icon can show more than the status of events, however; it can also show you whether or not your computer is connected to the server or is in the middle of a backup. In Chapter 6, we covered the various tray icon states. Table 11.1 shows the ones that specifically pertain to health notifications:

TABLE 11.1

Task Bar Health Notifications

Task Bar icon	Health Status
	The green icon indicates a healthy status. This tells you that there are no notifications to investigate
	This yellow icon is a warning that your computer or your server is at risk. You should connect to the Windows Home Server Console and click the Network Health button to learn what the problem is.
	This red icon appears when there is a critical notification. You should connect to the Windows Home Server Console immediately and click the Network Health button to learn what the problem is.

Enabling tray icon notifications

It is very likely that you don't want every user on every computer to receive task tray event notifications. Fortunately, they can be turned on or off. In order to receive event notifications in the task tray, you must enable them by right-clicking on the task tray icon and checking the Display Network Health Notifications item, shown in Figure 11.4.

NOTE If you want to enable or disable task tray notifications for a user with accounts on more than one computer, you will need to set it on each computer. Conversely, if you have multiple users on a single computer, you can set this setting independently for each of them. Generally, you should enable them for anyone who has access to the Console.

FIGURE 11.4

You can enable task tray notifications using the icon's context menu.

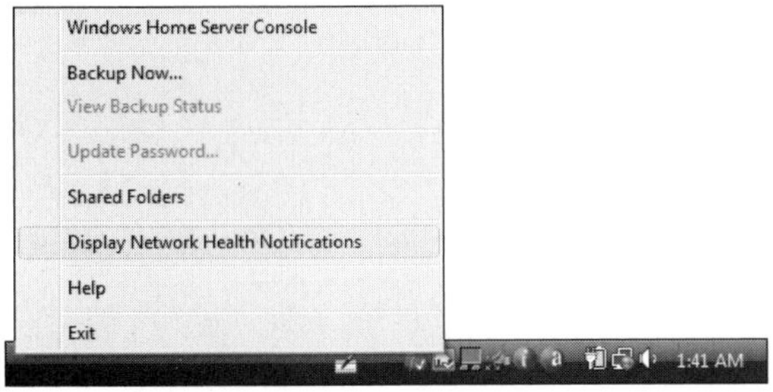

Windows Home Server Console
Backup Now...
View Backup Status
Update Password...
Shared Folders
Display Network Health Notifications
Help
Exit

When an event occurs that warrants sending a notification message, it automatically appears as a balloon text popup emanating from the tray icon, as shown in Figure 11.5. If there are multiple notifications active at the same time, you can cycle through them by right-clicking on the balloon text. If the notification indicates a Critical or At Risk state, you should log into the Console to investigate further.

TIP If the balloon text fades and disappears before you have a chance to read it, you can force it to appear again by unchecking the Display Network Health Notification menu item and then rechecking it.

FIGURE 11.5

A text balloon will pop up when a notification event occurs.

⚠ JENNY Backup Error ✕
The most recent backup for JENNY was not successful.
Click View Backups and then click Details to determine
why the backup was not successful. Use Backup Now to
try and back up again.

Addressing Home Server Health Notifications

Windows Home Server health notifications are ones that indicate an issue directly related to the server that must be addressed. These notifications range from significant server issues such as hardware or software failure, to more run of the mill stuff such as Windows Update notifications.

Monitoring storage space

As file storage in the form of backups and file sharing is one of the most important functions of Windows Home Server, notifications dealing with hard drives storage space are particularly important. Notifications are issued when your remaining storage drops below a certain percentage of the total storage pool size, with that percentage value depending on the size of your total storage pool size.

- **100GB or less:** At Risk (yellow) notification when free space is less than 12 percent of the total. Critical (red) notification when free space is less than 3 percent of the total.

- **101GB to 200GB:** At Risk (yellow) notification at 10 percent free space remaining. Critical (red) notification at 3 percent free space remaining.

- **201GB to 500GB:** At Risk (yellow) notification at 7 percent free space remaining. Critical (red) notification at 2 percent free space remaining.

- **501GB to 1000GB:** At Risk (yellow) notification at 4 percent free space remaining. Critical (red) notification at 2 percent free space remaining.

- **1001GB to 2000GB:** At Risk (yellow) notification at 3 percent free space remaining. Critical (red) notification at 1 percent free space remaining.

- **2001GB or more:** At Risk (yellow) notification at 2 percent free space remaining. Critical (red) notification at 1 percent free space remaining.

Identifying software problems

You may receive notifications if software running on your server is detected in an abnormal state. This can occur if Windows Home Server or an add-in isn't functioning correctly. Figure 11.6 shows an example.

FIGURE 11.6

An example of a software failure

Backup Service is not running.
Backup Service is not running on server FRED.

Detecting hard drive problems

If Windows Home Server detects a problem with one of your hard drives, you will receive a notification. The notifications are as follows:

- **At Risk (yellow):** A hard drive problem has been detected. This level of alert only applies to SMART (Self Monitoring, Analysis, and Reporting Technology) enabled hard drives only. Such hard drives are capable of reporting problems that may indicate a severe failure is likely soon. Click the Details button to see the full message.

- **Critical (red):** One or more hard drives have failed. You should check for loose cables, particularly in the case of external drives. With folder duplication technology, this error doesn't mean it's time to panic. An example is shown in Figure 11.7.

FIGURE 11.7

An example of a hard drive failure notification

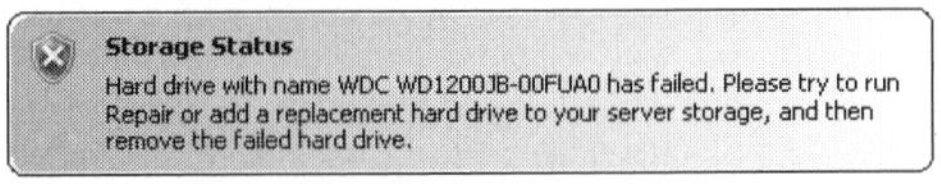

Storage Status
Hard drive with name WDC WD1200JB-00FUA0 has failed. Please try to run Repair or add a replacement hard drive to your server storage, and then remove the failed hard drive.

Monitoring shared folder duplication

If your shared folders have duplication enabled, there are some warnings that you might receive:

- **At Risk (yellow):** Your server does not have enough free storage remaining for shared folder duplication. If you get this warning, you should look for large folders that you may not really need duplicated, such as TV show recordings or other transient data. You can also add storage.

- **At Risk (yellow):** One or more of the files in a shared folder has a path name greater than 260 characters long. This limitation includes the length of the names of all subfolders in the file's path as well as the filename. Click the Details button to find out which file is causing the problem. An example of this notification is shown in Figure 11.8.

CROSS-REF More information about shared folders and folder duplication can be found in Chapter 12.

FIGURE 11.8

An example of a folder duplication notification

Storage Status
Duplication is failing for shared folder: Public. The folder may contain files with path names longer than 260 characters.
Details...

Updating Windows

Even when you have automatic Windows updates enabled, there are some that require your approval before they can be installed. These are usually security-related updates, and in keeping with that the notification is a critical one.

Critical (red) is a Windows update requiring approval has been downloaded, and it needs to be installed.

CROSS-REF See Chapter 8 for information on how to enable automatic Windows updates.

Monitoring the evaluation period

If you have downloaded the evaluation version of Windows Home Server, your installation is good for 120 days before you must upgrade to a fully licensed copy. You will receive the following notifications when your evaluation deadline is approaching:

- **At Risk (yellow):** You have 30 days or less remaining in your evaluation period.
- **Critical (red):** You have 15 days or less remaining in your evaluation period. Upgrade as soon as possible.

CROSS-REF To upgrade your evaluation version of Windows Home Server, you must reinstall the operating system with a licensed version. See the section on reinstallation in Chapter 5 for information on how to do this.

Product activation

Windows Home Server must be activated within 30 days of installation or first startup. Activation requires you to enter your product code to verify your license status. You will receive the following notifications as the deadline approaches:

- **At Risk (yellow):** You have 15 days or less to activate.
- **Critical (red):** You have 10 days or less to activate.

When you check the notification in the dialog box, it is updated with the number of days remaining, as shown in Figure 11.9.

FIGURE 11.9

You will be warned as your product activation deadline approaches.

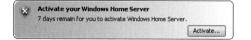

Activate your Windows Home Server
7 days remain for you to activate Windows Home Server.
[Activate...]

Identifying Home Computer Health Notifications

Windows Home Server not only monitors and reports its own health status, but it also monitors and reports on the status of the computers you have connected over the network. The notifications you can receive are dependent on the computer's operating system version. Computers running Windows XP can get notifications pertaining to backup status, while Vista computers can receive any of these notifications.

Backup status

One of the more common groups of notification messages you will likely see relate to backups. You will get notifications if backups fail or if they can't be started. The following notifications apply to backups:

- **At Risk (yellow):** Your computer has not been successfully backed up for at least five days. This tends to occur if computers are powered off during the normal backup time. If it happens regularly, you can change the times that backups are attempted in the Settings dialog box. An example of this is shown in Figure 11.10.

- **At Risk (yellow):** The most recent backup for this computer was unsuccessful. This can happen if the computer shuts down in the middle of the backup, or if the network connection between it and the server is unreliable.

- **At Risk (yellow):** [Computer name] has a new hard-drive volume. Do you want to automatically back up this volume? When you configured backups for your computer, you took into account backups for all existing volumes. When you add a new hard-drive volume (partition), Windows Home Server needs to know if you want it included in the backups.

- **Critical (red):** Your computer has not been successfully backed up for at least 15 days.

TIP If a computer is not going to be connecting to the server in a while, disable backups on the Computers and Backups tab. This will keep backup-related notifications from being reported for that computer.

CROSS-REF You can find information about configuring backups in Chapter 20.

FIGURE 11.10

Notifications are given for backup problems.

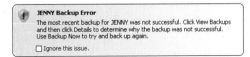

JENNY Backup Error
The most recent backup for JENNY was not successful. Click View Backups and then click Details to determine why the backup was not successful. Use Backup Now to try and back up again.

☐ Ignore this issue.

Windows updates

It is just as important to keep your other home computers up to date with Windows Update as it is with the server. Because of this, you will be notified if your Windows Vista computer has updates to be installed, or if automatic updates are turned off. The following notifications apply to updates:

- **At Risk (yellow):** Your computer has updates to install. You should log onto the Vista computer in question and run Windows Update.

- **Critical (red):** Your computer is configured to never check for Windows Updates. Some people don't like to have updates applied automatically, so they disable Windows Update completely. This is generally a bad idea — it's better to check for updates and notify you to download them, or (even better) to automatically download updates and notify you that they need to be installed. Figure 11.11 shows an example of this notification.

FIGURE 11.11

Windows Updates must be enabled to prevent this notification.

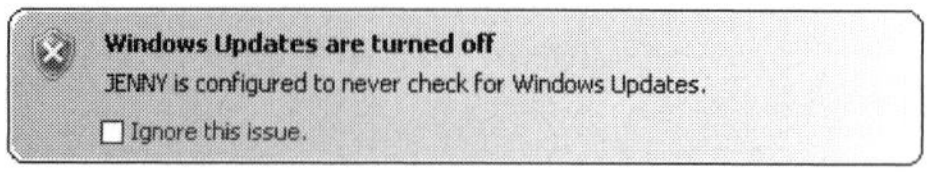

Firewall, antivirus, and spyware warnings

If your Vista computer is missing common security precautions, you will receive a critical alert to that effect. Notifications that you can receive are:

- **Critical (red):** Your computer has Windows Firewall turned off.

- **Critical (red):** Your computer does not have antivirus software. The antivirus software is not installed, is turned off, or is out of date. This catch-all notification alerts you to problems with your antivirus program. Log on to your Vista computer and investigate.

- **Critical (red):** Your computer does not have antispyware software. The antispyware software either is turned off or is out of date.

NOTE Vista includes a built-in antispyware program called Windows Defender. If you need help configuring it, consult Vista Help. If you need help with a third-party antivirus or antispyware program, consult that product's documentation.

Summary

Windows Home Server Network Health can help simplify the task of maintaining all of the computers in your household. With it, you can see at a glance if the server or your Vista-based computers have any problems that need your attention, and in some cases, you can resolve them. If your home computers run Windows Vista, you will be able to monitor even more, including security settings and Windows Update status.

There are two ways to check your network health. You can log onto the Console and check the status of the Network Health icon and dialog box, or you can enable health notifications on one or more of your home computers in the tray icon. Either way, you'll always be able to tell what is going on with your network and the computers on it.

Part III

File and Printer Sharing

Chapter 12

Understanding Shared Folders

I f you have networked home computers, undoubtedly you've had times when you needed access to files located on one computer from another one. Quite often this can be a headache-inducing experience — folder sharing in Windows can be complicated, especially when it comes to sharing files across different versions of Windows, or with users who don't have an account on each computer. It's also easy to lose track of which folders are shared on each computer.

Windows Home Server aims to change all that with its shared folders feature. While sharing folders over the network has been available since Windows 3.1 for Workgroups, it's never been as easy to set up and manage at a glance as it is now.

With shared folders, you create, remove, and set properties for all folders directly from the Shared Folders tab on the Console. You can see at a glance the status of all shared folders, what they are for, whether they make use of folder duplication, and how much storage is used on them.

To top things off, in many cases you don't even need to create shared folders, as Windows Home Server automatically creates them for user accounts and even provides built-in shared folders for everyone to use.

NOTE When reading about file servers and other specialized devices that offer shared folder services, you will often see them referred to as *NAS* devices. NAS stands for Network Addressable Storage, and is really just a fancy way of referring to shared folders.

Exploring the Built-In Shared Folders

Windows Home Server creates five standard shared folders automatically during installation. These folders are intended to be used for various specific purposes instead of the more general nature of other shared folders.

Using built-in shared folders

Three of Windows Home Server's built-in shared folders are intended to be used for media sharing. In addition, there are two other built-in shared folders created for software installation and general purpose file sharing for everyone on the network.

Music

The Music folder is one of the three media-oriented shared folders. It is intended to hold music files that you wish to make available over the network. Music files can either be accessed directly from the shared folder or streamed using media sharing features of Windows Home Server.

>  **Media file sharing is covered in detail starting with Chapter 25.**

Photos

The Photos folder is another media-oriented shared folder. Photo files stored here can be accessed directly or through media sharing.

Public

The Public folder is intended to be a general purpose folder that anyone can have access to for sharing files. This can be used to store software installation files, media files that you don't want to include in media sharing, household notes — pretty much anything you can think of.

Software

The Software folder contains software installation files for Windows Home Server. As we show in Chapter 6, the Software folder contains installation files for the Windows Home Server Connector software that is installed on Windows home computers. There is a Home PC Restore CD image file that you can use to create a bootable CD useful for restoring a computer from a backup.

This folder is also used as a holding place for installation files for Windows Home Server add-ins. You can conveniently download add-ins on one of your home computers and copy it here so that it can be installed through the console.

> **CROSS-REF** **See Chapter 23 for more information on the Restore CD. Chapter 32 provides information about installing Windows Home Server add-ins.**

Videos

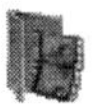

The Videos folder is the last of the three media-oriented shared folders. This folder can be used to host home videos and other video files. As with the other two media related shared folders, videos can either be streamed or accessed directly from this folder.

Understanding special features of built-in shared folders

Although the built-in shared folders behave in much the same way as other shared folders (those created for each user account and any you add yourself), there are some differences.

■ The built-in shared folders have special icons to distinguish them from other shared folders (shown in Figure 12.1).

■ Built-in shared folders cannot be renamed or removed.

■ New user accounts are given full access to all built-in shared folders by default. You must specifically change this for users you do not wish to have full access.

Other than those three differences, the built-in shared folders are managed in the same way as others on the Shared Folders tab of the Console.

FIGURE 12.1

Built-in shared folders have special icons to differentiate them from the others.

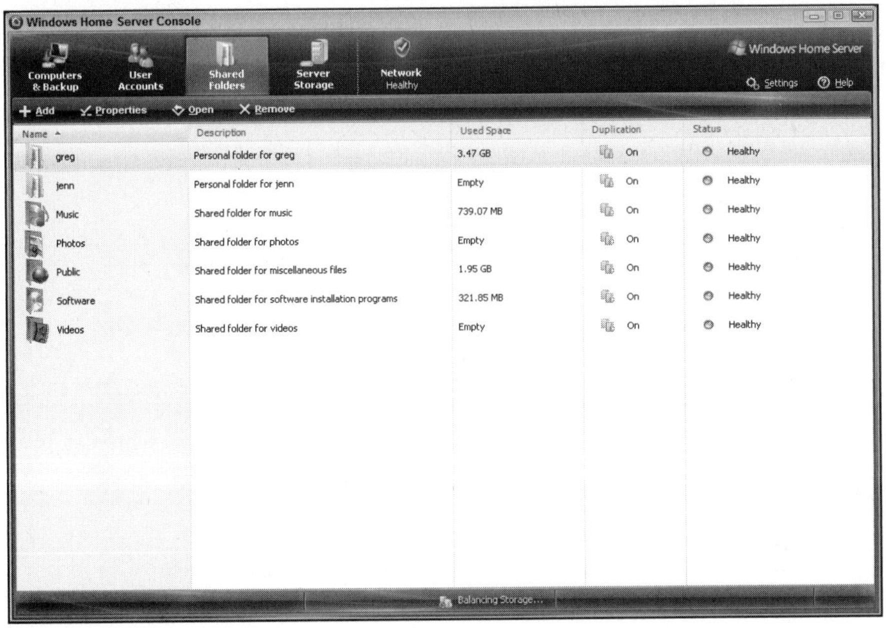

Accessing Personal Folders

When a user account is created, a personal shared folder is automatically created for them with the same name as their user account (as shown in Figure 12.2). This folder is intended to be used for general purpose file storage, and provides the following benefits versus storing the file locally:

- Files can be accessed from any computer that the user has an account on.
- The shared folders can take advantage of folder duplication, giving them additional protection from hardware failure.
- It's easy to control access to shared folders on the server through the Console.

CROSS-REF We discuss adding and managing user accounts in Chapter 9.

FIGURE 12.2

A personal shared folder is automatically created when a new user account is added.

Personal shared folders have a special connection to the user account they are created for. This connection allows Windows Home Server to automatically manage the folder in some limited ways. You can tell which user a personal shared folder was created for by looking at the User Access tab of the properties dialog, shown in Figure 12.3. The user's name appears in bolded text.

FIGURE 12.3

Shared folder user access properties highlight their owner's name in bold.

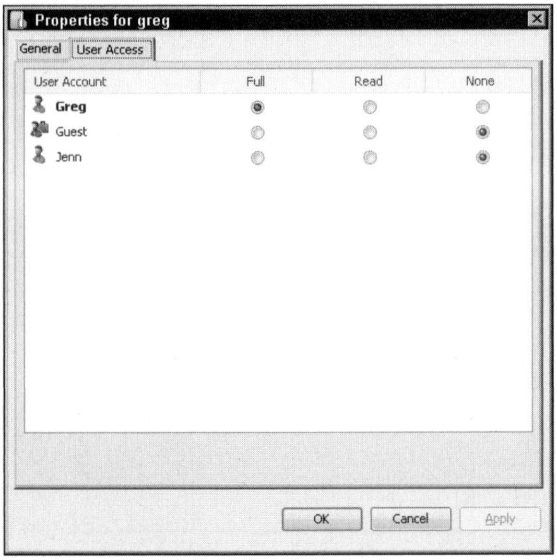

Maintaining Folders

A key advantage of using Windows Home Server for shared folders lies in how easy it makes the job of managing them. All shared folder management tasks are performed from the Console on the Shared Folders tab.

Adding folders

The built-in and personal shared folders should be enough for most general purpose uses. Even so, there may be times when you want to create additional shared folders. There are several reasons why you might want to do this; some possible uses include

- You want a shared folder with special user access, say, granting full access to two users, but not everyone on the server. You could, for example, add a folder to hold your financial data and give access to the adults in the household, but not the children.

- You have a server-based application (such as a custom Web site) and you wish to point it to a shared folder to make it easy for you to update content on it.

- You have a specialized backup application that can copy files to a shared server, and you want to keep the backup files separate from other shared files.

- You simply want to use additional personal shared folders to aid in organizing your files.

To add a new shared folder, follow these steps:

1. **Open the Console and click the Shared Folder tab.**
2. **Click the Add button on the toolbar to open the Add a Shared Folder dialog box (shown in Figure 12.4).**

Shared folders are created in the Console.

3. **Enter a name for the folder.** This must, of course, be a unique name from all the other shared folders.
4. **Enter a description for the folder.** While this is optional, we recommend that you do so to make it easy to remember what the folder is for when you glance at the Console display.
5. **Choose a folder duplication option.** The Enable Folder Duplication box is checked by default if you have more than one hard drive. If you don't want this folder to be duplicated, you should uncheck this to prevent it. Folder duplication is described later in this chapter.
6. **Click Next.**
7. **Choose the level of access you wish each user to have (shown in Figure 12.5).** By default, all user accounts other than the guest account get read-only access to the folder. One or more users should be given full access in order to allow files to be copied to the share.
8. **Click Finish to complete and then click Done to close the summary screen.**

CAUTION While it may be tempting to add folders in Windows Explorer, as you're used to doing for your local folders, you'll be doomed to disappointment. If you don't add folders within the Console, they won't be viewable as shared folders within the Console. This means you won't be able to control user access or take advantage of folder duplication. Whenever you're performing any sort of folder maintenance on the server, do it from within the Console.

FIGURE 12.5

Choose user access options for your new shared folder.

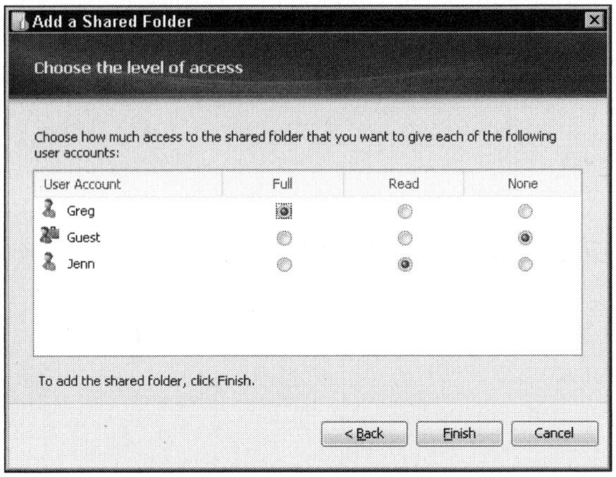

Add a Shared Folder

Choose the level of access

Choose how much access to the shared folder that you want to give each of the following user accounts:

User Account	Full	Read	None
Greg	●	○	○
Guest	○	○	●
Jenn	○	●	○

To add the shared folder, click Finish.

< Back | Finish | Cancel

Removing folders

There are times when you may want to remove a shared folder. As with adding folders, this should be done in the Console:

1. **In the Shared Folders tab in the Console, click the folder you want to eliminate.**
2. **Click the Remove button on the toolbar.**
3. **You will be given a warning about the contents of the folder being permanently deleted, as shown in Figure 12.6.** Click Finish to proceed with the removal.

FIGURE 12.6

Removing a shared folder.

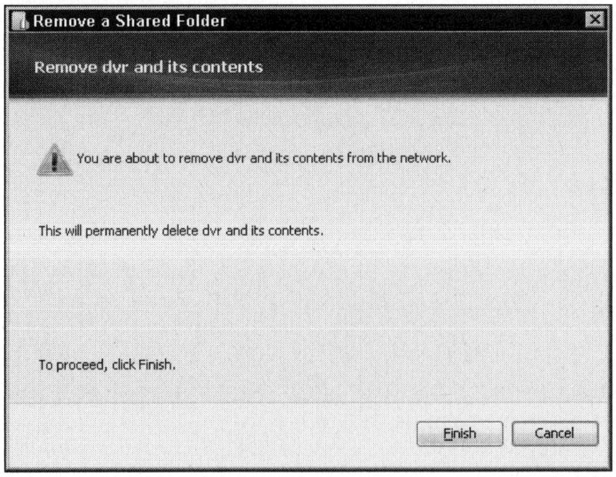

Remove a Shared Folder

Remove dvr and its contents

⚠ You are about to remove dvr and its contents from the network.

This will permanently delete dvr and its contents.

To proceed, click Finish.

Finish | Cancel

Setting shared folder properties

As your use of Windows Home Server changes, your shared folder needs may change along with it. You can change a folder's name (with the exception of the built-in shared folders), alter user access, and set whether or not folder duplication will be used on it.

To change the properties for a folder in the Console, follow these steps:

1. **From the Shared Folder tab, click the folder you wish to change.**

2. **Click the Properties button on the toolbar.**

3. **Enter the new information for the folder on the General tab, as shown in Figure 12.7.** You can change the name, description, and folder duplication status.

4. **Click the User Access tab, and make any desired changes.**

5. **Click OK when done.**

FIGURE 12.7

Changing shared folder properties

Viewing shared folder contents

You can use the Console to launch a Windows Explorer window for the shared folder path. This is a one of the quickest ways to see the contents of a shared folder if you happen to already be in the Console.

To open a shared folder from the Console, do the following:

1. **From the Shared Folder tab, click the folder to open.**
2. **Click Open on the toolbar.**

> **NOTE** The Open function to view shared folders from the Console will not work if you are using remote access. The only way to access shared folders remotely is through the shared folder link in remote access.

Viewing shared folder history

It can be helpful at times to see how folder usage has changed over time. You can see a graph showing the history a shared folder's storage use over time by right-clicking the folder name and choosing View History, as shown in Figure 12.8. This will show you when your teenager decided to go on a music downloading spree and fill up the server's hard drive.

You can choose a history range to display: the options are one week, one month, one year, and the full history of the folder.

> **NOTE** A shared folder must be at least one week old in order for you to view its history.

FIGURE 12.8

The folder history graph shows how a folder's storage size has changed.

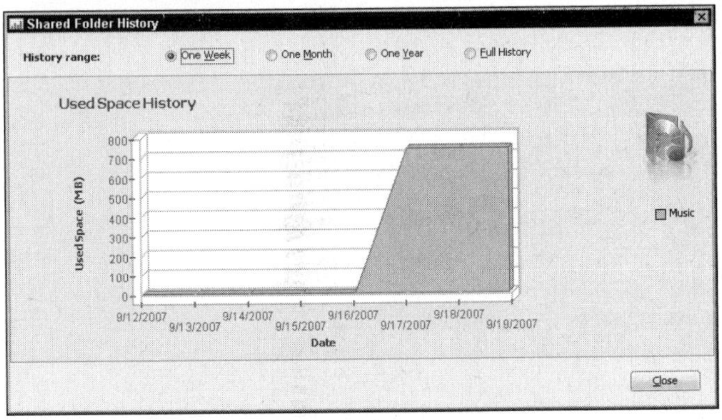

Duplicating Folders

When you entrust your valuable files to server storage, you want to make sure they'll be protected. In typical server environments, you could use a RAID (redundant array of independent disk) solution that mirrors the data stored on one hard drive with another one of the same size. This ensures that if one drive fails, the data is still safe on the other drive.

This is a reliable solution that works well; however, Windows Home Server goes one better by providing a feature called *folder duplication*. With folder duplication, the operating system intelligently distributes the files across multiple hard drives, automatically choosing which one to use. Because folder duplication can be set on a folder-by-folder basis, you don't have to enable it for folders that may contain large files that you intend to be temporary, such as digital video recorder (DVR) video recordings or large temporary files you may create while editing video or photos. The beauty of Windows Home Server's solution is that you can adjust your folder duplication to reach the optimum balance between folder protection and maximum storage capacity.

> **CAUTION** Folder duplication causes a lot of strange-looking folders to be created on the Data drive of the Home Server file system. It is advisable to not work with those files directly, as it can easily cause problems with operating system access to those files.

Discovering how folder duplication works

In order for folder duplication to work, your server must have at least two hard drives and enough space free on them for the duplicated files. When you add a second hard drive to your storage pool using Drive Extender, the Folder Duplication check box in the folder properties dialog box becomes enabled. All you need to do to activate folder duplication for a particular folder is to check this box, as shown in Figure 12.9.

FIGURE 12.9

Folder duplication is toggled on and off in the folder properties dialog.

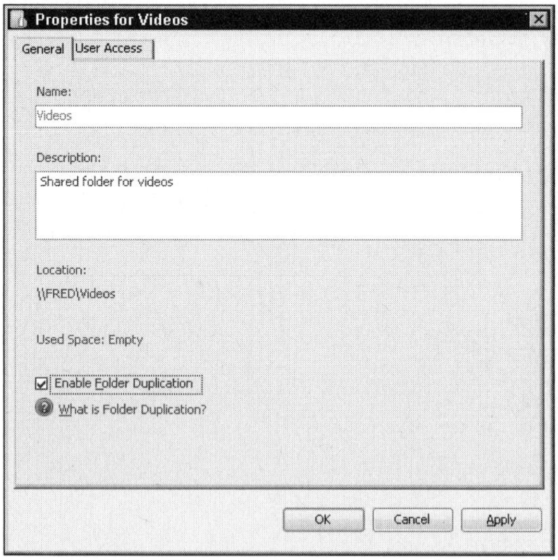

The status bar of the Console lets you know when folder duplication is taking place, as shown in Figure 12.10. When it shows the Balancing Storage indicator, the server has detected that a file has been written to a folder with duplication enabled, and it is busy copying the files to the backup folder on the other hard drive. When the status bar indicates that storage is balanced, the file duplication process is complete.

FIGURE 12.10

The status bar indicates the balancing status.

Using volume shadow copy services

A feature that Windows Home Server has inherited from Windows Server 2003 is Volume Shadow Copy services. This feature takes frequent snapshots of shared folders to allow you to revert to a previous version of a file in the event that you accidentally overwrite or delete it.

NOTE Shadow copy services are also utilized on your connected XP and Vista computers to perform backups.

On Windows Server 2003, the Volume Shadow Service (VSS) scheduler manages shadow copies. This scheduler is disabled in Windows Home Server and the Drive Extender program schedules shadow copies at 7 AM and 12 PM daily instead.

If you would like to force a shadow copy to be made at a different time, you may do so by following these steps:

1. **Log directly on to the server's desktop either using a keyboard and monitor attached to the server, or from a client computer using Remote Desktop.**

2. **Choose Start ⇨ All Programs ⇨ Administrative Tools ⇨ Computer Management to open the Computer Management window, shown in Figure 12.11.**

3. **Right-click the Shared Folders item and choose All Tasks ⇨ Configure Shadow Copies.**

4. **All the volumes on you computer will be listed, as shown in Figure 12.12, along with the number of shared folders hosted by each.** Any volume that doesn't have any shared folders on it is used for folder duplication purposes.

5. **Choose a volume with shares folders, and click Create Now.** This causes the shadow copy snapshot to be made at that point. Click OK when you are finished.

FIGURE 12.11

The Computer Management window is where shadow copy settings are managed.

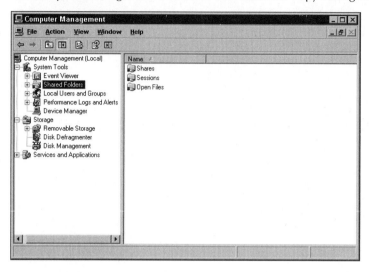

FIGURE 12.12

You can force a manual shadow copy to be made at any time.

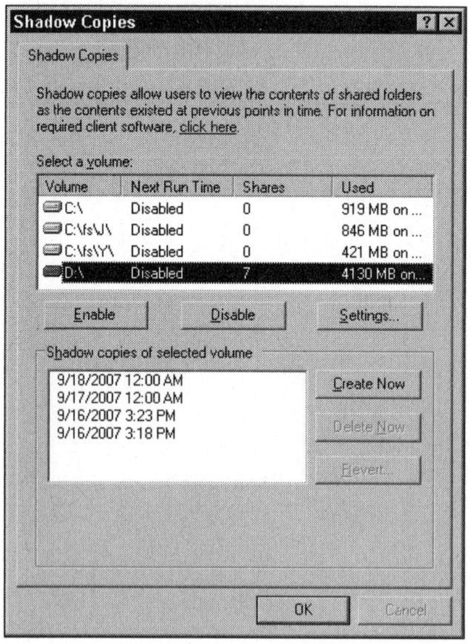

 You should notice that the shadow copies show as Disabled. This is intentionally done to allow Windows Home Server's drive extender software to manage shadow copies instead of the operating system. We don't recommend changing these settings.

CROSS-REF You can access the shadow copies made of your shared folders directly from your client computers. We discuss this in more detail in Chapter 13.

Summary

File sharing between networked computers is more important than ever; however, sharing folders between Windows computers is not always simple, especially when you're dealing with computers running different versions of Windows. Windows Home Server's shared folders feature makes it easier than ever for Windows-based home computers to set up and access shared files and folders.

Windows Home Server offers plenty in terms of standard shared folders. It includes built-in folders for sharing media files and software installation files, as well as a Public folder that all users have access to. User accounts are automatically given personal shared folders of their own, allowing users to securely access their files from any computer. In addition, you can create additional shared folders and control access to them as you desire, all from the Console.

To top things off, powerful features such as folder duplication and shadow copies put Windows Home Server a step above a plain old file server when it comes to protecting your important and precious files.

Chapter 13

Accessing Shared Folders and Files

I n Chapter 12, you learned about Windows Home Server shared folders and how to create and manage them. In this chapter, we'll show you how to go about accessing them from your home computers.

Windows File Sharing has been around for a long time — and solutions for accessing Windows file shares from non-Windows platforms have been necessary from the start. If you happen to own a Mac or a Linux computer, we will show you how to access shared folders and files from those platforms, as well.

Accessing from a Windows PC

More than likely, you are using a Windows computer running either XP or Vista to connect to your shared folders. Windows computers have a definite advantage when it comes to accessing your Home Server shared folders, as they speak the native file sharing protocol.

When you install the Connector on a Vista or XP client, you are given two distinct ways to access shared folders from the desktop, using either the desktop shortcut or the tray icon. In addition, you can use Windows Explorer to navigate to the server or to map a drive letter to a particular shared folder. This section shows you how.

Using the tray and desktop shortcuts

The tray icon that was installed with the connector includes a menu item to access the shared folders. Right-click on the tray icon and select the Shared

IN THIS CHAPTER

Accessing shared folders

Accessing from a Windows computer

Mapping a drive letter

Accessing shared folders from a Macintosh

Accessing shared folders from Linux

Folders item, as shown in Figure 13.1. This launches Windows Explorer, pointing to the server on the network, showing all of its shared folders.

Launch the shared folder window from the tray icon.

The built-in shared folders (Videos, Software, Public, Photos, and Music) are all accessed directly from this view. The user-specific shared folders are organized under a folder named Users.

You may also have noticed the Shared Folders on Server shortcut icon that was placed on your desktop when you installed the Connector. This is simply another way to launch the same view that is provided by the tray icon menu item. The redundancy exists to provide easy access to your shared folders whether you have a lot of open windows on your desktop or not. If you prefer using the tray, you can delete this icon from your desktop.

Using Windows Explorer

If you need to access the shared folders from a local computer that doesn't have the Connector installed, you can navigate to them using Windows Explorer. Follow these steps to navigate to the shared folders:

Using Windows Vista

1. **Click the Start button, and then click the Network button.** The computers on your network will be shown in the pane on the right in Explorer. One of them should be your server.

2. **Double click the server's icon.** If you are prompted for a username and password, enter your Home Server username and password. Alternatively, you can use Administrator for the username and the Windows Home Server administrator password.

Using Windows XP

1. **Click the Start button, and choose My Network Places.** You can right-click on it and choose Explore if you want to see the folder tree in Explorer.

2. **Click Entire Network.**

3. **Click Microsoft Windows Network.**

4. **Click the work group name that your server is on.** By default, it's in Workgroup.

5. **Double-click on the server name.** If you are prompted for a username and password, enter your Home Server username and password. Alternatively, you can use Administrator for the username and the Windows Home Server administrator password.

The shared folders will be displayed in Explorer, as shown in Figure 13.2.

FIGURE 13.2

You can use Explorer to navigate to the network shares.

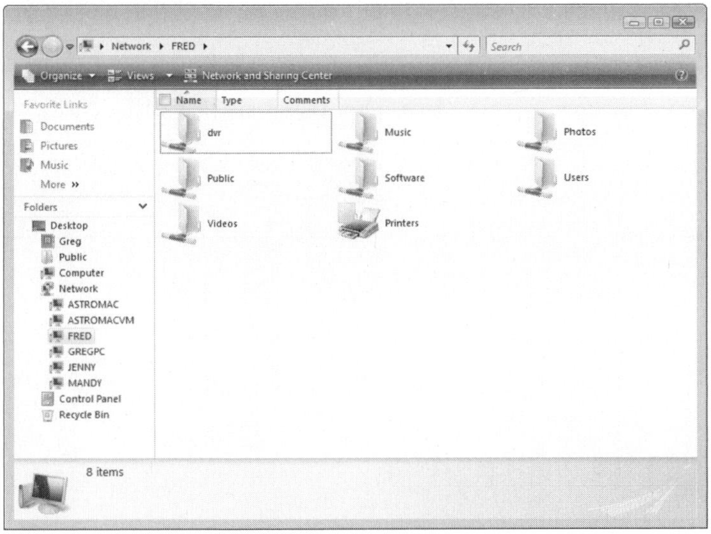

Browsing the network for servers isn't always reliable, so it is possible that your server isn't visible in Explorer in the Network section. Fortunately, you can enter the server name directly in the address bar in Explorer in both XP and Vista.

NOTE If the address bar isn't visible in Explorer on XP, choose View ➪ Toolbars and make sure Address Bar is checked. Sometimes you have to drag it into view — right-click on the toolbar and choose Unlock Toolbar if you are unable to move them.

To go directly to the server, enter two backslashes followed by the server name in the address bar. For instance, if your server was named Fred, you would type \\fred (case is not important) in the address bar.

Mapping a drive letter

If you would like to formalize your connection to a shared folder, you can map a drive letter to it. For instance, you might want to give every computer the same drive letter pointing to the Public share, or give every user the same drive letter pointing to his or her user shared folder. This gives you a shortcut to the folders that makes it easy to locate shared files from any program without having to browse through the network paths. The drive letter can even be automatically reconnected whenever you restart your computer. Follow these steps to map the drive:

1. **Navigate to the folder you would like to map to the drive in Explorer.**

2. **Right-click on the folder and choose Map Network Drive.** This opens the dialog box shown in Figure 13.3. Your folder will already be entered in the Folder field.

3. **Choose a drive letter from the Drive drop-down list.**

4. **Make sure that the Reconnect at logon box is checked if you would like to have this drive letter map retained when you log off or restart the computer.**

5. **If you aren't logged on using the same username and password that has access to the shared folder on the server, you can select the Connect using a different user name link to enter a different one.**

6. **Click Finish when you are done.**

FIGURE 13.3

Mapping a drive letter to a shared folder in Windows XP

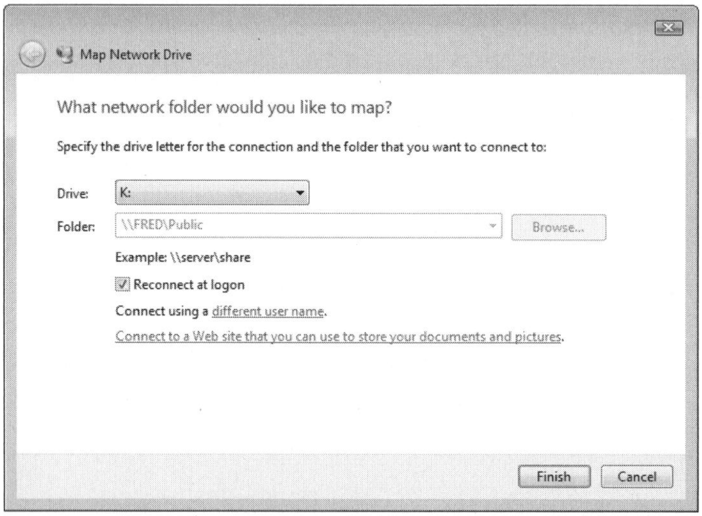

The mapped drive letters for shared folders are visible in Explorer just like any other drive, as shown in Figure 13.4.

FIGURE 13.4

You can access mapped drive letters in Explorer just like any other drive.

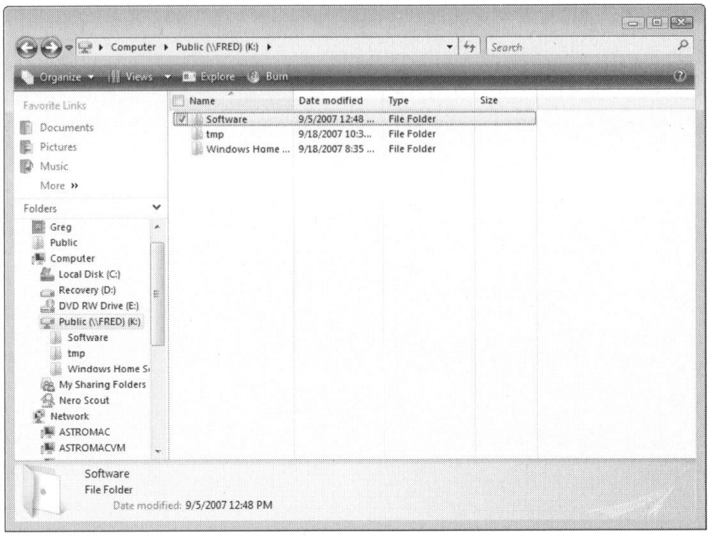

Accessing shadow copies

In the previous chapter, we described Volume Shadow Copy — the feature in Windows operating systems that provides timed snapshots of shared folders. These snapshot copies can be accessed from Windows Explorer when the computer has the Shadow Copy Client installed.

ON the WEB If you are running Windows 2000 or a pre-SP2 version of Windows XP, you will need to download and install the Shadow Copy Client. It can be found at http://technet.microsoft.com/en-us/windowsserver/bb405951.aspx.

Vista users should note that the Shadow Copy Client is not available for Home versions of Vista. You will need to be using the Business or Ultimate versions to be able to access previous shadow copies.

Fortunately, if you need to access shadow copies from an unsupported operating system (including Mac and Linux, as well as Home versions of Vista), you can connect to Windows Home Server using Remote Desktop, and use Explorer as described here.

To see the shadow copies for a shared folder, follow these steps:

1. **In Explorer, navigate to one of your shared folders as described earlier in this chapter.** If you want to see the previous versions for a subfolder only, navigate to it.

2. **Right-click on the folder name in the Explorer tree view or right-click in the empty space in the right side pane and choose Properties.** This step opens the Properties dialog.

3. Select the Previous Versions tab.

4. Any shadow copies that have been made for the folder are displayed, as shown in Figure 13.5.

FIGURE 13.5

Access shadow copies of shared folders in the Properties dialog.

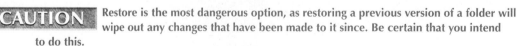

From the Previous Versions tab, you have three options for dealing with the shadow copies. Select one of the folder versions listed and choose one of these options:

■ **View:** This opens a special Explorer window pointing to the previous version you selected. From this window you can browse, open, and copy the files as you see fit. An example of this view is shown in Figure 13.6.

■ **Copy:** If you select Copy, you will be prompted to choose a destination folder to copy the files to. Use this option if you want to restore the previous version of a file to a different folder than it was in originally. Usually, you would do this to compare it with the current version.

■ **Restore:** If you know for a fact that you want to revert to the previous version of a file or a folder, choose this option.

CAUTION Restore is the most dangerous option, as restoring a previous version of a folder will wipe out any changes that have been made to it since. Be certain that you intend to do this.

FIGURE 13.6

You can use Explorer to browse previous versions of your files. Note that the date and time of the shadow copy appears in the address bar.

Accessing from a Mac

Mac computers have long been a popular choice, particularly among creative types who work with music, video and photo editing. These days, a growing number of people are choosing Macs for day-to-day computing, as well.

If you are a household that counts Macs among the mixed assortment of computers that need access to shared folders, rest easy. OS X has no trouble finding Windows file servers and connecting to shared folders.

Just as you saw with Windows, you can locate your shared folders using a Mac multiple ways. You can either browse to locate the server or you can navigate to it directly.

Browsing to your shared folders in OS X

Browsing the network to find your shared folders is very similar to the process used in Windows. Follow these steps to find your shared folders by browsing:

1. **Open the Finder.** Perhaps the simplest way is to click the Finder icon in the Dock.
2. **Choose Go ➪ Network from the menu.** If you are running OS X 10.4 or earlier, the Network browser window should present you with a list of workgroups in your home network. If you are running OS X 10.5 (Leopard), you will only see the computers, as Figure 13.7 shows. Leopard users should skip to Step 4.

FIGURE 13.7

The OS X Network browser lets you locate Windows computers.

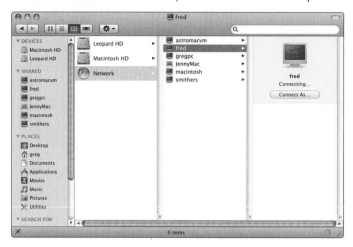

3. **Click on the workgroup that your server is located in.** By default, it will be Workgroup.

4. **You should see the server name in the middle column.** Select it and click the Connect button (In Leopard, Connect As), and you will be presented with an authentication window, as shown in Figure 13.8.

FIGURE 13.8

You must provide authentication to access Windows file shares.

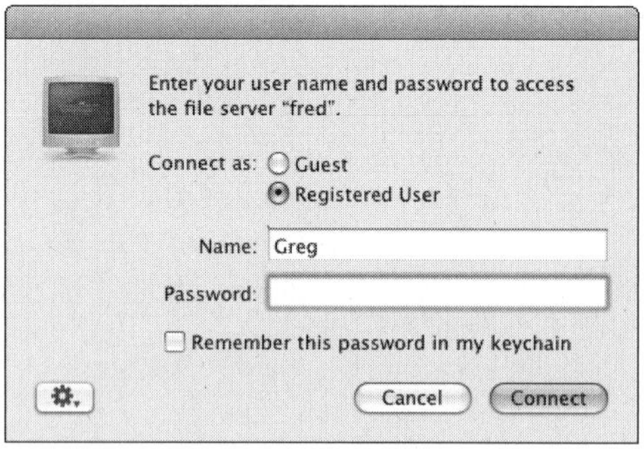

5. **Enter the username and password that you created on Windows Home Server.** If you want OS X to remember your password, click the checkbox to have it stored in the keychain. Click OK when done.

6. **You will be presented with a list of shared folders on the server, similar to those shown in Figure 13.9.** These are the top-level folders only. If you are running OS X 10.4 or earlier, you must mount the folder as a Mac volume. Pick one that the user you authenticated with has access to, and click OK.

FIGURE 13.9

Choose a shared folder to access.

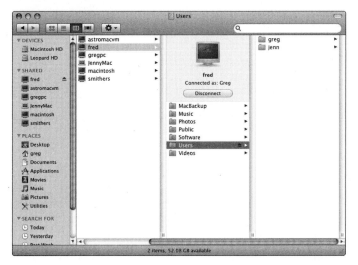

With OS X 10.4 and earlier, the folder you choose will be mounted and show up as a network mount point in the finder, as shown in Figure 13.10. With OSX 10.5 (Leopard), the server itself is the mounted volume in the Finder, and you can access shared folders directly, as shown in Figure 13.11. You can now access files in accordance to the level of access your account has been granted in the Windows Home Server Console.

FIGURE 13.10

In OS X 10.4, you must mount your shared folders in order to access files stored in it.

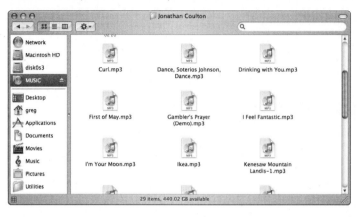

FIGURE 13.11

In OS X 10.5, servers are visible and can be mounted as volumes directly.

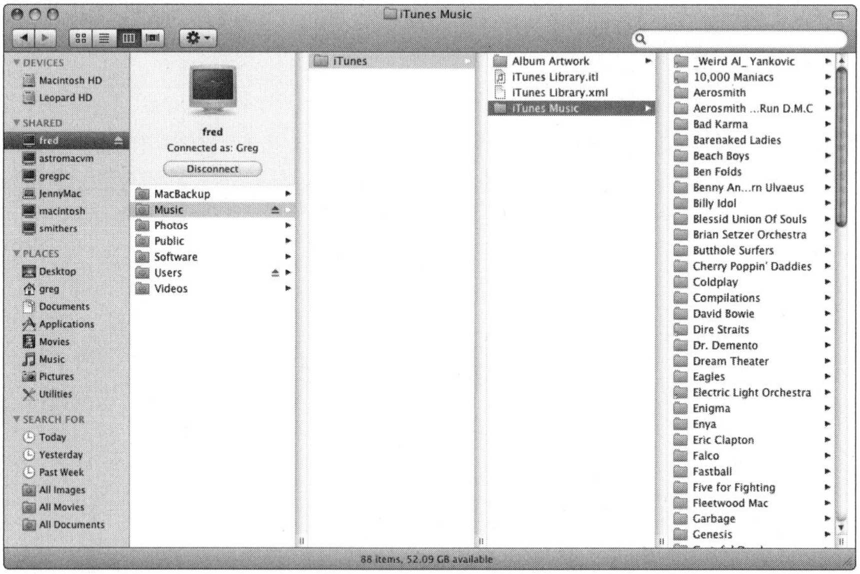

Navigating directly to a shared folder in OS X

If you're unable to find your server by browsing to it, you may still be able to access it. OS X offers a shortcut method of connecting directly to a server if you happen to know its name. Follow these steps to connect directly to the server:

1. **Open the Finder.**

2. **Choose Go ⇨ Connect to Server from the menu.**

3. **In the Connect to Server dialog, shown in Figure 13.12, enter the server address in the format** smb://<servername>. You can also navigate directly to a folder by appending to the address, smb://<servername>/<foldername>.

4. **If you would like to save this address in the Favorite Servers list, click the + button to the right of the address.**

5. **Click Connect.** Enter authentication details if prompted.

6. **If your address didn't include a folder name, you will be given a chance to choose one.** Pick it and click OK.

7. **The folder you choose will be mounted and accessible through the Finder, again subject to the access rights your user account has been granted.**

FIGURE 13.12

Connect directly to a server by entering the SMB (Server Message Blocks) address.

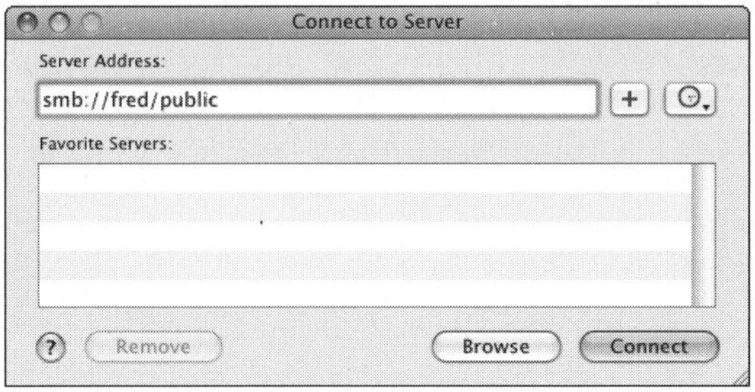

Explaining Server Message Blocks

SMB, or Server Message Blocks, is a network protocol used mainly by Windows computers to share resources, especially folders, files, and printers over a local area network. It is also responsible for browsing the network to see shares, and for authenticating access to them.

SMB actually has its origin back in the days of DOS as a part of LAN Manager, one of the first networking tools developed by Microsoft. In Windows, the protocol was first used with Windows For Workgroups, and every Windows OS since then has been able to make use of it from both a client and a server standpoint. SMB has also come to be referred to as CIFS (Common Internet File System).

Due to the popularity of Windows, other operating systems have often needed a way to access shared Windows resources. The Samba open source implementation of SMB is currently the most popular way to access SMB file shares from Linux, Mac OS X, and other Unix and Unix-like operating systems.

> **ON the WEB**   You can learn more about Samba at their official Web site located at us1.samba.org/samba.

Accessing from a Linux computer

Linux is another popular operating system among computer hobbyists, and it's not uncommon to see a Linux box or two in households with a lot of computers. There are quite a few different Linux distributions out there, with a wide range of capabilities and features. However, most current desktop-oriented Linux distributions include Samba and Winbind. These programs allow you to make connections to Windows shared folders and to find Windows servers on the network. This section shows you how to go about connecting to Windows shares on Fedora 7 from the GNOME desktop. The procedures are similar if you are using Ubuntu or other desktop Linux distributions.

> **NOTE**   In order to access Windows shared files from Linux, you must have the Samba client installed. Please consult your specific version of Linux to learn how to obtain and install the latest Samba package for your computer.

To access Windows shares from the desktop in Fedora, follow these steps:

1. **Choose Places ➪ Connect to Server from the desktop menu.** This opens the Connect to Server window shown in Figure 13.13.

2. **Choose Windows share as the service type.**

3. **Enter the server name in the Server field.**

4. **If you wish to connect directly to a specific shared folder, you can enter it in either the Share or Folder fields.**

5. **Enter your Windows Home Server username in the User Name field.** You can leave the Domain Name field blank, as your Home Server is not in a domain.

Fedora Linux connects to Windows file shares.

6. **Click Connect.**

7. **You will be prompted to authenticate, as shown in Figure 13.14.** Enter your user-name and password, and choose an option for remembering your password.

You must provide your Home Server authentication details to connect.

8. **Click Connect.** A window opens showing you your shared folders. This is shown in Figure 13.15.

FIGURE 13.15

Windows shared folders are available for perusal in Linux.

Summary

Windows Home Server shared folders uses the standard Windows file sharing protocol SMB, so it is easy to connect to them not only from Windows computers, but from other platforms as well. This versatility makes it easy to share files between your Windows-based computers as well as other computers, including OSX-based Macs and Linux computers.

Shared folders support for Volume Shadow copies means that you can access prior versions of your files if you happen to make a mistake and overwrite or delete one of them. If you've installed the Connector, no additional tools are necessary to recover shadow copies — the client interface is built right into Explorer.

Chapter 14

Installing and Sharing Printers

Even in households with more than one computer, very few people can justify having more than one printer. Of course, everyone needs to be able to print at least occasionally. This means that one computer must host the printer and share it on the network, and it can be a problem if that computer isn't turned on when a family member needs to print. The person using the computer that's directly connected to the printer often has to deal with annoying popup messages when someone tries to print or when the printer runs out of paper.

While you could buy a dedicated print server device and share a printer on the network that way, why not take advantage of your Windows Home Server box by giving it printer server duties, as well?

Printer sharing is not one of the advertised features of Windows Home Server, and the current release doesn't contain any printer management functions in the Console. The printer subsystem, however, comes straight from Windows Server 2003, and any printer that you can install under that operating system should work fine with Windows Home Server.

Installing a Printer

Installing a typical printer in Windows Home Server is usually a straightforward process, and this chapter gives you the information you need to install it.

Some printers, especially some consumer-level printers, can have installation procedures that vary from the norm. The instructions in this chapter are for a typical consumer multifunction fax/printer. If the instructions in this chapter don't work for you, follow the instructions provided by the printer manufacturer.

Obtaining drivers

Your printer undoubtedly came with a CD-ROM with printer drivers on it, and that is a good place to start. However, if you go to the manufacturer's Web site, you can often obtain newer printer drivers. As an added bonus, in many cases, downloaded drivers provide a simplified installation process that doesn't bog you down with extraneous photo-editing or fax applications.

NOTE   If your printer's installation makes it optional to install any extras such as photo-editing software, be sure to opt out of installing them. The chances of you editing photos on your headless Windows Home Server box are nil. Instead, in many cases, you can install these programs on your other home computers and use them to print to the remote printer. Consult the documentation that came with the printer.

Table 14.1 lists the URLs for U.S. Web sites for many of the most popular printer manufacturers. If you are located in another country, you may still be able to obtain a compatible driver from these sites; alternatively, go to the manufacturer's home page and locate the site pertaining to your region.

TABLE 14.1

Where to Find Printer Drivers

Manufacturer	Web Location for Consumer Printer Products
Brother	http://welcome.solutions.brother.com/bsc/Public/CountryTop.aspx?reg=us&c=us&lang=en
Epson	http://support.epson.net/page2.htm?country=USA
Canon	www.usa.canon.com/consumer/controller?act=ConsumerHomePageAct
Hewlett-Packard	http://welcome.hp.com/country/us/en/support.html
Lexmark	www.lexmark.com/lexmark/sequentialem/home/0,6959,204816596_652569466_0_en,00.html

Because Windows Home Server is based on Windows Server 2003, you should be able to use any driver that is listed as compatible with that operating system. In some cases, you may find that your printer only has drivers for Windows 2000. These drivers should work as well.

Figure 14.1 shows a typical Web site with driver downloads for a multifunction printer — in this case a Canon PIXMA MP830 multifunction printer. You can access the manufacturer's Web site from the server's desktop using Internet Explorer if you have a monitor and keyboard connected. Alternatively, download the drivers to one of your home computers and then copy it to the server using one of the shared folders (Software or Public, for instance).

FIGURE 14.1

Most printer drivers are available for download from the manufacturer's Web site.

Courtesy of Canon

In some cases, you'll need to install the printer driver before adding the printer; in other cases, you'll be able to point to the installation files or the installation CD while you're adding the printer. Again, you should consult the documentation that was provided with the printer or the driver for specific installation instructions.

Adding the printer

To add a printer to your server, you'll likely need to connect it to either a parallel port or a Universal Serial Bus (USB) port on the computer. In rare cases, you may need to use an RS-232 serial port. If you have a network printer, you can still install it through the server for easy sharing; however it will connect to your network hub instead of directly to the server.

CAUTION Although most desktop computers still include parallel ports, many newer computers, especially laptops, are forgoing these ports in favor of USB. If you find yourself in the situation where you have a parallel port printer and a USB-only server, you may be able to use a USB to parallel port adapter, available at most office supply and electronics stores, as well as online.

NOTE Some printers are able to install themselves entirely using Plug and Play. If you happen to have such a printer, you can bypass these steps and simply plug the printer in and the installation will start automatically.

Barring specific installation instructions to the contrary, you will add the printer in the Printer and Faxes control panel on the server. Follow these steps to install a locally connected printer:

1. **Log on to the server's desktop.** Using Remote Desktop from another computer will work fine.

2. **If your printer driver requires installation first, do so now following the manufacturer's instructions.**

3. Click Start ➪ Printers and Faxes to launch the panel, shown in Figure 14.2.

FIGURE 14.2

Add a printer through the Printers and Faxes control panel.

4. Double-click the Add Printer icon to launch the Add Printer Wizard, shown in Figure 14.3.

5. Click Next.

FIGURE 14.3

The Add Printer Wizard simplifies printer installation.

6. **Choose the Local printer attached to this computer option, shown in Figure 14.4.**

7. **If you want to have the wizard automatically detect your printer, check the Automatically detect and install my Plug and Play printer box.** In some cases, you will have needed to install the driver first, as described in Step 2. If, when you click Next, the wizard tells you that it can't find the printer, try installing the driver and then starting the wizard again.

8. **Click Next.** If your printer is detected by Plug and Play, it will be installed automatically. Skip to Step 15 to print a test page.

FIGURE 14.4

The wizard can automatically detect and install some Plug and Play printers.

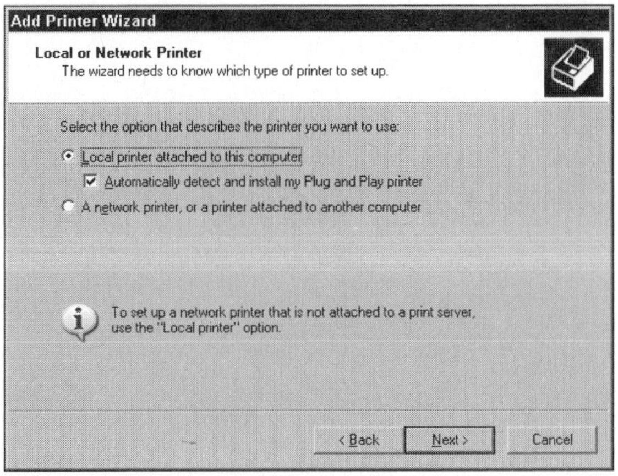

9. **If the printer can't be detected using Plug and Play, or you don't select that option, you can choose a manual installation.** You'll be prompted to choose a port, as shown in Figure 14.5. If your printer is attached to a parallel port, choose the default LPT1: option. If it is USB, choose the USB001 virtual port. If you have a network printer, it will require a new port. In these cases, select that option and choose Standard TCP/IP Port. When you have chosen a port, click Next.

FIGURE 14.5

Choose a port for your printer.

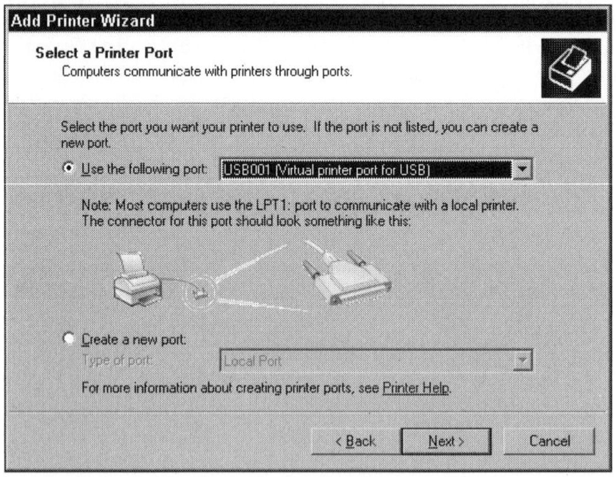

10. **Choose the manufacturer and model of your printer from the list, as shown in Figure 14.6.** In some cases, Windows Update will add additional printers to the list. If your printer isn't listed, but you have drivers for the printer on a disk, click the Have Disk button and follow the instructions. Click Next.

11. **If a driver is already installed for your printer, you will be given the option to use it or to replace it with a newer one.** Make a selection and click Next.

12. **Enter a name for the printer and click Next.**

13. **You will be given the option of sharing the printer or not.** Of course, because the whole purpose of this exercise is to share a printer, you should choose to share it. Enter a descriptive share name, or keep the default. Then click Next.

14. **Enter a location and comment for the printer if you think it will be helpful.** This is optional, as this is intended more for large office environments with many printers than for the home where you might have one or perhaps two. Click Next.

15. **Choose to print a test page or not.** It is advisable to print a test page to make sure that the printer is connected and functioning properly, so click Yes and click Next.

16. **Click Finish to exit the wizard and add the printer.**

FIGURE 14.6

Choose the manufacturer and model of your printer.

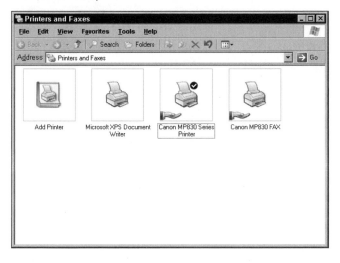

When the installation is complete, the printer will be visible in the Printers and Fax window, as shown in Figure 14.7. The printer icon indicates that the printer is shared by the extended hand under the icon. You may notice that this figure shows a second entry for the fax portion of the printer. If you have a multifunction printer that includes fax capabilities, you can repeat the Add Printer Wizard and install a printer that uses the fax driver for the printer. The fax driver will allow you to send documents directly from your computers to the fax without having to print a hard copy.

FIGURE 14.7

The new shared printer is now available for use.

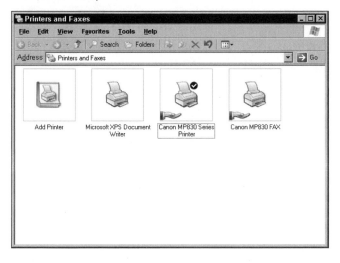

Setting Printer Options

After the printer is installed, there are some options that you may find useful. Right-click on the printer icon in the Printers and Fax panel, and choose Properties to launch the Printer Properties dialog, shown in Figure 14.8.

You can use printer properties to customize your printer's behavior.

Your particular printer's properties may vary somewhat, but here are some of the common options:

- **General:** This tab allows you to change the name of the printer and change the location and comment fields. You can also print a test page, or select the button to open the Printing Preferences dialog (see Figure 14.9) to select printer-specific properties such as print quality, paper type, color, and special effects. The option to print backwards from the last page to the first (so the printed pages are in the proper order when stacked in the output tray), a common choice, is usually found in the Printing Preferences dialog under Page Setup.

- **Sharing:** If you neglected to enable sharing when you installed the printer, you can rectify that using this tab. You can also change the share name.

- **Ports:** In most cases you won't need to change this, unless you move the printer to a different parallel port than you installed it on.

- **Advanced:** Here you can set availability times for the printer if you desire. You can also update your printer driver, and configure print job spooling (so that successive print jobs are queued after each other). You may elect to print a separator page for each print job as well, although this can be wasteful if your printer doesn't see a lot of use.

- **Color Management:** You can choose a different color profile from the default. Usually you will keep this at the default setting. Consult the printer documentation to determine the right color profile for your use.

- **Security:** You can restrict printer access to certain users or groups. Windows Home Server user accounts created through the Console belong to the Everyone group. You can add specific user accounts to this list if you want to restrict or grant special access to a user. Click Add and enter the user accounts name (see Figure 14.10).

- **Maintenance:** You'll find options for cleaning the print heads, print head alignment, and other printer-specific functions on this tab.

FIGURE 14.9

A typical printer-specific properties dialog.

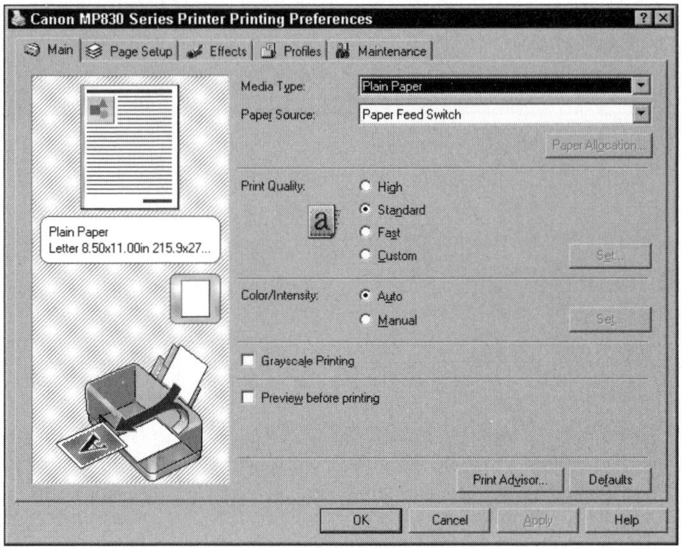

197

You can customize access rights for the printer for user accounts.

Mapping to a Shared Printer

Once you have completed installation of your printer and successfully printed a test page, half the battle is won. Now all that is left is mapping to the printer from the computers connected to the server. Mapping to the printer will differ somewhat depending on the operating system you are using.

Mapping from a Windows computer

On Windows Vista and XP, you map to your shared printer from the Printer control panel on your home computer. Install the printer by following these steps:

Windows Vista

1. Click Start ➪ Control Panel to access the control panel.

2. Choose Printer to open the Printers control panel, shown in Figure 14.11.

3. Click the Add a printer button on the toolbar.

4. Select Add a network, wireless, or Bluetooth printer, and click Next.

5. Shared printers on your network will be displayed, as shown in Figure 14.12. Choose the one you added to your server, and click Next.

6. **Vista will notify you if you need to install the printer driver, and warn you about the potential security risks of doing so.** Since you installed the driver yourself, this won't be a problem. Click Install Driver to proceed.

7. **When the installation is complete, click Next.** You will be presented with the option to print a test page. Do so if you like, and then click Finish to complete the installation.

FIGURE 14.11

Vista's Printer control panel looks slightly different than the one on Windows Home Server.

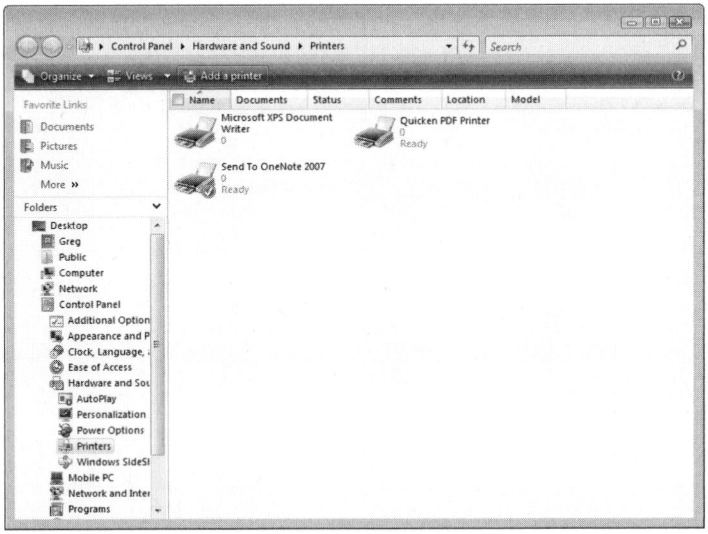

FIGURE 14.12

Browsing for a network printer in Vista

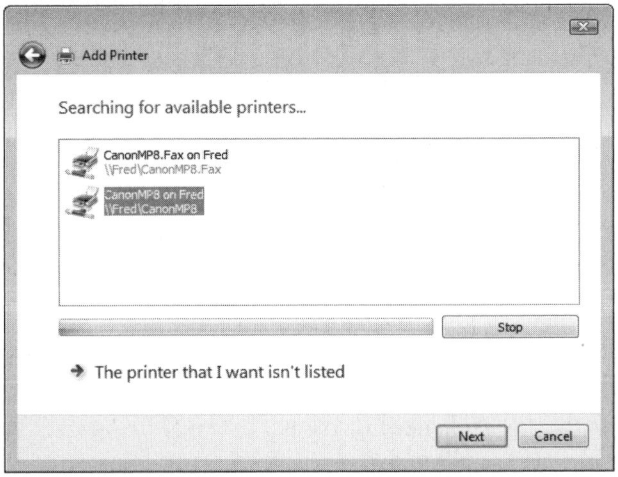

Windows XP

1. Click Start ⇨ Printers and Faxes to open the Printer control panel.

2. Double-click the Add Printer icon to launch the wizard. Click Next to start.

3. Choose the Add a Network printer, or a printer attached to another computer option, and click Next.

4. On the Specify a Printer page, choose the Browse for a Printer option and click Next.

5. Search for your server name and the printer underneath it, as shown in Figure 14.13. You may need to select the workgroup name that your server is in, and it may take a few seconds for all of the computers and printers to be populated on this list. Select the printer and click Next.

6. You will be warned about the dangers of installing an un-trusted printer driver. Because you have just installed the driver yourself, you can click Yes.

7. Choose whether you want the printer to be used as the default printer or not, and click Next.

8. Click Finish to complete the wizard and add the printer.

FIGURE 14.13

Browsing for a network printer in XP

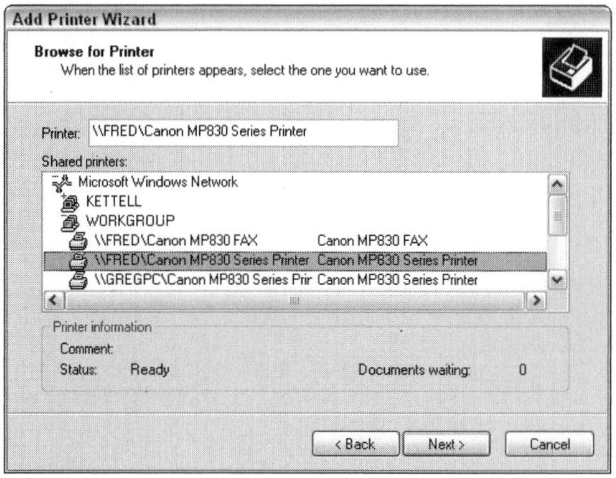

Mapping from a Mac

Printer sharing isn't limited to Windows computers. In many cases, Macs can get in on the action as well. Mapping to a Windows shared printer from a Mac is almost as easy as from Windows. Follow these steps to make the connection:

1. Open System Preferences from the Apple menu, and choose the Print & Fax option.
2. If the Print & Fax window is locked, click the lock at the bottom left and enter your password to unlock it.
3. Click the + button to launch the Printer Browser, shown in Figure 14.14.

FIGURE 14.14

Use the OS X Printer Browser to locate printers shared on the network.

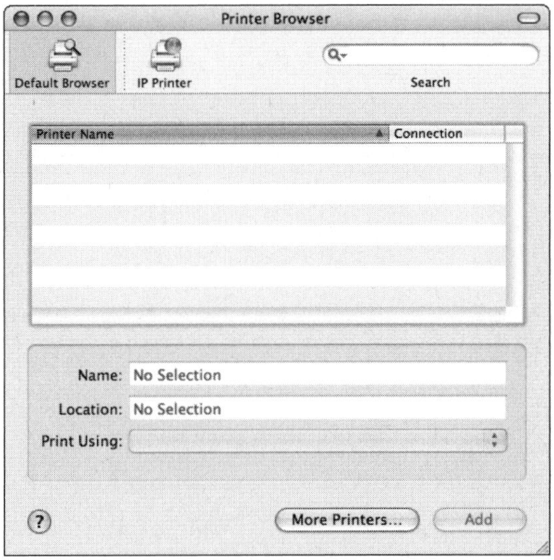

4. If the printer doesn't show up in the Printer Browser, click the More Printers button.
5. Choose Windows Printing and the workgroup that your Windows Home Server belongs to.
6. Select the name of the server when it appears, as shown in Figure 14.15. Click Choose.
7. **Enter a username and password to use to connect to the printer.** You should use your Windows Home Server credentials. Then click OK.
8. **You will then see the printers available on your server.** Choose it and click Add.
9. If you navigate back to the Print & Fax window in System Preferences, the printer will be visible, as shown in Figure 14.16.

FIGURE 14.15

Locate your server in the Printer Browser.

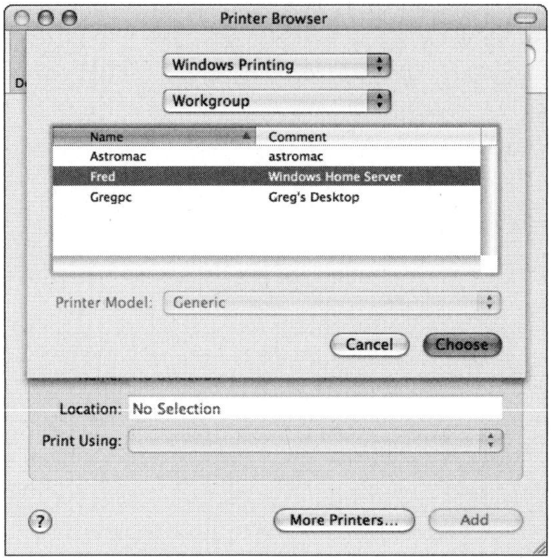

FIGURE 14.16

Your shared printer is ready to use in OS X.

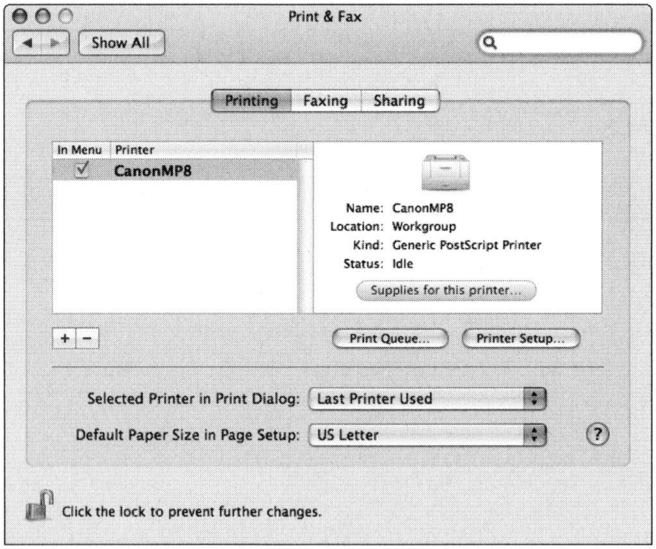

Summary

Printer sharing is one of the most useful functions that a home server can perform in a household with many users. Using your Windows Home Server as a print server frees up one of your computers from having to act in this capacity (and be on and available whenever somebody needs to print). It also ensures that you don't have to upgrade to a network printer or buy a standalone print server device.

When you install a shared printer over the network, the server supplies the device driver that the Windows client computer will need in order to print to it, making client computer installation under Windows a breeze. Likewise, the popularity of Windows has helped to ensure that shared printers, like shared folders, are accessible from a variety of different computer platforms, including Mac OS X.

Chapter 15

Sharing Data Between Computers

Perhaps you run a home-based business with deadlines and meetings with clients and suppliers. Maybe you just need to coordinate your busy schedules with your spouse and the kids. Maybe you even homeschool your children, and need a way to share lesson schedules and plans with them.

Households today are very diverse in the way they function, but they do have one thing in common — the need to share information with one another quickly, painlessly, and automatically.

While collaboration software is common in the workplace, it tends to rely on expensive infrastructure software such as Microsoft Exchange or Lotus Notes. These solutions work great, but they are impractical for the home due to their cost and the server resources that they require. There are, however, alternatives that are more viable for the home user that you can implement right on Windows Home Server.

In this chapter, we'll show you how to configure Windows Home Server's Web server to allow it to share calendar information and to act as a host for Microsoft SharePoint services. We'll also show you how to take advantage of your server's shared folders to share information in Microsoft OneNote, new in Office 2007.

Sharing Calendars

Microsoft Outlook is more than just an e-mail program. This popular program from the Microsoft Office suite is often used in corporate environments as a client for Microsoft's enterprise server called Exchange, where it offers collaboration features in addition to e-mail. These features include shared calendars, tasks, and contact lists. While those features are available for standalone Outlook users, the lack of sharing capability for most of the features make them quite a bit less useful.

Outlook's Calendar component, shown in Figure 15.1, is a nice exception to this rule. The Office 2007 version of this program includes the ability to share and subscribe to Internet Calendars published to the Web, using a standard known as iCalendar. iCalendar is supported by a large number of different calendar programs, including Lotus Notes, Google Calendar, and Mac OS X's iCal, which makes it possible to exchange scheduling information with a lot more than just other Outlook users.

FIGURE 15.1

Microsoft Office Outlook's Calendar

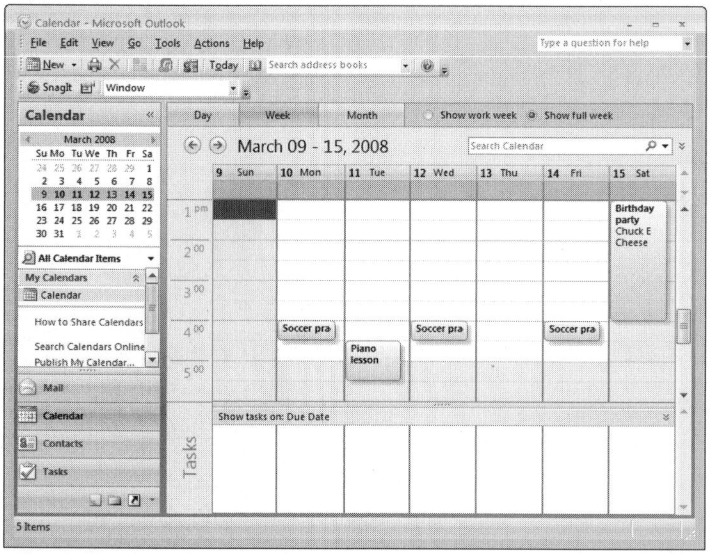

With iCalendar, you have two ways to share calendars with others. First, you can simply e-mail the iCalendar file (with an .ics extension) to all of the people that need the information. While this works well, it is only a snapshot of a calendar. It doesn't allow for automatic updates of the calendar entries when they change without the owner of the calendar sending it out all over again.

The second method for sharing iCalendar files is more intriguing. You can subscribe to calendars that are hosted on any accessible Web site, and have Outlook automatically check for updates periodically.

That's not all — when used in conjunction with a Web server that can support the WebDAV (Web-based Distributed Authoring and Versioning) protocol, Outlook can also publish your calendar to the Web. Windows Home Server's Internet Information Services (IIS) Web server is capable of doing just that. We'll walk you through the process of creating and configuring a Web site on your Windows Home Server for both publishing and subscribing to Internet calendars.

Configuring IIS

In order to publish iCalendar files directly to Windows Home Server, The IIS Web server must be configured to allow for the use of the WebDAV protocol. WebDAV is an extension to the Web's HTTP protocol that allows files to be uploaded, edited, and managed directly on a Web server without the hassles of having to transfer them to an FTP server.

Enabling WebDAV

The WebDAV protocol is included in Windows Home Server's implementation of IIS, but it is disabled by default. To enable it, you will need to log on to the server's desktop either directly or through Remote Desktop.

To enable WebDAV, follow these steps:

1. **Log on to the server's desktop, either directly, or through Remote Desktop, using the server administrator account.**

2. **Click Start ⇨ All Programs ⇨ Administrative Tools ⇨ Internet Information Services (IIS) Manager.**

3. **In the IIS Manager, shown in Figure 15.2, expand the server entry for the server in the tree on the left and click on the Web Service Extensions in the left pane.**

4. **Check the status of the WebDAV Web Service Extension from the list on the right.** If it shows Allowed, you can stop now as this means that WebDAV is already installed. If it shows as Prohibited, continue on to Step 5.

5. **Select the WebDAV item in the list.**

6. **Click the Allow button to enable WebDAV.**

CAUTION When you enable WebDAV for IIS, you have enabled it for the entire Web server and all of the sites that it hosts. Be careful when configuring other Web sites on your server to ensure that files can't be overwritten by making sure write access is turned off.

Enabling WebDAV in IIS will allow you to save files directly to the server.

Creating an iCalendar Web site

Now that you have the WebDAV protocol enabled, you need to create a Web site to use as a repository for iCalendar files. There are two steps involved in accomplishing this. First, you need to create a folder to use as a repository for the iCalendar files. Second, you need to create an IIS virtual directory to point to it.

Creating the folder

Your calendar files will need to be stored in a folder, and what better place to share them than in a shared folder on your server? Doing this ensures two things. First, you can grant users the ability to read or write from the folder using Windows Home Server's folder management feature. Second, it gives you access to the iCalendar files directly so that you can send them in e-mail as a snapshot if you like.

You have two choices when it comes to creating space on your shared folders: create a new shared folder just to store calendar entries, or create a folder on an existing shared folder such as Public. Either method is valid, but creating it on Public is somewhat simpler, so for this demonstration we'll show you how to do just that. Create a folder named Calendars in the Public shared folder, as shown in Figure 15.3.

FIGURE 15.3

You must create a folder to store the calendar entries; putting it on a shared folder offers some benefits.

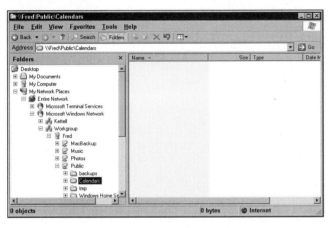

Creating the virtual directory

Now that you've created a folder to store the calendars, you need to tell IIS about it. You do this by creating a *virtual directory*, which is essentially an alias that IIS uses to refer to it within the Web site's own hierarchy.

A virtual directory can point to a local folder or a network share — you'll tell Windows Home Server to point to the share that you just created. The virtual directory can exist anywhere in the Web site hierarchy — you'll simplify it a bit by creating it under the existing Remote directory, which is already configured to require authentication and to use secure socket layer (SSL) connections.

NOTE Although you are configuring a secure iCalendar location, this is not mandatory, of course. You could just as easily place your calendar in a publicly accessible location so that others may access it. Consider the case of a professor sharing a class and office schedule with students, for example.

To create your virtual directory, follow these steps:

1. **Expand the Web Sites folder and then the Default Web Site folder (see Figure 15.2).**
2. **Right-click on the folder named Remote, and choose New ⇨ Virtual Directory.** This launches the Virtual Directory Creation Wizard, shown in Figure 15.4.

FIGURE 15.4

Use the Virtual Directory Creation Wizard to point IIS to your new calendar folder.

3. **Click Next.**

4. **Enter** Calendars **as your alias name and click Next.**

5. **Enter the path to your shared Calendars folder.** You can browse to it using the Browse button if you don't remember the exact path. Click Next.

6. **Leave the box checked to ensure that the authenticated user's credentials are used, as shown in Figure 15.5.** This will limit calendar updates to those who have write access to the share. Then click Next.

FIGURE 15.5

By using the authenticated user's credentials, you can control access to the calendars using Windows Home Server's shared folder permissions.

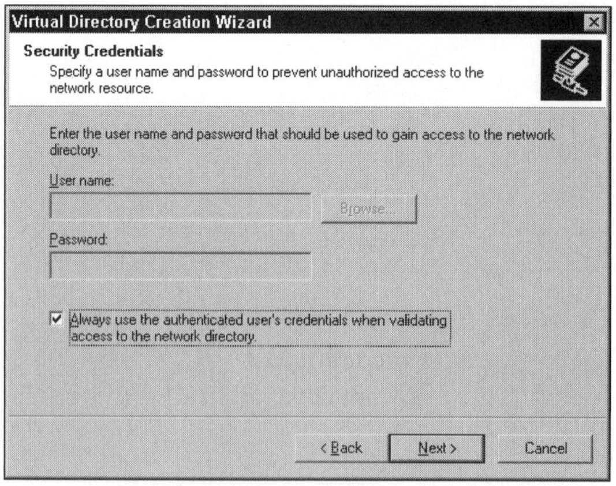

7. **In the Virtual Directory Access Permissions, make sure Read, Write, and Browse are checked as options.** This will allow authenticated users the ability to read and write files as well as view the contents of the folder in Internet Explorer. Click Next.

8. **Click Finish.** Your virtual directory has been created and is ready to use, and should be visible as one of the folders under Remote.

CROSS-REF For more information on configuring Web sites in IIS for Windows Home Server, see Chapter 35.

Testing your calendar share

Internet Explorer has the capability of opening WebDAV shared folders and then allowing files to be entered and modified in it. With this in mind, you should test your newly created virtual directory to make sure everything works as intended. Follow these steps:

1. **Open Internet Explorer on a client computer.**

2. **Choose File ⇨ Open.** You can press Ctrl+O if the menu bar isn't visible in Internet Explorer 7.

3. **In the Open dialog, check the Open as a Web Folder and enter the URL to your Calendar share, as Figure 15.6 shows.** Don't forget to use https as the protocol.

FIGURE 15.6

Open as Web Folder allows you to test WebDAV folders in Internet Explorer.

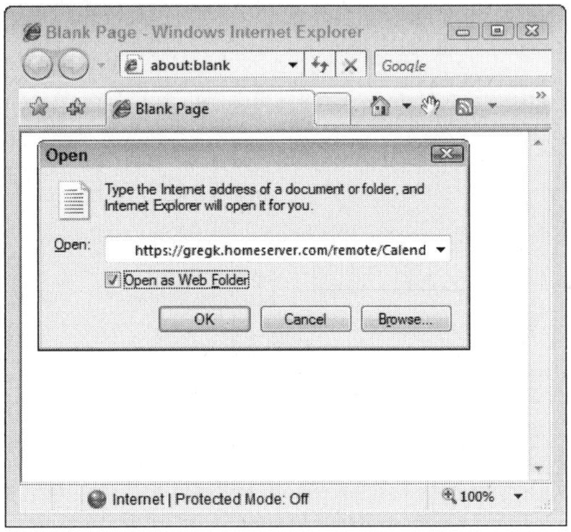

4. **When prompted, enter your user credentials.** This should be a user account that has write access to the shared folder that contains your Calendars folder.

When you use Internet Explorer to open a WebDAV folder as a Web folder rather than a Web page, you can work with the files in the folder much as you can with files in Windows Explorer. You can edit them directly from the Web site, copy and paste files to and from the folder, and rename and delete files too. To verify that your folder is set up with the proper permissions and that your account has the access level that you need, try it out by creating and copying a few files to the folder, as shown in Figure 15.7.

Now that you've created a writable WebDAV folder, you're ready to point Outlook and other calendar clients to it. We'll show you how to do that in the next section.

FIGURE 15.7

Test your writable WebDAV folder by creating or copying test files to it.

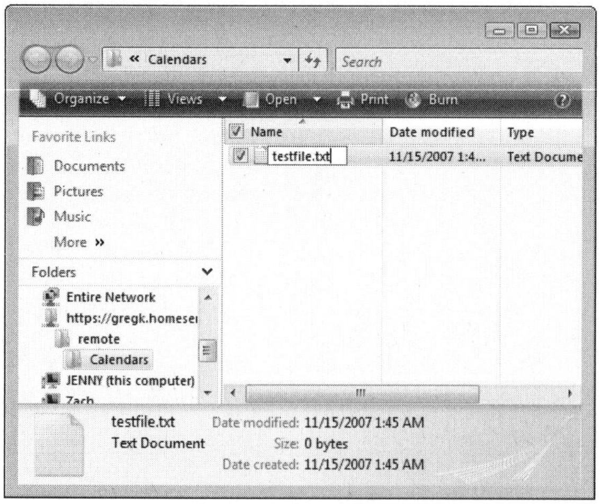

Publishing your calendar with Outlook 2007

Now that your calendar has a place to go home, you need to configure Outlook 2007 to save it there. There are a number of options when it comes to saving your calendar, ranging from saving it one time only (the equivalent of the e-mail snapshot calendar) to continually updating the server with updated information.

To publish your calendar in Outlook, do the following:

1. **Right-click on the Calendar entry on the navigation panel, and choose Publish to Internet followed by Publish to WebDAV Server, as shown in Figure 15.8.**

2. **Enter the URL of the folder that you created in the location field of the Publish Calendar dialog, shown in Figure 15.9.**

3. **Select a time span for publishing.** By default, calendar entries from 30 days in the past to 60 days in the future will be published.

4. **Choose a level of detail to display.** Options are Availability Only, Limited Details, and Full Details.

5. **Click the Advanced button, and choose whether you want this to be a single upload or an automatic update.** If automatic, check the Update Frequency check box so that Outlook knows to update based on the WebDAV server's recommended settings.

FIGURE 15.8

Select Publish to WebDAV server to share your calendar.

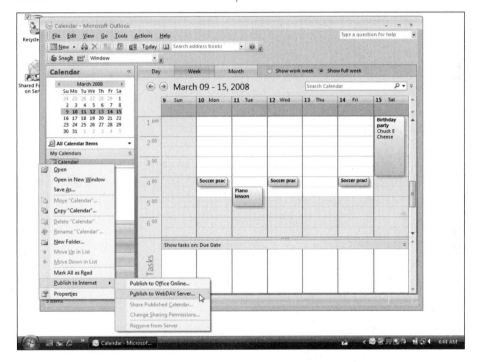

6. **Click OK.** Enter your authentication information if prompted. If you calendar is published successfully, you will be given an option to e-mail the link to interested parties.

FIGURE 15.9

Enter the location of your calendar-sharing Web folder.

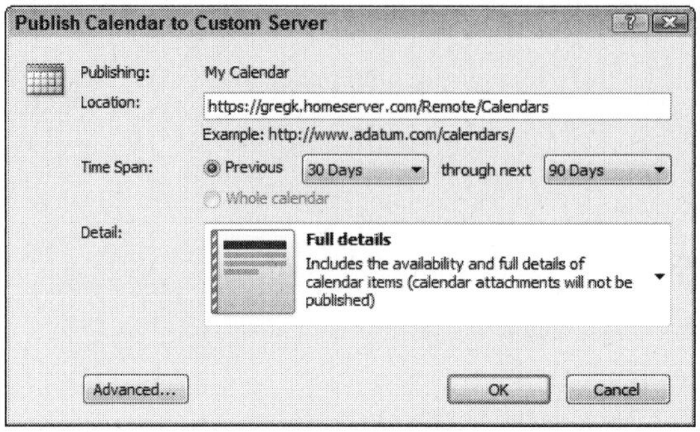

Subscribing to calendars with Outlook 2007

Now that you have your calendar published to the Web server, others can configure their Outlook clients to subscribe to the calendar. When subscribing, Outlook will check the server location regularly for changes to the calendar file and update its local copy when appropriate.

To subscribe to a calendar, follow these steps:

1. **Choose Tools ⇨ Account Settings from the Outlook menu.**

2. **Click the Internet Calendars tab.**

3. **Click the New button.**

4. **Enter the location of the calendar including the complete filename with the .ics extension.** Don't forget to use https as the protocol to access the site.

5. **In the Subscription Options dialog box, shown in Figure 15.10, enter a name for a local folder for the calendar.**

6. **Enter a description if you like.** You will be able to see this description in Outlook.

7. **If you would like to be able to download attachments stored with calendar entries, check that box.**

8. **Check the Update Limit box.** This tells Outlook to check the server at the frequency specified by the WebDAV server. Click OK when done.

Subscribed calendars are visible in the Outlook navigation window under the category Other Calendars. To view the calendar you have subscribed to, expand that box and check the box next to the calendar's name.

FIGURE 15.10

Set options for subscribing to an iCalendar.

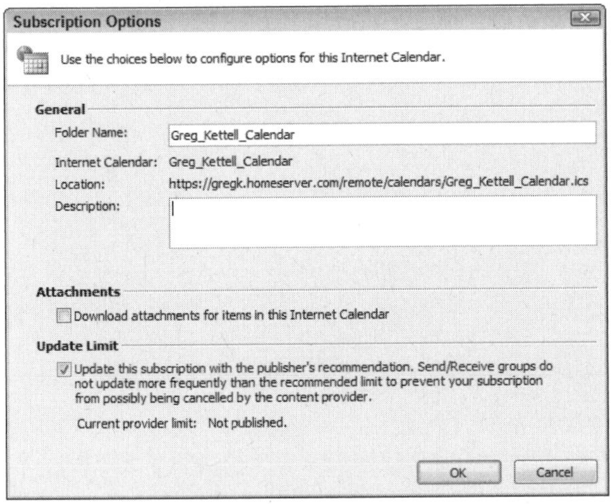

Unsubscribing to Calendars

If you decide you no longer wish to subscribe or publish a calendar, you can visit the Account Settings dialog box to remove them from the list.

To remove a subscribed calendar, click the Internet Calendars tab, shown in Figure 15.11. Highlight the calendar you wish to remove, and click the Remove button. Click Yes when prompted to remove the calendar from all computers that you use.

To stop publishing your calendar, click the Published Calendars tab, shown in Figure 15.12. Highlight the calendar and click Remote. The calendar will be removed from the server and no longer published.

FIGURE 15.11

Remove subscribed calendars in Outlook's Account Settings dialog box, on the Internet Calendars tab.

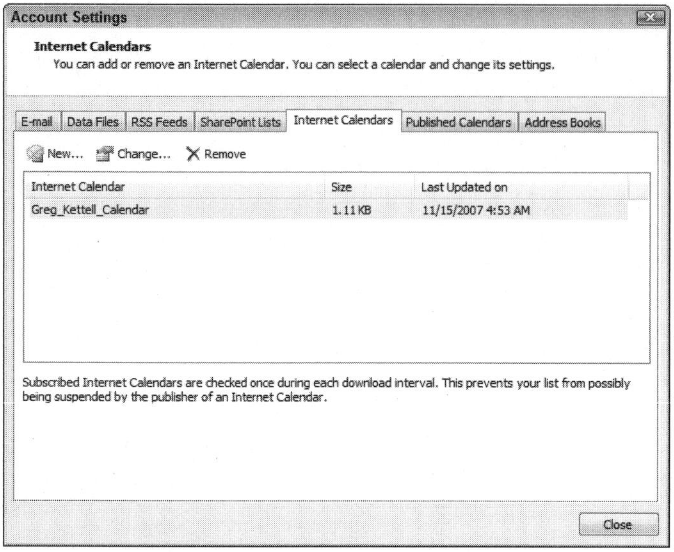

FIGURE 15.12

Remove published calendars in Outlook's Account Settings dialog box, on the Published Calendars tab.

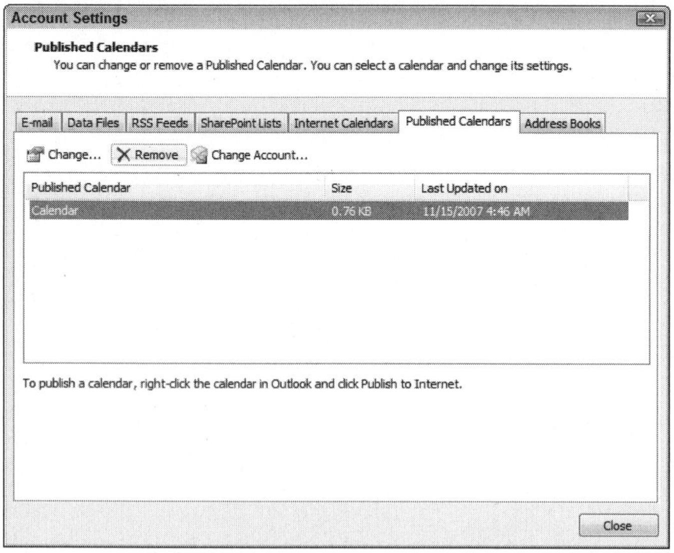

Using Windows Calendar

If you use Windows Vista, but don't have Microsoft Outlook, you are still in luck when it comes to sharing calendar data. Vista comes with a new program called Windows Calendar, shown in Figure 15.13, which offers much of the same capabilities as Outlook's calendar feature. These features include the ability to publish and subscribe to calendars hosted on a WebDAV-enabled Web server.

FIGURE 15.13

Vista includes the iCalendar-enabled Windows Calendar.

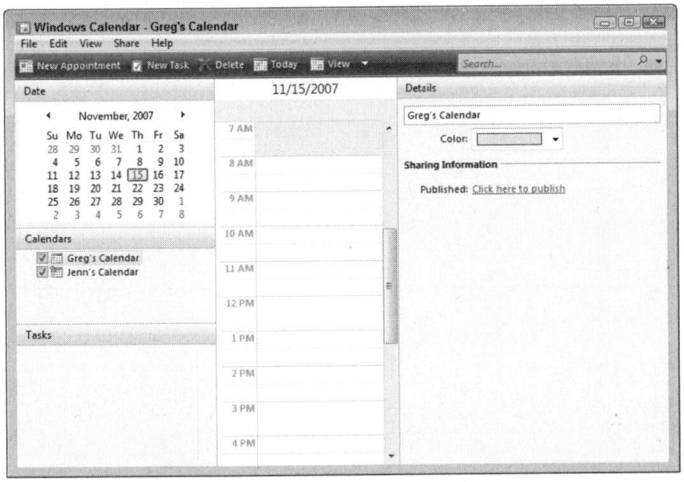

Windows Calendar is a simpler application than Outlook due to its focus on the single function of calendar maintenance. Because its primary focus isn't to connect to an Exchange server, the Internet Calendar sharing functions are more front-and-center rather than the afterthought they seem to be in Outlook.

Publishing with Windows Calendar

To publish your calendar, simply choose the Share ⇨ Publish menu item. In the Publish Calendar dialog box, shown in Figure 15.14, enter the location information for your WebDAV folder. You can also specify a name for the calendar, and choose the types of information that you want to include with the calendar, including notes, reminders, and tips.

Be sure to check the Automatically publish changes made to this calendar box if you want the calendar to be updated continually. Click the Publish button to submit the calendar to the server, and send the notification out to interested parties.

FIGURE 15.14

Windows Calendar publishing configuration contains features much like Outlook's.

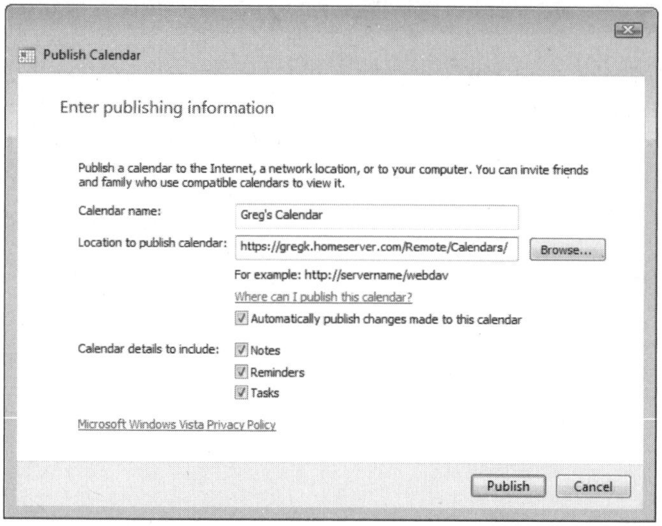

Subscribing with Windows Calendar

Subscribing to iCalendars using Windows Calendar is just as easy as publishing. Choose Share ⇨ Subscribe from the menu, and enter the pertinent information for the share in the Subscribe to a Calendar box.

First, enter the full path to the calendar, including the Web path and the complete filename with its extension, and click Next. Enter your authentication information when prompted.

Next, enter calendar subscription settings, as shown in Figure 15.15. You can choose a name to use for this calendar, an update interval ranging from never updating to once a week, and whether you want to receive reminders and tasks along with the calendar entries.

FIGURE 15.15

With calendar subscription settings, you can change the update frequency.

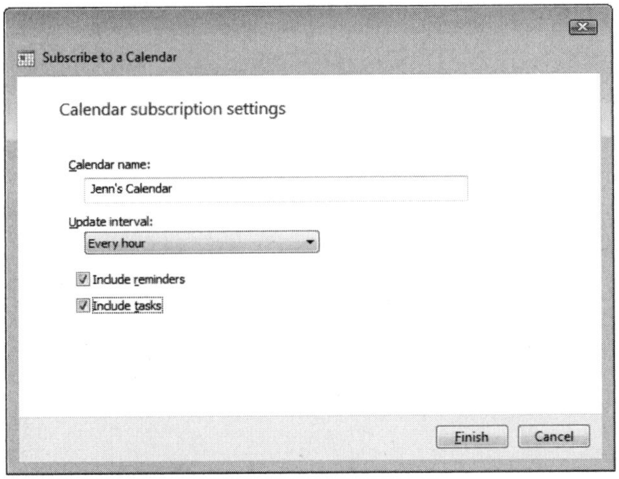

Sharing OneNote Notebooks

Calendars aren't the only things you can share on Windows Home Server. The shared folder feature makes it a convenient place to store collaborative documents from all sorts of applications.

Microsoft Office has included an application called OneNote since Office 2003. OneNote is a free-form database tool with the ability to store all manner of information, including notes, images, links, and more. It also includes the ability to share notes with others, either by e-mail or through the use of collaborative notebooks. OneNote is shown in Figure 15.16.

OneNote 2007 provides two notebook templates specifically for collaboration, although you are certainly not limited to that choice when you want to share a notebook. You can store notebooks created from any of the templates, including the Blank template, on a server share where they can be accessed by other OneNote users.

FIGURE 15.16

Microsoft OneNote 2007 is designed with multiuser collaboration in mind.

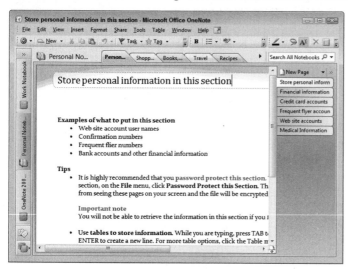

To create a shared notebook, follow these steps:

1. Create a folder on one of your Windows Home Server shared folders, either under Public or in a new shared folder.

2. In OneNote, choose File ⇨ New ⇨ Notebook from the main menu.

3. Specify a name for the notebook in the New Notebook Wizard, shown in Figure 15.17.

4. Choose a template to use as the basis for the notebook, and click Next.

5. On the Who will use this notebook page, shown in Figure 15.18, choose the option to allow multiple people to share the notebook.

6. Click in the On a server radio button to specify that you want to use a network file share and click Next.

7. **Enter the path to the shared folder path you created in Step 1.** This can either be a UNC path in the form of \\server\folder, or a shared folder mapped to a drive letter.

8. Click Create when complete.

FIGURE 15.17

Choose a template that gives your notebook the basic formatting that you need.

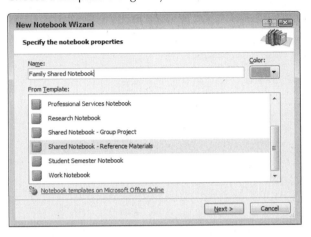

FIGURE 15.18

Specify sharing information when creating a new notebook.

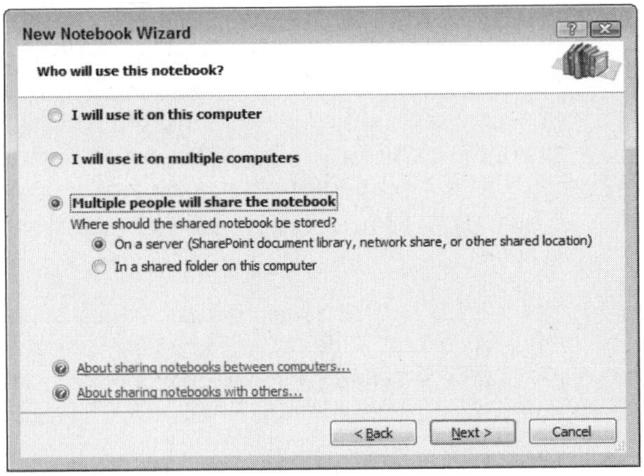

To open the notebook on other OneNote clients, follow these steps:

1. **Choose File ⇨ Open ⇨ Notebook from the main menu.**

2. **Enter the path to the notebook in the Open Notebook dialog.** You can browse to your network share using the My Network Places item on the navigation controls on the left side of the dialog box.

3. **Choose the folder that the notebook is located in, and click Open.** The folder opens, as shown in Figure 15.19.

FIGURE 15.19

Your new shared notebook is ready for use.

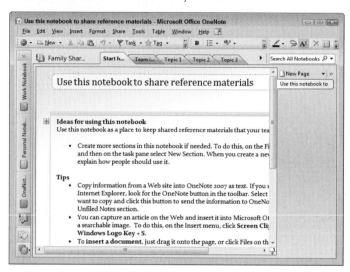

Summary

Collaboration and information sharing isn't just for the corporate world anymore. Today's busy families often need the same type of schedule synchronization and data sharing. Fortunately, you don't have to invest in an expensive enterprise-class collaboration server in order to share calendar schedules with other family members and friends. Instead, you can take advantage of features provided by your Windows Home Server, including folder sharing and WebDAV support in the IIS Web server to make it possible.

Microsoft Outlook and Windows Calendar are two programs that can take advantage of an Internet standard for calendar sharing called iCalendar. Both of these programs can publish calendars they create to a WebDAV-enabled Web site, with periodic automatic updates to ensure that the information on the server doesn't get stale. Other clients that support iCalendar can subscribe to the files on the Web server, and will automatically pull any updates down. While this method isn't real-time instantaneous, as using calendars on Exchange or Lotus Notes would be, it is far more useful than the standby of e-mailing static iCalendar update files to other users.

Calendars aren't the only data files that can be shared on Windows Home Server. Other documents can be stored there as well. Microsoft OneNote, for example, allows multiple users to collaborate on a notebook stored on a shared server as long as you specify the desire to share the notebook when you create it.

Chapter 16

Installing Server Applications

In building Windows Home Server, Microsoft packed just about every server application that they could think of that could be useful for the home user. Out of the box, Windows Home Server provides file server, Web server, media streaming services, backup services and also acts as a Remote Desktop gateway. Could you possibly need more functionality than that? Of course you could! That shiny new (or recycled) Windows Home Server machine is just begging for you to install additional server applications in order to get even more value and utility out of it. Your server is on 24/7, shouldn't you be able to use it 24/7 for all of your server application needs?

While the range of services that Windows Home Server offers is already impressive, there is no reason why you shouldn't install other server applications to get even more out of it. Here are a few ideas to consider:

- Hosting your own mail server
- Installing an antivirus management server
- Hosting a multiplayer game server

In this chapter, we'll show you how you can install each of these types of applications and gain more from your server.

Installing an E-mail Server

Is the e-mail service from your ISP (Internet Service Provider) not what you would consider reliable? Does it impose undue restrictions on you such as limiting e-mail attachment sizes? You could purchase an e-mail account from a third-party hosting company; however, with Windows Home Server in your home, you have another option.

There are a number of mail server solutions available for the Windows OS, including ones that are both open source and commercial. These systems will run on Windows Home Server, and can be a useful alternative to using your ISP's or a third-party's mail server, although it's definitely not a solution for everyone.

The benefits of running an e-mail server include the fact that you control it; you can create as many accounts as you wish, and you can control the restrictions on e-mail size yourself. As the server administrator, you can also see detailed logging information on all mail received or sent.

There are downsides and potential gotchas as well. Unless you have a static IP (Internet Protocol) address from your ISP, you will be limited to using your homeserver.com domain name as your mail server name. You are also subject to your ISP deciding to keep critical ports available to allow you to host an e-mail server. Finally, as server administrator you will be in charge of making sure the mail server is virus and spam free. Your home hosted mail service will be exactly as reliable as the server you run it on. Excessive downtime of your server or your Internet connection can result in your mail getting bounced back to the sender.

Installing hMailServer

If your willing to accept those risks, or want to install a mail server just to try it out or to use as a second or test e-mail account, we recommend an open source mail server called hMailServer. It will work well with Windows Home Server and incorporates a lot of functionality for a free system, including support for POP3 (Post Office Protocol version 3), SMTP (Simple Mail Transfer Protocol), and IMAP (Internet Message Access Protocol) mail protocols; support for distribution lists, antivirus/antispam, aliases; and more.

> **ON the WEB** You can find more information about hMailServer, and download the installation package from www.hmailserver.com.

Installing the package

After you've downloaded the most recent build of hMailServer, installation is very straight forward. Follow these steps:

1. **Log on to your server's desktop, either directly or via Remote Desktop.**

2. **Run the hMailServer executable to launch the hMailServer Setup Wizard, shown in Figure 16.1.** Click Next to begin.

3. **Choose a destination for the installation.** The default is in your `C:\Program Files` folder. Then click Next.

4. **Choose whether to install the Administrative tools and the Server, or just the Administrative tools, as shown in Figure 16.2.** For your Windows Home Server installation, choose both. You should also consider installing the Administration tools on another computer to manage your mail server remotely. Click Next.

5. **Choose whether to use the built in MySQL database, or to use an external database server.** If you have a different database server installed on your Windows Home Server computer, you may elect to use that. Supported database servers include MySQL and Microsoft SQL Server. Then click Next.

6. **Accept the default program shortcuts for the Start menu, and click Next.**

FIGURE 16.1

hMailServer lets you become your own postmaster.

FIGURE 16.2

You can install tools on another computer to administer the mail server.

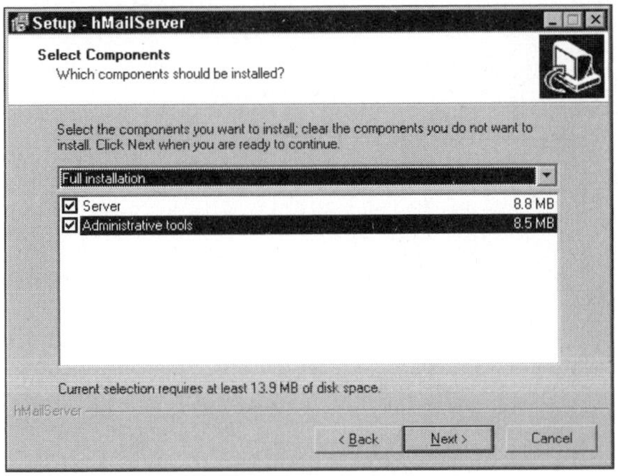

7. **Review your setup steps and click Install.** The installation will proceed.

8. **Enter a password for the mail server, and click Next.**

9. **Finally, click Finish to complete the installation.**

Opening ports

Mail server software uses three ports commonly: Port 25 for SMTP (for outbound mail), Port 143 for IMAP (for inbound mail), or 110 for. In order to use these services, the Windows Firewall must open these ports to allow other mail servers to connect to hMailServer. In addition, you should configure your router to forward those ports to your Windows Home Server computer.

The Windows Firewall applet, shown in Figure 16.3, is accessed through the control panel. Launch it by choosing Start ➪ Control Panel ➪ Windows Firewall. Once it is opened, click the Exceptions tab.

FIGURE 16.3

You need to open standard e-mail protocol ports to allow other mail servers to connect.

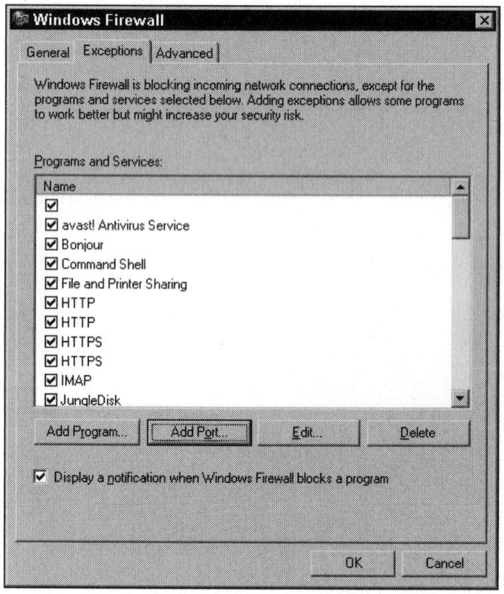

In the Windows Firewall panel, do the following to open the firewall ports:

1. **Click Add Port.**

2. **Enter** SMTP **for the port name.**

3. Enter 25 for the port number.

4. Leave the TCP radio button selected.

5. Click OK.

6. Repeat Steps 1 through 5 for POP3 (port 110) and IMAP (port 143).

7. Click OK in the Firewall panel to accept the changes.

Now, you need to configure the router to forward these ports to Windows Home Server. Figure 16.4 shows a typical router configuration screen for port forwarding configuration, but every router manufacturer's configuration procedure is a little bit different.

Configure your router to forward the same ports that you opened in the firewall: 25, 110, and 143.

TIP Port forwarding typically works best if you assign a static IP address or use a reserved DHCP (Dynamic Host Configuration Protocol) address so that it won't change. Consult your router's user's guide for information on reserving DHCP addresses.

FIGURE 16.4

Configure your router to forward ports to your server.

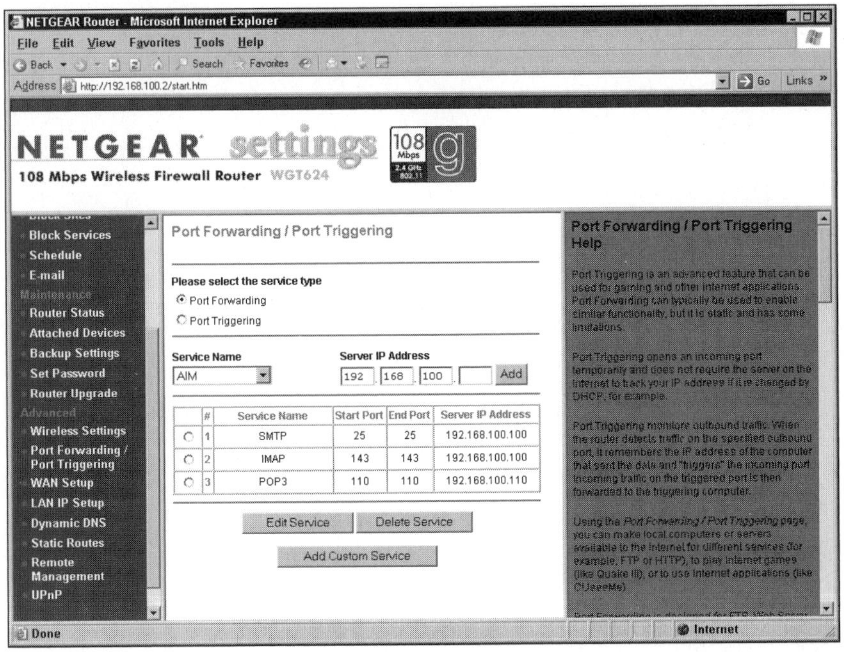

Configuring the server

Now that ports are opened, you need to configure hMailServer. You do this with the hMailServer Administrator, which you may have launched automatically after installation was complete. If not, it's available on the Start menu: Choose Start ➪ All Programs ➪ hMailServer ➪ hMailServer Administrator to launch it.

When you first run the Administrator, you are given the option to connect to the server running on localhost, as shown in Figure 16.5. Assuming that you're running Administrator on your Windows Home Server machine, this is the correct choice. If you run Administrator from another computer, click the Add button to add the link to your host.

FIGURE 16.5

Use the Administrator tool to configure hMailServer.

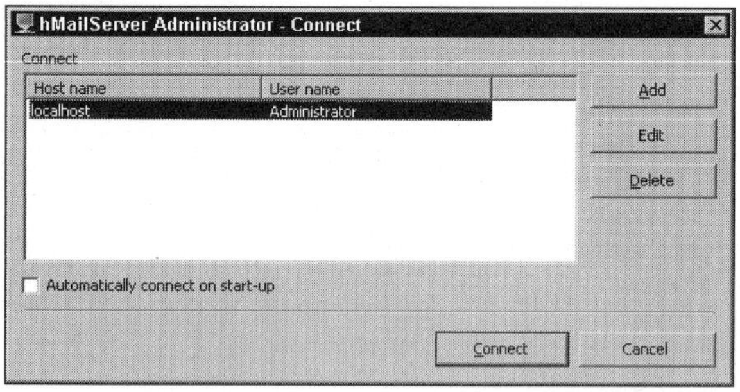

Click Connect if these settings are correct to connect to the server. When prompted, enter the password for the server that you specified when installing.

Once connected, you will be at the Welcome screen. The first thing you need to do is to configure your domain. Click the Add Domain button to go directly to the domain configuration screen, shown in Figure 16.6.

Enter your e-mail domain name. This should be the same as the domain used to access your Windows Home Server, as it will be used by sending e-mail systems to connect to your server. Enter this in the Domain Name field. While you are on this screen, take the time to configure a catch-all e-mail address such as postmaster. This will be used to handle all e-mail sent to your domain but not to a legitimate address. Click Save when done.

Next, you will add an e-mail account. When you expand the Domain tab and select the domain, you will see additional buttons for account management. Click the Add account button. On the Account screen, shown in Figure 16.7, enter an account address, a password, a maximum size for the user's e-mail storage, and whether you want the account to be able to act as an administrator for hMailServer. Click Save when done.

FIGURE 16.6

You must configure the domain used for your e-mail accounts. This should be the same as your Windows Home Server domain name.

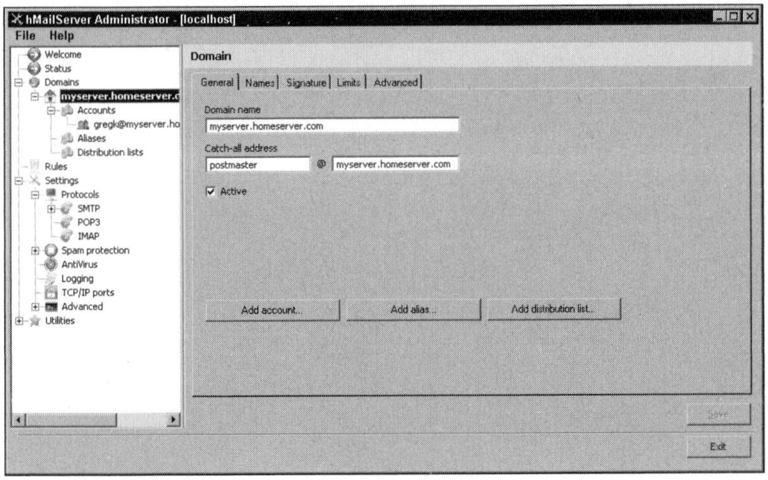

FIGURE 16.7

Create e-mail accounts for each user.

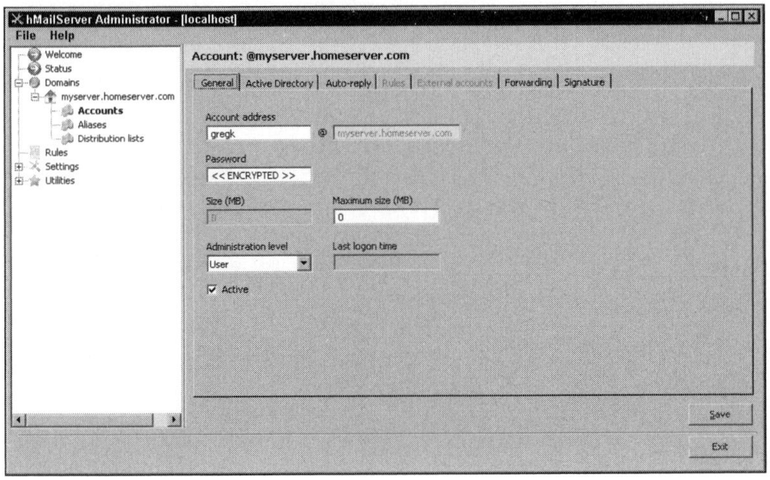

Finally, you need to configure the host name for SMTP. This is necessary because some e-mail servers are configured to reject e-mail if this is not set. Expand Settings followed by Protocols, and select SMTP. Then select the Delivery of e-mail tab, shown in Figure 16.8. Enter a value for the

Host name that equals the name you used for your domain configuration, and click Save when you are finished.

Your mail server is now configured with at least one user account on it. The next step is to verify the settings work by connecting with an e-mail client and sending a message.

FIGURE 16.8

Set the host name for SMTP to prevent other servers from rejecting your mail.

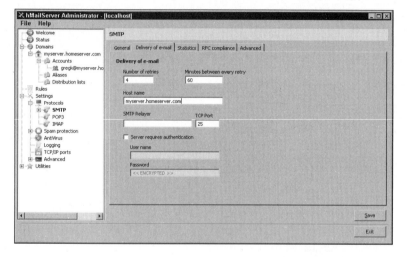

Testing your mail accounts

In order to test your e-mail server, you must use an e-mail client such as Outlook or Windows Mail (formerly known as Outlook Express) and create a new account profile for your server. To test using Windows Mail under Vista, do the following:

1. **Choose Tools ➪ Accounts from the menu.**

2. **Click the Mail tab.**

3. **Click the Add button, and choose Mail.**

4. **Enter your name and click Next.**

5. **Enter the e-mail address of an account you've created on hMailServer; that is,** myemail@myserver.homeserver.com, **as shown in Figure 16.9.** Click Next.

6. **Choose whether to use IMAP or POP3 as your incoming mail server protocol.** You enabled both on the server, so either should work.

FIGURE 16.9

Configure a mail client to test your mail server.

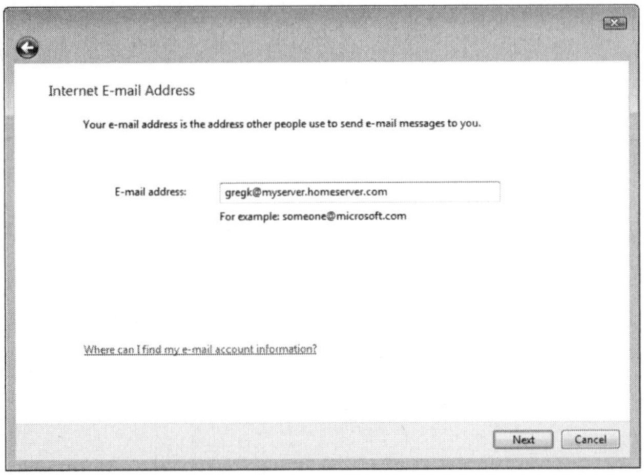

7. **Enter the incoming mail server.** This will be your dynamic domain name; that is, myserver.homeserver.com.

8. **Enter the outgoing mail (SMTP) server.** This will be the same as the incoming server. If a check box is visible stating that the outgoing server requires authentication, make sure to check it, as shown in Figure 16.10.

FIGURE 16.10

Choose your dynamic domain name as your mail server name.

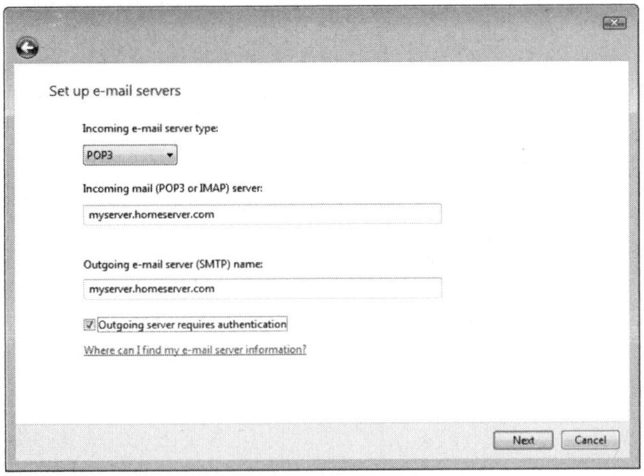

9. **Click Next.**

10. **Enter the account name and password that you created when you set up the account.**

11. **Click Next.** Make sure that Secure Password Authentication is not checked and click Next again.

12. **Click Finish.**

13. **Highlight the account and click the Properties button.**

14. **Click the Servers tab.**

15. **Under Outgoing Mail Server, check the My server requires authentication box.**

16. **Click OK.**

Now that your mail server is configured, try sending mail from it to another e-mail account, and then the other way around, as shown in Figure 16.11.

FIGURE 16.11

Send and receive mail using your new account to give it a try.

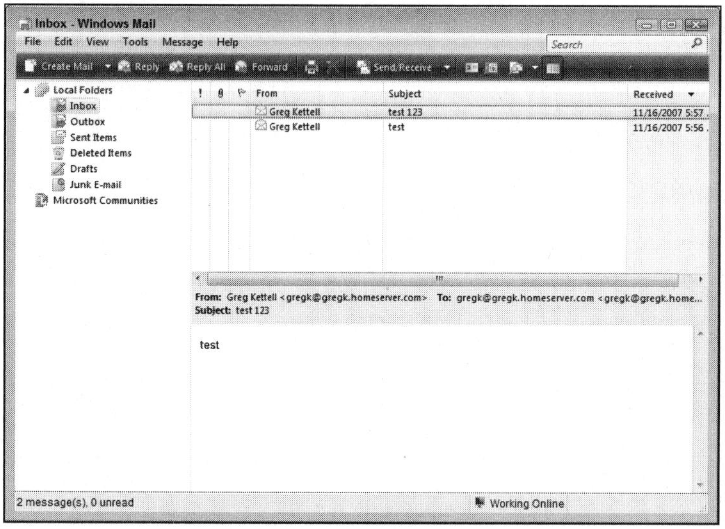

Installing Antivirus Software

As everybody knows by now, viruses and spyware are a huge problem that affects millions of computer users around the world. Running your computer without virus protection in this day and age is tantamount to an invitation for your computer to be overrun. Fortunately, there are plenty of antivirus solutions on the market, and one of our favorites, avast!, from ALWIL Software, has recently introduced an antivirus package especially for Windows Home Server that not only protects the server, but also allows for management of client computers as well.

ON the WEB Visit avast! `www.avast.com`. Downloads for avast! programs can be found at `www.avast.com/eng/programs.html`.

Installing avast!

The avast! solution for Windows Home Server involves downloading both a server component for your server, and client software to run on each of your Windows client computers. Download both versions from `www.avast.com`, and copy them to a shared folder accessible to your server and the clients, such as Public or Software.

Installing avast! Windows Home Server Edition

First, here are the steps you need to install the server component:

1. **Run the** `setup_av_whs.exe` **executable.** The setup will start, as shown in Figure 16.12.

FIGURE 16.12

Avast! antivirus is now available in a Windows Home Server edition.

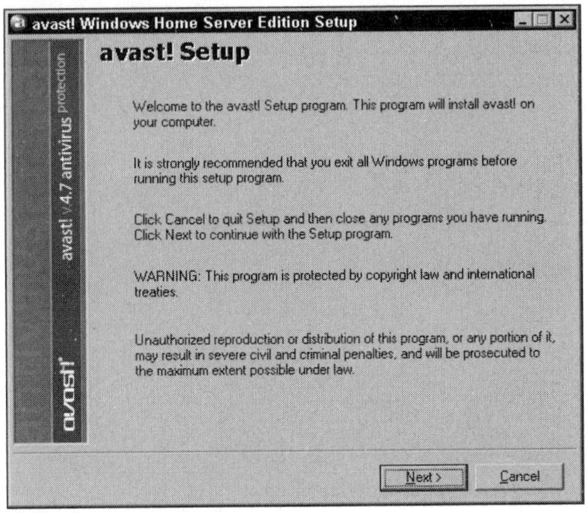

2. **Click Next, read the notes in the read me section, and then click Next again.**
3. **Read and indicate acceptance of the license agreement terms, and click Next.**
4. **Choose a destination directory.** The default choice is fine.

5. **Choose the type of install that you want.** Your choices are Typical, Minimal, and Custom. Typical installs all features other than the foreign language support. Minimal leaves out some of the less-used features to minimize the installation footprint. Custom lets you choose exactly what you want.

6. **If you have a license file from avast!, enter the path to it and click Load.** Otherwise, click the Demo button for a time-limited demonstration of the program.

7. **Click OK.**

8. **Review the installation information, as shown in Figure 16.13, and click Next to begin the installation.**

9. **Choose to restart now or later.** We recommend restarting right away.

FIGURE 16.13
_____

Review the installation information.

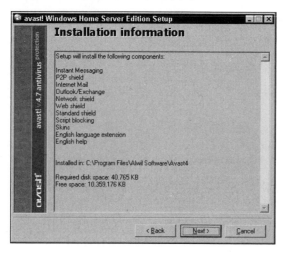

Installing the avast! client

With the server installation complete, you now need to install or upgrade client computers with the latest version of the avast! client application, which you can also download from www.avast.com. Run through the installation or upgrade wizard (shown in Figure 16.14) to complete the installation. Allow the computer to restart if necessary.

FIGURE 16.14

Install the latest version of the avast! client application.

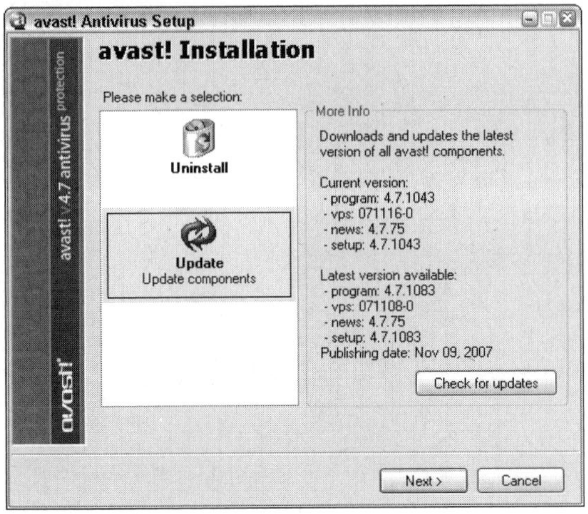

Managing avast! WHS edition

As a proper Windows Home Server application, you can manage avast! WHS edition entirely from the Windows Home Server Console.

After the installation is complete, the avast! antivirus tab is available on the Console, shown in Figure 16.15. This tab provides the means for configuring and monitoring avast! activity on the server as well as on all of the client computers with avast! installed.

Using the avast! console tab

The following buttons are available from the avast! tab:

- **Properties:** Allows you to view the antivirus settings for a selected computer. You can also access the properties by double-clicking on a computer.

- **Scan history:** Enables you to see the results of past virus scans on a client computer.

- **Refresh:** Updates the Console window with any changed client information.

- **Scan all:** Launches an immediate virus scan on all available clients. If a virus is found, it's a good idea to scan all of the computers on the network to ensure that they are clean, and this button provides the most convenient way to do this.

- **Licensing:** Provides a way to update license files and deploy them to all of your client computers.

- **Start main avast console:** Launches the avast! server console. This console is described later in the chapter.

FIGURE 16.15

You can use the new avast! antivirus tab on the Console to manage antivirus features on your client computers.

Setting computer antivirus properties

You can change antivirus settings for a computer by either double-clicking on it, or selecting it and clicking the Properties button. This launches the settings dialog for that computer, as shown in Figure 16.16.

You can use the three tabs available on this dialog, Scan Scheduler, Notifications, and Licensing. Scan Scheduler, to set up scheduled scan times for the computer or for the server. The Notifications tab provides you with information regarding problems on the clients. These can not only consist of virus detected messages, but also client problems such as errors encountered, license expiration, or simply problems because the client antivirus is turned off. The Licensing tab will give you information regarding the avast! licensing for that client. You can also enter new licensing information for that computer as you receive it from avast! after licensing the software.

NOTE The scheduler is not usable with the free avast! home edition. If you would like to take advantage of this feature, you will need to run the avast! professional edition instead. You can, however, use this tab to configure scan scheduling for the server itself.

If you schedule scans on the server, you should schedule them for a time outside of your backup windows, such as right afterwards. You should do this to prevent the scan from having an impact to the backup times.

FIGURE 16.16

You can configure antivirus settings for each client computer.

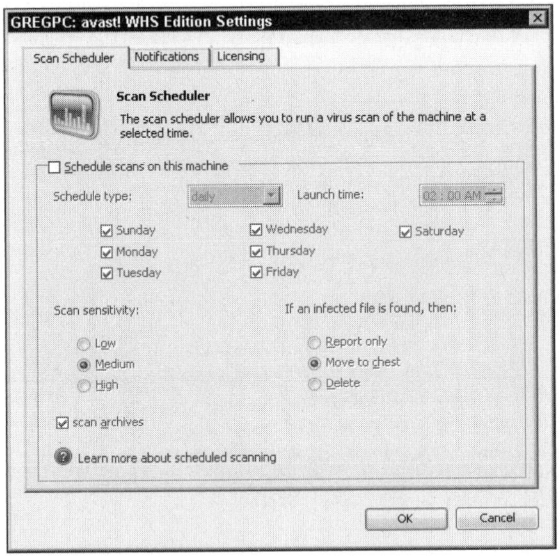

Launching the avast! console

You can do much more in terms of configuring the server with standard avast! console than with the Windows Home Server Console. Normally, you would have to log on to the server and view it from the server's desktop; however the avast! plug-in eliminates the need to do that in true Windows Home Server fashion — by launching it from a button on the Console.

The Start main avast console button launches the avast! console in the same Remote Desktop window that the Windows Home Server Console runs in, as shown in Figure 16.17. The avast! server console window simply pops up over top of the Windows Home Server Console, allowing configuration from anywhere that Remote Access can be done.

FIGURE 16.17

You can launch the avast! console directly from the Windows Home Server Console.

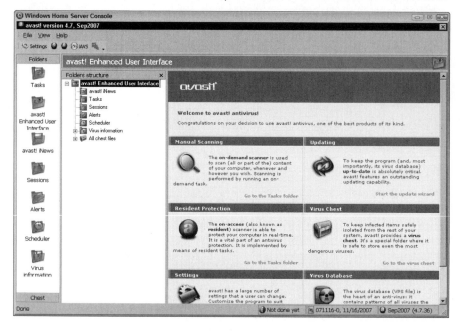

Hosting a Game Server

Whether you are an avid multiplayer gamer, or just like to play occasionally, you are probably aware of games that can operate with a standalone game server. A game server is used to host the game world and control the interactions between players, and is used so that performance of the client computers isn't hobbled or so that a person hosting the game on their local computer doesn't get any sort of unfair advantage.

To get the most out of running a game server, a dedicated computer is often used. However, depending on the hardware requirements of the game server you want to run, your Windows Home Server computer may be able to easily take on the chore.

NOTE   If you are expecting to host a game server that allows many users to connect from the Internet, you may have to rethink this strategy, as the bandwidth available to most residential ISP connections isn't sufficient. You will be better off using a public hosting server or leasing game server space from an Internet hosting company. If you just want to host a server for a few of your friends to connect from the Internet, or where all players will connect from inside your network, hosting the server on your Windows Home Server computer should work fine.

NOTE At the time of this writing, there are no game server add-ins for Windows Home Server. If you want to host a game server, you will have to do it from the server's desktop.

As an example of installing a game server, we'll walk you through the installation steps for a popular one, Steam from Valve Software, shown in Figure 16.18. Steam is a digital distribution system and multiplayer game communication platform used as a basis for more than 200 games, including the popular Counterstrike and Team Fortress multiplayer games, so getting Steam up and running will allow you to host a number of different games.

FIGURE 16.18

Install Steam locally on your Windows Home Server computer to host game servers for Counterstrike and others.

ON the WEB You can download Steam from Valve Software at `http://steampowered.com/v/index.php?area=getsteamnow&cc=US`. The download and steam account are free, but you will be charged for the games themselves.

Download Steam and install it. Using the default settings, it will be installed onto your C: drive. If your C: drive space is getting a little cramped, you can install it to one of your shared folder paths instead. Alternatively, you can add another hard drive, either internal or external, to your server, and format it using the Disk Management utility instead of adding it to the server storage pool.

CROSS-REF You can find information on using Disk Management in Chapter 34.

Follow these steps to install Steam on your Windows Home Server computer:

1. **Run the SteamIntall.msi program that you downloaded from Valve.**

2. **Follow the Steam Installation Wizard.** Enter your Valve account information when prompted, or create a new account if you don't currently have one.

3. **Sign into Steam and click the Tools tab.**

4. **Select either the Dedicated Server or the Source Dedicated Server items, and click the Install button on the lower-right side of the window.** Each dedicated server option hosts different games, so you may wish to install both. The server you choose will be automatically downloaded and installed, as shown in Figure 16.19.

FIGURE 16.19

Download the Source Dedicated Server component. Installation is automatic.

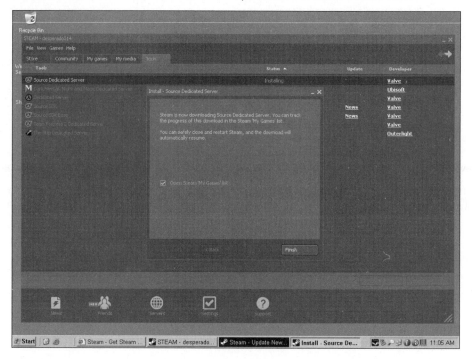

5. **When the download is complete, click the Launch button, which has replaced the Install button.**

6. **Click the Launch Tool button to launch the dedicated server.**

7. **Choose the game you'd like to host, as shown in Figure 16.20.**

8. Enter a password for the server that others will need to use to access it.

9. Click Start Server to begin hosting.

10. Connect to the server from client computers.

FIGURE 16.20

Choose the game you would like to host.

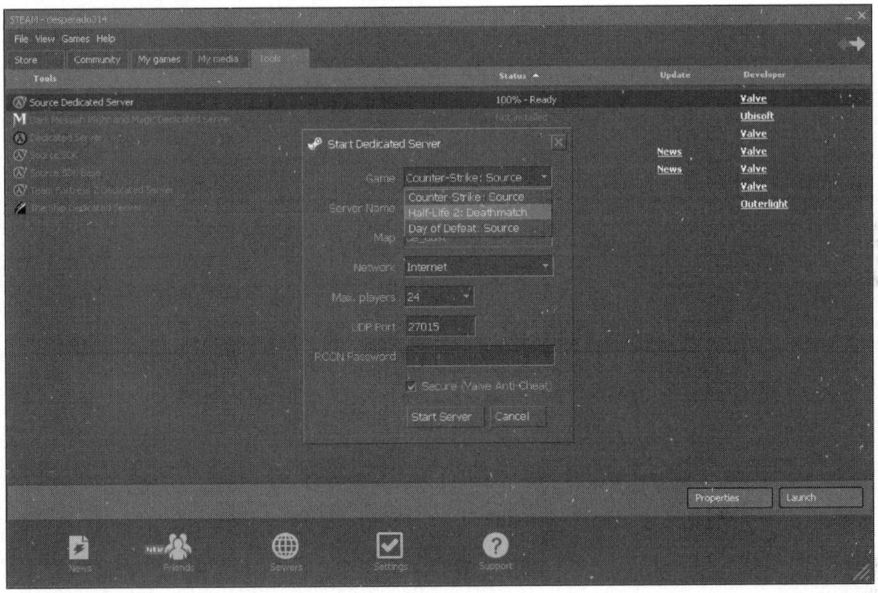

Summary

While Windows Home Server provides a large number of services right out of the box, that doesn't mean that you are limited to those functions. A variety of server applications are available that you can install on Windows Home Server just as with other versions of the Windows operating system.

One common server application that Windows Home Server does not provide is an e-mail server, given there is less of a need for one in the home environment than in, say, a small business. If you run your own business out of your home, or you simply have the desire to host your own e-mail server, several commercial and open source solutions work with Windows Home Server. One popular open source package, hMailServer, can provide you with as many IMAP, POP3, and SMTP e-mail accounts as you like. It also offers advanced features such as distribution lists, integration with antivirus scanners, and more.

Speaking of antivirus, Windows Home Server makes an ideal platform for hosting a server managed antivirus solution for you networked computers. One popular package is avast! from ALWIL Software. Not only can their antivirus software run on Windows Home Server, but they also provide a Windows Home Server add-in that lets you manage antivirus settings for both the server and clients on your network.

Windows Home Server can be a convenient platform for installing and running many other types of server applications as well. Game servers are one example. Game servers are used to host multiplayer online games without having to sacrifice the performance of one of the client computers by having it double as a server. Because they are only required to host the game world and network connections, game server computers can typically be run on computer hardware with less power than clients that also need graphics processing power.

Part IV

Remote Access

Chapter 17

Configuring Remote Access

H aving a server at home to hold all of your important files is nice, isn't it? The fact that you can access them from any computer in the house is a nice bonus. But what about when you aren't at home? It's not always possible to remember to copy files you might need onto your laptop — what you really need is a way to access your network from anywhere.

Fortunately, Windows Home Server includes a way to do just that. The Remote Access feature allows you to access all of the files stored in your server's shared folders. You are able to download, upload, rename, and delete files through a special remote access Web site hosted on your Home Server. You can even remotely manage your server through the Console and attach Remote Desktop to your computer's desktops.

In this chapter, we explain how to configure your router and your server to enable Remote Access, and show you how to get a free dynamic domain name. We also show you how to configure the Web server.

IN THIS CHAPTER

Explaining remote access

Configuring your router for remote access

Creating a custom domain

Accessing your Web site

Resolving blocked port problems

Explaining Remote Access

To make use of Remote Access, you need to have a few things configured on your network and on your server. Remote Access allows computers on the Internet that are external to your household network to connect to the server or to other computers on the network. In order for this access to work, your network router must be configured to forward requests from the Internet to the server. This is accomplished using a technique known as *port forwarding*. With port forwarding, your router is told to forward all requests that come on a particular port on to a computer on the network, in this case your

Windows Home Server computer. Figure 17.1 presents a network diagram that illustrates how Remote Access works.

In order to reach your household network, your ISP (Internet Service Provider) issues you an IP (Internet Protocol) address, a four-byte number used to route messages to and from your network. When these messages are passed to your network, your router is usually the first device to see them. The router must make the determination as to which computer (if any) on your network to forward the message on to.

An IP address can be considered somewhat analogous to a phone number, only instead of people calling people, it's used by computers to "call" other computers. You can extend this analogy further by thinking of a port as similar to a phone extension at a business. While a phone call will get you a specific business, you need to use the extension to reach the correct person. Similarly, while the IP address will direct computer messages to the correct network, the address must also be directed to a specific port because the server applications listen to this in order to ensure that the port gets the messages intended for it.

FIGURE 17.1

A Remote Access network diagram

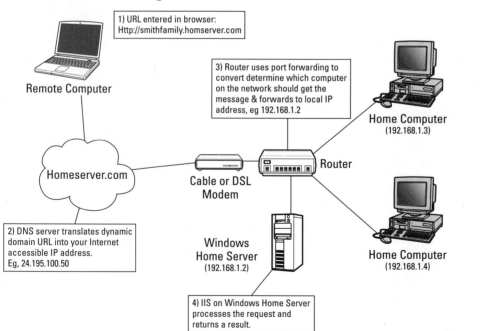

Windows Home Server utilizes several server applications that can listen for messages and respond to them. The important ones for remote access are Remote Web Workplace, which is a means for accessing Remote Desktop over the Web, and Internet Information Services (IIS), which is Microsoft's standard Web server application. Table 17.1 shows the ports used for each of these applications.

CROSS-REF Using Remote Desktop to manage Windows Home Server is discussed in Chapter 10.

TABLE 17.1

Windows Home Server Remote Access Ports

Port	Server Application and Purpose
80	IIS – Standard port used for nonencrypted Hyper Text Transfer Protocol (HTTP) Web requests.
443	IIS – Standard port used for encrypted Secure Socket Layer (SSL) HTTP Secure (HTTPS) Web requests.
4125	Remote Web Workplace – Port used to access Remote Desktop over the Internet.

Settings for Remote Access

What we are getting at with this discussion of port forwarding is that Windows Home Server and your router both have to be configured to support remote access in order for you to be able to access your files or control your computer. You do this in the Console, using the settings dialog's Remote Access tab, which is shown in Figure 17.2.

The settings available for remote access are as follows:

- **Web Site Connectivity:** This button controls access to the IIS server. The default setting is off. This must be turned on in order to access the server's Web sites.

- **Router:** This setting indicates the configuration status of the router. If the router supports Universal Plug and Play (UPnP), you can tell Windows Home Server to configure port forwarding automatically.

- **Domain Name:** In this setting, you can configure and see the status of the domain name that can be used to reach your server.

- **Web Site Settings:** In this setting, you can decide whether to use the default Windows Home Server Home Page or the Windows Home Server Remote Access page for your home page.

FIGURE 17.2

The Console Settings dialog is used to configure Remote Access.

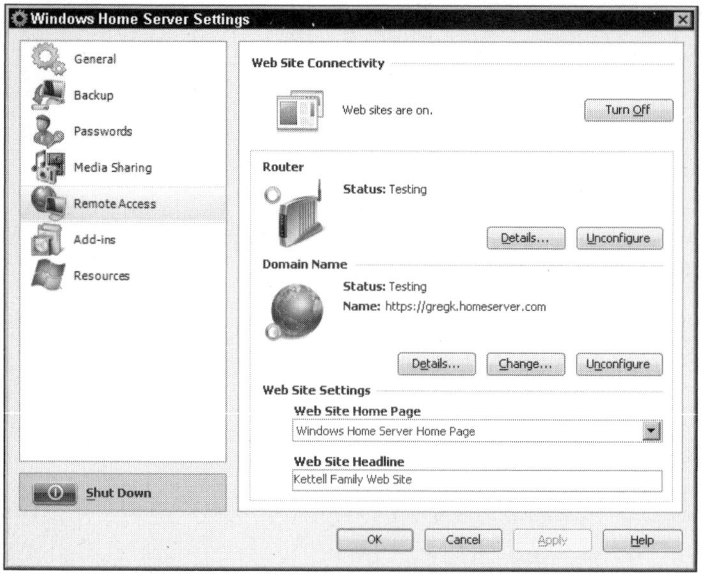

Controlling Web site connectivity

By default, your Windows Home Server is configured with Web site connectivity turned off. In order to access the Web server to allow remote folder access and remote computer control, this must be turned on. All of the other remote access settings are disabled as long as connectivity is turned off. Click the Turn On button to enable the connectivity.

Configuring your router

The router acts as a bridge between your household network and the Internet, and as we discussed, you need to configure port forwarding so that it knows which computer on your network to forward Web requests to. There are two ways to go about this: You can either have Windows Home Server attempt to configure the router automatically, or you can configure it manually yourself from the router's own Web interface.

Automatic configuration

If you are using a reasonably new router, it likely has the ability to have port forwarding configured automatically by a server, a capability known as UPnP. If your router has UPnP capability, you won't have to try to figure out how to configure port forwarding in its Web interface; you can let Windows Home Server configure port forwarding automatically. As a bonus, if your server is configured to use Dynamic Host Configuration Protocol (DHCP), it will update UPnP port forwarding with its new IP address automatically if it changes.

ON the WEB UPnP capability is part of a larger standard for allowing simple communication between consumer electronics devices, including home computer and networking equipment. It is promoted by the UPnP Forum (www.upnp.org).

To configure your router using UPnP, follow these steps:

1. **Log on to the Console.**

2. **Click the Settings button, followed by the Remote Access tab.**

3. **Click the Setup button in the router section.** Windows Home Server then attempts to automatically configure your router.

4. **You can follow the status of the configuration process by clicking the Details button.** The configuration progress is displayed, as shown in Figure 17.3.

FIGURE 17.3

You can automatically configure your router if it supports UPnP.

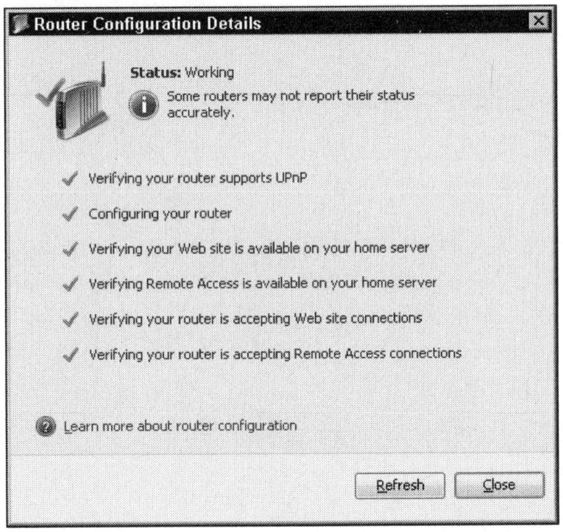

If you believe that your router does support UPnP, but the configuration process fails, you may simply have to enable it on the router. To do this, you will have to learn how to log on to the router's Web administration facility to make the change. Although specific instructions are not possible due to variations in routers, you can try the following steps:

1. **In your browser, enter the IP address for your router (for example, 192.168.0.1).**

TIP If you don't know the IP address for your router, you can find it using the ipconfig utility on one of your home computers. Open a command line prompt and enter ipconfig, and press Enter. The IP address displayed for your default gateway should be the same as the IP address of your router.

249

2. **You should be prompted for authentication.** If you don't know the administration username and password for your router, consult its documentation for the default settings.

3. **Locate the UPnP settings for your browser.** On a Linksys brand routers, it may be under the Password or Administration tab. On a NETGEAR router, there may be an UPnP selection on the left side menu. The NETGEAR UPnP settings are shown in Figure 17.4.

4. **Check the option to enable UPnP and click the Apply button (which may be labeled Save Settings or something similar) to make the changes.**

Once you have enabled UPnP, go back to the Console and try to configure the router again. If it still fails, you may need to try manually configuring port forwarding on the router. This is discussed in the next section.

FIGURE 17.4

You may need to enable UPnP in your router's Web administration facility.

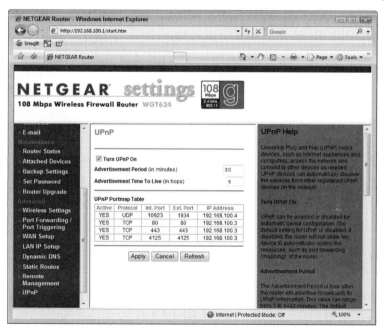

 There are a lot of routers out there, and each manufacturer has its own way of administering them. Consult your router's users manual if you need assistance in configuring it for port forwarding or UPnP.

Manual configuration

If your router doesn't support UPnP, you will have to configure port forwarding on the router manually. Although it isn't as easy as the UPnP process, it still isn't very difficult. You will need to use the router's Web administration facility as described in the previous section.

> **TIP** If you are going to configure port forwarding for your server on the router, I advise you to configure your server with a static IP address instead of a DHCP one. The procedure to accomplish this is discussed in Chapter 4.

The steps to configure port forwarding on your router will vary somewhat depending on the brand of router you have, but it should be similar to these steps:

1. **Enter the IP address for the router in a browser.** See the tip in the previous section for a way to obtain this IP address if you don't already know it.

2. **Enter your administration username and password.**

3. **Locate the port forwarding configuration settings for your router.** On a NETGEAR router, it may be located under Port Forwarding/Port Triggering on the menu on the left. On a Linksys router such as a WRT54G, it will be under the Applications and Gaming tab.

4. **Forward the following ports to your Windows Home Server computer.** In some cases these ports will have their standard service names available from a list. Figure 17.5 shows an example.

   - **Port 80:** You may be able to find this listed as a service name of HTTP.
   - **Port 443:** This may be listed as a service name of HTTPS.
   - **Port 4125:** Remote Web Workplace may not be listed as a service name.

5. **Click the Apply or Save Settings button depending on which one your router provides.**

6. **Some Linksys routers require an additional step.** Click the Security tab, uncheck the Block Anonymous Internet Requests box, and then click Save Settings. This is necessary to allow requests to be made from computers on the Internet. Some other brands of routers may have similar settings; consult the documentation to find out.

At this point port forwarding should be enabled for your computer.

FIGURE 17.5

You can manually configure port forwarding on your router if necessary.

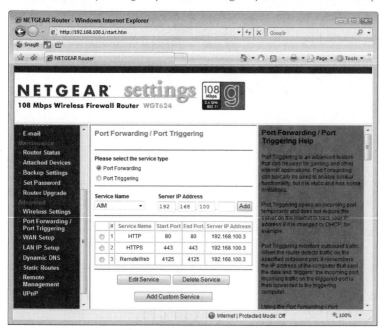

Configuring a domain name

A *domain name* is a unique identifier used to reach a computer over the Internet. A special server called a *domain name server* is used when a Web request is made to translate the requested domain name into an IP address. Most large Web sites reserve static (unchanging) IP addresses and can purchase domain names that point to it. Most residential ISP providers, however, do not provide static IP addresses to their customers unless they pay an extra fee. Most residential customers, therefore, have dynamically assigned IP addresses that can change at any time. This limitation makes it impossible to assign a standard domain name to point to a server behind a dynamically assigned IP address.

Fortunately, Windows Home Server provides a solution to this dilemma. In conjunction with Windows Live, you can create a free dynamic subdomain name to use to reach your network from the Internet. Microsoft has created a special domain, homeserver.com, just for Windows Home Server users. When you create your own domain, it will actually be a subdomain of homeserver.com.

NOTE Unfortunately, you can't use a domain name obtained from a traditional domain registrar such as Network Solutions, Go Daddy, or eNom to connect to your home network. Such domains are useful only with a static IP address. Most residential IP addresses are dynamically assigned and can change frequently.

Follow these steps to create a dynamic homeserver.com domain for your server:

1. Log on to the Console and open the Settings dialog.

2. Select the Remote Access tab.

3. **Click the Setup button in the Domain Name section (not the Setup button in the Router section if that is still visible).** This starts the Domain Name Setup Wizard (see Figure 17.6).

FIGURE 17.6

The Domain Name Setup Wizard is used to configure a dynamic domain name.

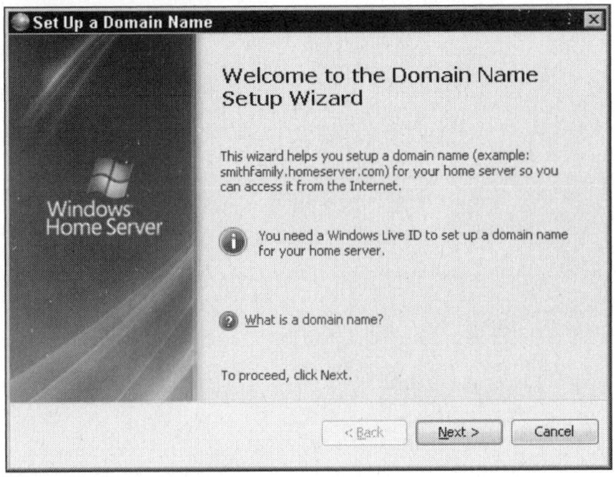

4. **Click Next.**

5. **Enter a Windows Live e-mail address and password.** This can be any e-mail account with Hotmail.com, Live.com, or MSN.com. If you don't have an account with any of those servers, you can create one by clicking the Get your Windows Live ID link and following the instructions there, as shown in Figure 17.7. Click Next when you are done.

6. **Read over the Windows Home Server Privacy Statement along with the Custom Domain addendum.** Select the I accept button when you are ready to proceed, and then click Next.

7. **Enter the name you would like to use for your custom domain in the box, shown in Figure 17.8.**

FIGURE 17.7

You must sign up for Windows Live in order to use the domain name feature.

FIGURE 17.8

Your custom domain will be assigned as a subdomain part of homeserver.com.

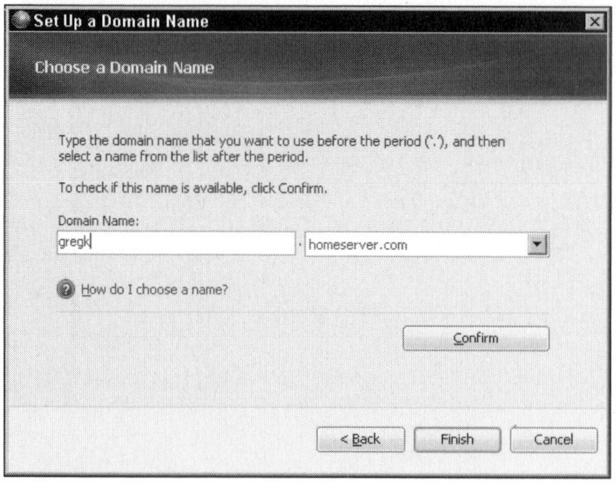

8. **Click the Confirm button to have Windows Home Server verify that your domain name is available.** If the name you choose is already in use, or is otherwise prohibited, you will see a popup notice to that effect, shown in Figure 17.9. Click Finish after you've entered a suitable domain name.

NOTE If you already have a custom domain name on homeserver.com, you can create a new one. However, only one domain name can be active at a time. If you create a new one, your old domain name will be deleted and will be available for use by anyone.

FIGURE 17.9

The Confirm button lets you know if your chosen domain is available.

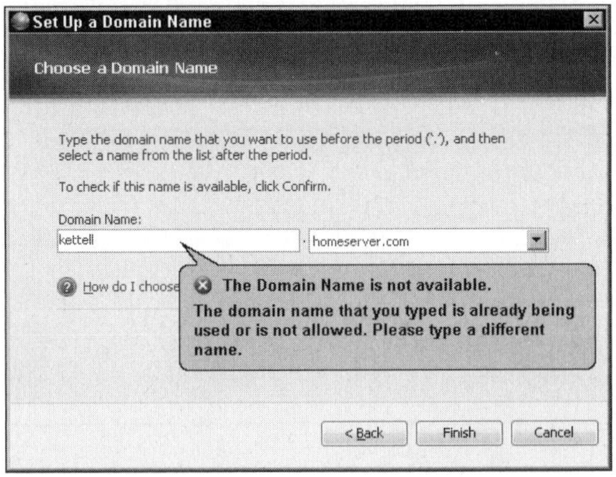

9. **Click Done to complete the configuration.** You should now be able to reach your server using the domain name over the Internet.

TIP Your domain name should be available quickly; however it can sometimes take a minute or two for a domain name change to be propagated to the domain name server. If you are unable to access your server right away after creating your custom domain, try again in a few minutes.

Configuring Web site settings

Your Windows Home Server Web site consists of essentially two different Web sites. There is a public site, reachable by anyone, and a remote access site, which requires signing in with a Windows Home Server user account with remote access enabled.

You can change which site shows by default when users visit your custom domain. If you have no intention of making a public Web site available, you can choose to have your domain go directly to the remote access site instead. You can also customize the title that is displayed for Web site.

To configure your Web site settings, do the following:

1. **In the Console, navigate to the Remote Access tab.**

2. **In the Web Site Settings section, choose which Web site to use as your home page from the Web Site Home Page drop-down list, shown in Figure 17.10.**

3. **Enter a custom Web site headline to use if you desire.** The changes will become available when you click OK.

FIGURE 17.10

You can choose which Web site to use as your home page.

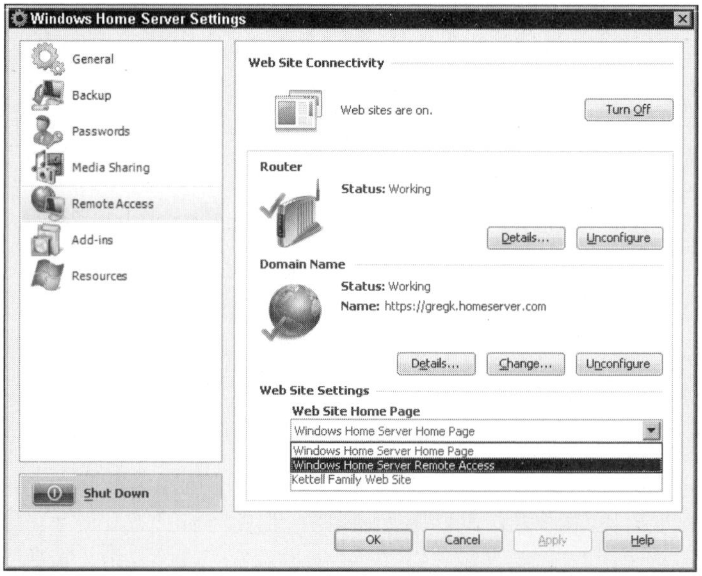

Accessing Your Web site

To access your Web site, all you need is a Web browser. Enter your dynamic domain name in the address bar, as shown in Figure 17.11.

FIGURE 17.11

Use a Web browser to access your server remotely.

The default Web site includes only a button to log on. Click the Log On button to access the Remote Access site, and enter the username and password of an account on your server that has remote access enabled. When you log on, you will see the Remote Access Web site shown in Figure 17.12.

NOTE   Although virtually any browser can be used to access your shared files, remote control of your computers requires Internet Explorer.

FIGURE 17.12

The Remote Access section of your Web site is where you will access shared files and computers.

Resolving Blocked Port Issues

If you are unable to make the connection to your Web site on port 80 or port 443, those ports may be blocked by your ISP.

ISP terms of service vary. Some ISPs prohibit hosting Web sites and other services from residential ISP accounts. If you are unable to connect to your server remotely, contact your ISP to see if there is a workaround or another plan you might be able to use.

If you are able to connect to your Web site through another port, such as 4443, you can configure Windows Home Server to use that port for your SSL (HTTPS) connection along with or instead of the default port setting of 443. Follow these steps to make port 4443 a viable port. If you choose a different port number, substitute it in these instructions:

1. **Configure your router to forward port 4443 to your server by following the manual port forwarding instructions earlier in this chapter.** Figure 17.13 shows this being done in the NETGEAR router Web administration.

2. **Log on to your Windows Home Server using Remote Desktop.** (You can log on to the server directly if it has a monitor and keyboard attached.)

FIGURE 17.13

You may be able to configure alternative ports for the Web server if existing ones are blocked.

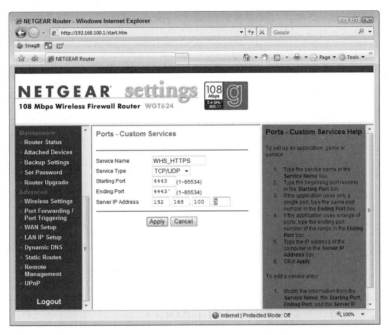

3. Click Start ⇨ Control Panel ⇨ Administrator Tools ⇨ Internet Information Services (IIS) Manager to launch the IIS management console, shown in Figure 17.14.

FIGURE 17.14

The IIS management console is used to customize Web site settings.

4. Expand the Web Sites folder in the tree on the left.

5. Right-click on the Default Web Site item, and choose Properties.

6. Select the Web Site tab, shown in Figure 17.15.

Default Web Site Properties can be overridden if necessary.

7. Click the Advanced button.

8. Click the Add button under Multiple SSL identities for this Web site.

9. Enter 4443 as the new SSL port to use and click OK. The new SSL port is added to the list, as shown in Figure 17.16.

10. Click OK to accept the setting change.

11. Click OK again to close the Default Web Site Properties dialog.

FIGURE 17.16

You can configure IIS to listen on a different port.

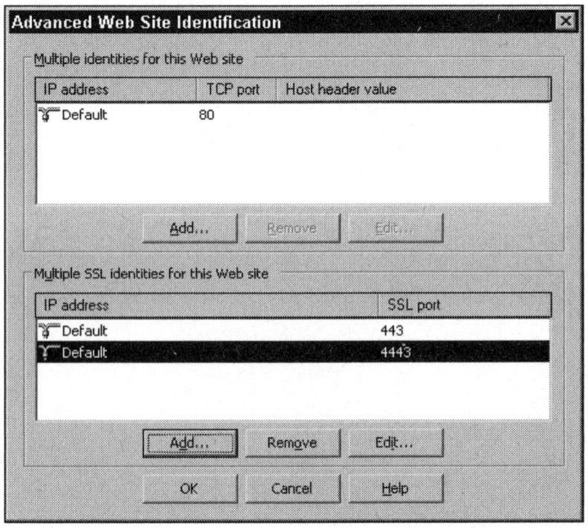

In addition to the IIS settings, you must also allow this port through the Windows Home Server firewall. Staying in Remote Desktop, do the following:

1. **Click Start ⇨ Control Panel ⇨ Windows Firewall.**
2. **On the General tab, make sure that the Don't Allow Exceptions checkbox is unchecked.**
3. **Select the Exceptions tab, shown in Figure 17.17.**
4. **Click Add Port.**
5. **Enter a name for the redirect.** WHS_HTTPS or something similar would work.
6. **Enter 4443 as the port number.**
7. **Click OK.** The exception you entered should now be shown in the Programs and Services list.

FIGURE 17.17

If you change the ports used to access your Web server, you must let the new port through the firewall.

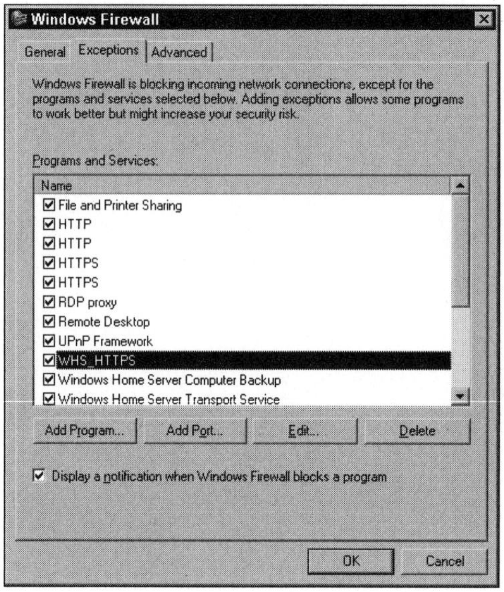

The new port you entered should be ready for use. There are now two differences in how you access your site.

- You must use https instead of http as the protocol prefix in your address.
- You must append the new port number to the end of the URL to access your site.

For example, if your custom domain is smithfamily.homeserver.com, and you change the default SSL port to 4443, you would enter the following into your browser to access it: https://smithfamily. homeserver.com:4443. Figure 17.18 shows how you would access your server using a different port in the URL.

FIGURE 17.18

Using a custom port for remote access. Notice the port number in the address.

Summary

Remote access is a powerful feature of Windows Home Server. With it, you are no longer limited to accessing your files and your home computers solely from inside your network. You can access your shared folders, manage your server, and, in some cases, even control your other computers via remote desktop.

Windows Home Server simplifies the process of setting up remote access by automatically configuring UPnP routers. However, if you have a router that doesn't support UPnP or you have unique port forwarding requirements, you can do that as well.

Along with your Windows Home Server purchase, you will receive a custom domain name from homeserver.com. This free domain name can be used to access your server's Web site and remote access tools from virtually anywhere.

In the next few chapters, we'll show you how to take advantage of remote access by showing you how to retrieve, upload, and delete files in your shared folders. We'll also show you how to access all of the computers on your network remotely.

Chapter 18

Accessing Shared Folders Remotely

After you've configured remote access, you are ready to start using it. One of the main things that you can do with shared folders is to access the files stored in your Windows Home Server shared folders. With this feature, you can access any file stored on a shared folder. While you don't have seamless access to the files using Windows Explorer, as you would when accessing your server locally, you do have plenty of control over the files. You can retrieve files, replace them, and rename and delete them. There is even a search facility to make it easy to find a particular file.

Shared folders are accessed remotely through a special remote access Web site hosted on your Windows Home Server machine. This Web site is always secure: it can only be accessed using the HTTPS protocol, ensuring that nobody can snoop on your files as they are being transferred.

Exploring Shared Folders

To access shared folders remotely, you may use just about any Web browser that supports file transfers, JavaScript, and Hyper Text Transfer Protocol Secure (HTTPS). It doesn't have to be on Windows, either. Macs, Linux boxes, game consoles, and even portable devices can be used to access your shared folders and work with the files contained therein.

To access shared folders, do the following:

1. **Enter the remote access Web site URL in your browser of choice.**

2. **If you have the Windows Home Server Home Page set as your home page, click the Log On button to navigate to the remote access logon page.**

3. Enter the username and password of a Windows Home Server account that has remote access enabled.

CROSS-REF   See Chapter 9 for information on creating user accounts and enabling them for remote access.

4. Click the Log On button.

5. Click the Shared Folders tab at the top of the page to access the Shared Folders Web site, shown in Figure 18.1.

FIGURE 18.1

The shared folder Web site

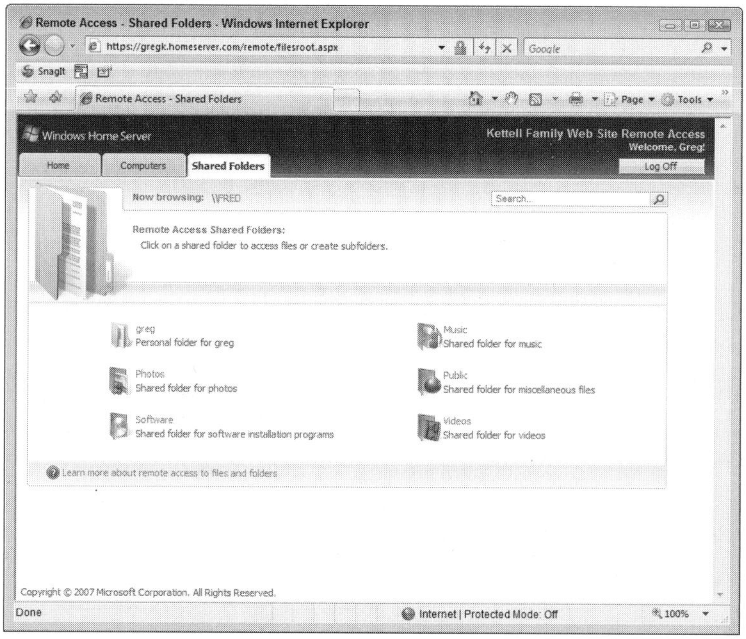

There are two ways you can find files. If you know which shared folder contains the file or files that you wish to access, you can browse directly to them. If you aren't sure where they are located, the search feature makes fast and easy work out of finding them. Both methods are described here.

Browsing shared folders

You can browse through shared folders almost as easily as when using Windows Explorer. The only thing missing is the tree view.

From the shared folder site root, click on the name of the shared folder you wish to access. This opens the folder browser page shown in Figure 18.2.

FIGURE 18.2

The folder browser lets you navigate through your shared folders and files.

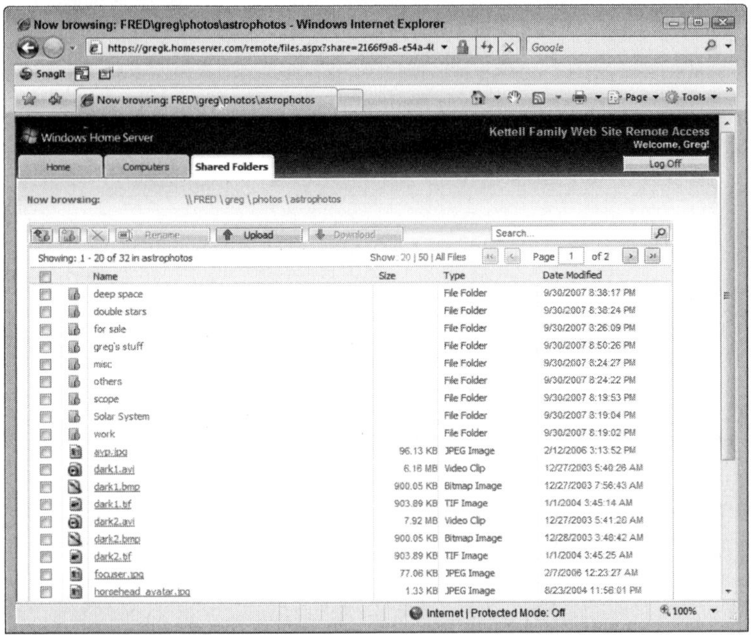

This folder contains several controls to assist you in browsing for files. They are as follows:

Breadcrumb links

The links showing the path at the top of the page, shown in Figure 18.3, allow you to navigate quickly through the folder hierarchy through several levels of parent folders.

FIGURE 18.3

Breadcrumb links make navigating the hierarchy a snap.

Toolbar

The toolbar, shown in Figure 18.4, is used to navigate, perform actions on files, and to search for files. The buttons are as follows:

- **Up to parent:** Navigates to the parent folder of the current one
- **New folder:** Allows you to create a new folder

- **Delete:** Allows you to delete the currently selected file
- **Rename:** Allows you to rename the currently selected file
- **Upload:** Uploads a file
- **Download:** Downloads the currently selected file
- **Search:** Searches shared folders for a filename

FIGURE 18.4

The toolbar is used for navigation and to perform actions on selected files.

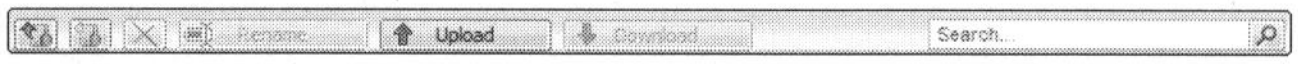

File listing

The file listing, shown in Figure 18.5, is the main feature of the folder browser. It contains a link for each subfolder and file in the folder, complete with an icon representing the file type. Files are displayed similar to the Windows Explorer detail view, with information about the file including size, type, and the date modified displayed as well.

Options above the file listing let you choose the number of files to show at a time. The default view shows 20 files at once, but you can choose to display 50 at once or All Files at once.

If there are more files than can be displayed in the current view, you can use the paging controls to page through the files.

FIGURE 18.5

The file listing mimics the details view of Windows Explorer.

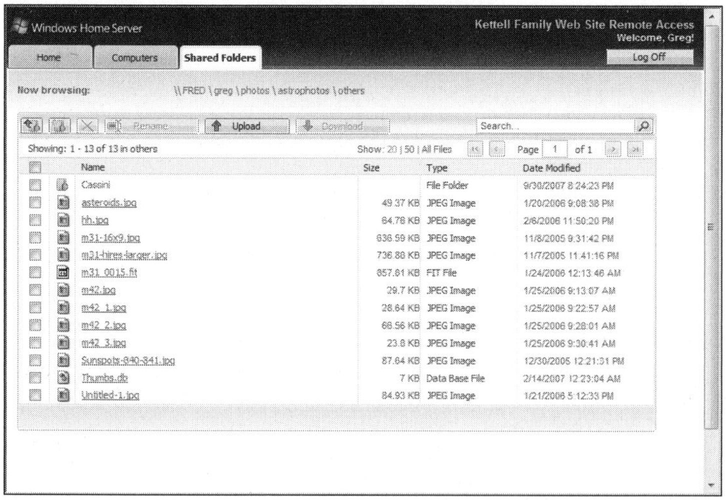

Sorting

The column headings of the file listing are links, and when you click them, the file listing will be resorted based on the column link, shown in Figure 18.6. Names and types are sorted alphabetically, file sizes are from smallest to largest, and dates are sorted from oldest to newest. Clicking the column heading again sorts the list again in the opposite order.

Subfolders are always sorted separately from files at the beginning or end of the list, depending on sort order.

FIGURE 18.6

Sorting the file listing is accomplished by clicking the column headings.

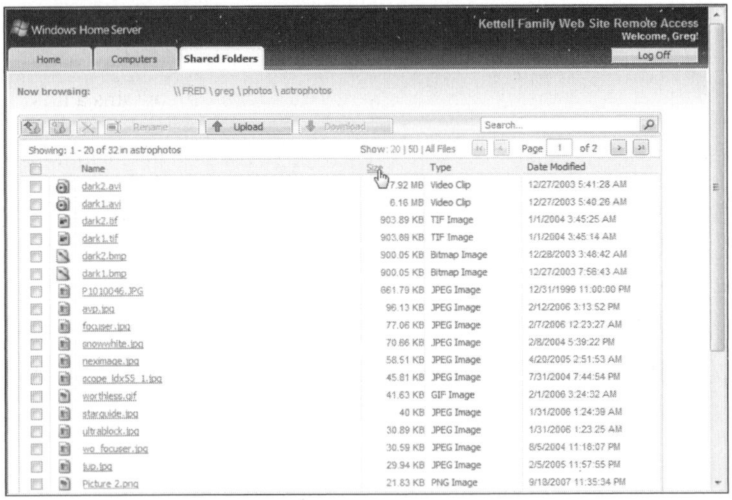

Searching for files

If you don't feel like browsing for your files, or you are not quite sure where a particular file is, you can search for it (see Figure 18.7). You can enter your search term a number of different ways:

- **Complete filename:** Only files matching a specific filename will be located. If the same file exists in multiple folders, all will be shown.

- **Partial filename:** You can enter part of a filename, and all will match. For example, enter **mp3** and it will find all of your shared mp3 files.

- **Wildcard search:** You can enter a filename with wildcard characters replacing some of the characters in the text. Use an asterisk (*) as a substitute for more than one character in a row, and a question mark (?) to substitute for a single character. For example, to search for all of your mp3 files that start with the letter b, you could search for "b*.mp3."

- **Document text search:** In addition to filename searches, the contents of documents and text files will be searched. If you are looking for a document that contains a particular word or phrase, you can enter it and documents in your shared folders will be searched.

FIGURE 18.7

The search facility makes quick work out of locating a particular file or all files matching a partial filename.

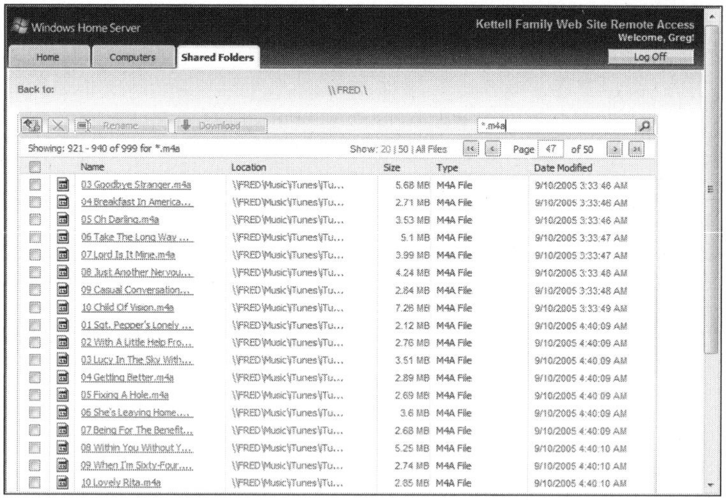

Managing Files

Browsing for files is nice and all, but by itself it is pretty useless. What you really want to do is to work with your files and folders. You want to be able to download your files from the server to work on them on your local computer, and when you are done with them, upload them back to the server. You may also need to perform folder or file maintenance.

Downloading files

In most cases, you will want to download a file from your server to a local computer to work with it. Whether it is a document or spreadsheet you need to work with, or music and video files that you want to play, your shared files are always right at hand.

Downloading a file is simple. Simply click on the link for the filename, and the browser will prompt you for a location to download the file to, as shown in Figure 18.8.

FIGURE 18.8

You can download files to work with them locally.

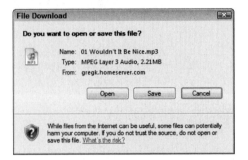

You can download more than one file at a time if you like. Simply check the box to the left of each file you wish to download. When you have selected all of the files, click the Download button on the toolbar. You can select folders as well as files.

The files you have selected will be placed into a single zip file, which you will download as you would any individual file. The zip file will be named after the folder you are downloading from or SearchResults.zip if you select the files from a search.

When the zip file has been downloaded, you can use Windows Explorer or any archive program that supports zip files (such as WinZip or WinRAR) to browse and extract the files (see Figure 18.9).

CAUTION While most aspects of remote access are speedy, the performance of the multiple file download feature can be very poor if you have more than a few files or large files to download. Use this feature with care.

FIGURE 18.9

Improve efficiency by downloading more than one file at a time.

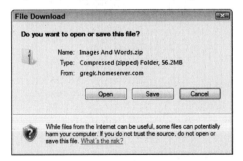

Uploading files

When you have finished working on a file, you will more than likely wish to upload it back to the server. You can upload new files as well.

To upload a file or files to the server, follow these steps:

1. **Click the Upload button on the toolbar.** This button is not visible when displaying search results — it must be used when browsing a folder. The Upload dialog will be displayed, as shown in Figure 18.10.

2. **Click the Browse button and search for the file you wish to upload.**

3. **If you wish to upload multiple files at once, click Browse again to locate an additional file.** Repeat for each additional file you want to upload.

4. **If files of the same name already exist on the server, you must check the Overwrite existing files checkbox.**

5. **When you have finished adding files, click the Upload button to have the files uploaded to the server.**

TIP   Although you can overwrite existing files when you upload, it is a good idea to rename your local file and upload the file using this different filename so that your original file isn't lost if something happens to the file in transit.

FIGURE 18.10

You can upload one or more files at a time.

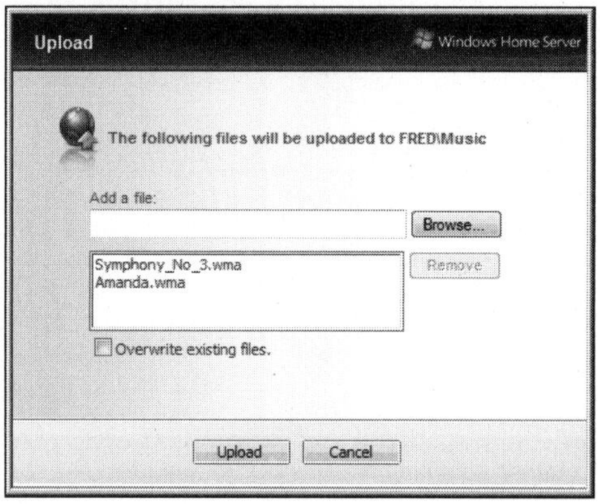

Working with other folder and file operations

Aside from uploading and downloading files, the folder browser page gives you additional control options for maintaining files and folders. You can delete them or rename them.

Deleting files and folders

To delete a file or folder, or a group of them, select them by checking the box next to the filename. If you want to select all of the files on a page, check the box at the top of the list to select all of the files at once.

When you have selected your files, click the Delete button (the red X) on the toolbar. You will be given a single warning, as shown in Figure 18.11, before the files are deleted.

CAUTION Once you delete a file, there is no way to recover it remotely. If you need to recover a deleted file, you will have to do it from inside the network using the shadow copy facility that we discussed in Chapter 13.

FIGURE 18.11

When deleting files remotely, you are given a warning to make sure that you have selected the correct files.

Renaming files and folders

The folder browser gives you have the ability to rename files and folders. To rename a file or folder, check the box to the left of its name and click the Rename button on the toolbar. This button is only enabled when you have a single file or folder selected — you cannot rename multiple items at once.

As Figure 18.12 shows, you will be prompted for a new name for the folder or file. Enter it and click OK.

FIGURE 18.12

You can rename folders and files.

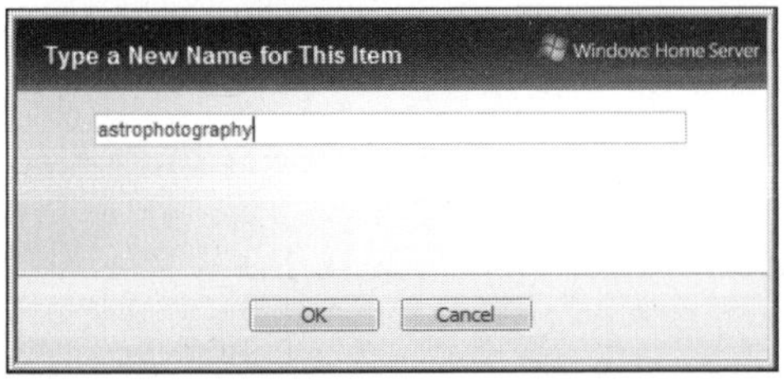

Summary

If you've ever been traveling or at work and realized that you needed a file that is on a computer at home, you will find the shared folder feature to be a godsend. The more of your files you place on your Windows Home Server shared folders, the more useful this feature becomes.

The folder browser page allows you to upload, download, and manage shared files in a way that is the next best thing to actually being on the server. Browsing through the folder hierarchy is quick and easy, and there is even a search facility that can quickly find a file no matter which shared folder it is in.

In the next chapter, we show you how to take advantage of the other feature of remote access — the ability to control your computers and manage your server from afar.

Chapter 19

Controlling Computers Remotely

I n Chapter 18, we showed you how to access your Windows Home Servers shared folders and Web site using the Remote Access feature. While this is indeed a terrific feature to have, there are times when you may need more than this. Suppose you need to access one of your client computers to check your mail, or your server to make changes to backup settings, but you aren't anywhere near your home network. Are you out of luck?

With the computer Remote Access feature, you are not. Using Internet Explorer, you can connect to the server and control the Console remotely, as if you were on your home network. In some cases, you can even connect to your client computers depending on the version of Windows they are running.

In this chapter, we show you how to do both of those things and even more. If you'd like the ability to use Remote Desktop to connect to your server's desktop rather than the Console, we'll show you how to do that. We also show you an alternative that you can use in the event that remote access is not a viable solution for your version of Windows.

About Remote Access to Computers

Remote access to computers makes use of a special Internet Explorer ActiveX control that uses your browser as a host for a Remote Desktop window. This window can be used to connect to your server's Console, or to other computers on your network depending on the operating system version and security settings that they are running. You can access the computers through the Remote Access section of your server's Web site, as shown in Figure 19.1.

> **NOTE** The Terminal Services ActiveX control used for Web-based Remote Desktop only works with Internet Explorer on Windows computers. You cannot use it on the Mac or from other systems. See the section in this chapter on using other remote control options for alternatives.

FIGURE 19.1

Access your computers and the Windows Home Server Console remotely with Remote Desktop.

Benefits of remote access

When you connect to your computers in this way, you are really using your Windows Home Server as a Remote Desktop gateway. It monitors incoming requests for remote access and forwards them on to the computers in question. The advantage of this solution over, say, just exposing each client's Remote Desktop to the Internet is twofold:

- **Added security:** Because you have to go through the Remote Access Web site to control your computers remotely, your Remote Desktop ports aren't exposed to the Internet for anyone to find.

- **Convenience:** If multiple computers on the network including the server were to allow Remote Desktop access through your router, they'd have to be configured to all listen on different ports, and your router would have to know how to forward each setting. With remote access to computers, the router only needs to know to forward Remote Desktop connections to the server, which brokers them out to other computers.

CROSS-REF   **Learn more about accessing computers with Remote Desktop in Chapter 10.**

Supported versions of Windows

Remote access to computers is a terrific feature for Windows Home Server; unfortunately Microsoft wasn't as prescient when it came to deciding which versions of their operating systems should be controllable remotely. The follow OS versions support Remote Desktop:

- Windows XP Professional Service Pack 2 (SP2)
- Windows XP Media Center Edition 2005
- Windows XP Tablet Edition Service Pack 2 (SP2)
- Vista Ultimate Edition
- Vista Business Edition
- Vista Enterprise Edition

Remote Desktop cannot be used with Windows XP or Vista Home, or Vista Premium editions.

Microsoft's seen Remote Desktop as more of a high-end business class feature, which is why it hasn't been available on the Home editions of XP or Vista, but the exclusion from the Vista Premium edition when it was available in XP Professional is a real head scratcher. As one of the most common versions of Vista that is bundled with computers being sold today, we hope they reconsider: without it, the benefits of remote access are greatly limited, and you will need to consider upgrading to Vista Ultimate edition.

If you are fortunate enough to have any of the supported operating systems on your home computers, you will be able to use remote access to computers to connect to them. If not, you will still be able to access the server's Console (and the desktop, as we'll explain). You can also take advantage of other tools to allow a similar capability, as we show later in the chapter.

Configuring Remote Access

In order to make use of remote access to computers, you need to make sure a few items are configured properly to support it. First, your router must be configured to forward the proper port to the server. Second, any computers that you wish to connect to must have Remote Desktop connections enabled.

Configuring your router

If your router has Universal Plug and Play (UPnP) capability, you should be able to configure it for remote access using the Console.

Otherwise, you will need to configure your router manually. Ports 80 (HTTP), 443 (HTTPS), and 4125 (Remote Web Workplace) will all need to be forwarded to your Windows Home Server's IP (Internet Protocol) address.

CROSS-REF Chapter 17 provides information on the steps necessary to configure your router for remote access. Refer to that chapter for specific instructions.

Configuring client computers

Client computers that you wish to access remotely must be configured to allow Remote Desktop connections. As we mentioned earlier, this is only possible on certain versions of XP and Vista. To enable Remote Desktop for your computers, follow the instructions for your operating system.

Configuring XP computers

Follow these steps to configure a Windows XP computer for remote access:

1. **Log on to the computer with an account that has administrator access.**
2. **Click Start, right-click on My Computer, and choose Properties.**
3. **In the System Properties dialog box, click the Remote tab, as shown in Figure 19.2.**
4. **Make sure that the Allow users to connect remotely to this computer box is checked.**
5. **Click the Select Remote Users button.**
6. **Choose the user accounts that should be allowed to access the computer remotely.** Accounts with administrator privileges are allowed to connect by default.
7. **Click OK when you're done.**
8. **Restart your computer to allow this setting to take affect.**

You need to make sure that the Windows Firewall (or any third-party firewall) is configured to allow Remote Desktop access. Follow these steps to enable the Remote Desktop port:

1. **Click Start ⇨ Control Panel.**
2. **In the Control panel, double-click the Windows Firewall icon.**
3. **Click the Exceptions tab.**
4. **Scroll down the list and ensure that Remote Desktop is checked (see Figure 19.3).** This should be set to allow port 3389 to connect; you can verify this by selecting Remote Desktop and clicking Edit.
5. **Click OK when done.**

FIGURE 19.2

Allow Remote Desktop support in the System Properties dialog box.

FIGURE 19.3

Open the Remote Desktop port in Windows Firewall.

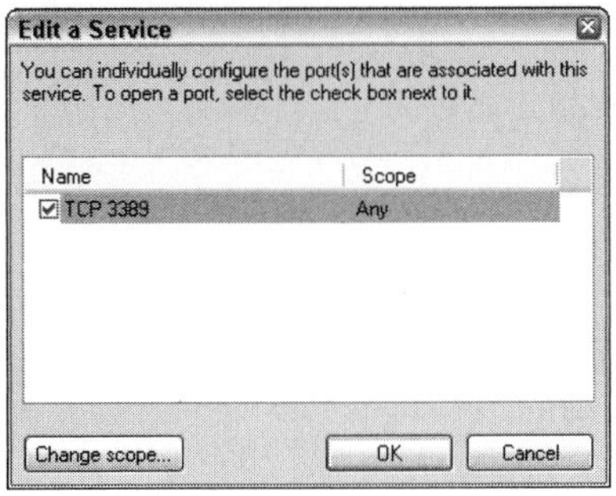

Configuring Vista computers

If you have Vista Ultimate, Business, or Enterprise, you can enable remote access by following these instructions:

1. **Log on to the computer with an account that has administrator access.**
2. **Click Start, right-click on Computer, and choose Properties.**

3. In the System Properties window, click the Remote tab (see Figure 19.4).

4. Click in the Allow connections from computers running any version of Remote Desktop radio button.

CAUTION Do not select Allow connections only from computers running Remote Desktop with Network Level Authentication. This option is not compatible with remote access from the Internet.

5. Click Select Users and add users that you would like to allow to connect remotely. Accounts in the administrator groups are allowed to connect by default.

6. Click OK when you're done.

7. Restart your computer to allow this setting to take affect.

FIGURE 19.4

Enable Remote Desktop in Windows Vista.

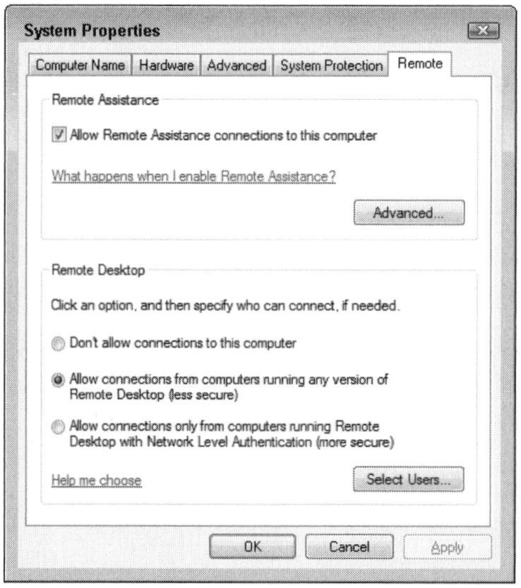

If you are using the Windows Firewall or a third-party firewall program, you need to make sure that the port used for Remote Desktop connections is enabled. Follow these steps to enable Remote Desktop in the Windows Firewall:

1. Choose Start ➪ Control Panel.

2. Click Security.

3. Click the Allow a program through Windows Firewall link.

4. Make sure the Remote Desktop item is checked, as shown in Figure 19.5.

FIGURE 19.5

Open the Remote Desktop port in Windows Firewall.

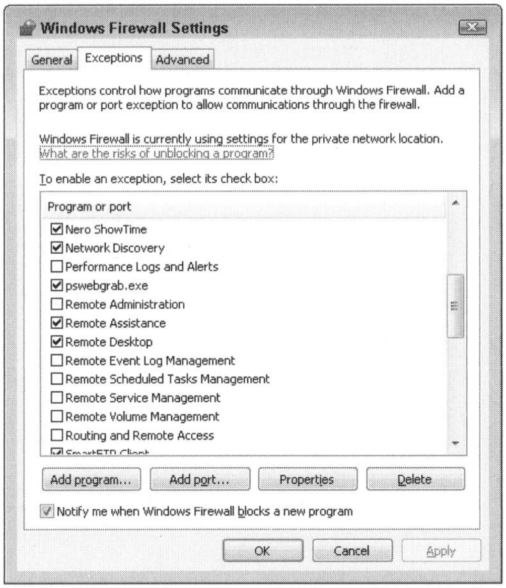

Accessing over the Internet

Remote access to your server and your computers is done through Internet Explorer, utilizing the Terminal Services ActiveX control, as we mentioned previously. Before you can do this, you must add your home server domain to your trusted sites zone in Internet Explorer.

Configuring Internet Explorer

To add your site to the Trusted Sites list, do the following:

1. **Choose Tools ➪ Internet Options from the menu bar.**

2. **Select the Security tab, as shown in Figure 19.6.**

3. **Click the Sites button.**

4. **Enter the domain for your Web site (if it isn't there already) and click the Add button.** Figure 19.7 shows a domain added to the Trusted Sites list in this way.

5. **Click Close and then click OK.**

FIGURE 19.6

The Security tab is used to add sites to your Trusted sites list.

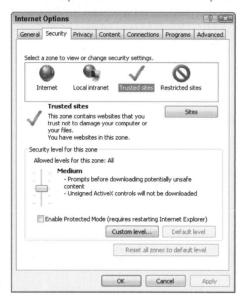

FIGURE 19.7

Open the Remote Desktop port in Windows Firewall.

CAUTION In order to secure your network, Windows Home Server utilizes a security certificate to ensure communication over the Internet through a Web browser is secure. When the Connector software is installed on a client computer, this certificate is automatically added to the trusted certificate list. Microsoft recommends that the best way to maintain security is to use a notebook computer that is added to the Windows Home Server when the Connector is installed. While you can access remotely from other computers, you can possibly expose your server or other computers to security risks.

Connecting to the Console

To connect to your Windows Home Server Console, access the remote access portion of your Web site by entering your domain. Click Logon, and enter a Windows Home Server user account that has remote access permissions. Select the Computers tab to see the list of computers attached to your network.

To connect to the Console, click the Connect to your Home Server link. You will be prompted for the Windows Home Server password—enter it in the space provided, and click OK.

If you are connecting via Internet Explorer 7, you will be prompted to acknowledge that you trust the computer you are connecting to, and that certain credentials will be exchanged, as shown in Figure 19.8. Click Yes to continue.

FIGURE 19.8

Acknowledge that you trust the computer you are connecting to.

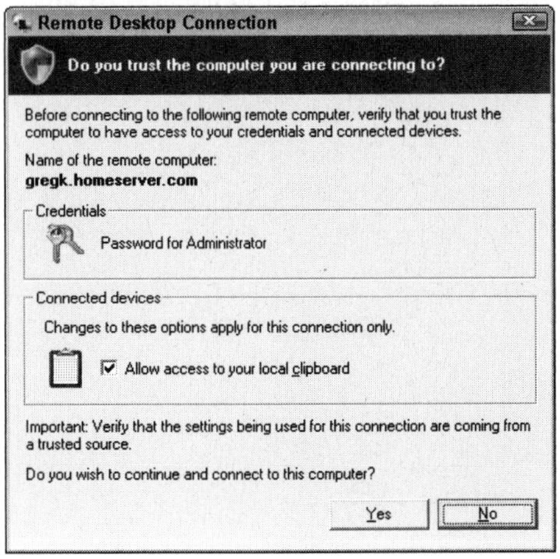

When you are connected to the Console remotely, as shown in Figure 19.9, you can do just about anything that you can do in the Console directly, with the exception of opening folders from the Shared Folders tab. You must access shared folders through the Shared Folders function of the Remote Access Web site instead.

When you have finished using the Console, you can end your remote access session by clicking the Disconnect button at the top of the window.

Accessing your computers

If you have computers that are able to be connected to via Remote Desktop, you will see a status message indication that they are available for connection on the Computers tab of the Remote Access Web site. You will only be able to select those computers. Click the computer name to connect to it.

FIGURE 19.9

Access the Console through remote access as if you were on your local network.

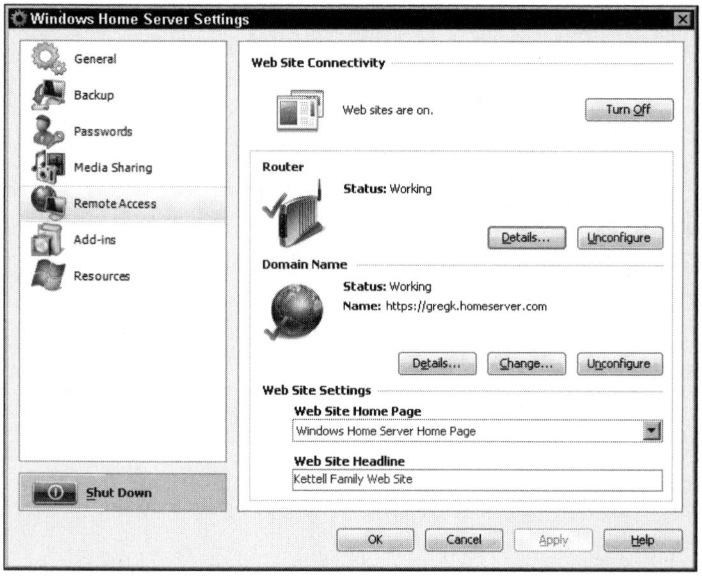

Connection options

To make the best use of the computers connection speed to the Internet, as well as to optimize the Remote Desktop connection, you will use the Connection Options dialog box, shown in Figure 19.10. You can set the following options from this window:

Connection Speed

Choose a connection speed that best matches your computer's current connection to the Internet. If you are connecting through a broadband connection (cable modem, DSL, corporate LAN, and so on), choose the Broadband option. If you are connecting through a slower connection such as dialup or ISDN, choose the Dialup option.

Screen size

Choose a screen size that best fits the display of the current computer. The Remote Desktop will be sized to match so that you don't have to scroll around as much on it.

Options for screen size include 640 x 480, 800 x 600, 1024 x 768, 1280 x 1024, 1600 x 1200, and Full Screen. The Full Screen option will size the connection to fit into your computer's entire screen, not just within the browser window.

Other settings

There are a few other options you can set. You can check to enable the remote computer to print to a local printer, choose to hear sounds from the remote computer, and enable file transfers. Choose your option and click OK.

FIGURE 19.10

When accessing computers remotely, you can configure some Remote Desktop settings.

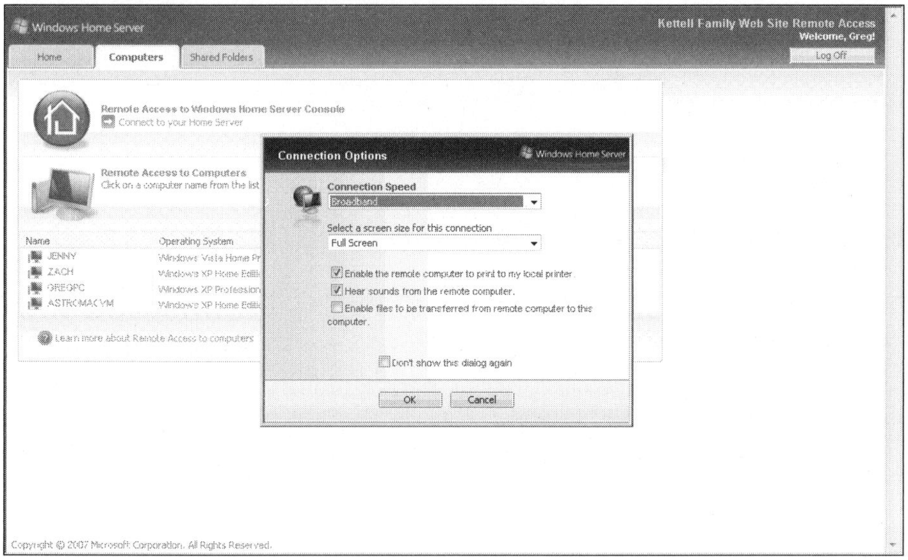

For anything other than a full screen connection, the Remote Desktop window appears inside the browser, as shown in Figure 19.11. You now access your remote computer as if you were sitting at the keyboard.

Click the Disconnect button at the top of the screen when you are ready to end the remote session.

FIGURE 19.11

Accessing a computer remotely through the browser

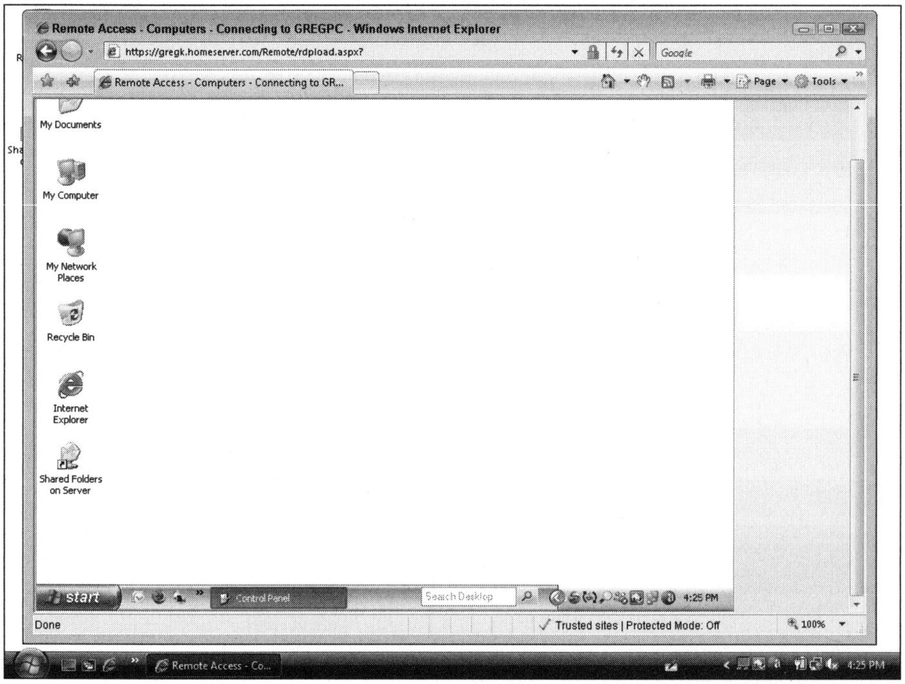

Connecting to the server's desktop

Remote Access, as it's configured out of the box, cannot connect directly to the server's desktop, as its connection is used to provide access to the Console instead. If you need access to the server's desktop for whatever reason, there are two ways you can go about it.

The daisy chain approach

First, you can chain Remote Desktop calls by first connecting to a supported client computer, and then connecting from there to the server. This works fine; however, there is a performance penalty because the desktop interface is getting redirected twice.

The old-fashioned port opening

Another option is to forward Port 3389 (the Remote Desktop port) on your router to your Windows Home Server. Then you can connect directly to the server using a standard Remote Desktop client instead of the one available from the browser. Keep in mind that this option is not as secure as the going through another computer.

The permanent solution

If you would rather always log in to the server's desktop instead of the Console (after all, you can access the Console from the desktop easily enough), you must make a change to the server's Web site configuration to allow it. Follow these steps:

1. **Log on to the server's desktop.**

2. **Open Windows Explorer by clicking Start ➪ Windows Explorer.**

3. **Browse to** `C:\Inetpub\remote`.

4. **Right-click on the** `rdpload.aspx`, **and open it with Notepad.**

5. **Search for the following line:**

   ```
   MsRdpClient.SecuredSettings.StartProgram =
       "HomeServerConsole.exe -b";
   ```

6. **Comment the line out, as shown in Figure 19.12, by putting a double slash at the beginning of the line.** This prevents Windows Home Server from overriding the normal Remote Desktop shell, Windows Explorer, with the Home Server Console.

7. **Save the edited file and then try connecting to the server again using the Remote Access Web site.**

FIGURE 19.12

Edit the server's Remote Desktop loading script to allow connections to the server's desktop.

Now, when you click the Connect to your Home Server link, you will connect to the server's Remote Desktop instead of to the Console, as shown in Figure 19.13.

Connect to the server's desktop instead of the Console by changing the Remote Desktop script.

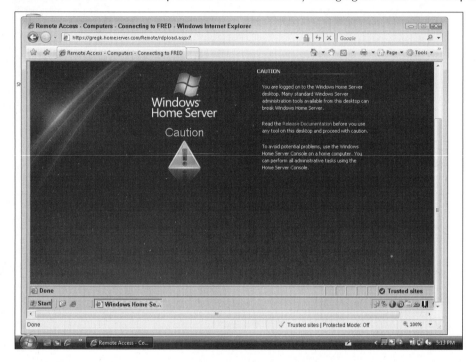

A Remote Desktop Alternative

If you have computers that cannot be accessed using Remote Desktop, and upgrading to a supported operating system is out of the question, you will have to look into third-party solutions if you want to be able to connect to them remotely.

You can use an open source program and protocol called VNC (Virtual Network Computing) to access computers on your network that can't be reached using Remote Desktop, including the Windows XP and Vista Home editions, and Vista Premium edition.

VNC is platform independent, and clients and servers exist for a huge number of operating systems and platforms. With a VNC server on your computer, you can access it remotely from any number of clients, including Macs, Linux boxes, handhelds, and more.

There are several versions of VNC available; some common ones for the Windows platform include RealVNC, TightVNC, and UltraVNC. All have free versions available. Our preference is for UltraVNC due to the ability to do file transfers, along with integrated Windows security.

ON the WEB **Find more information about the benefits of UltraVNC at www.uvnc.com/.**

The procedure for installing UltraVNC is as follows:

1. **Download the UltraVNC setup program.** This contains both client and server components.

2. **Install it on the server.** Choose to make it auto start as a service when prompted.

3. **In the server default properties window, shown in Figure 19.14, configure a port to use in the Incoming Connections section, and a default password under Authentication.**

FIGURE 19.14

The VNC server admin window is used to configure most server parameters.

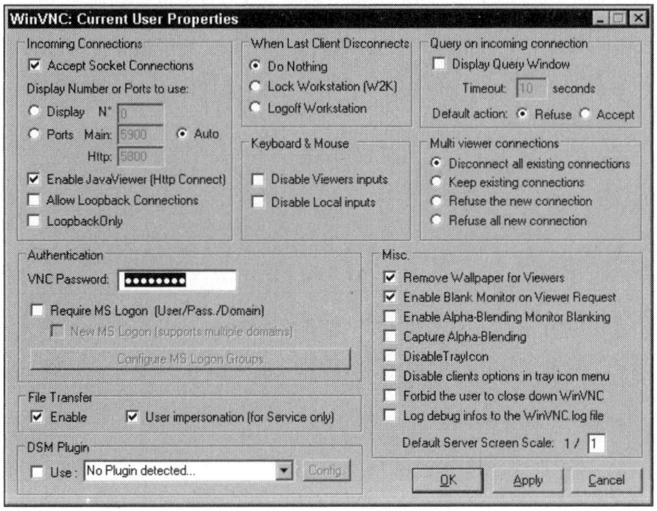

4. Make sure that the port that you choose is open in the Windows Firewall. The
   default port is 5900.

5. In your router configuration, forward the port you choose to the server.

6. Install VNC on a client computer.

7. Using the VNC viewer, connect to the server or to your homeserver.com domain,
   using the port that you configured on the server, as seen in Figure 19.15. Figure
   19.16 shows the client connected to a VNC server running on the Windows Home Server
   computer.

FIGURE 19.15

Use the client to connect to the domain and the port you specified.

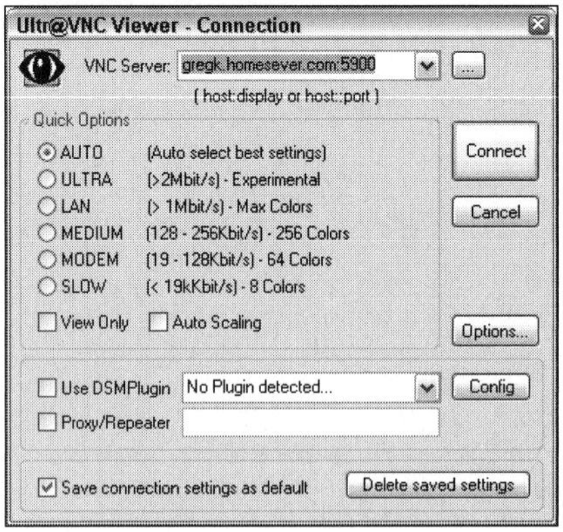

You can configure servers on all of your client computers, if you like. The only requirement if you
want to access them from the Internet is that you assign a different port number (that is, 5901,
5902, 903, and so on), and that you forward those ports to the correct computers on your router.

FIGURE 19.16

Connecting to the server via VNC

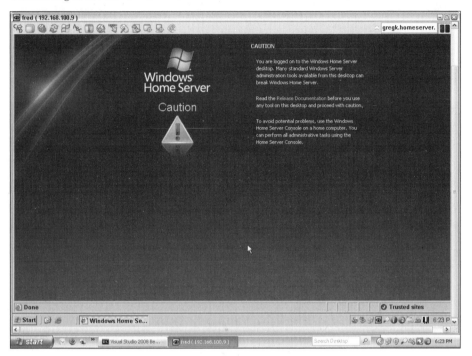

Summary

Remote Access means more than just getting access to your shared folders. If you have a compatible Widows operating system on your client computers, you can connect directly to its desktop using a browser-hosted ActiveX control for Terminal Services access.

In order to connect using Remote Desktop, you need to make sure that your router is configured to forward port 4125 to the server, that the client computers are running an appropriate Windows operating system, and that the client computers have Remote Desktop access enabled and the appropriate ports are opened in the firewall.

From the Remote Access Web site hosted by your Windows Home Server, you can connect to the Console or to any compatible computer.

If you would like to connect to the server's desktop remotely, you can go about it two basic ways. One option is to connect to another client computer and use the Remote Desktop client to connect to the server from there. The other option is to modify the Web settings so that you can connect directly to the server's desktop as well.

Part V

Creating Backups

Chapter 20

Configuring Backups

ousehold chores aren't much fun. Doing the dishes, folding the laundry—these are all chores that nobody likes to do and, too often, procrastinates doing. Computer chores are the same way. Everybody knows that they should back up their computer data regularly; they just neglect to do it. Even with hard drive storage as inexpensive as it is these days, it's still a pain to have to bother with hooking up an external drive and running backup software. What you need is an automatic backup system that just works and gets out of your way.

Windows Home Server's backup feature is designed to do just that. In fact, when you add a computer to the server, it automatically configures backups for you without you having to do a thing. However, you can still tweak backup settings to your heart's content for each of your computers.

Even better, Windows Home Server backups make use of technologies that can not only speed up your backups, but also can reduce the amount of server storage needed for backups as well.

Windows Home Server backups are almost as useful as having a robot to do the dishes and the laundry.

Understanding Backups

The backup feature of Windows Home Server is designed to be as easy to use as possible in order to encourage users to back up their systems. When the Connector is installed on client computers, it is automatically scheduled for daily backups of all files. For most users, this is satisfactory and no further configuration will be necessary. You can, however, make adjustments to some backup settings, as we'll describe later in this chapter.

By default, backups are scheduled to run between midnight and 6:00 a.m. Client computers are backed up one at a time, and computers that are on standby or hibernating will be awaken to perform their scheduled backup, and returned to sleep afterwards. The scheduled backup time window can be changed in the Windows Home Server Console, as we will show later in this chapter.

NOTE Computers must be running on AC power in order to have their automatic backups run. Laptop computers that are on battery power will not be restored from standby to run the backup. You *can* run a backup manually for a computer on battery power. It is up to you to make sure that you have enough battery power remaining to complete the backup, though.

Backup Features

Windows Home Server backups have a number of advantages over other backup solutions that might rely on an external hard drive, optical discs, or tape drives. The biggest advantage, of course, is that it works all Windows computers on your network and not just a single computer.

Windows Home Server backups are very efficient, making use of a technology developed for business Windows Server products called Single Instance Storage, which ensures that files that have multiple copies on a file system are actually only stored once, as Figure 20.1 shows. This is beneficial for backups in two ways:

- **Between daily backups, very few files tend to change as compared to the total number of files on the hard drive.** With Single Instance Storage, multiple complete system backups can be made daily, with only the files that have actually changed copied to the server. Files that haven't changed are simply saved as pointers to the common existing files.

- **Computers in the same household often have many files in common.** They often run the same operating system versions and have many of the same applications installed on them. Dynamic linked libraries and other files are often shared between computers. Single Instance Storage can ensure that files that are common between computers are only stored once as well.

Single Instance Storage is an improvement over backup systems that rely on storing both complete as well as partial backups in that it isn't necessary to refer to the complete backup when restoring. The complete backup also does not need to be kept around in order to restore the backup. Instead, when an older backup is deleted as a part of backup maintenance, the references to the shared files are removed rather than the files themselves. The file instance itself won't actually be removed from the server until the last reference to it is removed as well.

FIGURE 20.1

Single Instance Storage technology makes backups efficient by only including files when they've changed. Files that haven't changed are accessed seamlessly.

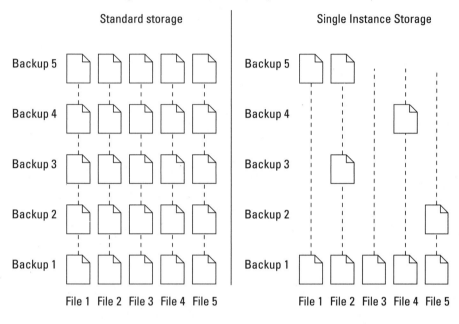

Exploring Backup Settings

Some of the backup customization that you can do in Windows Home Server are changes to the global settings that affect all backups. You make these configuration changes in the Settings window, as shown in Figure 20.2. In this window, you can change your schedule backup window, adjust the length of time backups are retained, and perform a manual backup cleanup.

Scheduling backups

By default, automatic backups will occur between midnight and 6:00 AM. During this window, all of the computers that are powered on and connected to the server (via the connector software) will be backed up one at a time. If you have laptop computers that are in standby or hibernate mode, they will be automatically powered on during their scheduled backup time and returned to sleep after the backup is computer, provided they are running on AC power.

FIGURE 20.2

Global backup setting changes are made in the Settings window.

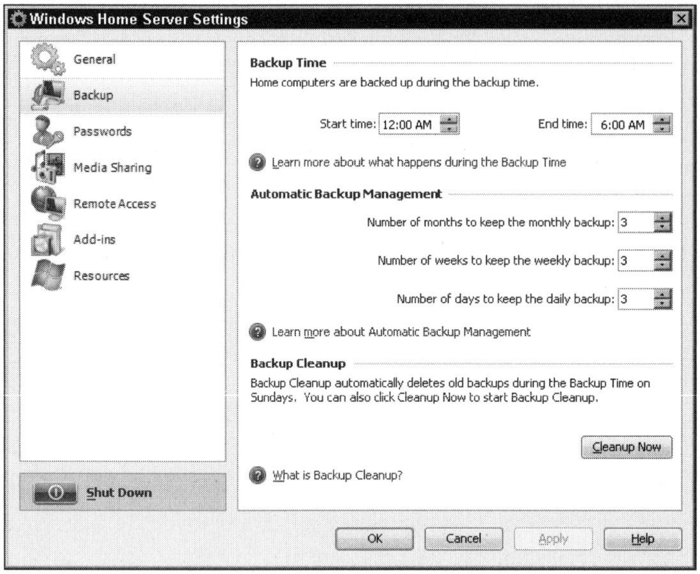

Although this time window should be satisfactory for most users, there are several reasons why you might want to change this setting. You should choose a time period when your computers aren't in use. If you are a night owl and frequently use your computers late at night, you might want to reschedule your backups for the morning or afternoon. If you power off your computers at night, you should schedule backups to occur during a time that you have your computers turned on. To set the backup time, do the following:

1. **Open and log onto the Console.**
2. **Click the Settings button.**
3. **Click the Backup button on the left side of the Settings dialog.**
4. **Click on the Start time control and use the up and down arrows to select the starting time.** You can select the AM with the mouse or by pressing left or right arrow keys to adjust whether to set to AM or PM. Figure 20.3 shows the time being set.
5. **Do the same for the End time.**

NOTE   You can only set the start and end times to the nearest hour, and they cannot set them to the same time.

FIGURE 20.3

Set your backup start and stop window to times that are convenient for you.

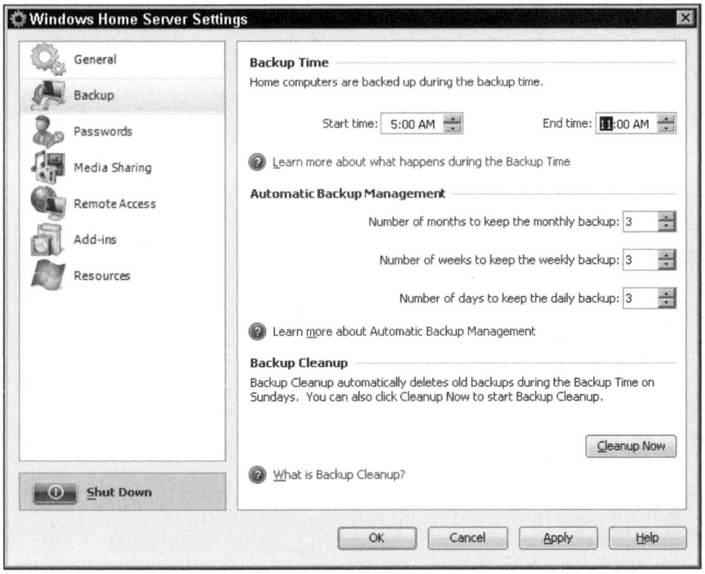

The backup time window is used for other maintenance tasks as well as backups. The following actions occur during the window:

- Automatic backups are performed on all computers sequentially.
- If enabled, Windows Updates are installed on the server if they are available, and the server restarted if necessary.
- On Sundays, Backup Cleanup is run to remove old expired backups.

Managing backup retention

Backups are performed every day, and while an individual daily backup doesn't usually take up much server storage, eventually you want old backups to be cleaned up and removed. Windows Home Server has flexible backup management that lets you keep daily, weekly, and monthly backups:

- **Daily backups:** This setting specifies how many daily backups to keep. This can range from 1 to 90 days.
- **Weekly backups:** The first backup of each week is kept as the weekly backup. You can use this setting to control the number of weekly backups to retain. Possible values are 0 to 52 weeks. A setting of 0 means no weekly backups will be kept.

■ **Monthly backups:** The first backup of each month is considered the monthly backup. This setting allows you to set the number of monthly backups to retain from between 0 and 120 months. A setting of 0 means no monthly backups will be kept.

To configure a backup management setting, click the one you wish to change (Monthly, Weekly, or Daily), and use the up and down arrows to increase or decrease the time, as shown in Figure 20.4.

NOTE These backup management settings refer to the number of backups that are retained in each category, and not necessarily sequential days, weeks, or months. If your computer is offline, has backups disabled, or otherwise misses a scheduled backup, Windows Home Server will still keep the specified number of daily, weekly, and monthly backups.

The configurability of the backup management lets you control backups the way you want. For instance, if you prefer to keep weekly backups instead of monthly backups, you can increase the weekly backup retention and lower the monthly backups to zero.

TIP The default settings are designed to provide a good balance between flexibility and server storage. If you are unsure of what you want to use for backup settings, you may want to begin with the default settings and adjust them later when you gain more familiarity with your own usage patterns and the amount of storage your backups are taking up.

FIGURE 20.4

Backup management settings allow you to configure backup retention.

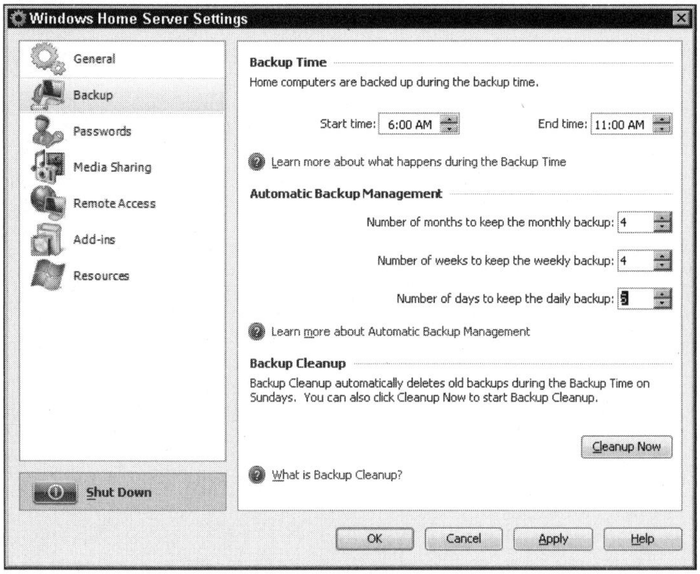

Cleaning up backups

The backup cleanup process runs every Sunday during the backup window time. If for some reason you want to clean up backups right away, you can use the Cleanup Now button to run the cleanup process immediately, as shown in Figure 20.5.

Running a manual cleanup isn't usually necessary; however there are times when it is justified:

■ If you adjust your backup management settings to retain fewer backups in order to use less server storage, you may want to run the cleanup right away to take advantage of the improved storage limit.

■ If the automatic cleanup doesn't run successfully on Sunday due to an error or the server being down, you may want to run the manual cleanup when you bring the server back up.

■ If you change the retention of an individual backup to be removed at the next cleanup, you may want it to be removed right away.

CROSS-REF Retention settings for individual backups are discussed in Chapter 21.

FIGURE 20.5

Run a manual backup cleanup when you change backup management settings.

Viewing Backup Storage Use

With all of daily, weekly, and monthly backups you are retaining, you may be wondering how to tell just how much server storage space is being used for backups at any particular time. Fortunately, you can tell at a glance on the Server Storage tab, shown in Figure 20.6. The pie chart on the right-hand side of the screen gives you immediate visual feedback as to the percentage of storage in use as backup storage, and the legend underneath shows you exactly how much is in use.

If you think that backups are taking too much of your server storage, you can reduce the number of backups kept by your backup management settings.

FIGURE 20.6

You can tell at a glance how much storage your backups are taking on the Server Storage tab.

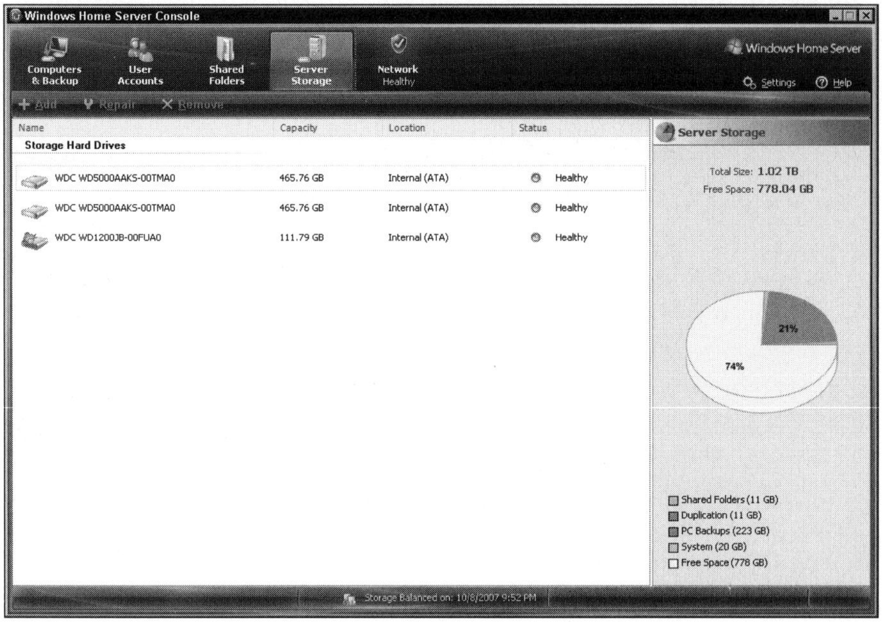

Summary

Backups are one of the most critical and yet often one of the most neglected of household computer chores. With Windows Home Server, however, backups are no longer a chore and for the most part just happen automatically behind the scenes. Your only job is to check them once in a while to make sure they are occurring on schedule.

If for whatever reason you need to make a change to the backup settings, you can do so in the Settings dialog. You can adjust the backup start and stop times to better fit with the times that your computers are powered on or not heavily used. You can adjust the backup retention settings to keep more or fewer backups based on your personal preferences or to make better use of the server storage you have available. You can also run manual backup cleanups.

That takes care of the global backup settings. In the next chapter, we show you how to go further by configuring backups for each your individual computers.

Chapter 21

Backing Up Windows Computers

In Chapter 20, we discuss some of the benefits of Windows Home Server's backup capability, and how to configure the global backup settings that apply to all of your computer backups. Now you know how to get all of your Windows computers connected to the server and backed up. Great! Really, that is most of the battle. However, you can still go a little further with backups by customizing the backup configuration of each computer. You can decide exactly which drives and folders to include in each computer's backups.

On top of the backup configuration settings, Windows Home Server gives you some handy backup management tools. You can browse all of the backups for a computer, as well as decide to manually override the default backup management settings by either keeping a particular backup indefinitely or forcing it to be deleted during the next backup cleanup event.

Manual backups are another option. Manual backups allow you to make a backup at any time without having to wait for the scheduled backup time. This makes backups not only a tool for system recovery, but also a way to freeze your system to an exact point before you do something major to it, such as installing a new hard drive or a Windows service pack.

IN THIS CHAPTER

Configuring backups

Determining what to include in a backup

Performing manual backups

Disabling automatic backups

Viewing backup details

Configuring Computer Backups

The Computers & Backup tab, shown in Figure 21.1, lets you manage the backup process on your client computers. Every Windows computer that you add to the server appears in the list on this tab, along with its current backup status.

FIGURE 21.1

Manage backups in the Console's Computers & Backup tab.

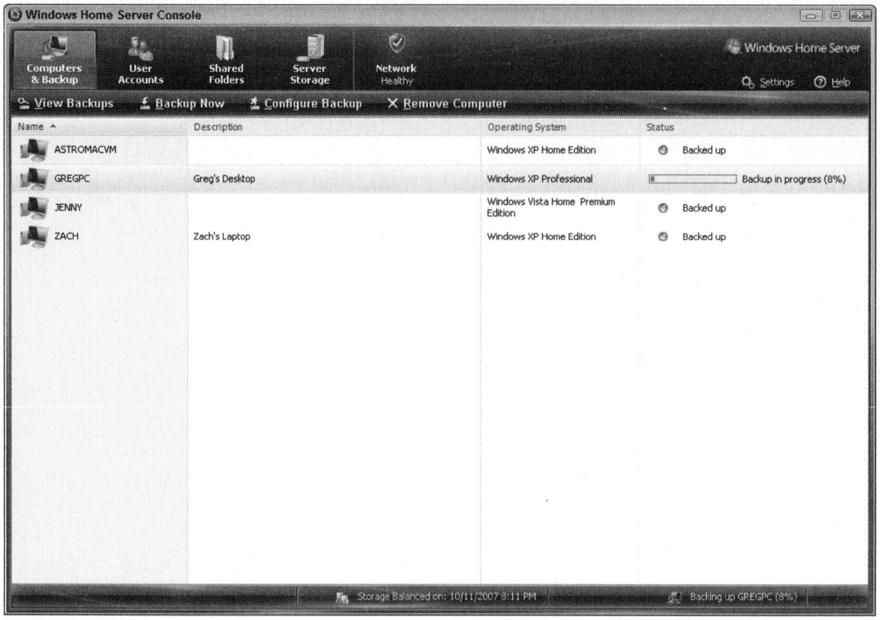

By default, Windows Home Server backs up your entire computer, with the exception of a few folders that are deemed expendable, such as the temp directory or the browser cache.

You don't have to do anything to accept this setting, but if you prefer to tweak everything you can, Windows Home Server gives you the ability to go a bit farther with the Backup Configuration Wizard.

Running the Backup Configuration Wizard

The Backup Configuration Wizard is the main backup configuration tool in Windows Home Server. Although it doesn't offer a lot in terms of configuration settings, it does make it easy to choose folders and files that you want to exclude from the backup.

To run the Backup Configuration Wizard, follow these steps:

1. In the Console, select the Computers & Backup tab.
2. Select a computer from the list.
3. Click the Configure Backup button on the toolbar to launch the wizard, shown in Figure 21.2.
4. Click Next to proceed.

FIGURE 21.2

You can use the Backup Configuration Wizard to customize backups for each of your client computers.

5. **Choose the volumes you wish to include in the backup, as shown in Figure 21.3.** You can only choose NTFS (New Technology File System) formatted volumes. Click Next.

NOTE NTFS is the standard file system for XP and Vista computers. Older Windows file system standards such as FAT and FAT32 lack features that allow the backup function to work efficiently, so they are not supported.

6. **If you would like to exclude additional folders, click the Add button, and select a folder to exclude (from the list of folders, as shown in Figure 21.4).**

FIGURE 21.3

You can back up any NTFS formatted volume attached to your computer.

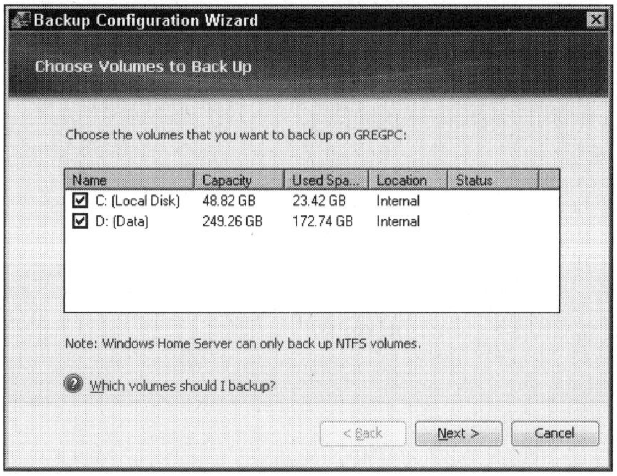

FIGURE 21.4

You may choose to exclude folders with files you don't want backed up to save storage space.

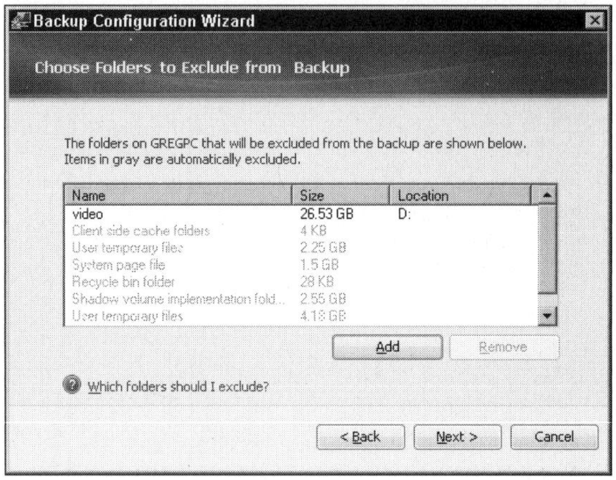

7. **If you would like to exclude additional folders, repeat Step 6.** Click Next when you are done.

8. **Your configuration is now complete!** You will see a summary page showing you the number of excluded folders and how much server storage space a backup will be expected to take. Click Done to close the window. You can run the Backup Configuration Wizard again any time you want to change the excluded files settings.

Deciding what to include in the backup

The backups made by Windows Home Server can be used to completely restore a computer to a working state if, for example, the hard drive needs to be replaced. In order to be able to restore a computer from the Restore CD, you must include the System volume (drive) in the backup. The System volume (typically Drive C) includes the Windows OS and the files necessary to boot the computer. If you have other volumes with data on them, you will have to make the call as to whether they need to be included in backups.

Any volume that contains valuable, irreplaceable files should certainly be included in the backup.

Some computers include a special recovery volume (typically on Drive D) that can be used to restore the computer to the out-of-the-box configuration. Your Windows Home Server backups give you a similar capability, so you may elect not to include this drive, especially if it is also provided on a separate DVD-ROM.

TV recordings are an example of files that you probably don't want to include in your backup. If you are using your computer as a digital video recorder (DVR), the TV recording files will be created and deleted often. Backups take longer because the difference between the computers current state and its existing backups will be larger, requiring more files to be copied every night. Backups will take up more storage on the server as well, given that a constantly changing TV recording lineup won't be able to take much advantage of the single instance store technology. Exclude such files, or, better yet, store them on the server in the Videos shared folder so you can stream them throughout your house.

CROSS-REF See Chapter 20 for more information on single instance store and how it is used in Windows Home Server backups. For information on streaming video with Windows Home Server, see Chapters 25 through 30.

Performing Manual Backups

For the most part you can simply let the automatic backups happen on schedule and not worry about them too much. There may be some times, however, when you'll want to kick off a backup manually:

- **If your computer hasn't been backed up automatically for a while, which can happen if it's been turned off during the backup window.**

- **You are replacing the old hard drive, and you want to be able to restore a complete backup onto the new hard drive.**

- **When you first add a computer to the server.** Initial backups tend to take much longer than subsequent ones, so you may prefer to start a backup right away so that other computer backups won't be impacted.

Whatever your reason, you don't have to wait for the daily backup if you don't want to. You can run a manual backup at any time from the Console or from the client computer itself. Follow these easy steps to do a manual backup from the Console:

1. **Click on the Computers & Backup tab.**

2. **Select the computer to back up in the list.**

3. **Click the Backup Now button on the toolbar.**

4. **You will be prompted to give the backup a description.** Using a description can be helpful in identifying the backup later when you want to restore it, but it's not essential. You can leave it with the default description of Manual Backup if you like.

To do a manual backup directly from the client computer, right-click on the tray icon and choose the Backup Now option, as shown in Figure 21.5. You can give the backup a description just as with manual backups from the Console.

FIGURE 21.5
_____

You can force a manual backup at any time from the tray icon.

Viewing backup progress

You can view the status of a backup in progress, whether automatic or manual, from the Console or from the client computer. In the Console, the backup progress can be monitored directly on the Computers & Backup tab, as shown in Figure 21.6.

On the client computer that is being backed up, you can tell that a backup is in progress when the tray icon turns blue. There are two options for viewing the progress of a backup on the client computer. First, you can simply hover the mouse pointer over the tray icon to see the percentage complete at a glance.

You can get a more complete picture of the backup status by double-clicking on the tray icon. The Backup Status dialog, shown in Figure 21.7, gives you a little more information. For example, it will give you some indication of which step is currently being performed, or let you know if the server is waiting on another computer's backup to finish.

NOTE Manual backups are not automatically managed by your retention settings, which means that they will be kept until you either mark them to be managed automatically, or mark them to be deleted at during the next backup cleanup action.

Occasionally, backups will fail to complete. These can occur for a number of reasons: A wireless connection disconnects, a computer is shut down in the middle of a backup, or the computer crashes in the middle of the backup. When this occurs, the status of the backups will be visible in the Status column of the Computers & Backup tab. A Network Health notification is also issued when a backup fails; however these are considered non-critical and hence these messages can be disabled.

FIGURE 21.6

You can monitor backup progress in the Console.

FIGURE 21.7

You can also view the backup status on the client computer by double-clicking the tray icon when it is blue.

Disabling and Enabling Backups

Sometimes you may not want a computer to be backed up automatically. You may decide that the only backups you want are those that you create manually. For instance, if you have a computer that you use as a Media Center PC, you may just want to configure it the way you want and only back it up when you update the system. It may not be worthwhile to back up a laptop or other computer that you rarely turn on or connect to the network.

With Windows Home Server backups, this is not a problem. On the Computers & Backup tab, you can right-click on a computer and choose Turn Off Backups to disable them, as Figure 21.8 shows. The computer will show as Off in the Status column.

To enable automatic backups again, right-click on the computer and choose Turn On Backups.

> **TIP**
>
> The Help file that comes with Windows Home Server states that manual backups can be performed even if backups are turned off. At the time of this writing, our testing with a pre-release version of the software shows this not to be the case. Manual backups can be started but they error out before they can complete.

FIGURE 21.8

You can disable backups for computers you don't want backed up automatically.

Working with Backups

Your computer is now being backed up every night. Or is it? If you would like to see details of your backups, browse them to look for an old file, or change the backup management settings for your backups, you can do so in the Computers & Backup tab by selecting one of your home computers and clicking the Console's View Backups button.

NOTE Backups can fail for various reasons. A computer might be powered off in the middle of a backup, or a spotty wireless network connection might prevent the computer from maintaining a connection to the server. It is recommended that you check your backups once in a while to make sure that they are occurring.

The View Backups dialog, shown in Figure 21.9, shows a list of the backups for your computer. The list is ordered by date, newest to oldest by default; however you can click on the column headings to change the sort order if you like, which can be handy if you have a lot of backups.

FIGURE 21.9

View Backups lets you keep track of how your computer's backups are being maintained.

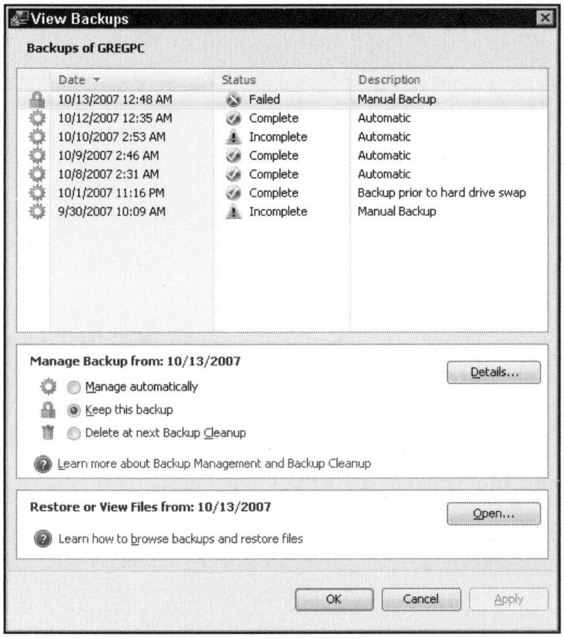

The list will show the following information:

- **Management icon:** This icon tells you how the backup is being managed.
- **Date:** The date and time the backup was started.
- **Status:** Tells you whether or not the backup completed successfully.
- **Description:** The default values for the description are Automatic or Manual Backup, depending on whether the backup was done automatically or manually. This can also be a custom description if you entered one while doing a manual backup or on the Backup Details screen.

Checking backup status

The Status indicator on the View Backups list is probably the most important thing to keep track of when monitoring your backups. These indicators can alert you to problems that could be keeping you from having a successful backup. Possible values for the status are:

- **Complete:** The backup completed successfully.

- **Complete with Errors:** The backup completed, but there was a problem backing up one or more files. The problem files will be listed, and you should investigate them to see what the problem is. In some cases, running chkdsk can fix corrupted files on a disk.

- **Incomplete:** Backups that successfully back up one or more volumes, but fail on others will be listed as Incomplete. The Backup Details screen will give you more information on which volume failed to be backed up, and why.

- **In Progress:** A backup that is currently running appears with this status.

- **Failed**: As we mentioned, backups can fail for a variety of reasons ranging from network problems to a lack of storage on the server or on the client computer itself.

Managing backup retention

The View Backups dialog lets you control how backups are maintained. There are three possible choices for this feature. The icon on the left shows the current status of the backup. If you select a backup, you can set its management status to one of the following:

- **Manage automatically:** This setting tells Windows Home Server to manage the backup as part of the normal cleanup process that runs during each Sunday's backup window. Backups with this setting will be managed according to the values entered in the Settings dialog. This is the default setting for automatic backups.

- **Keep this backup:** Backups with this setting will be kept indefinitely. This is the default setting for manual backups. It is a good idea to visit the View Backups dialog after performing a manual backup in order to verify the backup completed successfully.

- **Delete at next Backup Cleanup:** This setting tells Windows Home Server to delete this backup during the next Sunday cleanup, regardless of whether it would have been deleted anyway due to the management settings.

> **TIP** If you want backups to be deleted right away, choose the Delete at next Backup Cleanup option, and run a manual cleanup by clicking the Cleanup Now button in the Backup section of the Settings dialog.

Viewing backup details

Clicking the Details button brings up the Backup Details dialog, shown in Figure 21.10. This dialog gives you a lot of useful information regarding the backup, including how long the backup took, information about the volumes backed up, and the size of the files excluded from the backup. If any files were not backed up, they will appear in this dialog as well.

FIGURE 21.10

You can view details pertaining to each of your backups.

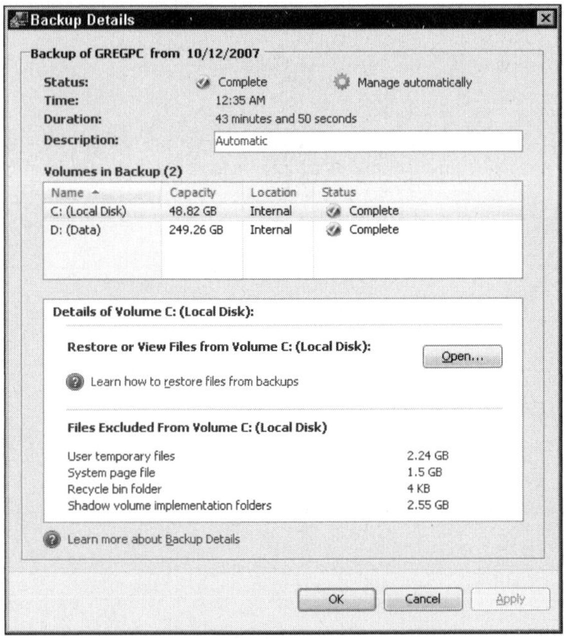

The following items are displayed in the Backup Details dialog:

- **Status:** The status of the backup. This will be the same as the status displayed on the View Backups dialog.

- **Management icon:** This is the management setting from the View Backups dialog. (Keep this backup, Manage automatically, or Delete at next Backup Cleanup.)

- **Time:** The time of day the backup was started. (The date is shown at the top of the window.)

- **Duration:** How much time elapsed while completing the backup.

- **Description:** The description of the backup, either Automatic or Manual, or a custom name. You can give a backup a new description in this field.

- **Volumes in Backup:** A list of the volumes included in the backup, including the volume's name (with drive letter), capacity, whether it's an internal or an external volume (such as with a removable drive), and the status of the backup for that particular volume. Select a volume by clicking on it to see its details.

> **NOTE** It is possible to have a backup complete successfully for one volume and not for others. In these cases, the backups of the successful volumes are still valid and useable for restoring files.

■ **Details:** This panel gives you details about the currently selected volume. Information shown here includes files that were excluded from the backup and their size, as well as any files that couldn't be backed up for one reason or another. This section also includes the Open button, which allows you to view files from the backup.

You can use the Backup Details dialog to show you how a failed or incomplete backup may have gone wrong. Select the volume that the backup failed on to see a description of why the failure occurred, as shown in Figure 21.11. Failed volumes will typically have the Open button disabled, but you will be able to open other volumes in the backup.

FIGURE 21.11

You can browse incomplete and failed backups to see the most likely cause of the problem.

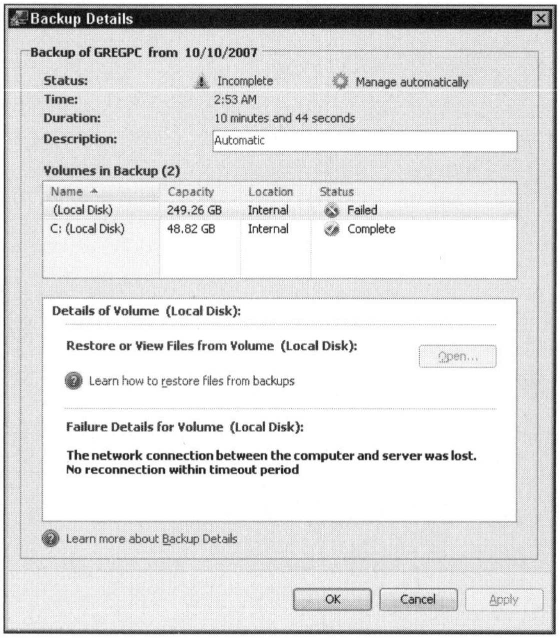

Viewing Backup Failure Notifications

It'd be nice to know immediately when a backup fails, wouldn't it? Well, of course, you are able to do this. If you have Display Network Health Notifications enabled on the tray icon on connected computers, you will receive a notification whenever an error occurs during a backup. As Figure 21.12 shows, if you go into the Console, the Network At Risk button shows the warning icon, and clicking it shows you what caused the error.

Backup notifications may become annoying if they occur frequently. Of course, ideally you should fix the problem that is causing the backup errors, but that is not always possible. Fortunately, backup errors are not considered critical, so you can deal with them by disabling them in the Home Network Health dialog. Simply check the Ignore this issue box when viewing the network health, and your tray icon no longer turns red because of this issue. The issue is still there and you can see it in the Network Health dialog if you need to see it again.

FIGURE 21.12

Network health notifications keep you apprised of any backup mishaps.

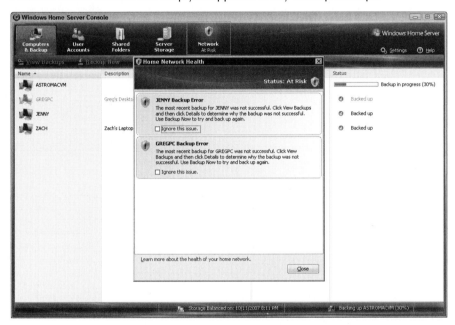

Summary

The backup feature in Windows Home Server is simple to use — in fact, you hardly have to do anything at all to have all of your computers fully backed up every night by Windows Home Server. Once you've joined the computer to the server, the backups just happen. In order to get the most out of your backups, however, you can get down to the details by customizing exactly what is backed up on each of your computers, and how to manage those backups. You can choose to not back up computers entirely, or only have one volume on a multivolume computer backed up. You can also manage your backups in the Console, choosing how long to keep them.

In the next chapter, we show you how to restore files from the backups you have created — from a single file or two from a backup all the way to a full-blown complete system restoration.

Once you have backups in place, the peace of mind it will give you will make you wonder how you ever got along without them.

Chapter 22

Restoring Backups

Now that you are using Windows Home Server to create backups for all of your home computers, the peace of mind that comes from having your valuable files protected is invaluable. With your Windows Home Server backups, you now have a way to recover your computers from just about anything. You can now remedy everything from a single accidentally deleted file up to a catastrophic hardware failure.

As you saw in Chapter 21, the Console's View Backups and Backup Details dialogs each have a button that gives you access to the files in a backup. In this chapter, we show you how to browse these files, as well as how to recover them.

Most importantly, we show you how you can use the Restore CD to recover from a disaster such as a catastrophic hard drive failure, which would necessitate a complete restore from your most recent backup.

Finally, we show you how to recover the device drivers that Windows Home Server includes with each backup, and use them when restoring your computer by some means other than the Restore CD.

Viewing Backed Up Files

When we discuss the View Backups and Backup Details dialogs in Chapter 21, we make a passing reference to the Open button on both dialogs that allows you to view and restore files from each backup. Here, we address this Open button further.

Opening backups

If a backup only includes a single volume (drive) from the source computer, both Open buttons operate in the same way and will automatically load the file browser for that volume.

For backups with multiple volumes, the behavior of the two Open buttons is slightly different. On the View Backups dialog, you can only select a backup to browse. When you click the Open button, you will be asked which volume you want to open, as shown in Figure 22.1.

If a backup includes multiple volumes, you must choose the one you wish to open.

On the Backup Details dialog, shown in Figure 22.2, you must first select the volume that you want to browse, and then click the Open button.

NOTE   Backups that are failed or incomplete will often still have the Open button enabled. However, when you select a volume to restore, you will be informed that the backup cannot be opened. This is normal.

FIGURE 22.2

The Backup Details dialog lets you go directly to browsing a volume.

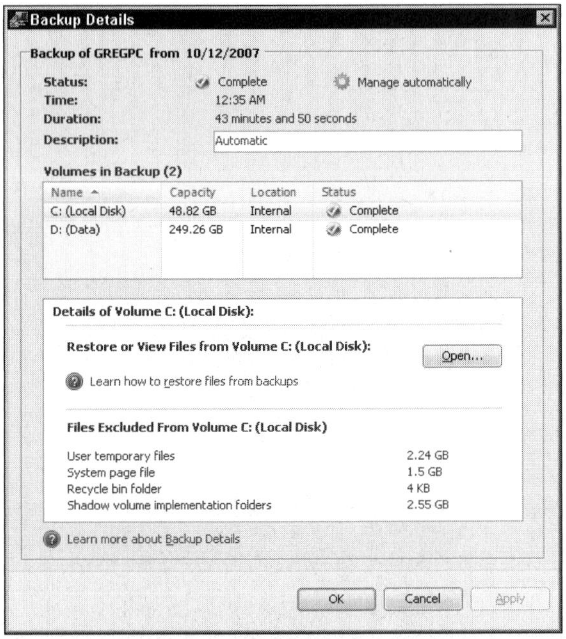

You can't view or open backups from the Console if it is running Home Server's desktop. You must run the Console on a client computer, although it doesn't necessarily have to be the computer that the files were backed up from in the first place.

At some point when the backup is opened, you may be prompted to restart your computer. This prompt comes up because a component must be installed on your computer in order to view the backups in Windows Explorer. You can safely ignore this prompt and still view files, as the Opening Backup message box shows in Figure 22.3. It can take a while to open a backup, especially if it is large. Be patient.

In Windows Vista, you will be prompted to install the device necessary to talk to the backup service. Make sure you choose Install when prompted.

FIGURE 22.3

When opening a backup, you are given a progress update.

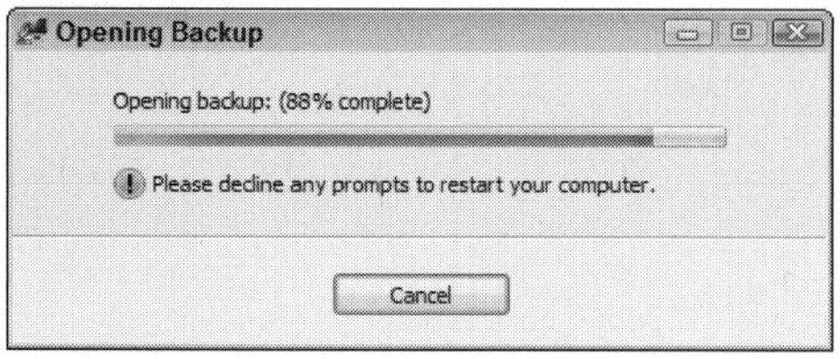

Browsing files

When the volume backup is open, it is mounted to a drive letter on the computer that opened it. This drive letter is typically Drive Z:. If Drive Z: is already in use, it will move up the alphabet until it finds a drive letter that is available and use that instead.

CAUTION The drive mount for the backup restore is only temporary. Although you can access it using other Windows Explorer windows, the drive will be disconnected when you close the original window.

A special Explorer window is opened pointing to the new drive, shown in Figure 22.4. From here, you can browse the folders and files and see them as they existed at the time the backup was made. As you might expect, this volume is write protected. You can only restore backups; you can't change them.

If you have Explorer set to view hidden files and folders, you may notice several additional files in the root of the backup. These files, named Home_Server_Accessible, Home_Server_Unaccessible, and Home_Server_Unaccessible_2, are special files that are put in place for Windows Home Server's use.

Another addition is the Windows Home Server Drivers for Restore folder. This folder contains drivers that may be needed by the restoration process to access the hard drive and to access the network in order to see the backup. We discuss how to use these drivers later in this chapter.

Restoring Files and Folders

The rest of the files and folders in the backup are the ones from your computer. You can browse them as with any drive in Explorer, and copy them to another drive to restore them. You can restore entire folders or even the entire drive in this manner.

FIGURE 22.4

When opening a backup, you are given a progress update along with a message to not restart your computer.

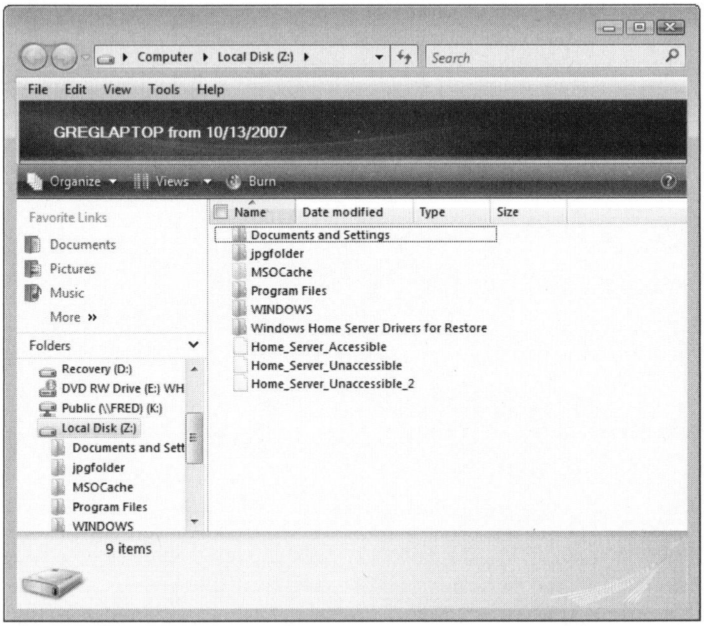

Follow these steps to restore a folder (or multiple folders), up to and including the entire drive:

1. **Verify that the destination drive has enough space for the files you are copying.** If you are restoring an entire volume, you may want to copy it to an empty drive.

2. **Find out how much space is needed for the files you want to restore in Explorer.** Simply select the file or folder you are planning to restore. (You can select multiple files or folder in the usual way: hold the Shift key to select a range or the Ctrl key to select individual items. Press Ctrl+A to select all of the files and folders in the current Explorer window.)

3. **Right-click on the selection and choose Properties.** The file sizes will be tallied up and shown, as in Figure 22.5. If there are a lot of files selected, this can take awhile.

TIP You can quickly find out how much space an entire volume uses by right-clicking on the drive letter for the volume and choosing Properties. If the Folders pane in Explorer is not visible, click the Folders button to see the folder hierarchy including the drive letter.

FIGURE 22.5

Make sure you have enough available storage space in which to restore your files.

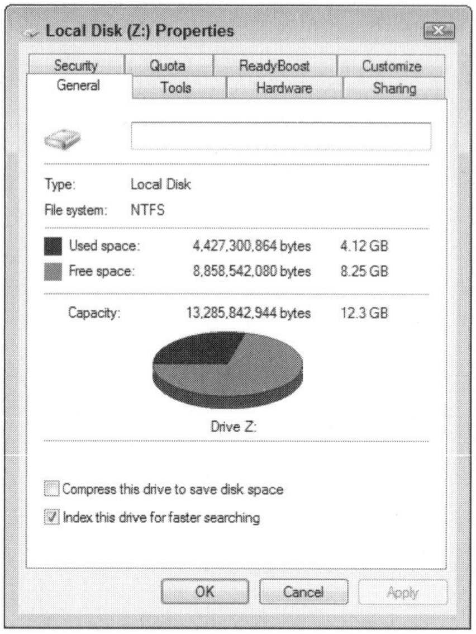

4. **With the files and folders to copy still selected, copy to the clipboard by choosing Edit ➪ Copy from the menu in Explorer, or by pressing Ctrl+C.**

5. **Navigate to the destination drive in Explorer.** You may find opening another Explorer window to be more convenient, especially if you are going to want to copy more files.

6. **Select Edit ➪ Paste from the destination folder's Explorer window.** The files are copied as with any other Windows file copy, as shown in Figure 22.6.

7. **If you wish to copy additional files, repeat the steps starting from Step 2.**

FIGURE 22.6

Restoring files is as simple as performing a file copy in Explorer.

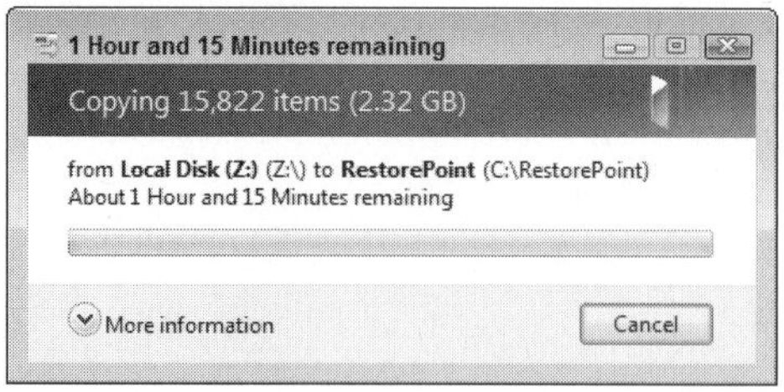

Using the Restore CD

If you need to recover the system volume of a computer, the process is a little more involved. Windows Home Server provides a Restore CD that you can use to boot from in order to allow the system volume to be restored. This can be useful for a number of circumstances:

- Your system volume is corrupted, either due to a software problem or even a virus.
- You suffer a catastrophic hardware failure, particularly a hard drive failure.
- You are upgrading your computer's hard drive and want to restore files to a new, larger volume.
- You are evaluating software or new operating system releases and decide that you want to restore the computer to the state it was in before you installed it.

Whatever reason you may have to restore the system volume can be accommodated.

CAUTION Restoring a system volume to a different computer is not recommended. Device drivers for the new computer are likely to differ significantly from those for the original computer, and such a restored system may either not boot at all or suffer from problems if it does.

Copying device drivers

In order to prepare for the system drive restoration, it is a good idea to copy the drivers from the Windows Home Server Drivers for Restore folder. Follow the directions listed in the previous section to open the most recent backup for the computer you are restoring, and copy the entire Windows Home Server Drivers for Restore folder to it, as shown in Figure 22.7. If you don't have a USB flash drive, you can use a floppy disc or some other removable drive type assuming the files fit on it.

NOTE If the computer you are restoring is not functioning, you can use another computer to copy the drivers (other than the Windows Home Server, that is). Just make sure that you get the drivers from a backup for the computer being restored.

FIGURE 22.7

Copy device drivers to a USB flash drive so that you can use them with the Restore CD.

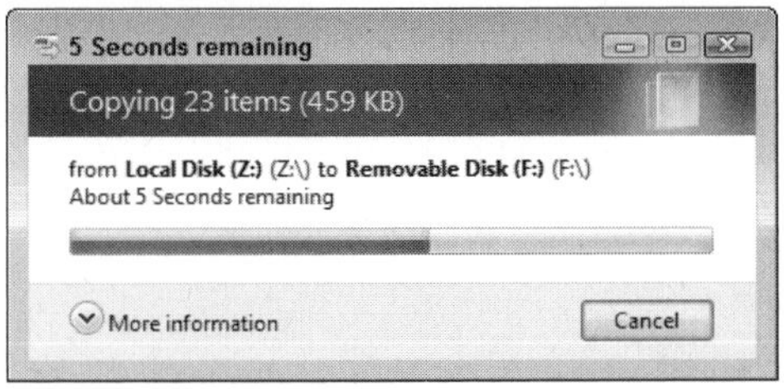

Once this is complete, you are ready to restore the system. If you copied the files from a different computer, be sure to remove the USB flash drive from the computer you copied the drivers from, and insert it into a USB slot on the computer being restored.

Preparing the Restore CD

The system volume on your computer contains the files that the computer normally boots from. If you are restoring the system volume, these files are either not there or need to be replaced with those from the backup. Therefore, you must use something else to boot the computer — the Restore CD that is included with Windows Home Server. If you have this CD at hand, skip ahead to Using the Restore CD. If not, read on for information on creating a replacement.

If you do not have the Restore CD that was included with Windows Home Server, you can create a new one. Windows Home Server handily includes a CD image file (`.iso`) that you can use to burn a new CD. All you need is a computer with a recordable optical drive (CD-R, CD-RW, DVD-R, or DVD-RW) and a blank CD. You will also need software capable of creating a CD from an ISO file.

You can use popular software such as Nero Burning Rom or Roxio Easy Media Creator. If you don't have one of these commercial applications, a number of tools are available for download that you can use to burn an ISO file. One way to do it is with the CDBurn command line utility included in the Windows 2003 Resource Kit Tools. ISO Recorder, which has a graphical user interface, is another popular utility.

ON the WEB You can find the Windows 2003 Resource Kit Tools at the following URL: `www.microsoft.com/downloads/details.aspx?familyid=9d467a69-57ff-4ae7-96ee-b18c4790cffd&displaylang=en`. Rather than type in that long URL, though, you can just go to the Microsoft.com home page and search for *CDBurn*. Note: These tools will work on Windows 2003 or XP.

ISO recorder can be found at `http://isorecorder.alexfeinman.com/isorecorder.htm`. ISO Recorder is compatible with Windows XP, 2003, or Vista.

Follow these steps to create the replacement Restore CD.

1. **On the computer that has the CD burner, open Explorer and navigate to the Software shared folder on your server.**

2. Verify that the `restorecd.iso` file is in the Home PC Restore CD folder. You may be able to burn the file directly from this folder, but if you have a slow or intermittent network connection, you can copy it to your local computer.

3. **Insert a blank CD into your CD-R drive.**

4. **Load your CD burning software.** If you are using ISO recorder, you can simply right-click on the restorecd.iso file and choose Copy image to CD, shown in Figure 22.8.

5. **Follow the instructions that came with your recording software to burn the ISO file.**

CAUTION Make sure that you are using the option to create a CD from the image file, as opposed to simply copying the image file to the CD. In Nero, for instance, the option to burn an image is the Recorder ⇨ Burn Image menu item. With Roxio Easy Media Creator, it's under File ⇨ Create Disc from Image in the Creator Classic application.

After you have located or created a Restore CD and copied your drivers to a USB flash drive, you are ready to restore a computer's system volume.

FIGURE 22.8

You can use the restorecd.iso file to create a replacement Restore CD.

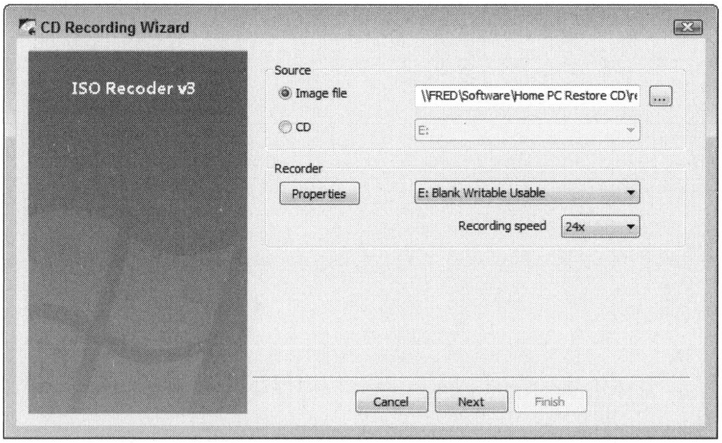

Using the Restore CD

In order to use the Restore CD, it must be able to boot from the CD or DVD drive. Although most computers created in the last several years are capable of doing this, you may need to configure the computer's BIOS (Basic Input/Output System) to allow a CD to boot.

CROSS-REF See Chapter 5 for more information on configuring your computer to boot from the CD or DVD drive. Although that chapter contains instructions for installing Windows Home Server, the steps for configuring a computer's BIOS to allow booting from a CD are applicable to most computers.

One thing to keep in mind is that the networking interface of the Restore CD is not capable of configuring wireless settings and connecting to a WiFi network. You will need to use a network cable to connect the computer directly to your router in order to restore.

Once you have verified that your computer is capable of booting from the CD, follow these steps to restore your system volume:

1. **Insert the Restore CD into the drive and power on the computer.**

2. **During the power on self test, if a bootable CD is found in the drive, you may be prompted to press a key to boot from it.** Press a key if you are prompted to do so.

3. **Wait for the installer to load.**

4. **Choose your time and keyboard formats.**

5. **You will eventually see a notice indicating the devices that have been found on the computer, as shown in Figure 22.9.** You need to have a network device as well as a storage device. If you are sure that you don't need any additional drivers, you can click Continue. Otherwise, click the Show Details button.

FIGURE 22.9

Loading the Restore CD

6. **A list of current devices is listed, as shown in Figure 22.10.** Click Install Drivers.

7. **Insert the USB Flash drive or floppy disk.** Wait for several seconds to give the computer time to mount the device, and click the Scan button. After a while any appropriate drivers are found.

8. **Click OK to add the device drivers found to the list of standard devices.** The installation program will need to find your storage and network devices in order to continue.

9. **Click the Continue button to proceed.** The Restore Computer Wizard, seen in Figure 22.11, is launched. The wizard will now locate your server.

10. **Click Next to continue.**

11. **Enter the password for your server.** You can click the hint button to see the hint if you like. Click Next.

FIGURE 22.10

A list of devices is displayed.

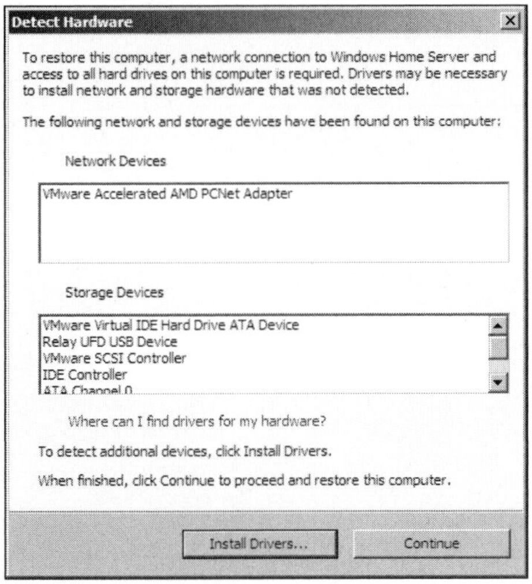

FIGURE 22.11

The Restore Computer Wizard will guide you thorough the restoration.

12. **Choose the computer to restore from in the drop-down list.** Do not restore a system volume to a different computer, unless it is identical hardware. However, you can restore it to another volume on your hard drive. Click Next.

13. **You will see a list of backups for the computer, shown in Figure 22.12.** You can use the Details button to see more information about a particular backup if you like. Select one and click Next.

FIGURE 22.12

Choose the backup that you would like to restore. In most cases you will want the most recent successful one.

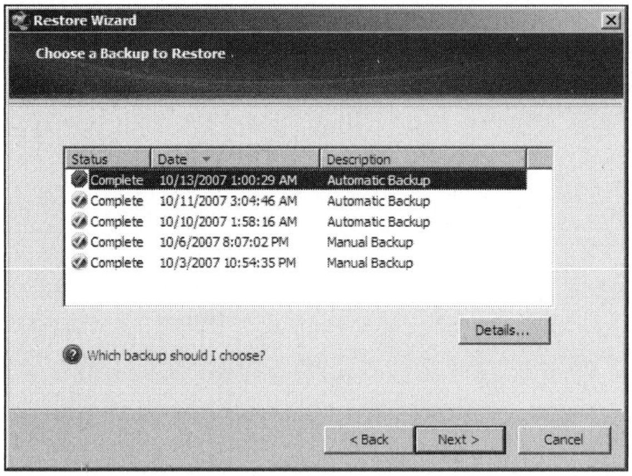

14. **If you are installing to a new hard drive, it won't be partitioned correctly for restoration.** You will be warned that there are no initialized discs found. If this happens, click the Run Disk Manager button. Otherwise, skip to Step 19.

15. **Disk Manager, shown in Figure 22.13, shows you a list of drives on your computer.** Make sure the new drive is selected and click OK.

FIGURE 22.13

Use Disk Manager to partition a new hard drive.

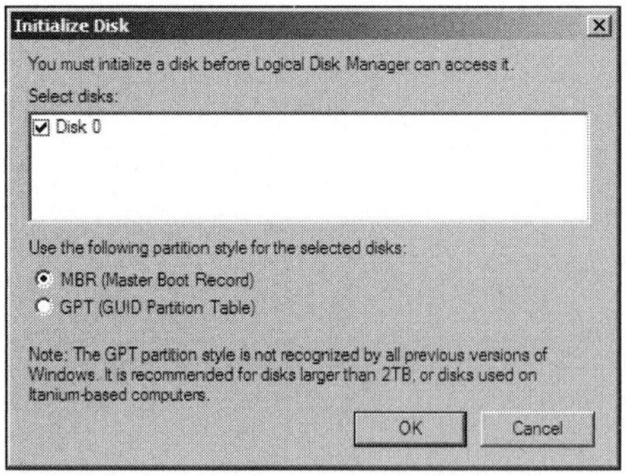

16. **Right-click on the disk in Disk Manager and choose Create Partition.**

17. **Follow the Simple Volume Wizard, shown in Figure 22.14, to create a new volume on the hard drive.** Be sure to create a partition large enough to accommodate your restore. A good rule of thumb is to create one as large as the previous drive was or larger. Assign the same drive letter that the original system volume used (typically C), and select NTFS as the file system type. You can check the Quick Format box to speed up the task of formatting the disk, although if it is a brand new disk, you may elect not to do this in order to check the disk for errors during the format.

FIGURE 22.14

You use the Simple Volume Wizard to initialize a brand new hard drive.

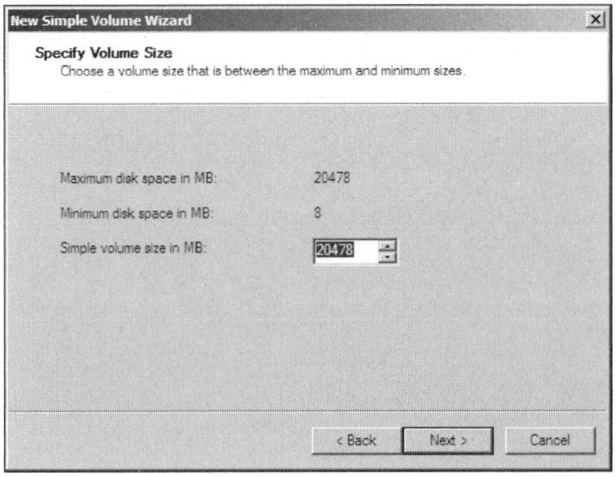

18. **Once the disk is initialized, you can close the Disk Manager by clicking the Close box on the upper right.** Then click Next to continue the Restore Wizard.

19. **Choose a source volume from the backup and a destination volume on this computer.** You won't have a choice of multiple destination volumes if there is only one. Then click Next.

20. **This is the point of no return; after you click Next the destination volume will be overwritten with the backup.** If you are only doing a "dry run" restore, stop here. Otherwise, click Next to continue.

21. **The restoration progress bar shows you how long the restore will take.** Once it is completed, you will be presented with the Restore Successfully Completed screen, shown in Figure 22.15. Congratulations! Click the Finish button to restart the computer.

FIGURE 22.15

Congratulations! You have successfully restored your computer.

Occasionally, the Restore CD will not allow you to restore a computer due to issues with either the storage or network drivers. Finding this out when you desperately need to restore a crashed computer is not a good thing. We recommend that you figure out in advance whether or not this will be a problem by doing a "dry run" restore, just to make sure that the wizard can work with your device drivers and find the home server on the network. Simply stop the restore at the point where the Restore Wizard warns you that proceeding further will result in the destination volumes being deleted.

Summary

The peace of mind that comes from having your important computer files backed up is even greater when you know just how easy it is to restore files, folders, or even entire computers from the backup. With Windows Home Server, you can mount backups and work with the files contained in them in the same way that you can work with files from any drive. To restore, you can just use normal Windows file copying methods to copy from the backup to a local drive. You can even restore backed up files to a completely different computer if you like.

In addition to restoring files, you can use the Restore CD to restore the entire system volume on a computer. This feature allows you to recover from a catastrophic hard drive failure or software corruption, or just restore to a known good configuration after testing new software or operating systems.

While the Restore feature built in to Windows Home Server is a great solution for your Windows PCs, it doesn't help much with other computers such as Macs. Not to worry — there are ways to do backups from other platforms as well. In the next chapter, we show you how to create backups from Macs as well as other computers.

Chapter 23

Backing Up Mac Computers

As we've shown, Windows Home Server backups are a great way to manage the chore of keeping your Windows XP and Vista computers backed up. For the most part, all you have to do to start doing daily backups is install the Windows Home Server Connector software on each computer.

Households with not only multiple computers, but also multiple types of computers are becoming more and more common. Apple Macs, in particular, seem to have escaped the niche market of creative types that they've occupied for a while. The fact that they now have reasonable ways of running Windows software (via Boot Camp, Parallels, and VM Ware) is helping to fuel their adoption too.

In the newest Mac OS X release, Apple has introduced a new backup feature of its own. This program, dubbed Time Machine, is designed to do much the same thing that Windows Home Server backups do, with some differences. Instead of taking a backup snapshot of your hard drive each night, it actually creates hourly backups by making incremental backups of any files as they are changed, so you can go back and recover a file that you may have overwritten or deleted during the same day.

While Time Machine is designed to store its backups on an external drive, you can also specify a server share as a backup destination. This is where Windows Home Server can come into play. We expect many of you who own both Windows Home Server and an odd Mac or two to want to take advantage of this feature, as it lets you keep all of your backups in one place, safe on your Windows Home Server.

Time Machine is a great new feature in the newest version of Mac OS X 10.5 (Leopard), but are you out of luck if you haven't made the jump to that

OS yet? Not really, there are other Mac backup solutions out there that can save to a network share — we touch on those in this chapter as well.

Creating a Mac Backup Share

The first step in configuring Windows Home Server to act as a backup repository for Time Machine (or other backup application) is to create a shared folder. We recommend that you create a shared folder specifically to hold Mac backups. This keeps them separate from other public or private shared folders, both for security and to reduce the chance of accidental corruption of the backup files.

Follow these steps to create a backup share specifically for Mac backups.

1. **Log on to the Windows Home Server Console.**

2. **Click the Shared Folders tab.**

3. **Click the Add button.**

4. **Give the folder a name and a description (such as Mac Backups, or Sandy's Time Machine Backups).**

5. **Decide whether or not you want to use folder duplication.** If you don't, uncheck the Enable Folder Duplication box. Keep in mind that your Time Machine backups are going to be taking up a lot of space, and using folder duplication will double it. On the other hand, your Time Machine backups will be protected from a hardware failure if they are duplicated.

6. **Click Next.**

7. **Choose the level of access to give each user account.** Because Time Machine will only need to use one username to create its backups, we recommend that you only give one user account full access. This can be your existing user account, although you can create a user account just for this purpose.

8. **Click Finish to add the folder.**

> **NOTE** If you want to change any of the shared folder preferences later, such as to enable or disable folder duplication, or to change the user accounts that can access it, you can do so by double-clicking on the folder in the Console, as shown in Figure 23.1.

> **CROSS-REF** Chapter 12 introduces the Windows Home Server shared folder feature, and describes in detail how to create and manage them. Chapter 13 shows you how to access them, in particular from a Mac.

Now that you've created the shared folder, you need to make sure that you can access it from the Mac. Note that the Finder sidebar in Leopard has a new Shared section that lists accessible servers. If you can see the server listed there, you should be able to navigate to the Backup share you created. This is shown in Figure 23.2. If you can access the shared folder, try copying a file to it to make sure that you have both read and write access to the folder.

> **CROSS-REF** Follow the instructions in Chapter 13 for accessing shared folders if you need assistance in doing this.

FIGURE 23.1

Use Windows Home Server to create a shared folder for use as a repository for Mac backups.

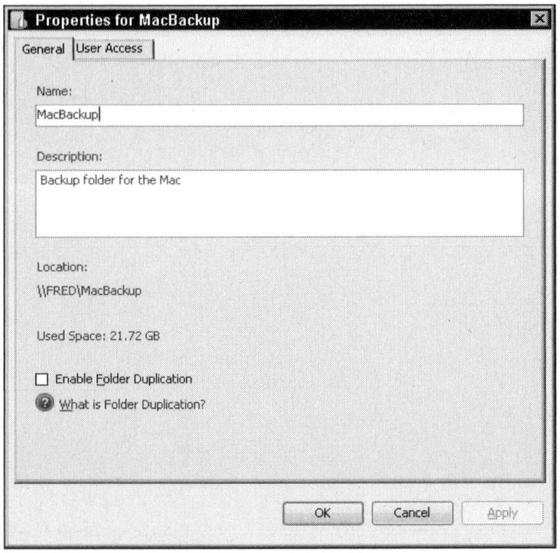

FIGURE 23.2

Access the shared folder that you created on the server.

Configuring Time Machine

You can change Time Machine settings in the System Preferences. You can access this by choosing System Preferences from the Apple menu, or by right-clicking the Time Machine icon in the dock and choosing Preferences. The Time Machine preferences window is shown in Figure 23.3.

There are not a lot of options to choose from in Time Machine. You can choose to turn it on or off, choose a destination disk, and choose folders or disks to exclude from the backup.

FIGURE 23.3

You configure Time Machine in System Preferences.

Enabling network folders for Time Machine

By default, Leopard doesn't allow Time Machine backups to be stored on a network shared folder. This of course prevents you from using Windows Home Server shared folders as a destination for Time Machine without some tweaking of the system settings.

To enable sharing to the backup shared folder you created, you need to perform the following steps:

1. **Open the Terminal utility.** You can find it in the Utilities folder. Choose Go ➪ Utilities from the Finder menu, and then double-click the Terminal icon.

2. **Enter the following on one line:** `defaults write com.apple.systempreferences TMShowUnsupportedNetworkVolumes 1`

3. **Press Enter.** You should now be able to use mounted shared folders as destination drives for Time Machine.

Setting the destination disk

You will use the shared folder that you created in the previous section to hold your Time Machine backups. Click the Change Disk button to access the list of potentially usable drives to use. If your shared folder is still mounted, it should be visible in this list, as shown in Figure 23.4.

The backup disk you selected now appears in the Time Machine Preferences window, along with information on the amount of space available on the disk.

Time Machine automatically schedules the next backup to occur two minutes after choosing a new destination disk. If you are not ready for the backup to begin — for instance, if you would like to have a chance to select drives and folders to exclude from the backup — turn Time Machine off using the switch.

> **NOTE** The first backup Time Machine backs up your entire system. As you might expect, it will take a long time to complete. The hourly incremental backups are much quicker.

FIGURE 23.4

Choose the disk to use for backups. Make sure that you choose the shared folder you created for backups.

Macintosh HD	79.4 GB
MacBook Backup	30.9 GB
Photos (fred)	31.4 GB
MacBackup (fred)	31.4 GB
Public (fred)	30.6 GB
None	

Cancel   Use for Backup

Setting other configuration options

Click the Options button to choose other configuration settings. You can choose folders and disks to exclude from the backup, and choose whether or not to have Time Machine alert you when the backup disk is full, as shown in Figure 23.5.

By default, disks other than your boot partition are excluded. You can include them by clicking the –(minus) button to remove them from the exclude list. If you would like to exclude other disks from the backup, click the + (plus) button and browse to the folder. Then click the Exclude button to add that folder to the list.

You can have Time Machine warn you when backups are deleted by selecting that option. If you don't have Time Machine notify you, your oldest backups will be deleted without warning when the backup drive is full.

FIGURE 23.5

Time Machine options include notifying you when the backup drive is full and excluding other drives and folders from the backup.

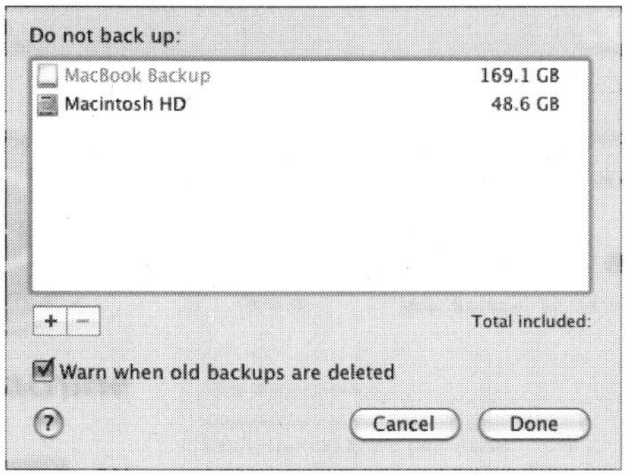

Do not back up:	
☐ MacBook Backup	169.1 GB
▨ Macintosh HD	48.6 GB

+ −   Total included:

☑ Warn when old backups are deleted

⑦   (Cancel) (Done)

Allocating storage space

Time Machine backups are simple. Just point to an external hard drive or network share, and it does all the work. As you may have noticed, there is a noticeable lack of backup options. There is a downside to this simplicity, however — Apple neglected to include any way to limit the size of the backups or even provide a way to prune older backups. Time Machine is designed to use up all of the free space on the destination hard drive before it starts deleting older backups.

Fortunately, the issue is partly solved when you use a network share as your backup destination. Time Machine is unable to use your Windows-formatted destination drive directly, so it creates a disk image on the folder automatically, using a *sparse bundle* image. A sparse bundle image is a disk image that looks like a huge disk to Leopard when it is mounted, but only occupies a small amount of space in reality until the drive is filled.

NOTE In our testing with Time Machine, if left to its own devices, it appears to create a sparse bundle image of about twice the maximum storage capacity of the folder that contains it. For example, if your shared folder is reporting 50GB free, a spare bundle image with a maximum size of about 100GB will be created. That might not seem practical, but in reality it doesn't matter much, as the actual reported free space in the image is the same as the folder that contains it.

As we mentioned, the issue is only partly solved by letting Time Machine create the sparse bundle image, because Time Machine doesn't give you the option of specifying the maximum size to use. Because of this, it will still eventually use up all available storage filling up the disk image. There is a way around this, however — you can create the disk image yourself and specify whatever maximum size you desire, and make Time Machine use that image for backups instead of the one that it created.

Creating a new disk image

Leopard includes a utility called, quite simply, Disk Utility. You may have used Disk Utility in the past to create images of CDs and DVD-ROMs or of hard-drives, but you can use it to create empty disk images as well. This is the tool that you need to use to create your own sparse bundle disk image for Time Machine. Follow these steps to create the disk image:

1. **Open Disk Utility.** You can find it in the Utilities folder. Choose Go ➪ Utilities from the Finder menu and then double-click the Disk Utility icon.

2. **In Disk Utility, shown in Figure 23.6, make sure none of the disks are selected on the left side and then click the New Image icon in the toolbar.**

FIGURE 23.6

You can use Disk Utility to create a disk image for Time Machine sized just the way you want it.

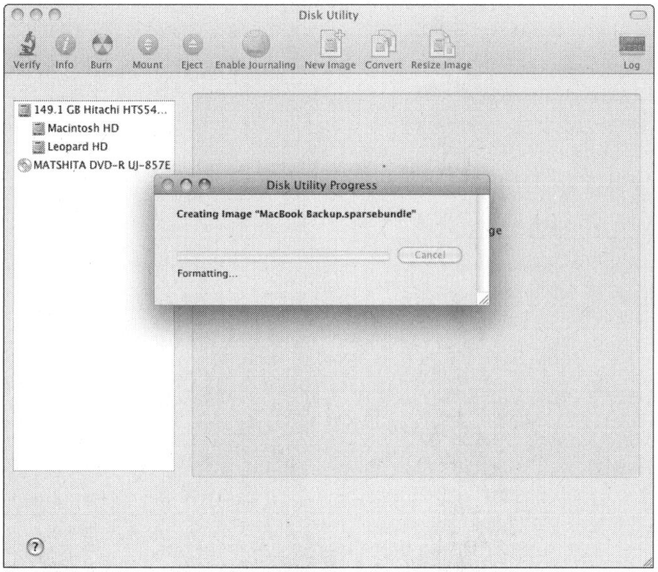

3. **Disk Utility will pop up a window where you can specify the parameters for the new image.** Navigate to your shared backup folder, shown in Figure 23.7.

4. **Choose a name for the share.** Choose a descriptive name for the image and enter it in the Save As box. Don't save the image just yet.

5. **Enter a volume name.** This should be the same as the volume name that Time Machine's sparse bundle was created with, and will be `Backup of <computername>`, where <computername> is the name of your Mac.

6. **Choose** Sparse bundle disk image **in the Image Format drop-down list.**

7. **Choose a volume size.** In order to back up your entire hard drive, it will have to be at least as large as that. If you tend to keep your drive full, we recommend that you create an image that is 1.5 to 2 times as large. To do this, choose Custom as your volume size, and enter the size of the disk you wish to use. Make sure you choose GB before you enter a size in Gigabytes.

8. **The Volume format should be Mac OS Extended (journaled).** This should be the default setting.

9. **Choose none for the encryption standard.** This is the default value.

10. **Leave the Partitions value as Single partition - Apple Partition Map.**

11. **Click the Create button.** The disk image will be created.

FIGURE 23.7

Create a disk image sized just the way you want it.

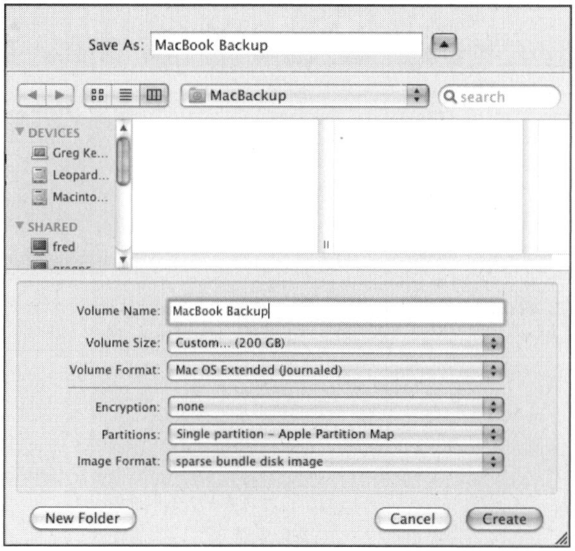

In order to use your new disk image as your Time Machine destination, we need to do two things with it. First of all, we need to copy the contents of the existing backup to it using Disk Utility. Second, we need to rename it to be the same as the sparse bundle image that Time Machine created so that it will use it. Follow these steps to copy the data:

1. **In the Finder, navigate to both of the sparse bundles and open them.** This will mount the drives in Finder so that we can see them in other applications.

2. **Launch Disk Utility.** You may still have it open from the previous step.

3. **Find the volume for the image you created.** You may need to expand the disk image to see it.

4. **Right-click on the volume, and choose Restore.**

5. **Drag the volume from the image created by Time Machine into the Restore dialog.**

6. **Click the Restore button to start the restoration.**

Once the restoration is complete, you need to rename the new sparse image so that Time Machine will see it. Unmount both disks by Right-clicking on them and choosing Eject. Then, navigate to the backup shared folder in the Finder, and rename the backups as follows:

1. **Rename the backup file created by Time Machine to something else.** Be sure to write the original name down, as you will need it for the next step.

2. **Rename the disk image you created to have the same name as the original Time Machine image.**

3. **Restart Time Machine in the System Preferences.** The next available backup should go to the new image.

4. **When you are convinced Time Machine can successfully backup to the new image, you can delete the old one.**

That was a lot of work just to get Time Machine working, but worth it if you want to be able to use a network share with it. Hopefully, as Time Machine matures it will gain the ability to make use of a network share without having to jump through hoops to get there.

Restoring Time Machine Backups

Once you configure Time Machine, your files will be backed up automatically whenever they change, every hour as long as the computer is powered on.

In order to see your past backup, Apple went a step beyond typical backup utilities in the presentation department. A Finder window with previous versions stretching off into the distance, along with a time line on the right side of the screen lets you see conceptually where in time you are. This interface is shown in Figure 23.8.

Restoring individual files

To access the Time Machine interface, click the Time Machine button in the dock. Select a position in the time line, or use the arrow buttons on the lower right to move forward and backward one version at a time. At any time you can browse the files as they existed at that point in time.

To restore a file or a group of files, select them in the Finder window for that backup, and click the Restore button. If a file exists in the same location in the folder, you have the option of overwriting it, keeping the original file (meaning the one currently on the hard drive), or keeping both.

FIGURE 23.8

Time Machine gives you a splashy interface for browsing your backups.

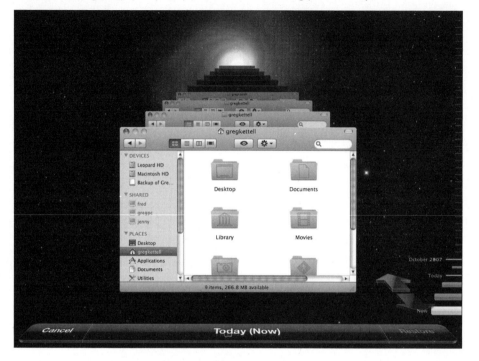

Restoring the system

Time Machine backups, much like with Windows Home Server backups, are intended to be usable for a "bare metal" restore. If for some reason your Mac's hard drive fails, you should only be out less than an hour's worth of work if your Time Machine backups are up to date.

Unfortunately, there doesn't appear to be a way to restore a complete backup from a network-shared Time Machine backup. There are, however, two other options — using the Migration Assistant to restore from the Time Machine backup, or copying the Time Machine backup drive image to an external drive and restoring from that.

Restoring from an external drive

One method for making use of your Time Machine backups for a system restore is to copy your backup drive image to an external drive, and then restore the files on the Mac.

The best way to do this is on the server itself: Log on to your Windows Home Server computer's desktop, and open your backup shared folder in Explorer. Plug in an external hard drive (a USB 2.0 drive will work fine). Keep in mind that the drive you choose will have to be large enough to hold the entire backup image. Note that Leopard can read from FAT32 or NTFS formatted disks.

Select all of the files in the backup shared folder (using Ctrl+A in Explorer) and copy them to the shared drive, as shown in Figure 23.9.

FIGURE 23.9

You can copy your disk image to an external drive for restoring files.

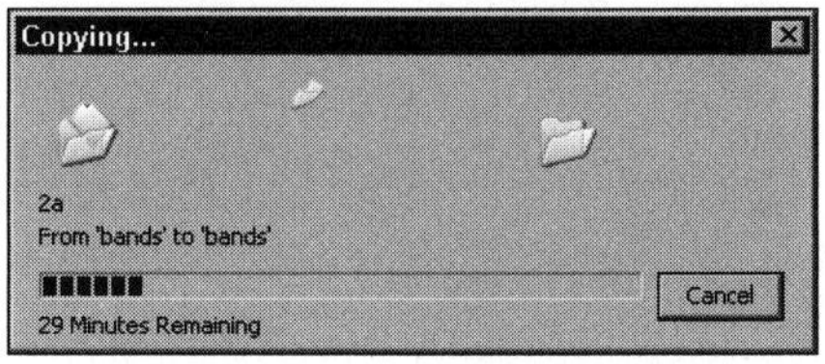

Follow these steps to restore from the external disk:

1. **Plug the external disk into the Mac you are restoring.**

2. **Boot with the Leopard installation DVD.** Hold down the Option button while booting, and choose the DVD when prompted.

3. **Choose a language for the installation.**

4. **At the Welcome screen, choose Utilities ⇨ Restores System From Backup from the menu.**

5. **Click Continue on the Restore Your System screen.**

6. **Select the disk image from the Select a Backup Source list when it appears and then click Continue.**

7. **Choose a backup date and time to restore from and click Continue.**

8. **Select the destination volume, which should be your new hard drive.**

9. **Click Restore to restore from the backup.**

Restoring using Migration Assistant

All Macs include a utility called Migration Assistant that allows you to copy your files and applications from an old Mac to a new one. With OS X 10.5 Leopard, Migration Assistant has gained the ability to restore these items from Time Machine backup as well.

To restore a Time Machine backup from Migration Assistant to a new hard drive, do the following:

1. **Install a fresh copy of OS X Leopard on the new hard drive.**

2. **Make sure you can access the backup disk image in the Finder.** Double-click on it to mount it.

3. **Launch Migration Assistant.** This is found in the Utilities folder.

4. **Choose to restore from a Time Machine backup, as shown in Figure 23.10.** Click Continue.

FIGURE 23.10

Migration Assistant makes it possible for you to recover your user data from a Time Machine backup.

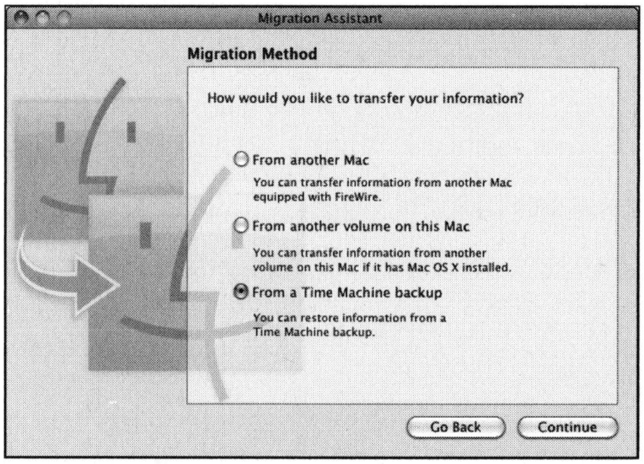

5. **Choose the mounted disk image as the system to transfer and click Continue.**

6. **After the image is scanned, it lets you choose which user to restore.** Make a choice and click Continue.

7. **Select the items to restore, including Applications and Files and Folders, as shown in Figure 23.11.** In most cases you will want to restore all of them. Then click Continue.

8. **After the files are restored, reconfigure Time Machine to start backing up again.**

FIGURE 23.11

Choose what you want to restore from the Migration Assistant Wizard.

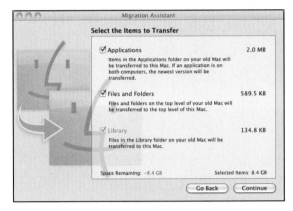

Backing Up Older Macs

Unfortunately, Time Machine is only available on Mac OS X 10.5 Leopard, and is not available for older versions of that OS. In our opinion, this feature alone is well worth the upgrade to Leopard, but for whatever reason you may not wish to do so yet.

Fortunately, there are both commercial and freeware/shareware backup solutions for older Mac computers that will work with a network shared folder. Here is a brief look at a couple of them.

iBackup

iBackup, shown in Figure 23.12, is a DonateWare backup utility that is very flexible in terms of backup scheduling. It will support backing up to multiple devices as well. This means you can schedule a full system backup to a Windows Home Server share, but also back up some folders (such as your Documents folder) to another location or even a remote drive such as .Mac iDisk. There is no charge to use iBackup; however, donations are accepted.

ON the WEB You can find iBackup at `www.grapefruit.ch/iBackup/`.

SuperDuper!

SuperDuper! is offered in both free and pay versions. The free version lets you back up and clone drives to a disk image on either an external hard drive or on a network share. The pay version includes additional features such as scheduling, Smart Update (which performs an incremental update on an existing backup), and scripting. SuperDuper! at work is shown in Figure 23.13.

FIGURE 23.12

iBackup is a free but powerful backup utility for Mac OS X machines.

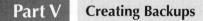

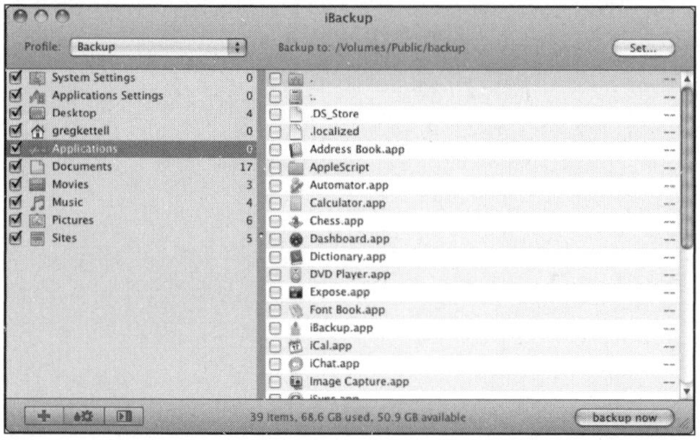

FIGURE 23.13

SuperDuper! Is a backup solution for older Macs, and it still works with Leopard.

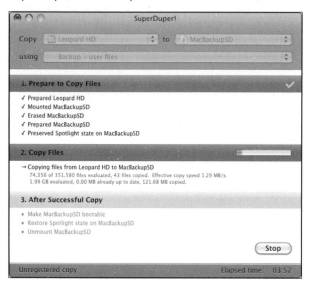

ON the WEB You can find Shirt Pocket's SuperDuper! at www.shirt-pocket.com.

Summary

Windows Home Server's backup feature is terrific, but if you also own Macintosh computers, you are not left out in the cold when it comes to using Windows Home Server for backups. Time Machine, a feature of OS X 10.5 Leopard, can make use of a network share on Windows Home Server as its backup repository.

To configure Time Machine to work with Windows Home Server, you should first create a shared folder specifically for the backups. While you could use an existing share, such as the public share, a special folder will allow you to tailor settings such as user access and folder duplication specifically for the Mac backups.

Once you've created a share, you need to create a disk image for Time Machine to save to. If you don't, Time Machine will create a disk image automatically, and it will expand to use all of the storage space on the shared folder by default. Disk Utility will allow you to create the sparse bundle disk image that you need quickly.

Time Machine backups are browsed using a special user interface that lets you page forward and backwards through your files, choosing to restore files from any backup point in the past. You can also do whole system restore, but this will require you to copy the disk image files to an external drive that you can then plug into the Mac.

You can, however, make use of the Migration Assistant utility to recover all files from an existing Time Machine backup in the event your Mac needs a complete hard drive replacement.

Chapter 24

Backing Up Server Folders

We've discussed the importance of backing up your computer files, and how Windows Home Server backups can allow for anything from the restoration of a single file all the way to bare-metal recovery of a crashed computer. We've also shown how the folder duplication feature of Windows Home Server shared folders allows you to ensure your shared files can survive even if one of your server's hard drives croaks.

As reliable as using multiple disks can be, however, your server could still be subjected to a catastrophic failure, costing you everything that you've stored on it. Extreme weather conditions such as lightning or hurricanes, fire, or even theft can leave you without any recourse for restoring the files stored on your home server. Replacing the server is easy. Losing years of personal and irreplaceable data can be impossible.

At this point, you may be wondering how you can protect the files on the server itself? In fact, you have several options depending on your budget and your backup and recovery needs. These options range from backing up some or all of your shared folders to backing up your entire Windows Home Server system. To protect against a household catastrophe, you can take your backup media off-site so that it will always be recoverable.

In this chapter, we show you a few of the options that you have for backups along with the pros and cons of each solution.

Deciding What to Include

The most important thing to consider when deciding on a backup strategy is what to include. This is doubly important on Windows Home Server because many of your files are stored multiple times due to the folder duplication feature.

Just about every backup solution lets you choose to include or exclude specific folders on your system, and you should take advantage of this to customize a backup set that is right for you and your chosen backup solution.

Full system backups

The choice of which files to back up depends on your choice of a backup solution as well. If you use a hard drive or a tape drive backup solution, and it has the capacity to back up the entire server, go ahead and do it — you should be able to restore the entire system in the event of a failure. Unfortunately, there are no full system backup utilities that are guaranteed to work with Windows Home Server. It is important that any such service be Windows Home Server aware, because it is absolutely critical when restoring an image to get all of the myriad of storage devices mapped to the correct place for Windows Home Server to function.

Shared folder backups

Given most of the important files that you store on Windows Home Server are in the shared folders, you should consider, at a minimum, backing up these folders. For bandwidth limited backups, such as online backups, you should choose shared folders based on their content. For instance, you may want to include your user or public shared folders, as well as photos and videos that you have created. On the other hand, you may not wish to include a folder used to store large video files from a digital video recorder (DVR).

Therefore, the recommendation is to back up the shared folders. Just make sure that any files that you need to be able to restore the server (such as add-in Microsoft Software Installers, or MSIs, and installation files for other programs) are stored on one of your shared folders.

Backing Up to an Online Service

An increasing number of options for online backup and recovery have become available with the advent of ubiquitous broadband Internet connections. While this option is obviously not going to be as fast as a local backup, it can be a convenient option for those with modest backup needs.

The advantages of online backup and recovery options is the fact that your backed up files are always available as they are just a click away over an Internet link. Your backups are by their very nature off-site, so no matter what happens to your local server, you will still be able to recover your files later.

Downsides to online backups are, of course, the fact that the speed is limited to the maximum throughput that you can get from your Internet connection, which is usually a factor of twenty or more slower than most local area network (LAN) connections. This limits the amount of data that you can practically store over such shares, and makes online backups most useful for archiving files that you may have stored in your shared folders. Backups of your entire Windows Home Server box, including the backups from other computers, will not be feasible.

NOTE Several online backup providers are only designed to work with Windows XP or Vista. Installation on a server OS such as Windows Home Server requires a server or professional license. This section only includes providers proven to work with Windows Home Server.

Let's go over a few of the options available for online backups.

Using KeepVault

KeepVault is an Internet-hosted backup service for Windows computers. One of their newest products is a backup and restore add-in for Windows Home Server that makes it easy to archive the files in your shared folders to the Internet. KeepVault's Web site is shown in Figure 24.1.

At the time of this writing, KeepVault is a subscription-based service that requires an annual commitment. This subscription price, however, allows for virtually unlimited server storage. Unfortunately, they do not currently offer a trial mode so that you can see how it works in advance.

ON the WEB Take a look at KeepVault, view their current pricing, or subscribe to the service at www.keepvault.com.

Installing and backing up to KeepVault

KeepVault is installed as a Windows Home Server add-in with a custom Console tab. When you subscribe to the service, you are given your account credentials. Install KeepVault according to these instructions.

1. **Download the KeepVault Windows Home Server add-in.**
2. **Install it through the Console's Settings window, on the Add-ins tab.** The Console must be restarted after the installation is complete in order to make the new tab visible.
3. **Click the KeepVault tab on the Console.**
4. **Choose the server shared folders that you would like to keep protected.** The KeepVault service ensures that all files are archived to the KeepVault server along with any changes that are made in the future.

FIGURE 24.1

KeepVault allows you to back up your Windows Home Server shared folders online.

Restoring from KeepVault

In the event of a catastrophic Windows Home Server failure, you can restore the files and folders that you archived with KeepVault. Follow these steps to recover your system and its shared folders in the event a total replacement is required:

1. Install new Windows Home Server hardware and operating system.
2. Download and install the KeepVault add-in.
3. Enter your subscription e-mail address and KeepVault serial number to gain access to your files.
4. Click the KeepVault tab in the Windows Home Server Console.
5. Click the Restore Files option to recover the files.

Using IDrive-E

IDrive-E is another Internet-hosted backup service. While they don't provide custom support for Windows Home Server through the use of an add-in, you aren't limited to shared folders as you are with the KeepVault solution. With Window IDrive-E, you can back up any file on the server that you like.

IDrive-E is available at reasonable monthly rates for the professional version. There is also a free 2 GB basic version with the full functionality included. While this isn't enough to do any sort of serious backup, it is enough to use as a trial amount to see if you like it.

ON the WEB You can download and install IDrive-E from www.idrive.com. Check here for more information about the product and current pricing.

Installing IDrive-E

After signing up, download the IDrive-E application to your Windows Home Server machine. Follow these steps to install it:

1. **Run the IDrive-ESetup.exe program from the server's desktop to launch the IDrive-E Setup Wizard, shown in Figure 24.2.** Click Next to begin.

FIGURE 24.2

Install IDrive-E using the setup wizard.

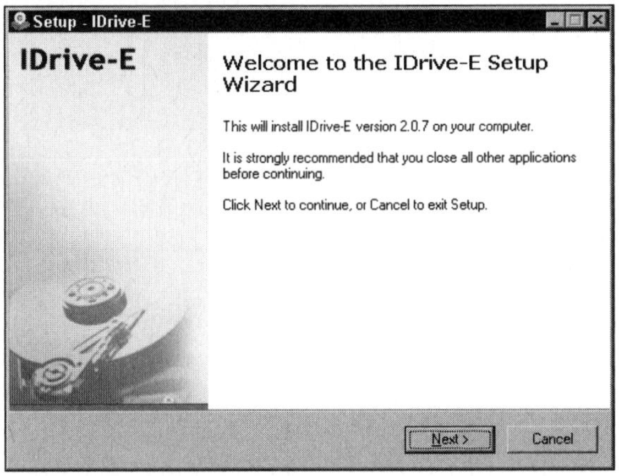

2. **Accept the license agreement and click Next.**
3. **Accept the default location for the installation,** C:\Program Files\IDriveE. Click Next. The installation will now proceed.
4. **Click Finish when it is complete.**

Choosing what to back up with IDrive-E

When installation is complete, an IDrive-E icon is created on your desktop. Double-click this icon to run the program. The first time you run it, you are prompted for your account information. Once it is entered and verified, you will see the IDrive-E Classic interface, shown in Figure 24.3.

FIGURE 24.3

IDrive-E is an online backup solution that works for Windows Home Server shares.

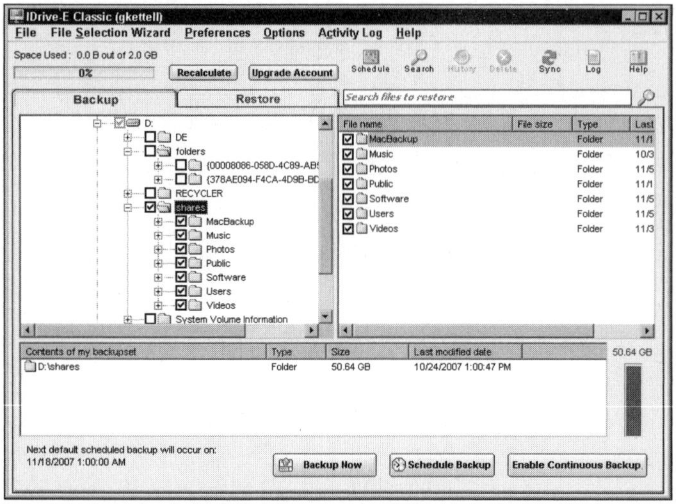

You can choose what to back up with IDrive-E by browsing the folder tree on the left, placing a check next to the folders you are backing up. More than likely, the files that you will want to back up the most are your shared folders, but IDrive can't see shared folders unless you map a drive letter to them first.

While this is an option, another is to back up directly from the shared folder located in D:\shares. Once you've chosen the files you want to back up, use one of the following options to perform the backup.

Backup Now

The Backup Now button will start a backup immediately, launching the Backing up window shown in Figure 24.4. All files and folder selected in the IDrive-E interface will be backed up, up to any server storage limits you may have.

Schedule Backup

Your most likely backup scenario will be to schedule automatic backups of your server to run on a nightly basis. Click the Schedule Backup button to run the scheduler, shown in Figure 24.5.

FIGURE 24.4

Backup Now lets you perform an immediate backup of all files whenever you choose.

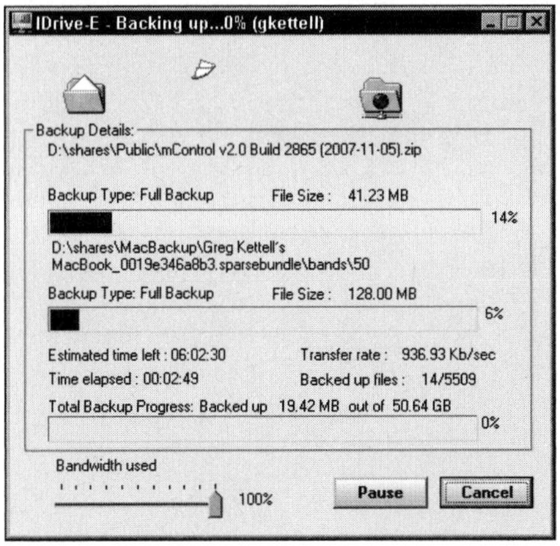

The default server backup time is daily at 1:00 AM. As this is within the default Windows Home Server backup window, you may wish to reschedule so as to not impact the speed of both backups by having them run at the same time. Click in the Use Custom Backup Time radio button to enable the calendar and time controls for selecting your own custom time. There are some other options for the scheduler as well, and they are described as follows:

■ **Email notification options:** You can choose to have a notification e-mailed to you on the completion (or failure) of a backup with status information.

■ **Desktop notification:** A status file will be linked to your Windows Home Server desktop that you can look at to check the results of a scheduled backup.

■ **Backup when idle:** This option backs up the computer only when it is sitting idle, which means when nobody is logged on to the computer's desktop. Given Windows Home Server is seldom used from the desktop, this option can remain disabled.

■ **Automatic power off after scheduled backup:** This option is intended for desktop computers, not servers. Leave it unchecked.

■ **Start the missed scheduled backup when the computer is turned on:** This is another option intended for desktops.

Click OK to save the backup schedule.

FIGURE 24.5

IDrive-E is an online backup solution that will work for Windows Home Server shares.

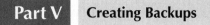

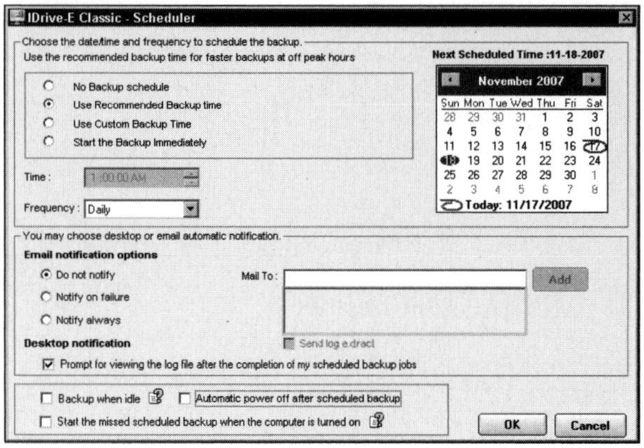

Enable Continuous Backup

The Enable Continuous Backup option monitors your folders, looking for small files (under 50 MB) that have been changed within the past 10 minutes. These files will be automatically backed up.

Restoring IDrive Backups

Files that have been backed up using IDrive can be restored using the Restore tab of the IDrive-E Classic interface, shown in Figure 24.6. To restore, follow these steps:

1. Choose the backup date and time from the drop-down list at the bottom right of the dialog.

2. Select the folders or files to restore in the tree view.

3. Click the Restore Now button.

FIGURE 24.6

Browse the backup to select folders to restore.

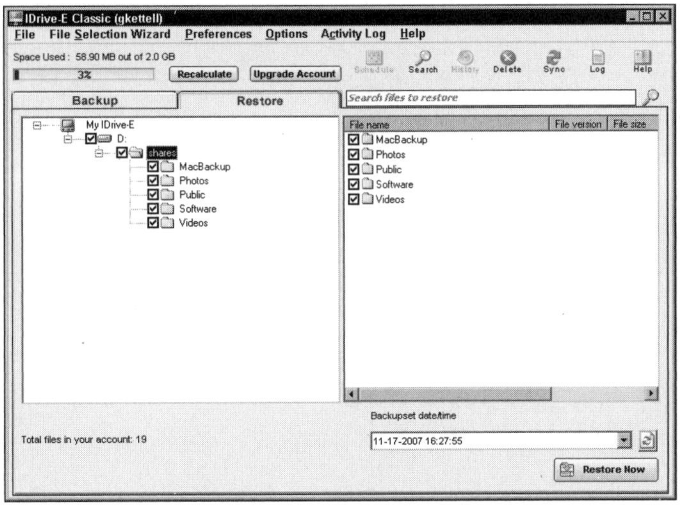

Using Jungle Disk

Jungle Disk is an online storage system based on Amazon.com's Simple Storage Service (S3). S3 is a pay-as-you-go service that lets you store as much information as you like — however, you are charged a fee per gigabyte (GB) storage and per terabyte (TB) transfer rates. As a front end for S3, Jungle Disk allows you to store and access your files from Amazon data centers all over the country.

ON the WEB Find out more information about Jungle Disk and how to use it at `www.jungle disk.com`. If you would like to learn more about the Amazon S3 service on which it is based, visit `http://aws.amazon.com/s3`.

At the time of this writing, Jungle Disk has promised a Windows Home Server add-in version of the program, though it is not yet available. Find more information about Jungle Disk for Windows Home Server at `www.jungledisk.com/whs.shtml`.

Installing Jungle Disk

In order to use Jungle Disk, you must sign up for the Amazon S3 service. There will also be a one-time charge for the Jungle Disk program itself, although a free trial is available.

Download Jungle Disk for Windows, and transfer it to your Windows Home Server computer. Run the `JungleDiskInstaller.exe` program and follow the steps in the installation wizard. The first step is the licensing agreement, shown in Figure 24.7.

FIGURE 24.7

Jungle Disk is a front end for Amazon's S3 storage service.

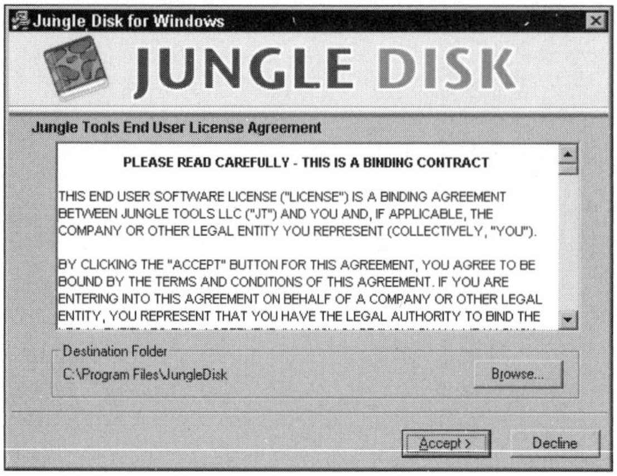

1. Accept the license terms.

2. Accept the option to run Jungle Disk automatically on startup.

3. If you don't have an Amazon S3 account, leave the option enabled to launch the signup page.

4. Click Finish.

5. Follow the signup instructions for Amazon S3 if you need to.

6. **In the Jungle Disk configuration, enter your S3 Access Key ID and your Secret Access Key, as shown in Figure 24.8.** You can choose a custom Bucket Name if you like; this allows you to differentiate files from your Windows Home Server backup with those from another computer.

CAUTION   Jungle Disk attempts to bind its My Jungle Disk to http port 80 by default. Since this port is used by Internet Information Services to provide access to Web content, including Remote Access, Jungle Disk cannot map the drive.

As a workaround, you can download a product called WebDrive from `www.webdrive.com`, and create a WebDAV drive mapped to `http://localhost:2667` to access your Jungle Disk in Windows Explorer, but this is not a free solution. Until the Windows Home Server edition of Jungle Disk is available, you can make due with accessing the Web interface using the `http://local host:2667` URL.

FIGURE 24.8

Enter your Amazon S3 information.

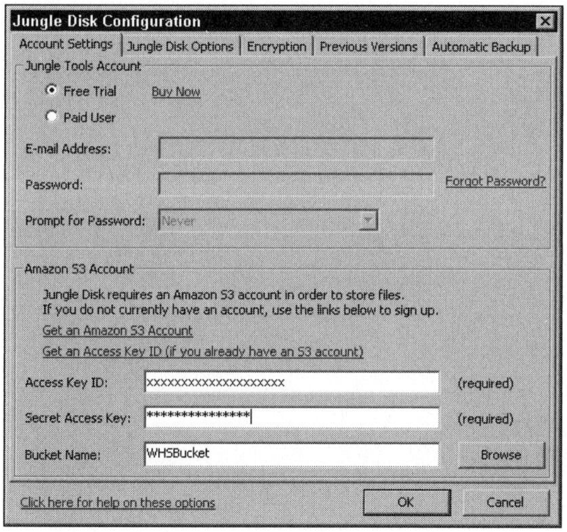

Backing Up Files

To perform backups in Jungle Disk, you must first choose which folders and files to include. Follow these steps:

1. **Open the Jungle Disk Activity Monitor through the Start Menu or through the tray icon.**

2. **Choose Backup ⇨ Configure Automatic Backup from the menu.**

3. **Click the Automatic Backup tab, shown in Figure 24.9.**

4. **Choose a time interval for your backups in the Automatically backup my files every list.** If you choose a daily or longer interval, choose the backup time using the slider control that appears.

5. **Click Add to add a folder to the backup.**

6. **Choose Entire Directory, and click Next.**

7. **Browse to or enter the path to the shared folder you wish to back up; such as, \\servername\public, as shown in Figure 24.10.** Then click OK.

FIGURE 24.9

Select files and folders to back up in the Jungle Disk Configuration dialog box.

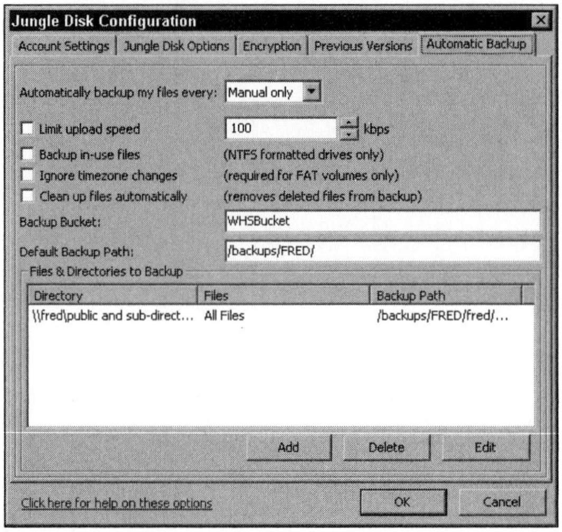

FIGURE 24.10

Browse your drives to choose folders to include in the backup.

8. **If you want to back up all files, leave that option checked.** If you only want to include or exclude certain file types, choose those options and then the file extensions to include or exclude. Click Next when done.

9. **Enter a list of directories (folders) and files to exclude from the backup, if any.** Click Next.

10. **Enter a backup path.** We recommend that you leave the default path set so that your files are organized on your Jungle Disk in an easy-to-find manner.

11. **Click Backup Preview if you would like to see which files will be included in the backup and how much space they will occupy on the server.**

12. **Repeats Steps 5 through 11 for each folder you wish to include in the backup.**

13. **Click OK when done.**

Once you have chosen the files to back up, you can either wait for your automatic backup to take place, or do a manual backup. Choose Backup ➪ Start Backup now to begin. The activity monitor shown in Figure 24.11 tracks your progress.

FIGURE 24.11

The Jungle Disk Activity Monitor displays your backup status.

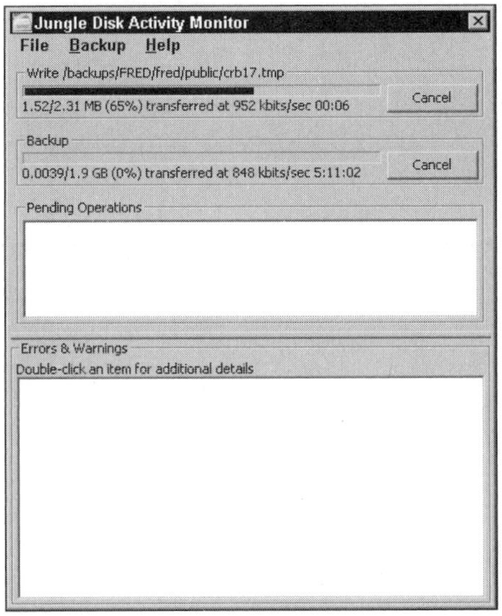

Restoring with Jungle Disk

To restore files from a Jungle Disk backup, do the following:

1. **Choose Backup ➪ Restore from the Jungle Disk Activity Monitor to open the Restore files dialog box, shown in Figure 24.12.**

2. **Browse the file tree and select either a file or a folder to restore.**

3. **Click Restore selected folder to add a folder, or double-click on a filename to add a file to the Restore list.**

4. Repeat Steps 2 and 3 for all folders and files you wish to restore.

5. Click Start Restore to begin the restoration.

FIGURE 24.12

The Jungle Disk Activity Monitor and the Restore files screen.

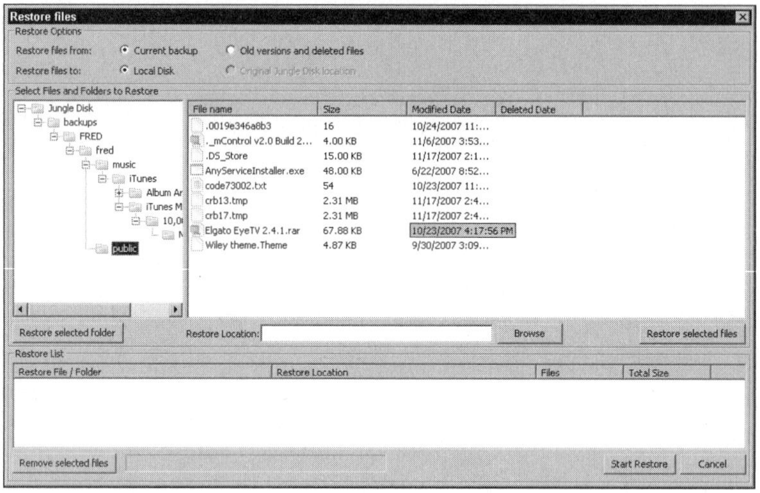

Backing Up to an External Hard Drive

If you don't relish the idea of paying a monthly fee for an online backup service, or are concerned about someone else having control over your precious data, you can opt for the tried-and-true local backup option. This option will require you to use an external disk or tape drive.

The advantage of the local backup as opposed to the online option is that local backups and restores are much faster, particularly when you are doing a full-system backup. The downside is that you have to remove your external disk from your house in order for it to be truly secure. After all, the same misfortune that could befall your Windows Home Server computer could also affect your backup device.

To back up to an external (USB) drive, you can use the Windows Backup and Restore Wizard to select folders (including shared folders) to back up. First, you need an external disk formatted with the (NTFS) file system. You can do this in Disk Manager (accessible by choosing Start ⇨ Administrate Tools ⇨ Computer Management, and then selecting Disk Management). Create a single partition on the disk and format it as NTFS, as shown in Figure 24.13.

FIGURE 24.13

Format your backup disk with the NTFS file system.

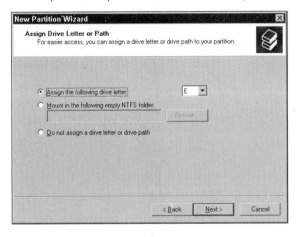

CAUTION   When you attach an external disk to the server, it is shown on the Server Storage tab in the Console. Leave it in the Non Storage Hard Drive category, as adding it to the storage pool will erase any data saved on the disk.

Scheduling backups

After you have a disk formatted with these options, make note of the drive letter that Windows Home Server assigns to the disk. You will need to know it to use it as a backup destination.

Follow these steps to configure a backup:

1. **Run the Backup or Restore Wizard by choosing Start ⇨ Accessories ⇨ System Tools ⇨ Backup.** Click Next.

2. **Choose Back up files and settings.** Click Next.

3. **Choose Let me choose what to back up.** Click Next.

4. **Using the Items to Back Up window, select the folders and files you want to include in the backup.** You can browse to a network path and choose your shared folders, as shown in Figure 24.14. Click Next when done.

5. **Choose the drive letter for the external drive that you have attached, as shown in Figure 24.15, and click Next.**

FIGURE 24.14

Use the Backup or Restore Wizard to configure a backup.

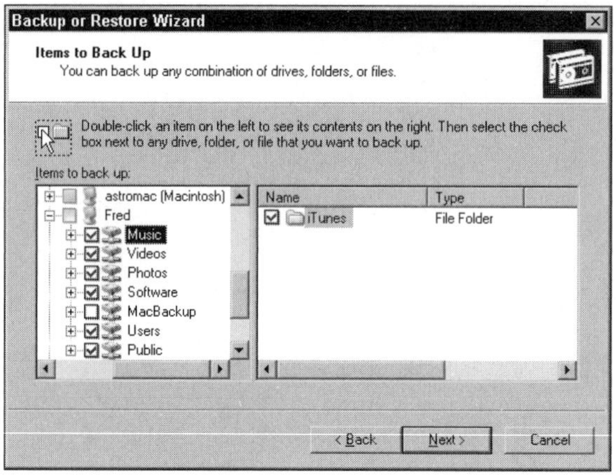

FIGURE 24.15

Format your backup disk with the NTFS file system.

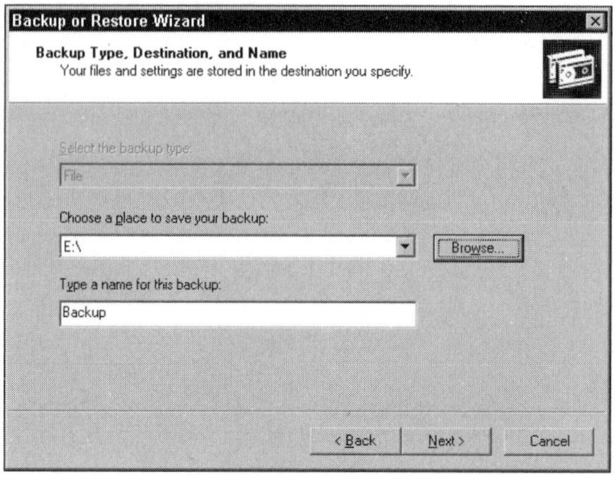

6. **On the Completing the Backup or Restore Wizard page, click the Advanced button to schedule this backup.**

7. **Select the type of backup.** Normal will back up all of the files. Click Next.

8. **Choose whether you want to verify the data after the backup.** We recommend this option; because the backup will be unattended, you won't notice the extra time. Click Next.

9. **Choose whether to append the backup to existing backups, or to replace the existing backup.** If it is a normal backup, choose replace. Click Next.

10. **Choose whether to run the backup now or to schedule it to run later.** If you schedule it for later, enter a name for the backup so you can see it in the scheduler. Click Schedule to choose a time to run the backup, and click OK.

11. **Choose an account to use to schedule the backup.** The Administrator account that you are logged in as is entered as the default. Enter the password and confirm, and then click OK. The backup name and schedule are entered, as shown in Figure 24.16.

FIGURE 24.16

Choose a name and scheduled time for the backup.

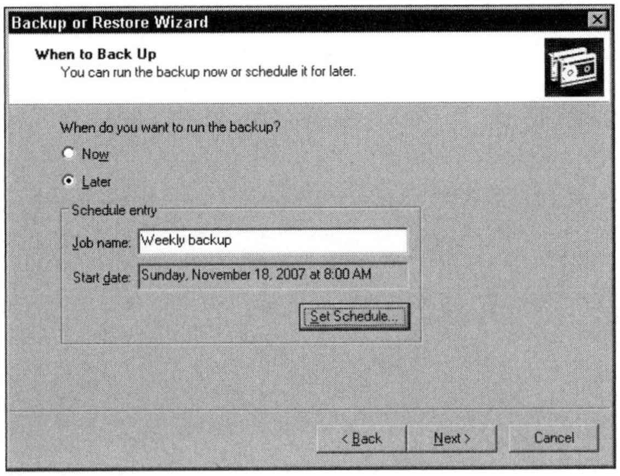

12. **On the final wizard page, shown in Figure 24.17, click Finish to schedule the backup.**

Restoring backups

Restoring your backups is the reverse of scheduling them. Follow these steps:

1. **Start the Restore Wizard by choosing Start ⇨ All Programs ⇨ Accessories ⇨ System Tools ⇨ Backup. Click Next.**

2. **Choose Restore files and settings, and click Next.**

3. **Browse your backup folders, and choose the files and folders to restore.** Click Next.

4. **If you want to restore the files to a different location, click Advanced.** Choose Alternate location, and browse to where you want the files. Click Next.

5. **Choose whether restored files should leave existing files of the same name, replace existing files if they are older than the backup, or simply replace existing files.** Click Next.

6. **Choose whether to restore security settings, junction points, and mount points.** Click Next.

7. **Click Finish to restore the files.**

FIGURE 24.17

Finalize the backup to schedule the task.

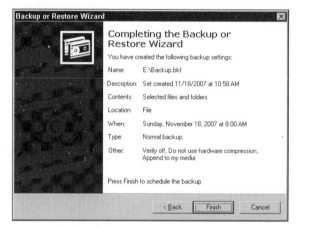

Changing scheduled backup tasks

Your backup schedules aren't set in stone. If you would like to delete or temporarily disable a scheduled backup, or change the time when it runs, use the Windows Task Scheduler, shown in Figure 24.18.

To modify a scheduled backup, follow these steps:

1. **Click Start ➪ Control Panel.**

2. **Right-click on Scheduled Tasks and click Open.**

3. **Double-click the task you wish to change.** This will open the task properties dialog.

4. **If you would like to disable the task, uncheck the Enabled checkbox.** Disabling the backup is preferable to deleting it if you only want backups stopped temporarily.

5. **Click the Schedule tab to edit the task start time and frequency.** On this tab, you can choose how often to run the task (daily, weekly, monthly, and so on) as well as choose the time of day you would like the task to run.

6. **Click OK to accept your backup task changes.**

FIGURE 24.18

Use the task scheduler to make adjustments to your backup schedules.

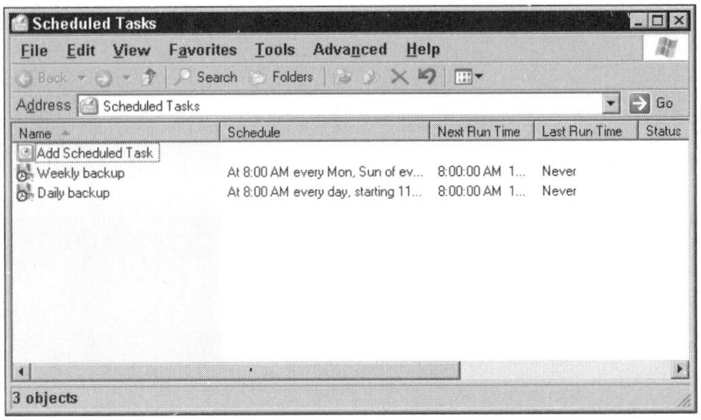

Summary

Windows Home Server has your client computer backup and recovery needs covered. With Windows Home Server backups, you can restore just a few files all the way up to a bare-metal recovery of the computer. Folder duplication adds a layer of protection to the server itself, ensuring that shared folders that make use of this feature can be recovered in the event of a single hard-drive failure.

Recovery from more than this isn't included in the Windows Home Server package. If you would like to be able to back up files on the server itself, you will need to employ a third-party removable hardware or online backup system to archive your files.

The decision of what to back up depends on the backup method that you choose, which is based on ease of recovery and your budget. You can choose a solution that only backs up your shared folder content or choose a solution that can recover a server from its bare metal (wiped clean) state.

Online backups through a service are one option. Although they're slow and involve a monthly fee that can range from trivial to expensive, online backups can be the safest choice because your backups occur behind the scenes to a safe location. You don't have to remember to keep taking the backup drive with you when you leave the house to protect your backup data.

Hard-drive backups are the simplest way to go for local backups. You don't need any additional software; simply use the Backup and Restore utility that is included with Windows Home Server to configure and schedule the backups. Back up to an external disk or tape drive so that you can take the media with you, ensuring that a localized catastrophe won't eradicate your backups.

Part VI

Building a Media Hub

Chapter 25

Configuring Media Library Sharing

From computers, to game consoles, to dedicated media players, it seems that almost every new electronic device announced for the home offers the capability to stream media. These devices all need to stream their media from somewhere — and just as streaming clients are proliferating, so are media servers.

Windows Home Server is getting into the media streaming server act as well by offering a Windows Media Connect (WMC) compatible media server that can stream files to most UPnP AV/DLNA compatible devices. (If you are confused about that alphabet soup we just described, don't worry — this chapter clears things up a bit regarding the TLAs [Three Letter Acronyms] of the media streaming world.)

Suffice it to say that with Windows Home Server media streaming, you can share your music files, photos, and even video files with a wide variety of connected devices.

For example, if you have a game console such as the Microsoft Xbox 360 or the Sony PlayStation 3, then you probably already know that these devices are much more than mere game players — they are multimedia powerhouses capable of working with all sorts of media content, including media streamed from your server. Some other Consumer Electronics (CE) devices are also capable of streaming media.

Explaining the Terms

You may have been confused about the acronyms we threw out at you in the opening paragraph. That's quite understandable; we're confused by them sometimes, too! Before we get too far into this chapter, though, it's a good idea to present you with a list of terms and their meanings:

- **CE:** Consumer electronics. CE companies build living room entertainment devices such as set top boxes, DVD players, VCRs, and so on. CE companies include Sony, Toshiba, Samsung, and Panasonic, among others.

- **DLNA:** The Digital Living Network Alliance. The DLNA is a consortium of major CE companies, computer companies, and mobile device manufacturers dedicated to defining interoperability standards for media interoperability between such devices. Client devices that support DLNA should be able to stream media from DLNA-enabled servers, including Windows Home Server.

- **HME:** Home Media Ecosystem. This is Microsoft's latest term for WMC technology.

- **MCE:** Media Center Edition software for Windows XP MCE and Vista Premium/Ultimate editions. MCE serves as the backbone for home theater PCs. Windows Home Server does not support MCE at the present time; however, you can use server media shares to store MCE-acquired content.

- **MCX:** Media Center Extenders. These are devices designed to serve as extensions to MCE computers. Such devices are not automatically compatible with Windows Home Server unless they also support WMC technology. The Xbox 360 is an example of an MCX device that can work with both types of content.

- **Renderer:** Another name for a playback device. It *renders* the streamed video on a screen.

- **UPnP AV:** Audio and Video interoperability protocols defined by the Universal Plug and Play Forum. These protocols form the basis of DLNA certification.

- **WMC:** Windows Media Connect. This is Microsoft's UPnP AV compatible protocol used in such products as Windows Media Player, Xbox 360, Windows Vista, and last but not least, Windows Home Server.

ON the WEB Specifications for the UPnP AV standards can be found on the UPnP Forum's Web site at `www.upnp.org/specs/av`. The Digital Living Network Alliance can be found at `www.dlna.org/en/industry/home`.

Enabling Media Streaming

As we've mentioned, Windows Home Server provides three shared folders specifically for media streaming. They are the Music, Photos, and Videos shared folders, and they cannot be removed. While authorized users can place content into these folders and use software that accesses media directly from these folders (such as iTunes or the Zune client software), you can't use the server's media streaming capabilities until you enable them. You do this in the Settings panel of the Console, shown in Figure 25.1. Follow these steps to enable streaming media:

1. Log onto the Console.
2. Click the Settings button to access the Settings panel.

3. Click the Media Sharing button on the left side of the Settings panel.

4. Select the On radio buttons for the folders you wish to enable media sharing for. You can enable sharing for the Music, Photos, and Videos folders independently.

FIGURE 25.1

You must enable media streaming in the Console.

That's all there is to it! Now your server can stream whatever supported media content you can fit onto the folders. Now, we'll take a look at some of the specific content that you can share.

Sharing Photos

Photos used to be easy — you'd fill up a roll of film with your family photos, take it to be developed, and then (after everybody had oohed and aahed over the pictures) put into a shoebox for safe keeping. As funny as that sounds, at least they were organized somewhat. Today with digital cameras everywhere, even in our cellular phones and PDAs (Personal Data Assistants), it's easy to get disorganized. With the Photos shared folder in Windows Home Server, you now have a single giant digital shoebox to hold all of your family photos. With folder duplication, they are safe from potential hardware failure. Best of all, with media streaming you can now access your photos from just about anywhere in the house.

Windows Home Server supports most of the common image file types and can stream them to clients. Table 25.1 presents a list of them.

TABLE 25.1

Supported Photo Formats

Format	File Extensions
Bitmap	.bmp
Graphics Interchange Format	.gif
Joint Photographic Experts Group	.jpeg .jpg
Portable Network Graphics	.png
Tagged Image File Format	.tif, .tiff

Photos shared in Windows Home Server can be streamed and displayed in any supported client. Figure 25.2 shows Windows Media Player 11 (Vista version) accessing a photo share from Windows Home Server.

NOTE The Windows XP version of Windows Media Player 11 doesn't contain a WMC client, and so it is unable to view media streamed from Windows Home Server. In order to stream media to a Windows XP machine, you need to use different client software. Nero Showtime and the On2Share plug-in for Winamp and Windows Media player are two popular programs that will do this.

FIGURE 25.2

Photo sharing can be used to stream a variety of image file types.

Sharing Music

It doesn't seem all that long ago that people lugged portable CD players around. Now, however, everybody has ripped their CD collections to mp3s or other formats. Windows Home Server can centralize everybody's music in one central location in the Music folder. You can even include playlist files so that the kids' music (or so they call it) won't accidentally be played by the adults, and vice versa. Table 25.2 shows the audio file formats that are streamable by Windows Home Server.

TABLE 25.2

Supported Audio Formats

Format	File Extensions
Advanced System Format	.asf
mp3	.mp3
Wave	.wav
Windows Media Audio	.wma

If you have music in other formats, such as the Advanced Audio Coding (AAC) format iTunes uses, you must first convert it to a supported format with a compatible program. iTunes itself can convert music files to mp3s as long as they weren't purchased in the iTunes store.

NOTE Music that is copy protected with Digital Rights Management (DRM) encryption cannot be streamed from Windows Home Server, as it has no way to verify the recipient of the music is the legitimate purchaser. Music files of this type can be stored on Windows Home Server, and played back from the share by the PC that is licensed to play them.

Sharing Video

Digital video is starting to become as ubiquitous as digital photographs and music. Homemade video comes from digital camcorders and even cellular phones, and DVRs (digital video recorders) and MCE-based home theater computers are a lot more commonplace. All of this content has to go somewhere (and video files can be quite large); a Windows Home Server with its potentially huge amount of storage seems like the perfect place (see Figure 25.3). Table 25.3 shows video formats supported by Windows Home Server.

Supported Video Formats

Format	File Extensions
Audio/Video Interleave	.avi
Microsoft Recorded TV show (from MCE)	.dvr-ms
MPEG-1	.mpg, .mpeg
MPEG-2	.mpg, .mpeg, .mp2
Windows Media Video	.wmv

 **NOTE** High definition content (video of 1280 × 720 or 1920 × 1080 resolution) requires a significant amount of bandwidth to move across the network. Don't be too surprised if the video stutters and skips, especially over a wireless network. It's not Windows Home Server's fault.

FIGURE 25.3

DVR content can be stored on the Video shared folder for streaming to a compatible player.

Understanding Security

As you know by now, access to shared folders is configurable through the Console, as shown in Figure 25.4. There you can grant rights to specific users. While some users may gain full read and write access, others may get read-only access. Still other users (such as the Guest account) may not have any access at all.

It's important to know, however, that when you enable a media folder for streaming, this security system is bypassed. Anybody on your local network who has a device or software capable of streaming media will gain access to all of it. If you have some content that you'd like to limit access to, you should put it in a shared folder other than a media folder, and limit access to the shared folder.

Media shared folder security is configured in the Console.

Going Beyond WMC

WMC, the basis of Windows Home Server's media sharing, is great — but in some ways it's rather limited. What if you need support for more file types, such as AAC for audio or MPEG-4 video? It just won't handle that. You'll have to convert all of your files to one of the formats supported by WMC. There is also the possibility that your client may not support the video formats that Windows Home Server is capable of providing. Is there a solution to this dilemma?

Yes, there is. You can completely replace the functionality provided by Windows Home Server's media sharing with a third-party application such as Nero Media Home, or our choice, TVersity.

CAUTION This is advanced functionality. Do not attempt this if you aren't comfortable with working with Windows services, user accounts, or granting administrator rights. At the time of this writing, TVersity is beta software at release version 0.9.10.8. Use it at your own risk.

ON the WEB You can find out more information about TVersity, and download it at www. tversity.com.

Exploring TVersity

Like WMC, TVersity is a UPnP AV/DLNA media server, but it goes beyond the functionality provided in Windows Home Server. Using TVersity will give you the following features over and above WMC:

■ **Transcoding:** TVersity can convert audio and video files on the fly to a format suitable for streaming to your client devices/renderers.

■ **Automatic client recognition:** Many of the more popular client devices are recognized, and transcoding options are adjusted to fit their requirements.

■ **Live Internet TV and radio:** Freely available TV stations on the Internet such as Bloomberg TV and audio including BBC World Service, CNN Live, and more (see Figure 25.5) are available.

■ **Multiple source folders:** Windows Home Server's media streaming is limited to the single Photo, Video and Music folders. TVersity lets you add as many of each as you want, and allows you to specify multiple media types for each folder.

■ **More supported formats:** MPEG-4, Ogg Vorbis, FLAC, QuickTime, Real Video, Flash, and more.

The transcoding features, real time or not, are a big help in dealing with format compatibility issues that always seem to arise when dealing with media formats. The other features, including streaming TV and radio channels, are just icing on the cake.

Installing TVersity

TVersity can be a little intimidating to install, especially if you are not used to working in a Windows Server environment. However, the steps to install are pretty straightforward. There are two things that prevent the install from being simple: First is the fact that it needs to read files from network shares (the same shares you access to put content on the server). The default installation process assigns the TVersity service to use an account that doesn't have access to server shares. The other is that the Windows Firewall blocks TVersity requests, and so it has to be told to allow the application.

FIGURE 25.5

TVersity offers streaming digital radio and TV from the Internet.

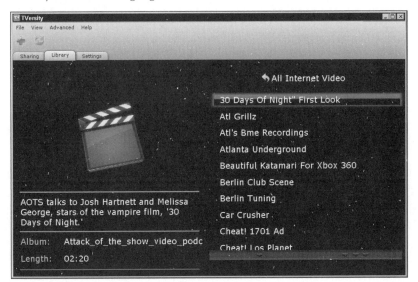

Follow these steps to install TVersity:

1. **Download TVersity from** www.tversity.com **and copy it to the server.** You can use the Software shared folder for this.

2. **Log onto the server via Remote Desktop as administrator.**

3. **Run the installation file** TVseritySetup.exe.

4. **Step through the wizard by clicking the Next button.** Accept the license agreement when prompted.

5. **Choose the default path for the installation.** All Windows Home Server programs should be installed to Drive C:.

6. **Click Install to begin the installation.**

7. **When the installation is finished, if you would like to install components necessary for transcoding, leave that option checked and then click Finish.** This screen is shown in Figure 25.6.

8. **If you chose to install the transcoding components, follow the wizard and accept the defaults.** You will install the codecs and the ffdshow components.

FIGURE 25.6

The TVersity installation allows you to install optional components for transcoding audio and video.

Next, you need to create an account to use as a service account, and set the service to use it. Follow these steps:

1. Click Start ➪ Control Panel ➪ Administrative Tools ➪ Computer Management to open the management console, shown in Figure 25.7.

FIGURE 25.7

The Computer Management console is used to add a new service user account.

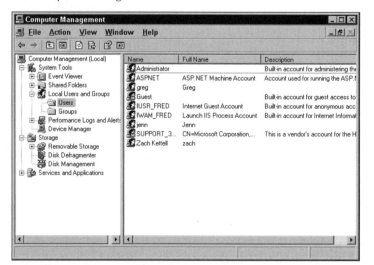

2. **Expand the Local Users and Groups item, and click on Users.**

3. **Choose Action ➪ New User.**

4. **Enter the account name** TVersityService. Enter a password.

5. **Uncheck the User must change password at next logon box.**

6. **Check the User cannot change password and Password never expires boxes.**

7. **Click Create to add the account, followed by Close.**

8. **Double-click the TVersityService account in the list.**

9. **Select the Member Of tab.**

10. **Click the Add button.**

11. **Enter** Administrators **in the box, as shown in Figure 25.8.**

FIGURE 25.8

The service account you are creating must be given administrator rights.

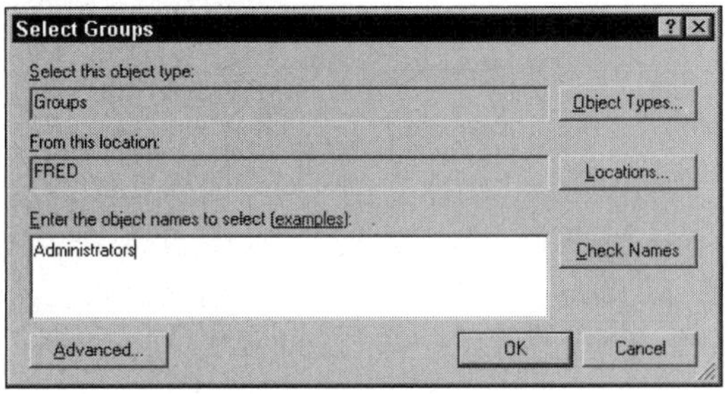

12. **Click OK, and then click OK again.**

13. **Back in the Computer Management console, expand the Services and Applications item.** Then select Services.

14. **Scroll down the service list until you find the TVersityMediaServer service.** You might find it easier to click the Standard tab first.

15. **Double-click on the TVersityMediaServer service name.**

16. **Click the Log On tab.**

17. **Click the This Account radio button.**

18. **Enter the username (**TVserityService**) and password you created in Step 4.** Then click OK.

19. **Right-click on the service name and choose Restart, as shown in Figure 25.9.**

FIGURE 25.9

You must give the service account you are creating administrator rights.

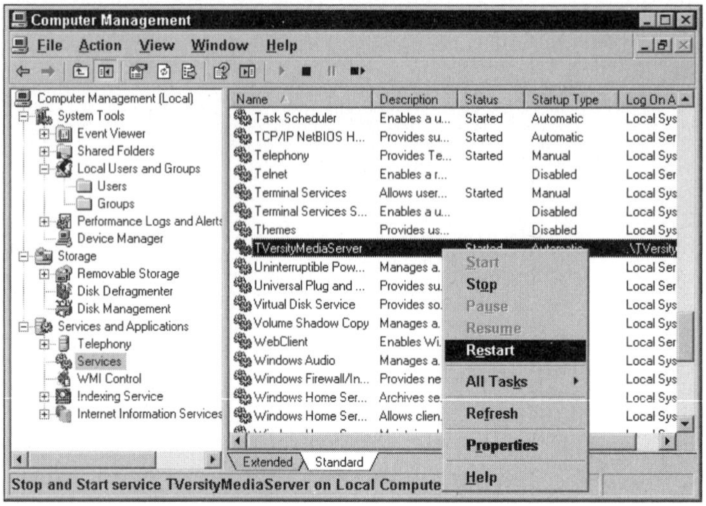

Next, configure Windows Firewall:

1. Choose Start ⇨ Control Panel ⇨ Windows Firewall.

2. Click the Exceptions tab.

3. Click Add Program.

4. Click Browse, and browse to C:\Program Files\TVersity\Media Server\MediaServer.exe.

5. Click Open.

6. Click OK.

7. Click Add Port.

8. Enter a name (TVersity is fine), and enter `41952` for the port.

9. Click OK and then click OK again to exit the firewall.

Phew! At this point, TVersity is installed and ready to be configured. Double-click the TVersity icon in the notification area (system tray).

On the Sharing tab, make sure Home Media is selected, and click the + button. The enter each of your shared folders using the UNC nomenclature `\\<servername>\folder`, as seen in Figure 25.10.

FIGURE 25.10

You can add as many shared folders as you like to the TVersity library.

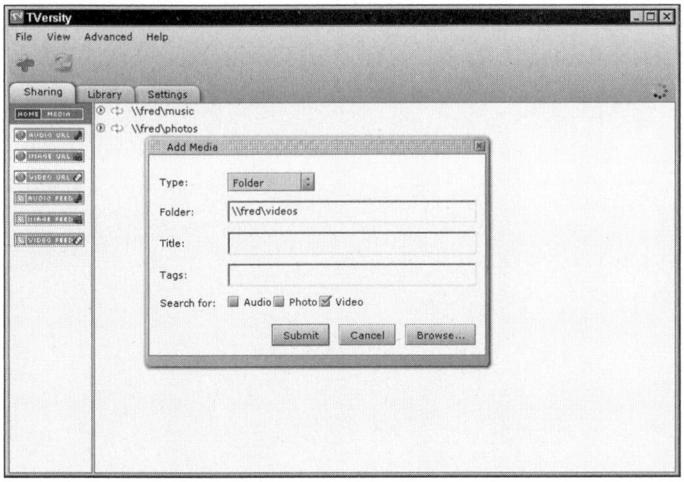

If all went well, TVersity will be sharing your media files, and you should be able to see them in your favorite UPnP AV client. If you can't, retrace these steps.

TIP When you install TVersity in this manner, you will see two media servers in each client: the original Windows Home Server one as well as the TVersity one. You can leave this as it is, or disable the WMC service if you don't want to see that on the clients any more.

Summary

Media sharing is a hot topic as more and more devices from the computer, CE, and mobile device arena are converging into genuine multipurpose devices. Fortunately, all three of these industries are working together to develop standards for interoperability between such devices, as it greatly increases the usefulness of a product such as Windows Home Server.

Windows Home Server supports a version of WMC that contains Microsoft's implementation of UPnP AV DLNA standards. These standards allow Windows Home Server to stream media to a wide variety of devices including computers, game consoles, and even some mobile devices. Those devices that can't use UPnP AV to stream media but can access network shares can gain access to media shares that way.

If the built-in WMC functionality isn't enough for you, there are third-party UPnP AV/DLNA servers you can install on your Windows Home Server machine. TVersity is one such program; you can install it under Windows Home Server, but a lot of the necessary steps are still a manual process. Hopefully somebody soon will come up with an Add-in that makes installation easier!

Now that we've explained what Windows Home Server can do in terms of streaming media, it is time to take a look at the other end of the pipe. In the next several chapters, we explore how to access shared media content on Xbox 360, PlayStation 3, and other devices.

Chapter 26

Connecting an Xbox 360

For a long time, companies in both the consumer electronics and the computer industries have been talking about *convergence devices*. Convergence devices are those that leverage their technological sophistication to do a job that in the past would have required a different device. Well, convergence devices are now sneaking into our living rooms in the form of game consoles. Given the tremendous amount of computing and graphics horsepower that goes into today's consoles, from multi-core CPUs, high definition video, network connectivity and storage, it's no surprise that these devices are leading the pack when it comes to convergence.

Microsoft's Xbox 360, the second generation game console, is a case in point. It contains a custom 3.2 gigahertz (GHz) triple core PowerPC processor, as well as a custom ATI graphics processor. Add a hard drive and an Ethernet port, and it's a multimedia machine that is able to do a lot more than just play games.

You can get media content on to the Xbox 360 in a number of ways. You can download it from Xbox Live Marketplace, or view it from an attached USB device. Two of the more exciting ways to view content on the 360 are via its streaming media support. The 360 has the ability to act as a media center extender for XP Media Center Edition and Vista MCE content. In addition, it can stream photos, music, and videos from Universal Plug and Play/Digital Living Network Alliance (UPnP/DLNA) servers including Windows Home Server, and as you may have guessed, that capability is the focus of this chapter.

Understanding Xbox 360 Playback Formats

The Xbox 360 supports streaming of music, photos, and videos, but not all of the video formats that are supported by Windows Home Server can be played on the 360. First, we'll go over what is supported, and then we'll show you how you can get around the video limitations.

Supported image formats

Fortunately, all of the image formats supported by Windows Home Server will work with the Xbox 360. They consist of the following:

- Bitmap (.bmp)
- Graphics Interchange Format (.gif)
- Joint Photographic Experts Group (.jpg, .jpeg)
- Portable Network Graphics (.png)
- Tagged Image File Format (.tif, .tiff)

Supported audio formats

The audio formats that are playable on the 360 also match up with what can be streamed from Windows Home Server:

- Advanced System Format (.asf)
- MPEG1 Layer 3 (.mp3)
- Wave (.wav)
- Windows Media Audio (.wma)

In addition to the audio formats, playlists are supported in the following formats:

- Windows Media Playlist (.wpl)
- MP3 Playlist (.m3u)

Supported video formats

Video support is where the Xbox 360 comes up short. While the Media Center Extender application on the 360 can stream all sorts of files from Windows Media Center PCs, its UPnP streaming compatibility list is rather limited. While the Spring 2007 update added H.264 and MPEG-4 formats (commonly used for QuickTime among others), these formats are not supported by Windows Home Server. That leaves one video format that both systems have in common: Windows Media Video (WMV).

So how can you take advantage of the video formats that you might already have, such as MPEG1 or MPEG2, QuickTime (MOV), DivX, or XviD files? You need a transcoder that is capable of playing them back. As we discussed in the previous chapter, TVersity is capable of serving video to an Xbox 360 while transcoding on the fly to the WMV format. Another option is to transcode your files in advance using a tool such as WinAVI.

Transcoding with TVersity

In the last chapter, we showed you how to go about installing and running TVersity on your Windows Home Server box as an alternative streaming media server. This is a very nice option when the Xbox 360 is your client, as TVersity was designed to transcode video on the fly.

When you connect an Xbox 360 to a TVersity server, it automatically transcodes video requests into the WMV format that the 360 supports. To look at or change the settings that TVersity is using, log on to your Windows Home Server desktop and launch TVersity from the icon in the system tray. Click the Settings tab, and then click the Transcoder button to see the transcoding settings, as shown in Figure 26.1.

FIGURE 26.1

TVersity can transcode video on the fly.

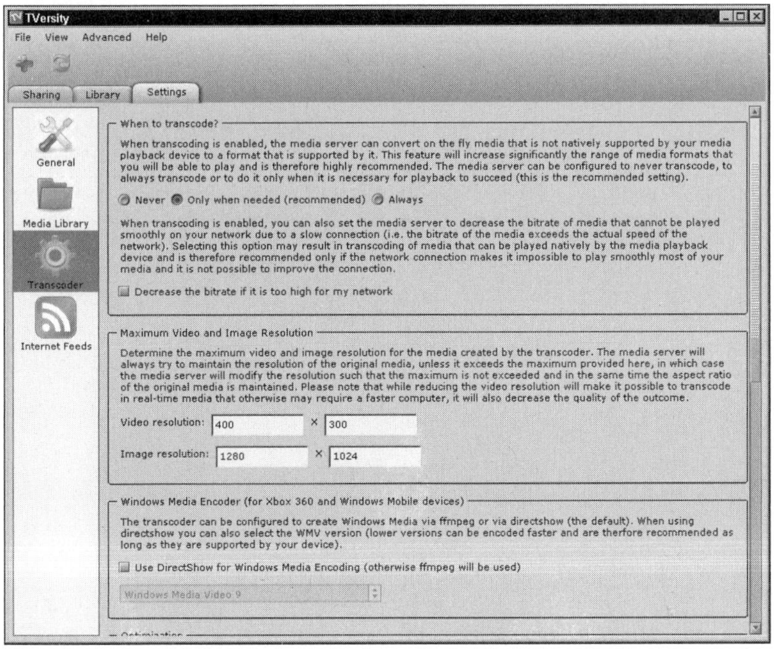

You may have to restart the TVersity service after making transcoding changes — you can do so by right-clicking on the TVersity icon in the system tray and choosing Restart Service.

Transcoding on the fly works well; however, as you might expect there are some downsides with this approach. For one thing, it can require a significant amount of CPU power, especially when transcoding high-resolution video. If you are using an old PC as your Windows Home Server box, it might not be up to the task of doing this. It also can sometimes take up to a minute or so for the video to actually start when you press play, due to the fact that TVersity has to cache the video in advance in order to stream without pauses.

Transcoding video files manually

If you would rather keep your Windows Home Server vanilla and not resort to installing a third-party UPnP server to stream video, there is another approach you can take to get your video files into the WMV format that the Xbox understands. You can transcode the video yourself.

WinAVI is a commercial utility that can transcode video from any format that is playable in Windows Media Player into AVI, Real Media, DVD, and for our needs here, WMV. WinAVI's basic interface is pretty straightforward; it is shown in Figure 26.2. You can let it automatically choose a format for the output, or you can click the Advanced button, where you can change parameters of the encoding, from the dimensions of the output to the bit rate. Some experimentation will be in order to come up with settings that will work well with your unique network.

ON the WEB Download a trial version of WinAVI from `www.winavi.com`.

FIGURE 26.2

WinAVI can batch transcode your video files into WMV to stream to the Xbox 360.

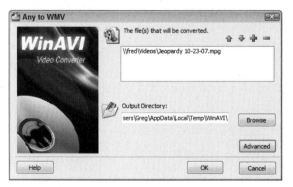

Making the Connection

The Xbox 360 includes a 100 Megabits per second (Mbps) Ethernet port, but not built in Wi-Fi. You can, however, purchase an adapter — either a third-party wireless bridge or a so-called game adapter, or Microsoft's own USB wireless adapter.

> **NOTE** If you purchase Microsoft's Xbox wireless adapter, you can configure your wireless settings in the Xbox's menus directly. A third-party wireless bridge can be used, but you'll have to connect it to a computer first in order to configure it.

Configuring the network connection

Network settings are configured in the System blade (360 lingo for tabbed page) of the Xbox dashboard interface, as shown in Figure 26.3. By default, the Xbox is configured to use Dynamic Host Configuration Protocol (DHCP), so if you plug it directly into your router, it should be able to automatically obtain the proper network configuration from the router.

FIGURE 26.3

Connect your Xbox to the network on the System blade on the dashboard.

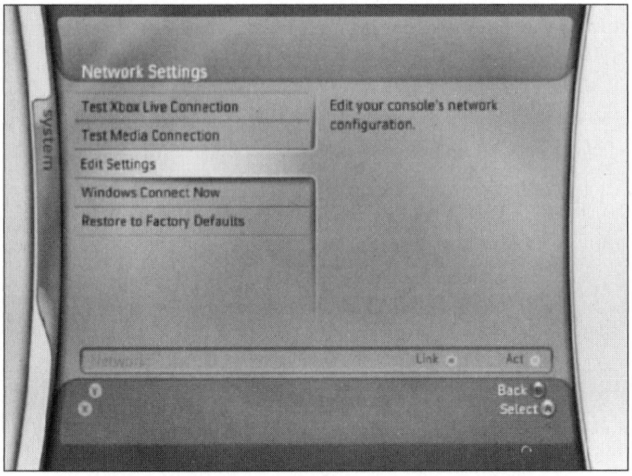

If your network settings are more unusual, you can select the IP somewhat unusually; there are some additional options you can set.

Address settings

If for some reason you do not use DHCP on your router, you can manually configure your Xbox 360 to use a static Internet Protocol (IP) address. You do this on the Network Settings blade. Follow these steps to set a static IP address:

1. Navigate to the Network Settings blade in the dashboard.

2. Select Edit Settings.

3. In the Edit Settings window, highlight the IP address block, as shown in Figure 26.4, and select it.

4. Select Manual on the Edit IP Settings screen.

FIGURE 26.4

You can enter a static IP address if you are not using DHCP.

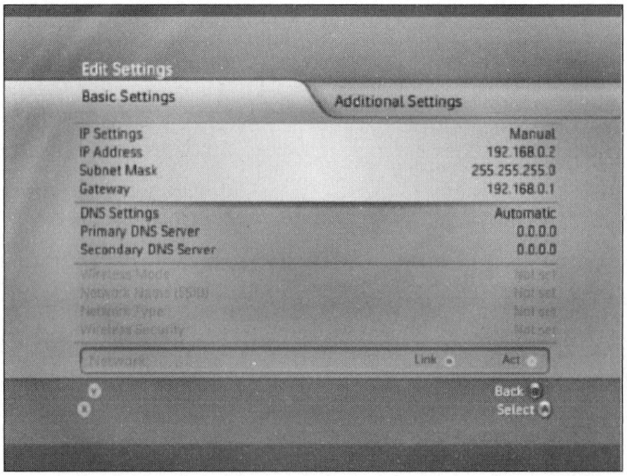

5. **Select IP Address, and enter a new address using the on-screen keyboard.** This should be an unused IP address on your home subnet. Press Select when done.

6. **Select Subnet Mask, and enter a value for it.** If your home network only uses the last octet value of the IP range, this will likely be 255.255.255.0. Press Select when done.

7. **Select Gateway, and enter the IP address for the gateway.** In most cases, your router will be your gateway device, controlling what gets sent to the outside world and what stays inside your local network. Generally, this will be the IP address of your router.

8. **Select Done when you have entered your settings.**

DNS settings

If your router isn't set up to act as a Domain Name Server (DNS) you can configure the Xbox 360 to manually add one as well. If your router does handle DNS resolution, you can leave this setting set to Automatic.

The DNS settings are on the Edit Settings window, right below the address settings. Select it to move to the Edit DNS Settings screen. Select Manual on the Edit DNS Settings screen. You can manually enter a primary or secondary DNS IP address. These addresses should have been provided by your ISP when your network was first set up.

Wireless settings

If you have a Microsoft Xbox 360 wireless adapter, you can modify your wireless settings as well. You can find these wireless settings on the Edit Settings window right below the DNS settings. You can configure the normal wireless settings, including the Service Set Identifier (SSID) and the type of security (WEP, Wireless Encryption Protocol or Wired Equivalent Privacy, or WPA, Wi-Fi Protected Access) and the passkey that your access point is configured to use.

> **NOTE** If the wireless settings are grayed out, it indicates that you don't have a wireless adapter attached, or that it is faulty.

Windows Connect Now

The Windows Connect Now feature, accessible from the Network Settings screen, is a nifty feature that allows you to copy wireless network settings from a Windows computer running XP SP2 or higher, if you have a compatible router.

Additional settings

The additional settings tab on the Network Settings screen allows you to configure your Xbox 360 to use other types of network settings, such as Point-to-Point Protocol over Ethernet (PPPoE). These settings are mostly useful if you are going to hook your Xbox up directly to a cable or Digital Subscriber Line (DSL) modem, rather than through a router, and so they'd be of no use in connecting to Windows Home Server.

> **ON the WEB** You can read more about Windows Connect Now at www.microsoft.com/
> windowsxp/using/networking/getstarted/windowsconnectnow.mspx,
> and specifically how it pertains to the Xbox at www.xbox.com/en-US/support/
> connecttolive/xbox360/connectionmethods/troubleshootliveconnection-
> windowsconnect.htm.

Testing your connection

Whether you configure your network settings manually or let your router automatically assign them, you will need to test the connection before you attempt to connect to Windows Home Server. The dashboard has a convenient item to do just that. Whenever you make a change to a network setting, you are forced to test. However, if you are using the default settings, follow these steps to test your network connection:

1. Navigate to the Network Settings blade.

2. **Select Test Media Connection.** The test will run and test each component of your connection, starting with your network adapter or your wireless adapter, your IP address, and whether or not you have specified a PC to use as the media server. Because you chose a PC media server to connect to, it should fail at this step, as shown in Figure 26.5.

If it fails prior to the PC Selected step, you can select the More Info button associated with the item that failed for details. The Edit Settings button provides a shortcut directly to the network settings.

FIGURE 26.5

Test your connection to verify that your network settings are correct.

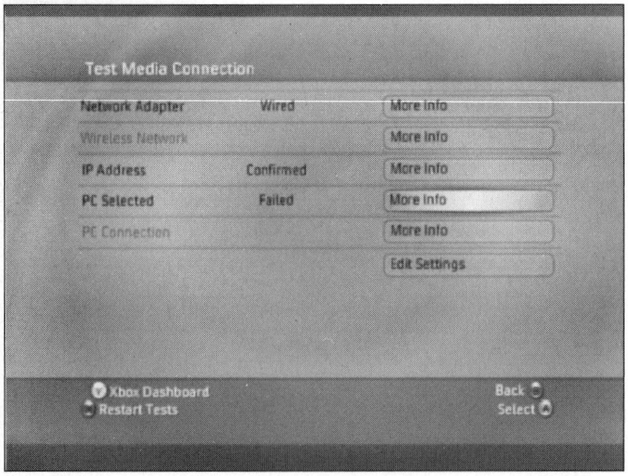

Connecting to Windows Home Server

If you are reconfiguring your Xbox to use a different computer than it was previously configured to use, you must disconnect. The Xbox can only be configured to stream media from one server at a time. In order to change the server you are using, follow these steps:

1. Navigate to the System blade.

2. Select the Computers menu item.

3. **The Windows-based PC option will show you which server you are connected to, as shown in Figure 26.6.** Select it by pressing A.

4. **Press A again to disconnect the computer.**

FIGURE 26.6

From the System blade, you can view an existing attached computer, or select it to disconnect.

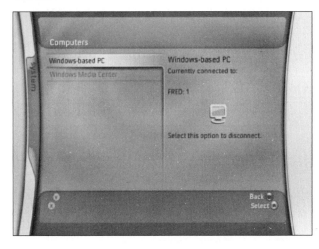

Now, you are ready to attach to your Windows Home Server computer. Unlike the other network-related settings, you don't do this in the System blade. You will have to navigate to the Media blade to proceed. This blade is shown in Figure 26.7. Once there, do the following:

1. **Choose one of the options on the Media blade that pertains to the type of media stored on the server.** Valid choices are Music, Pictures, and Video. Do not choose Media Center, as that is for use with Media Center PCs and not UPnP computers like Windows Home Server.

2. **You will be presented with two options, Console and Computer.** Choose Computer and press A to select.

3. **You will see a warning that you must first download audio and video software on the PC that will be used as the server.** Because you are using Windows Home Server, which already has the necessary components in place, acknowledge this message by selecting the Yes, continue option.

4. **On the Windows Based PC screen, you should see your Windows Home Server computer, along with any other UPnP servers you might have on the network, such as Windows Media Player 11 running on XP or Vista computers, as shown in Figure 26.8.**

5. **Select your Windows Home Server computer.** (If you've installed TVersity or some other media server, you can select it instead.)

6. **You should immediately connect and go to the media content.** If not, or if you didn't see your server as an option to choose, there has been a problem with your configuration on either the server or the Xbox. At this point, you can rerun the connection test, or try to connect to a different UPnP server.

FIGURE 26.7

The Media blade is your portal to your server's streamed content, and also where you configure the computer to attach to.

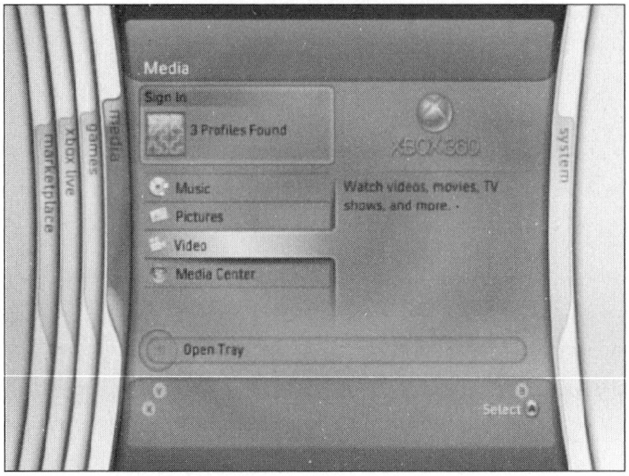

FIGURE 26.8

You can connect to a variety of different UPnP servers besides your Windows Home Server. As you can see here, we still have both our standard connection and a TVersity connection running.

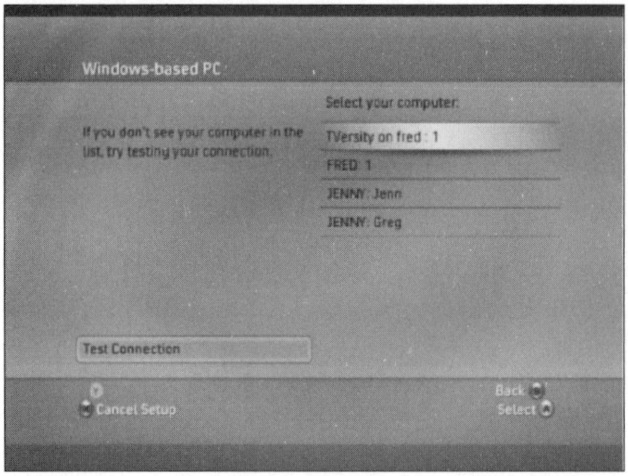

Assuming you were successful, you are now ready for streaming. We'll discuss what to do with these videos in the next section.

Streaming Media

The Media blade is where you will access your videos, music, and photos. After you've chosen a computer connection to use for one of these items, it will be used for all of them. In order to change to a different computer, or server on that computer, you will have to disconnect the existing one first as we described earlier.

Viewing pictures

There are differences in the way different types of media are presented. Pictures are presented in nested folders, mimicking the directory structure of the share they are on, as shown in Figure 26.9. You can either navigate these folders to select pictures to view individually, or you can view a slide show of the current folder's photos and those of any subfolders. When viewing a slide show, press the B button to return to the photo viewer.

FIGURE 26.9

View a photo slide show using pictures in a specific subfolder.

Playing music

Music is organized a bit differently. Music files can contain *metadata*, which is information identifying the song, the artist who is performing it, the genre of music it is, and a lot more. This metadata is usually either added manually by whoever rips the CD, or by automated metadata tools. The

Xbox lets you access your music by artist, by a sorted list of album titles, a sorted list of all songs, and by the genre of the music, as Figure 26.10 shows. You can even use playlists that were derived from Windows Media Player.

You can select an item in a category, such as an album title or an artist's name, and play all of the songs in that category.

FIGURE 26.10

You can browse through multiple folders of music, or choose to view based on album, artist, or other criteria if it exists in your media file metadata.

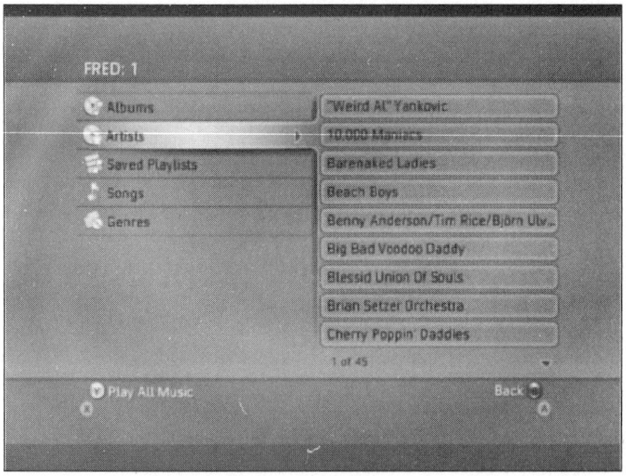

Streaming video

Videos can have similar metadata, and you can choose to view them by genre, folders, or playlists, as shown in Figure 26.11. Given a lot of video content can come from a DVR (digital video recorder) of some type, sorting by date added is a nice option. You can also choose to view All Video, in which case it will be sorted alphabetically.

Video streaming, unlike photos and music, can be very difficult to get working correctly. This is primarily due to the large bandwidth that a streaming video needs. If you see lots of stutters and halts while you're playing a streaming video, it's likely that your network doesn't have enough bandwidth carry that particular file.

If you have your heart set on a particular file playing, your choices are pretty limited. You can try using an on-the-fly transcoding server like TVersity, or transcode the files yourself using WinAVI or some other similar utility.

FIGURE 26.11

You can choose to sort video titles by various metadata parameters.

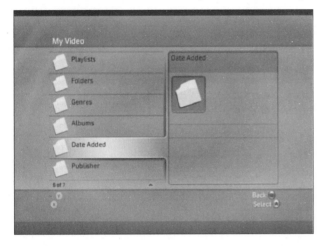

Summary

Game consoles have evolved into multimedia powerhouses that can do a lot more than just play games. Given the nature of their fast CPUs and advanced graphics architecture, playing them back is a cake walk.

The Xbox 360 has an easy to navigate interface called the dashboard. By sliding through tabs to access different parts of the system, you can easily hone in on the settings you need to change in order to see your Windows Home Server's shared media files.

When playing back video files, the Xbox 360 is limited to only one file format that is supported by Windows Home Server's UPnP implementation: WMV. To play back video files of a different type, you will either have to transcode (convert) them into the WMV format, or use a replacement media server such as TVersity that can transcode the videos on the fly while you are playing them.

When it comes to streaming media from Windows Home Server, the Xbox 360 doesn't get all of the fun. Its competitor in the video game race, the Sony PlayStation 3 (PS3), has some impressive multimedia credentials of its own. In the next chapter, we'll take a look at how to configure a PS3 to talk to Windows Home Server.

Chapter 27

Connecting a PlayStation 3

W hen it comes to being a great game console/convergence device, the Xbox 360 isn't the only game in town. Sony's PlayStation 3 (PS3) is another device in the fiercely competitive console market that has everything but the kitchen sink, it seems, in terms of media playback capabilities.

Sony's third-generation game console was designed from the ground up as a media powerhouse. Its custom Cell processor along with a custom NVIDIA graphics processor provides the horsepower. The 20 GB or larger hard drive, a Blu-ray optical drive, and built-in networking (including Wi-Fi in some models) means that Sony thought of every way they could to allow owners to get media content onto the machine.

The media streaming in the PS3 is accomplished using the Universal Plug and Play (UPnP) protocols espoused by the Digital Living Network Alliance (DLNA), which Sony, like Microsoft, is a member of. Fortunately, the UPnP protocols are also the basis for the media sharing features of Windows Home Server. This is fortunate because it means that the "universal" in the name is factual—the compatibility between products of two otherwise competitive companies means that the consumers are the ones who win.

In this chapter, we show you how you can take advantage of the PS3's media streaming features, and we show you what it takes to do so from your Windows Home Server machine.

Explaining PlayStation 3 Playback Formats

The PS3 can stream quite a few different audio, video, and image formats. However, like the Xbox, it is limited in the number of formats it can stream from Windows Home Server. The biggest limitation is that the PS3 cannot stream Microsoft proprietary formats such as Windows Media Video (WMV) and Windows Media Audio (WMA). If you need to stream these formats, you'll have to either convert them to a supported format or install a transcoding media server such as Nero MediaHome or TVersity on your Windows Home Server.

NOTE Media streaming in the PS3 was enabled in the 1.8 version of the firmware released in May 2007. If your console has an older version, you can obtain the new firmware by going to the System Update item in the Settings menu in the Xcross Media Bar (XMB) once your PS3 is connected to the Internet.

Supported image formats

The image formats supported by Windows Home Server match up favorably with those supported by the PS3. All of the most common image formats are supported.

The supported formats are as follows:

- Bitmap (.bmp)
- Graphics Interchange Format (.gif)
- Joint Photographic Experts Group (.jpg, .jpeg)
- Portable Network Graphics (.png)
- Tagged Image File Format (.tif, .tiff)

Supported audio formats

Audio formats supported by the PS3 include some Sony proprietary formats (such as Adaptive Transform Acoustic Coding, or ATRAC) that are not supported by Windows Home Server, but also a fair number of formats that are supported.

- AAC (.m4a)
- ATRAC (.at3)
- MPEG1 Layer 3 (.mp3)
- WAVE (.wav)
- Windows Media Audio (.wma)

Supported video formats

Video formats is an area where the PS3 enjoys quite a bit of support; however, in some ways it's as limited as the Xbox 360, especially if you want to stream video from Windows Home Server. Video formats supported by the PS3 include

- MPEG-1 (.mpg)
- MPEG-2 (.mpg, .mp2, .ts)
- H.264 (.mkv, .mp4)
- MPEG-4 (.mp4)
- AVC (.mov, .m2ts, .avc)

Of the supported video formats, Windows Home Server only supports MPEG-1 and MPEG-2. Videos encoded as AVI, WMV, or ASF formats must be converted to one of the supported formats.

While the MPEG formats are among the most widely supported video codecs (coder/decoder) around (MPEG-1 is used for Video CD format, and MPEG-2 is the video format used on DVD and HDTV broadcasts in North America), they are not as efficient as many of the newer codecs, including H.264, AVC, and MPEG-4. On the other hand, decoding MPEG-1 and MPEG-2 video is simpler. As with unsupported file formats on the Xbox 360, you can use a media server such as TVersity to transcode (convert from one video codec to another).

Transcoding with TVersity

Just as we showed with the Xbox 360, you can install a third-party streaming media server onto your Windows Home Server machine and have it transcode video files into a format that your client device will support. In the case of the PS3, you will want to encode video as MPEG-1 or MPEG-2, or one of the MPEG-4 variants (H.264, AVC). The MPEG formats are simpler to encode, but the higher bandwidth requirements mean that you will need a bigger network pipe in order to make use of the video. As with most things to do with streaming video, trial and error will be necessary to determine just what your particular network setup will be able to handle. TVersity's transcoding menu is shown in Figure 27.1.

CROSS-REF You can read more about TVersity and installing a third-party media server in Chapter 25.

You may have to restart the TVersity service after making transcoding changes — you can do so by right-clicking the TVersity icon in the system tray and choosing Restart Service.

Transcoding on the fly works well; however, as you might expect, there are some downsides with this approach. For one thing, it can requires a significant amount of CPU power, especially when transcoding high-resolution video. If you are using an old PC as your Windows Home Server box, it might not be up to the task of doing this. If you are using a newer dual core system, it will do better.

As with the Xbox 360, transcoded media can sometimes take a minute or so to start, due to the fact that TVersity has to cache the video in advance in order to stream without pauses.

ON the WEB   You can find the latest tips on configuring TVersity for the PS3 (and other devices) on the support page at `http://tversity.com/support`.

FIGURE 27.1

TVersity's transcoding options let you tweak your file streaming performance.

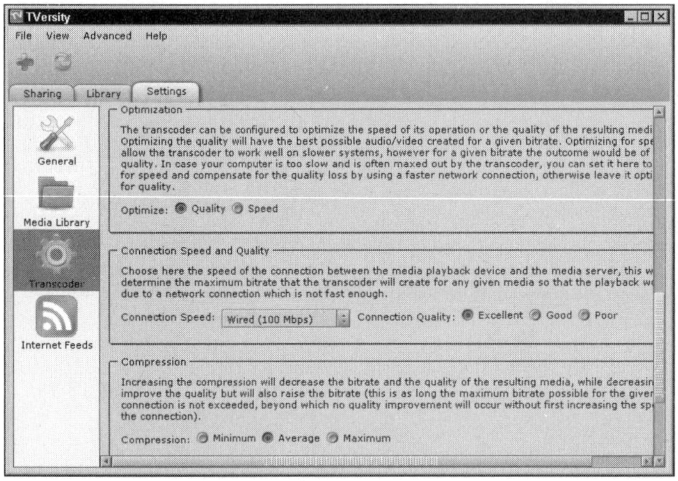

Transcoding video files manually

For transcoding video files for the PS3, you can use a number of different third-party tools. WinAVI, the utility we discussed for use with the Xbox 360, will work for the PS3, However, the only format that it supports for the PS3 is MPEG-2, so if you have a bunch of video files that are encoded with the more efficient MPEG-4 based codecs, converting them to a larger MPEG-2 video file may not seem like the best course of action. Aside from WinAVI, there are a number of different options.

Red Kawa PS3 Video 9

Red Kawa's video converters are designed to take the guesswork out of converting video for several different client platforms, including the PS3. Their application converts video files such as AVI, WMV, and others in to a format that the PS3 will recognize. (They also have versions for the Xbox 360, among other platforms.)

ON the WEB   You can find Red Kawa's PS3 Video 9 application at `www.redkawa.com/videoconverters/ps3video9/`.

Nero Ultra Edition 8

The latest version of Nero's terrific suite of disc burning and video authoring tools includes Nero Recode 2, a utility for converting all sorts of video into other formats. Choose MP4 AVC Standard for the PS3's video, as shown in Figure 27.2.

Nero Ultra Edition 8 also includes the latest version of Nero Media Home, which is a media server product similar to TVersity that can also convert media on the fly.

FIGURE 27.2

Nero Recode 2 can transcode video for the PS3 and a lot more.

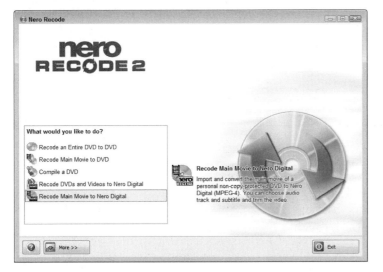

Making the Connection

The PS3 console includes a 100 Mbps Ethernet port. Some models include built-in 802.11g compatible Wi-Fi as well. You can use either of these connections to get your PS3 onto to the network, but if you can manage to use a hard-wired connection, you should enjoy fewer problems with video streaming, particularly with high-definition material.

CROSS-REF If you own a PS3 without a Wi-Fi adapter, and you still want it to connect wirelessly, you can by a third-party wireless bridge, or a game adapter. See Chapter 4 for information on the various network equipment you can use in your Windows Home Server network.

Configuring the network connection

The PlayStation's interface, called the Xcross Media Bar (XMB) is unique interface developed by Sony for several of their products, including the PS3 and the PlayStation Portable (PSP) portable game unit. The main menu, if you will, is a series of icons you scroll through using the controller's directional pad. For each main menu item, there is a vertical menu that contains the options for that menu item. This interface is designed to require fewer button pushes than a traditional menu-based Graphical User Interface (GUI).

Network settings are changed in the Settings menu, at the very bottom of the list, as shown in Figure 27.3.

FIGURE 27.3

Locate Network Settings in the Settings menu of the XMB.

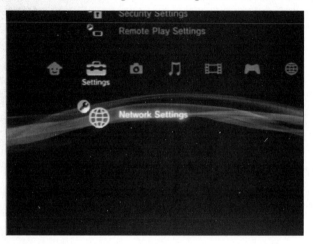

You have several options for configuring the network settings. You can either have the PS3 attempt to do everything automatically via Dynamic Host Configuration Protocol (DHCP), or you can configure settings manually. Select the Network Settings link using the X button on the controller. Here is a description of each of the items in the Network Settings menu.

Settings and Connection Status List

The first item on the list is useful for viewing the status of your network connection. Although the connection will be tested any time you change the settings, it is always helpful to go back and review your settings or see if a problem has developed.

As shown in Figure 27.4, this menu shows you your current network connection type and all of the current parameters, such as whether the info was obtained via DHCP (Automatic) or Static (Manual) settings, the IP address, subnet mask, default router (gateway) and DNS servers to use, and other somewhat more advanced settings such as the MTU (maximum transmission unit, the size of an individual block your router can handle), and your NAT (Network Address Translation) setting, which is mostly useful from an online game standpoint.

There are no settings to be made on this screen. Once you've reviewed your settings, press the circle button to move back.

Network Settings and Connection lets you see if your connection is good.

Internet Connection

The Internet Connection menu item is used to toggle the connection on and off. You can use this to disable networking if you don't want the PS3 to use it for some period of time. There are no other options for this menu.

Internet Connection Settings

This menu item is where you configure network connections, both wired and wireless. To configure your network settings, follow these steps for a wired connection:

1. Click the Internet Connection Settings item in the XMB.

2. **If you are already connected, you will be asked if you want to disconnect.** Click Yes.

3. **Click Wired Connection.**

4. **If you would like to have the PS3 try to configure the network settings automatically, select the Easy configuration mode.** This is the recommended option the first time you go through this menu. The PS3 verifies that you can do DHCP. If successful, press X to save and skip to Step 12.

5. **If you want to set your network settings manually, choose the Custom option for the Address Settings.**

6. **Choose an operating mode for the network device: Auto-Detect or Manual.** Choosing manual gives you the option to specify the duplex and speed settings of your connection. In most cases you will want to use the Auto-Detect option.

7. **Choose an IP Address Setting: Automatic or Manual.** The Automatic setting configures the network to obtain settings using DHCP. With the Manual option, you have to enter them yourself.

NOTE You should only use the Point-to-Point Protocol over Ethernet (PPPoE) setting if your PS3 is connecting directly to a cable or Digital Subscriber Line (DSL) modem and your ISP has provided you with settings to use. In a networked home environment, such settings will be done by the device that connects to the modem— which in most cases will be your router.

8. **If you chose Manual for IP Address Settings, enter the IP address, subnet mask, default router address, and at least one DNS server address (primary), as shown in Figure 27.5.** Use the X button to change individual items, and the directional pad to move to the next item when done. Once you have entered all required values, you can press right on the directional pad to go to the next menu.

FIGURE 27.5

Enter network information manually if you don't have a DHCP server.

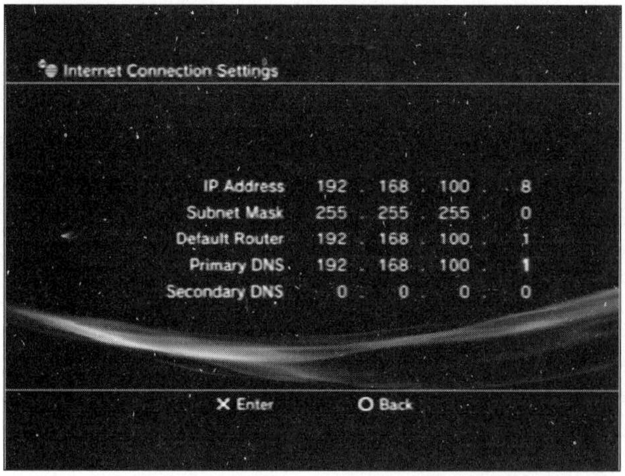

9. **Choose Automatic for the MTU size.** This will not need to be changed in most cases.

10. **You can enter a proxy server to use for Internet connections.** For most home users, you can leave this disabled. If your ISP requires you to connect through a proxy server, enter the provided information here.

11. **Choose a UPnP setting.** This will be used to check to see if your router supports automatic configuration using UPnP. If your router supports it, choose Enable.

12. **Review your settings, and press X to save.** If you notice a problem, you can back up through the process to correct it.

13. **Press X to test the connection.**

Configuring a wireless connection is similar to configuring a wired connection, with a few additional steps to enter the wireless settings. Follow these instructions to configure a wireless one:

1. **Choose a Wireless connection on the Select a Configuration screen.**

2. **Choose whether to Scan or Enter Manually your WLAN settings.** If you choose Scan, the PS3 searches the local airspace looking for Service Set Identifier (SSID) values. Choose yours when it comes up and skip to Step 4.

3. **If your SSID is not being broadcast, you must enter it manually.** Choose Enter Manually and do so.

4. **Choose a wireless security type to match your router's settings.** The WPA-PSK option is your best bet for security.

5. **Enter the WEP or WPA key if you chose on of those security settings.** Press X to enter the onscreen keyboard. Press Start when done.

6. **You can now configure the network address settings.** Jump to Step 4 in the manual configuration and complete it.

Internet Connection Test

The Internet Connection Test menu item simply repeats the test that was done when you configured your network settings. If there is a problem with the connection, rerunning this test may help you track down where the error is. Figure 27.6 shows the Internet Connection Test screen.

FIGURE 27.6

Test your connection to verify that your network settings are correct.

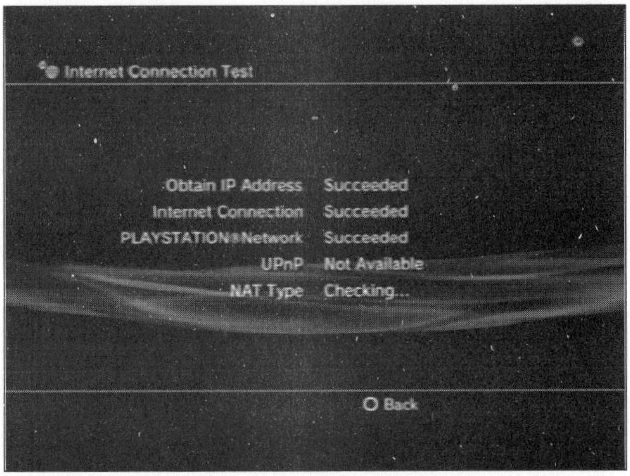

Media Server Connection

The Media Server Connection icon lets you enable or disable the automatic discover and connection to media servers such as Windows Home Server or Windows Media Player 11. If you disable this setting, you will still be able to use the Internet connection; however media servers will no longer show in the Photos, Music, or Videos folders.

Connecting to Windows Home Server

Unlike the Xbox, which needs to be told which media share to access, the PS3 automatically detects all that it finds on the network once you enable the media server connection and perform a search. The Search for Media Servers item is available under each of the Photo, Music, and Video folders. Figure 27.7 shows the result of a media server search in the photo folders.

FIGURE 27.7

Search for Media Servers will return all of the servers it finds on the network.

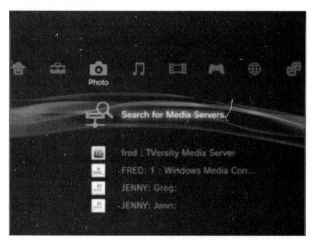

Streaming Media

Media streaming is done through the menu items created for each of your servers; however, you must access pictures from the Photo XMB item, music from the Music item, and video from the Video item.

Viewing pictures

As with the Xbox 360, pictures can be displayed in a variety of ways. With the Windows Home Server media server, you have the following options for organizing them:

- **Album:** This setting displays each folder of photos found on the server as a separate album. The albums themselves are not nested, even if the photo folders they are built from are. They are listed alphabetically.

- **All Pictures:** Every picture found on the server is displayed in alphabetically order.

- **Date Taken:** The date stamp on each picture is used to sort them into a folder containing all photos from that date.

- **Folders:** Like the album setting, photos are grouped according to the folder they are in on the server. The nested folder structure is maintained, however.

Figure 27.8 shows a list of photos in a subfolder. In order to view the photos, either select them individually, or press Start on the controller to begin a slide show.

FIGURE 27.8

View a photo slide show using pictures in a specific subfolder.

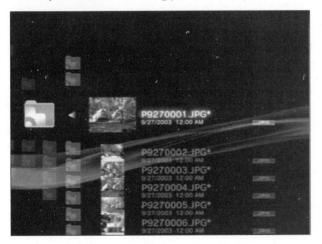

Playing music

As with the Xbox 360, you can order music according to its metadata. With Windows Home Server's media server, you can sort music in the following ways:

- **Album:** Sort the music according to the album it's from, without any regard for the artist or genre. All albums are displayed in a list.

- **All Music:** All of the songs in your Music shared folder will be listed alphabetically.

- **Artist:** Songs are sorted by artist. All songs by a particular artist are listed alphabetically, unfortunately with no regard for the album they are on.

- **Folders:** You can browse your music as it exists on the server, with the folder organization left intact.
- **Genre:** Music is sorted according to genre, with songs listed alphabetically under the genre defined in their metadata.
- **Playlist:** Playlist files (.wpl or .m3u) on the server are used to generate lists of songs.

Figure 27.9 shows the interface for viewing music.

TIP Using a third-party media server such as TVersity can give you more options for sorting. For example, in addition to the above options, you can choose to sort based on Artist followed by Album, or Genre/Artist/Album, and more.

FIGURE 27.9

You can browse through multiple folders of music, or choose to view based on album, artist, or other criteria if they exist in your media file metadata.

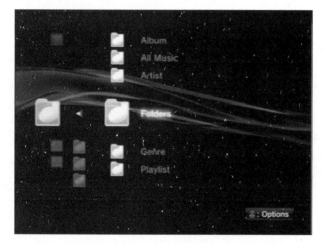

Streaming video

Videos can have similar metadata, and you can choose to view them by genre, folders, or playlists, as shown in Figure 27.10. Video content can come from a DVR (digital video recorder) so sorting recorded TV programs according to the date added is a nice option. You can also choose to view All Video, in which case they will be sorted alphabetically.

As we pointed out in Chapter 26 when discussing the Xbox 360, video streaming can be very difficult to get working correctly. This is primarily due to the large bandwidth that a streaming video needs. If you see lots of stutters and halts while you're playing a streaming video, it's likely that your network doesn't have enough bandwidth to carry that particular file.

FIGURE 27.10

Video files have some unique sort options, such as the publisher and date added.

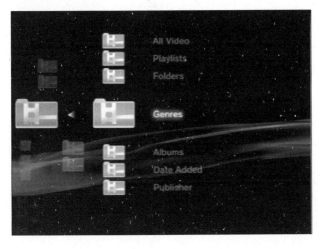

As with the Xbox, transcoding video ahead of time is still an option, or you can use a media server capable of transcoding on the fly, such as TVersity or Nero Media Home. If you can't seem to get a video to stream or you aren't happy with the loss of quality that transcoding offers, you have one additional option with the PS3 — local copying.

Copying media files

If you continually have network problems streaming media, the PS3 has an ace in the hole. Instead of streaming the video, you can copy it to the PS3's hard drive and play it from there.

To copy a file or even a folder full of files to the PS3's hard drive, highlight the item in the menu, and press the Options (Triangle) button. Then choose Copy.

You can even copy multiple files at once. Choose Copy Multiple from the Options menu, and you are presented with the interface shown in Figure 27.11. Select multiple images by checking them, or click the Select All button. Then highlight the OK button and click Select.

FIGURE 27.11

You can copy files to the PS3's hard drive in order to play them without the limitations of streaming.

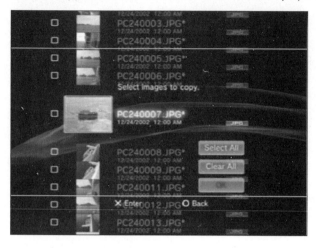

Summary

The Sony PS3 is another game console with impressive multimedia playback credentials, and its ability to stream a variety of video formats from a networked server makes it a natural match for Windows Home Server. If you own both a PS3 and a Windows Home Server, you owe it to yourself to introduce them.

The PlayStation's navigation system, called the XMB, makes it easy to navigate through all of your media content without having to navigate through a lot of different menus. Setting your network connection to allow you to communicate with the server is simple as well.

The PS3 can see all of your networked servers at one time — you don't have to force it to choose just one. If you have your Windows Home Server set up to use both its native media sharing and a third-party application like TVersity, this can be a big plus. You'll also be able to see any other UPnP servers, such as PCs running Windows Media Player or Windows Media Connect.

While game consoles make great clients for Windows Home Server's media sharing, they aren't the only devices that can make use of it. In the next chapter, we give you an idea of some other devices that you can use.

Chapter 28

Connecting Computers and Other Devices

The promise of the digitally connected home is here. Now things that you may never have thought of can link over the network and access your photos, music, and even video.

We've shown in the last two chapters that game consoles can make formidable clients for streaming content from Windows Home Server. While this is true, it certainly isn't all there is to the story. There is an ever-increasing array of devices that can stream media from a Windows Home Server's Universal Plug and Play (UPnP) media server.

UPnP compatible devices are popping up everywhere, and range from music playing devices to network-enabled picture frames.

Now that your Windows Home Server is serving up video, music, and photos 24/7, you might be interested in knowing more about the various types of devices that you can use to play your content.

Accessing PC Clients

When you think about potential clients for Windows Home Server media streaming, your home computers are one of the first things that come to mind. Sure, you can map a network share to your Music or Video folder and play them directly from the files, but wouldn't it be nice to take advantage of the organization according to metadata that a media server provides? With UPnP client software, you access Windows Home Server's media server just like any other client device does.

When you look for UPnP clients for Windows computers as well as for other platforms, it becomes apparent that while there are some capable applications out there, there aren't as many as you might think. Most of the UPnP software for Windows and the Mac are geared towards server capabilities, to enable streaming from the computer to a client device instead. So let's cut the wheat from the chaff and point out some UPnP clients that you can use to enjoy media streamed to your PC.

Windows Media Player 11 (Vista)

The ubiquitous Windows Media Player, shown in Figure 28.1, has had UPnP server capabilities since version 10, when Windows Media Connect (WMC) technology was integrated into it. Until recently, however, it hasn't been able to operate as a client, which to us seemed slightly backwards for a player application. This has finally been corrected with Windows Media Player 11 for Vista, which includes a UPnP client that is well integrated into the media library functionality.

In order to use the UPnP Client in Windows Media Player, you must first enable media searching. Click the Library button at the top, and then choose Media Sharing. Make sure that the Find media that others are sharing check box is checked, and then click OK.

FIGURE 28.1

Windows Media Player 11 on Vista can stream UPnP media from Windows Home Server.

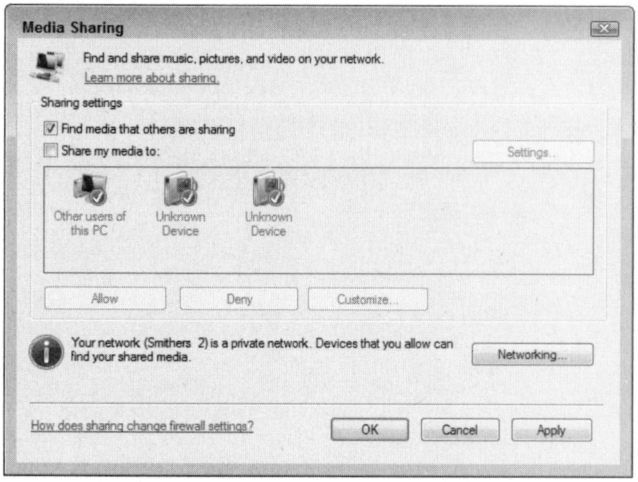

 You can find Microsoft's Web site for Windows Media Player 11 at `www.microsoft.com/windows/products/winfamily/mediaplayer/default.mspx`.

Nero ShowTime

Nero ShowTime (shown in Figure 28.2) is part of the Nero 8 Ultra Edition suite, and is the client companion to Nero MediaHome, their UPnP media server application. Besides UPnP media streaming, it serves as Nero's client application for viewing DVDs, listening to CDs, and playing locally stored media files.

To locate content from media servers, you must right click anywhere on the controller or media viewing window, and choose Select Source ⇨ Media Files from the pop-up menu, or press Ctrl+O.

In the Playlist window, click the Browser tab. Your media servers should be visible under the MediaHome Network entry, shown in Figure 28.3.

NOTE Nero ShowTime will stream music and video content; however, it will not stream photos.

FIGURE 28.2

Nero Showtime is an all-purpose media player with UPnP AV client capabilities.

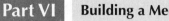

FIGURE 28.3

You can browse Nero ShowTime's UPnP media servers on the Playlist window.

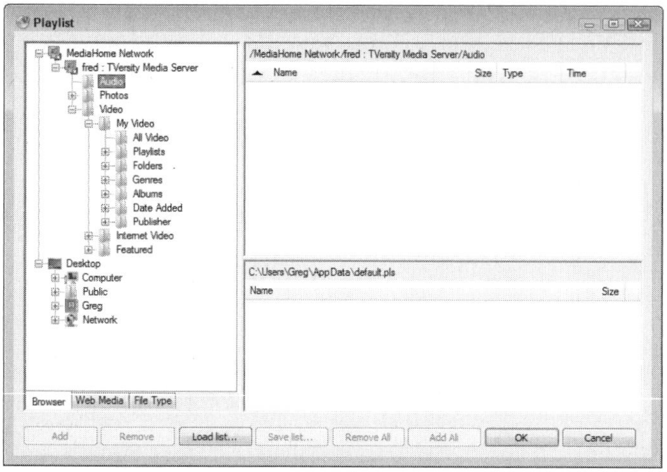

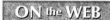

NOTE In our testing, ShowTime version 4 does not appear to recognize WMC-based media servers, including Windows Home Server's built-in media server, or Windows Media Player 11. It does work with TVersity and Nero's own MediaHome server. ShowTime 2 from Nero 6 does recognize the Windows Home Server media server.

ON the WEB You can find out more information about Nero ShowTime and the entire Nero Ultra Suite at www.nero.com.

Enabling Wi-Fi Photo Frames

One of the more creative uses for streaming media has to be the Wi-Fi enabled photo frame. Just a few years ago such devices would have seemed like something out of a science fiction novel.

Digital photo frames aren't entirely new — they've been around almost as long as digital photography, although the earlier models were pretty limited compared to the models you can get today. The newer devices typically include a 7 to 10 inch LCD display, a slot for reading camera memory cards, and a way to share photos over the Web or over phone lines.

Additional features can include music playback, and even access to RSS (Really Simple Syndication) feeds or weather and stock tickers. Most importantly, from our perspective, is the fact that many of these network-enabled photo frames allow pictures to be streamed to them from a UPnP media server such as Windows Home Server.

It's not possible to cover all of the available models of Wi-Fi–enabled digital photo frames on the market in this book, and due to the fact that models are constantly being introduced and discontinued, it's perhaps pointless. We do want to point out a couple that are currently available just to give you an idea of the technology available right now.

ON the WEB You can find an entire Web site devoted to wireless picture frames, with reviews, news, and more at www.wirelesspictureframe.com.

Kodak EasyShare EX-811 and EX-1011

Kodak produces quite a few digital photo frames, however not all of them are Wi-Fi enabled. The 8-inch EX-811 and the 10-inch EX-1011 frames (shown in Figure 28.4) are able to connect to your network wirelessly, and are capable of streaming photos from WMC-based UPnP servers, such as the one included with Windows Home Server.

FIGURE 28.4

The Kodak EasyShare digital photo frame will stream pictures right from the server.

Photo courtesy of Kodak.

Both frames include an 800 × 480 resolution widescreen LCD display and 802.11b/g wireless, and support a variety of memory cards.

ON the WEB
You'll find information about Kodak digital picture frames at the Kodak home page at www.kodak.com.

Momento Model 70 and Model 100

The Momento Models 70 and 100, shown in Figure 28.5, include 7-inch and 10-inch 800 × 480 TFT LCD displays, respectively. Like the Kodak frames, they can be used to stream photos from a WMC-based UPnP server over an 802.11b/g wireless connection.

An intriguing option of these frames is their support of Vista SideShow. SideShow is technology that allows Vista-based computers to drive external displays, showing information from your Vista gadgets.

FIGURE 28.5

A Momento digital photo frame can display your family photos in a slideshow.

Photo courtesy A Living Picture, PLC.

ON the WEB
Learn more about the Momento digital frames at http://alivingpicture.com.

Network Music and Video Players

As with digital photo frames, network music players have been around for a few years now. However, there may be one or two people out there who aren't familiar with these devices. Most of them can stream audio from a variety of sources, including UPnP/WMC servers and Internet radio stations. Here is an overview of a few popular devices.

CAUTION   You should be aware that not all network music players support the UPnP standard and act as a UPnP client. Some, like the popular Squeezebox from Slim Systems, requires using proprietary software. Check the specs before you buy if your goal is to have a device work with Windows Home Server.

Roku SoundBridge

The Roku SoundBridge family of devices, shown in Figure 28.6, is notable for their unique, stylish design and ability to handle a wide variety of streaming audio sources. You can connect it to Windows Home Server to stream audio, but that's not all. You can stream Internet radio stations as well as music from a number of other sources. It has earned Microsoft's PlaysForSure certification, which allows it to play WMA (Windows Media Audio) DRM (Digital Rights Management) music files from such sources as Rhapsody, Napster, and MuchMusic. It can also share non-DRM music from Apple iTunes.

FIGURE 28.6

The Roku SoundBridge and SoundBridge Radio devices stream music from Windows Home Server and more.

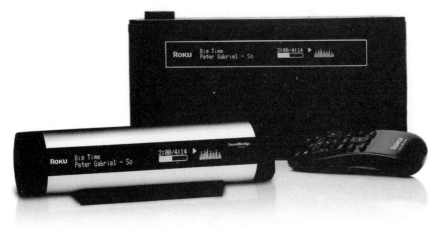

Photo courtesy of Roku Labs.

There are currently three models of the Roku SoundBridge — the M500, the M1001, and the R1000. The M500 and M1001 are network-media-only players, while the R1000 adds AM/FM radio capabilities. All of the SoundBridge models can stream audio over an 802.11b/g Wi-Fi connection.

ON the WEB You can get more information about the Roku SoundBridge family of players at www.rokulabs.com.

Network music players are great for streaming audio from your server, and given they only stream music files, they will work over most networks. If you have a network fast enough to handle streaming video, you may decide to add a device that can stream video as well — even high-definition video is possible over a fast connection.

D-Link MediaLounge DSM-750 Player

Don't have a game console that can play high-definition video, or simply want a device dedicated to that task? One option is the D-Link MediaLounge. This device will stream video up to high-definition quality if your network is suited for it. (802.11n or wired Ethernet is required.)

The DSM-750, shown in Figure 28.7, supports a wide range of different server options, including the ubiquitous UPnP solution provided by Windows Home Server. As a Windows Media Extender device, it can also stream content from Windows Media Center computers (such as Vista Premium or Ultimate, or XP Media Center Edition). Windows Media Video formatted streaming video is supported, which allows Windows Home Server's built-in media server to provide video. There is also support for popular DivX and Xvid protocols, although you will need a third-party media server software such as TVersity in order to stream those formats from Windows Home Server.

> **ON the WEB**   Learn more about the DLink MediaLounge DSM-750 at www.dlink.com/ products/?pid=547&sec=1.

FIGURE 28.7

The D-Link MediaLounge DSM-750 will stream from UPnP servers as well as from Windows Media Center computers.

Photo courtesy of D-Link

Summary

Game consoles aren't the only devices that are capable of streaming digital media content from Windows Home Server. A large and growing number of devices, ranging from satellite receivers to picture frames that have the ability to stream media, exist.

If you are running a Windows PC, your options for a UPnP client seem rather limited. Fortunately for Vista users, Microsoft has finally added media streaming capabilities into Windows Media Player 11. While that's great if you are using Vista, it's not if you are still running XP. There are, however, other software options for you to consider.

Aside from computers, devices such as digital picture frames, standalone music playback devices, and even satellite TV receivers are adding media streaming capabilities in order to increase their value.

Chapter 29

Configuring Music Players

I f you enjoy music, you probably have a portable music player, perhaps even two or more. Even if you don't, if you are in a household with several people, it's a good bet that at least someone in the house does.

The mp3 revolution of the early 2000s has caused a sea of change in the way people listen to their music. We used to be tied to our CD collections and tape copies, and we were constantly scattering our music collection between the home stereo, the car, and portable players. No longer — all of that has been replaced by a device that can hold multiple gigabytes worth of music files, all that fits in our shirt pockets and can be played anywhere we are.

For a family that owns multiple music players, however, a new problem has arisen. Everybody has their own music library on their own computer, without any simple way of sharing songs. This can be wasteful, as multiple copies of individual songs take up a lot of space on each computer.

You are probably wondering if you can use Windows Home Server with your portable music player, and if there is any advantage to doing so. The answer, of course, is yes, you certainly can, especially if you are willing to take the time to set things up to work properly. In this chapter, we'll show you how to take advantage of the server's file sharing capabilities and always-on nature to share your music library with other computer users on the network.

Enhancing the Use of Your iPod

The iPod family of music players has been the world's most popular player for a number of years now, and that doesn't show any signs of slowing down. Never ones to rest on their laurels, Apple is constantly refreshing the iPod line to keep it both innovative and stylish. Figure 29.1 shows the latest additions to the iPod family — the iPod touch and the iPod Classic.

FIGURE 29.1

Apple's iPod is the world's best-selling brand of portable music player.

Photo courtesy of Apple.

Installing iTunes on Windows Home Server

Installing iTunes (Apple's application used to manage your music library and sync it to your iPod) is pretty straightforward; in fact, if you have an iPod you've no doubt done it before, perhaps several times. Is there any difference when installing it on Windows Home Server? Well, yes and no. The installation process is for the most part identical. However, there are some things you need to keep in mind.

First of all, your Windows Home Server box may not have the hardware that a typical PC does, particularly when it comes to audio and video drivers — so you might not actually be able to play music on the server. Second of all, you will need to keep your iTunes library on a shared folder rather than on a local hard drive. Finally, while you might want iTunes to run on Windows Home Server to share your music files, you probably don't want to have to log on to the server to use iTunes to browse the iTunes music store or rip CDs. Instead, you will probably want to update your iTunes folder from a more convenient location. With these things in mind, here are the steps to follow to install iTunes on your Windows Home Server machine. Perform these steps on the server — accessing it through Remote Desktop is fine.

1. **If you have an existing iTunes library you'd like to start with, copy it to the Music share on your server.** Your iTunes folder is usually found in your My Music folder. If you don't have an existing iTunes library, create empty folders on your Music share: iTunes with a subfolder of iTunes Music.

2. **Insert the iTunes CD into the server's drive.** Alternatively, download the latest version of iTunes directly from Apple.

ON the WEB You can obtain the most recent version of iTunes from Apple at www.apple.com/itunes. You should download this from a computer other than the Windows Home Server machine and then copy it to a shared drive.

3. **Run the setup if it doesn't start automatically.** The installer shown in Figure 29.2 is launched.

FIGURE 29.2

iTunes can be installed on the server.

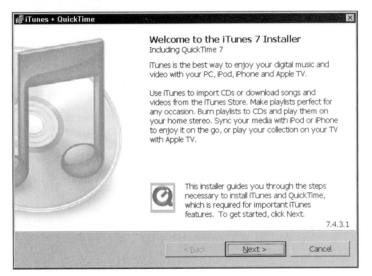

4. **Click Next to move through the iTunes Wizard.** Accept all of the defaults, especially the destination folder path of C:\Program Files\iTunes.

5. **Click Install to begin the installation, it will progress until completion, as shown in Figure 29.3.**

FIGURE 29.3

The iTunes installer in progress

6. **Leave the box checked to launch iTunes and click Finish.**

NOTE   You might see a warning similar to the one shown in Figure 29.4, indicating that iTunes has detected a problem with your audio configuration. You can be safely ignore it, because you will not be playing back music on the server itself.

7. **If all went well, iTunes launches to a blank library, as shown in Figure 29.5.**

FIGURE 29.4

On Windows Home Server, iTunes may not like the lack of audio playback capability. This can be safely ignored.

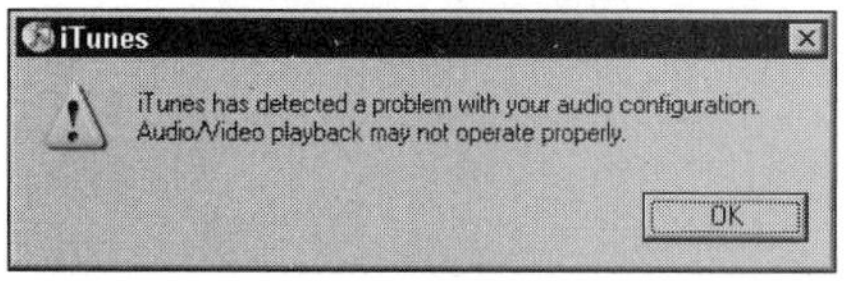

iTunes installs to a clean slate.

The next step that you will need to do is to map a drive letter to the Music shared folder on the server. This is necessary because when you specify the UNC path (for example, \\fserver\Music\), it often gets translated back in to the real drive path (such as D:\shares\Music), and it's not a good idea to write files directly to that path as it can interfere with Windows Home Server's ability to manage the files through folder duplication. To map a drive letter, do the following:

1. **Open Windows Explorer by choosing Start ⇨ Windows Explorer.**

2. **Choose Tools ⇨ Map Network Drive, as shown in Figure 29.6.**

Map your music folder to a drive letter to ensure you're not writing to the data drive directly.

3. **Choose a drive letter from the drop-down list.** (We chose P:, for Pod.)

4. **Enter the path to the shared music folder (for example, \\server\music), as shown in Figure 29.7.** Be sure to leave Reconnect at logon checked so that your drive letter will be maintained when you need to log on again.

5. **Click Finish to map the drive.**

6. **Verify that the P: drive contains the same contents as the** \\<server>\Music folder.

FIGURE 29.7

Choose a drive letter that isn't used by anything else. Leave Reconnect at logon checked.

Next, you need to configure iTunes to point to the new destination folder. To do this, you need to change the iTunes preferences. Follow these steps:

1. **Launch iTunes on the server.**

2. **Choose Edit ➪ Preferences. A dialog box appears.**

3. **Click the Advanced tab (see Figure 29.8).**

4. **Click Change to alter the iTunes music folder location.**

5. **Browse to your iTunes Music path.** If you put yours on the P: drive, the path should be P:\iTunes\iTunes Music.

6. **If you have existing files to import from those folders, make sure that Copy files to iTunes music folder when adding to library is unchecked.** Leaving this checked causes a corruption of your iTunes music folder by creating a second copy of each song in it.

7. **Make sure that the Keep iTunes Music folder organized box is checked.** This helps ensure that new additions to the library are done in an orderly fashion.

8. **Click OK.**

FIGURE 29.8

Point iTunes to your shared drive.

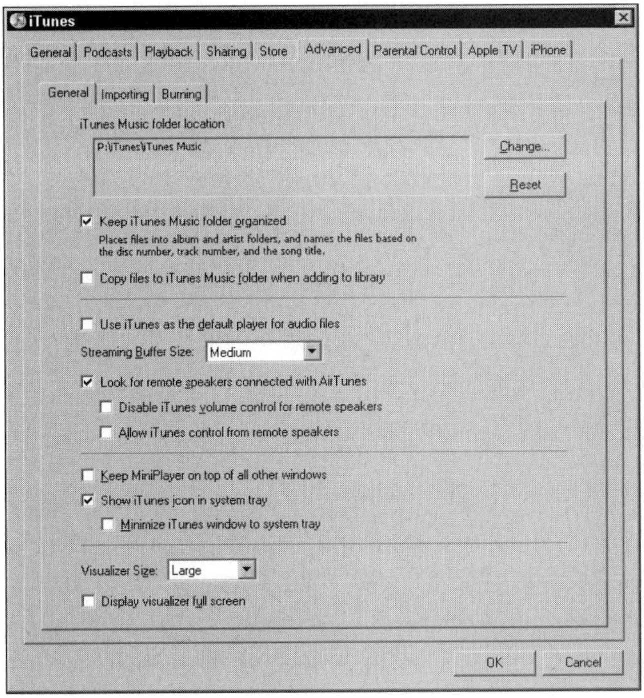

You are now ready to import your music files into the server's library. The easiest way to do this is to drag the iTunes Music folder onto iTunes, as shown in Figure 29.9.

If you want other computer's iTunes installation to share the same music files, repeat the previous steps on each of them. Each computer will then have its own iTunes library database, but will reference the same music files. The separate iTunes library will allow each user to customize her own playlists, rank songs, and sync to her iPod.

There is a problem, however. If one computer adds or deletes files from their library, the files themselves will be changed, but the iTunes libraries on your other computers won't know about the changes. New files won't be visible in the play list, and deleted files will still be visible but unplayable. What you need is a way to refresh the iTunes database when a change is made to the music library.

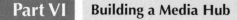

FIGURE 29.9

Add your iTunes music to your library with a simple drag and drop.

Using the iTunes Library Updater

Fortunately, a free utility can sync iTunes with any changes made to the library. This utility, called the iTunes Library Updater, will scan the music folders for any changes, and then sync them automatically to the library. The iTunes Library Updater (iTLU) is shown in Figure 29.10.

ON the WEB Download the iTLU at http://www.sofotex.com/iTunes-Library-Updater-(iTLU)-download_L31772.html.

FIGURE 29.10

The iTLU will keep iTunes in sync with changes to the music folders.

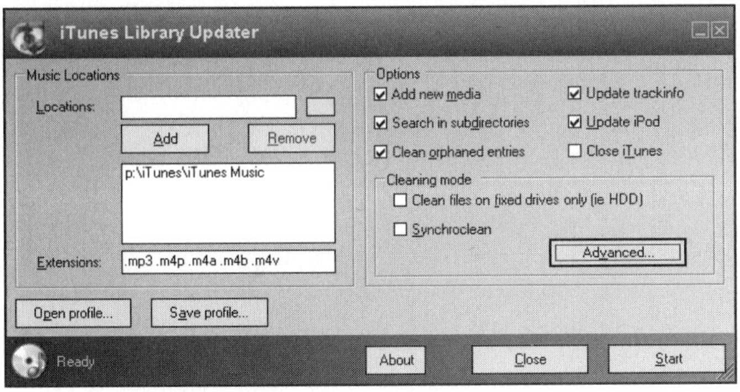

Install iTLU using the default settings on whichever computer needs to be brought in sync. Then, follow these steps to synchronize your library.

1. **In the location box, enter the path to your music files (for example, P:\iTunes\iTunes Music).** Click Add.

2. **Check the appropriate boxes on the right.** Add new media, Search in subdirectories, Clean orphaned entries, Update trackinfo should all be checked.

3. **If you would like an attached iPod to be automatically updated, check Update iPod.**

4. **Save the profile to a descriptive name.**

5. **Click Start to update iTunes.** If iTunes is not running, it will be launched in order to perform the update.

In addition to the graphical user interface (GUI) mode, there is also a command line interface to iTLU. The great thing about the command line utility is that it can be scripted to automatically update iTunes even if you aren't around. This makes it perfect for an unattended iTunes installation on the server. The command line utility at work is shown in Figure 29.11.

Scheduling the iTLU

You can use the Windows task scheduler to schedule a regular daily update of the iTLU utility. Follow these steps to accomplish this.

FIGURE 29.11

The command line version of iTLU is scriptable so that you can perform scheduled updates.

1. **Create a profile and execute it in the GUI to make sure it works.**

2. **Create a batch file in a convenient location.** We suggest the P: drive (or whichever drive letter you assigned to the music share). Name the file something descriptive, such as RUN_ITLA.BAT.

3. **Add the following line to the batch file, with the path and filename you called the profile you saved from the GUI for the** /p **parameter:**

   ```
   itluconsole /p:"P:\iTunes\myprofile.itlu"
   ```

4. **Save the batch file.**

5. **Open the Windows Task Scheduler; it can be found in the Control Panel.** Click Scheduled Tasks to launch the Scheduled Task Wizard, as shown in Figure 29.12.

6. **Click Browse and locate your batch file.**

7. **Make sure Daily is set as the update frequency, as shown in Figure 29.13.**

8. **Click Next.**

9. **Choose a time for the batch file to run.** I recommend that you choose a time that is outside the server's backup window as both are disk-intensive operations.

10. **Make sure the box to run the task every day is checked.**

11. **Click Next.**

12. **Choose a username to run the job under.** The default user name is Administrator.

13. **Enter the password twice, and then click Next.**

14. **Click Finish to schedule the task.**

Congratulations, your server is now set to update its iTunes library based on the actual files in the shared folder. You can repeat this for any other Windows computer on the network to keep them all updated.

FIGURE 29.12

Browse for your batch file, and set it to run daily.

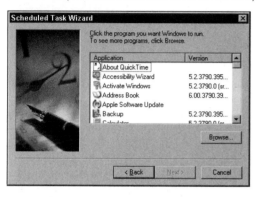

FIGURE 29.13

Schedule your batch job to run daily.

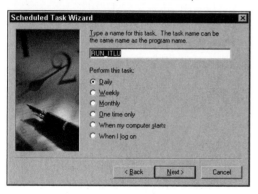

Sharing your iTunes library

You may be wondering why we had you install iTunes on the server in the first place, if it is going to be unattended. The answer is that you can use iTunes as a streaming media server, albeit not one that uses the Universal Plug and Play (UPnP) protocol that we discuss in previous chapters. There are, however, devices that are compatible with the iTunes network sharing, including iTunes itself. Figure 29.14 shows the iTunes accessing a shared library over the network.

FIGURE 29.14

Sharing your iTunes library means that any iTunes instance on the network can play music from the server's library.

Follow these steps to enable sharing:

1. Launch iTunes on the server.
2. Choose Edit ➪ Preferences.
3. Click the Sharing tab, shown in Figure 29.15.
4. Check the box labeled Share my library on my local network.
5. Click the General tab.
6. Enter a descriptive name for your server in the Shared Name field.
7. Click OK.

FIGURE 29.15

Sharing your iTunes library means that any iTunes instance on the network can play music from the server's library.

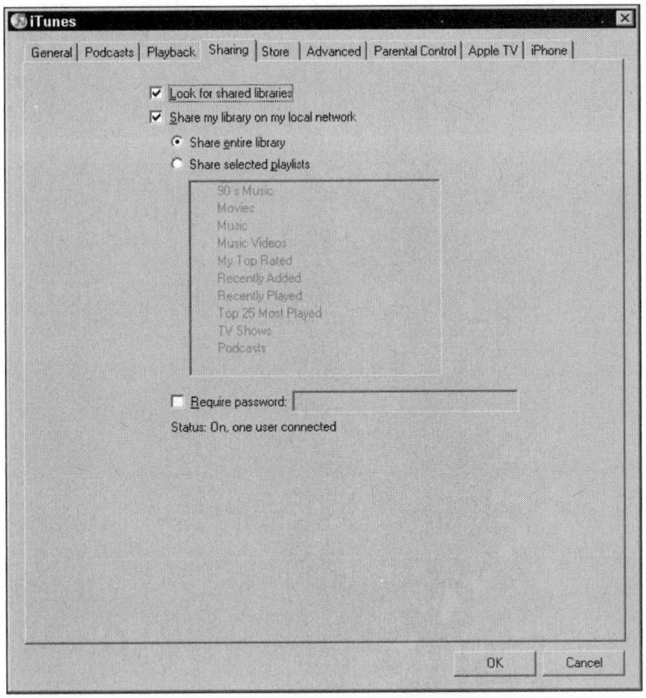

Using Your Zune

If you've recently purchased a Zune (shown in Figure 29.16), welcome to the Social. Well, at least that's what the marketing guys say. If the Zune is your thing, you may be happy to know that you can get even more out of your Zune by letting it get social with your server.

There are some major limitations when it comes to the Zune and Windows Home Server. The Zune software cannot be installed on a Windows 2003-based platform such as Windows Home Server, so sharing via that application cannot be done in the same way that you can with iTunes. There are a few unique things you can do with the Zune software though; take a look at them.

FIGURE 29.16

The Zune is Microsoft's answer to the iPod.

Photo courtesy of Microsoft.

Watching server folders

When you first install the Zune software, it will search your computer looking for all of the compatible media files it can find. It won't search network shared folders; however you can add them to the library. The Zune software will periodically check folders for new music and automatically add them to the library.

To add a network path to the Zune library path, do the following:

1. **Launch the Zune software.**
2. **Choose Options ⇨ Add Folder to Library.**
3. **In the Add Folder to Library window, shown in Figure 29.17, click Add Folder.**
4. **Browse for the folder or enter the path directly.** For network shares, you can use a mapped drive letter, or just a UNC path (such as, \\<server>\Music).
5. **Click OK.**

If you add the Music share from Windows Home Server, you will automatically get access to all of the music that is put on the server. You will even automatically get access to music from an iTunes library if you happen to also have an iPod and follow the instructions presented earlier in this chapter!

FIGURE 29.17

You can add server shared folders to the search path.

Ripping music to the server

If you want the Zune software to automatically rip CD content to the server so that it is accessible by any device capable of streaming it, you can change the default folder used for ripping. Follow these steps to change the folder:

1. **Choose Options ⇨ Rip ⇨ More Options.**

2. **In the Rip Options dialog, click the Change button next to the path shown.**

3. **Either browse to the server path or enter it directly (see Figure 29.18).** Click OK when done.

4. **Change any of the other ripping settings.** For maximum compatibility, choose mp3 as the format.

FIGURE 29.18

Change Rip settings so that new music automatically goes onto the server.

Summary

With the explosion of portable digital music devices, the task of managing your music collection has changed from keeping track of where your CDs are to keeping your mp3 files organized. Windows Home Server can help. Not only can you use it as a shared repository that any music player software can use to store the files, but also you can also install software directly onto the server to give it added functionality.

Although Apple's iTunes software is not designed for a multiuser environment, it can be made to point to a server share as the location of its music files, which means that instances of iTunes running on different computers can all share music. There is a catch, however — iTunes will not be able to track any changes to the music files unless the changes were done from inside iTunes. Fortunately, a third-party application can come to the rescue by forcing iTunes to sync with the music folder.

Another use for iTunes is as an alternative streaming media server. You can install iTunes directly on the server and stream music and video to iTunes running on other computers as well as other iTunes-compatible devices.

Microsoft's Zune software does iTunes one better by making it easier to manage the library. You can specify a server path as both a location to search for new music files and a destination for ripped files. The Zune can even scan your iTunes music folder and add any songs that are Zune-playable to its library.

Chapter 30

Working with Mobile Devices

People are increasingly more and more on the move, and they want to keep in contact while doing so. Today, we have more options than ever when it comes to using personal electronics to access information, in the form of mobile devices such as personal data assistants (PDAs) and smart phones.

If you have a Windows Mobile-based device, you can make use of software that has been created especially for Windows Home Server that will allow you to do such things as stream music to your device, and access your shared files, and this can be done from anywhere you are able to connect to the Internet using Wi-Fi or even through a wireless data access plan.

In this chapter, we present a few of the options that are available to those of you who are Windows Mobile device users that can provide even more value to your Windows Home Server investment.

IN THIS CHAPTER

Using Windows Mobile devices

Using LobsterTunes

Using Pocket Player

Establishing Remote access

Using Home Base

Using the Terminal Services client

Bringing Music to Windows Mobile

Modern wireless PDAs and smart phones are multipurpose convergence devices. They deliver traditional PDA functions such as calendar and portable document viewing and editing, Web browsing, and remote real-time e-mail access, and now, with flash memory cards dropping in price, they can even do a great job as portable media players.

It's easy enough to transfer music files to your Windows Mobile device using ActiveSync (or Windows Mobile Device Center in Vista). If, however, you'd like to take advantage of the music streaming capabilities of Windows Home Server to play music over your Wi-Fi network or elsewhere, you can do so with one of these applications.

Using LobsterTunes

LobsterTunes, from Electric Pocket Ltd. (shown in Figure 30.1) is a media player application for Windows Mobile devices that does a whole lot more than just play the music that is already on your Windows Mobile device. It is also capable of streaming music from a Universal Plug and Play (UPnP) audio source (such as Windows Home Server) over a Wi-Fi connection, play music from Internet radio stations, and even search out album art and biographical information on artists.

FIGURE 30.1

LobsterTunes can stream music to your Windows Mobile device.

Installing the LobsterTunes add-in

The LobsterTunes add-in is installed like other add-ins, from the Windows Home Server console. Follow these steps to do the install:

1. Download the free 7-day trial `LobsterTunes4WHS.msi` file from `http://lobstertunes.com/download.php`.

2. Copy the `LobsterTunes4WHS.msi` file to your server's `Software\Addins` folder.

3. In the Console, open the Settings dialog and select the Add-ins item.

4. Select the Available tab, Lobster should be visible in the list, as shown in Figure 30.2.

5. Click the Install button for the Lobster add-in. The LobsterTunes service will be installed on your server.

FIGURE 30.2

LobsterTunes includes a Windows Home Server add-in that is installed through the Console.

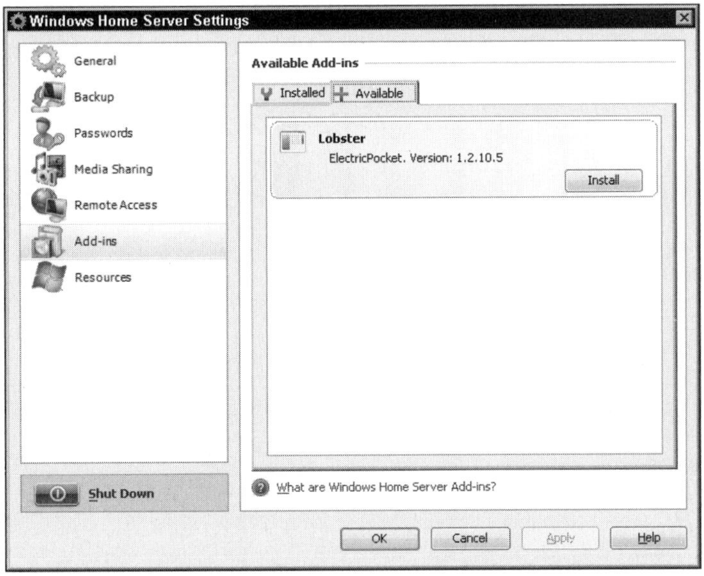

After the add-in is installed, you must install the client application on the computer that you use to sync with your Windows Mobile device. This client application is installed in the server's Public share, in the Lobster subfolder.

The next time that you sync with your device, LobsterTunes will be downloaded and installed on it.

Using LobsterTunes to stream media

LobsterTunes will automatically locate your Windows Home Server, along with any UPnP servers that it happens to find on your network. To stream music, do the following:

1. **Launch Lobster.**
2. **Select the My Music tab.**
3. **You will see your UPnP servers, including Windows Home Server in the list, and you can browse through and play your music.** This is shown in Figure 30.3.

ON the WEB   Find out more information about LobsterTunes (and download a free trial version) at www.lobstertunes.com.

Browse your UPnP servers just like any other folder.

LobsterTunes isn't the only media player for Windows Mobile devices that is capable of streaming media from Windows Home Server, but it is the first player to specifically target the Windows Home Server platform as a music server with the creation of the add-in.

Using Pocket Player 3.5

Pocket Player 3.5 (shown in Figure 30.4) from Conduits Technologies is another popular media player that is capable of streaming music from a variety of sources, including Internet radio, legacy Windows streaming protocols such as Multimedia Messaging Service (MMS), and Shoutcast. Not least among its features is the capability to stream music over UPnP servers, including Windows Home Server, when you install the optional UPnP plug-in.

Pocket Player 3.5.is another UPnP-capable streaming media player.

By itself, Pocket Player is comparable to other devices on your network that can access your UPnP servers in that it'll work just as long as you are connecting through your own network.

ON the WEB You can download a 30-day full-featured demo of Pocket Player 3.5 from Conduit's Web site (`www.conduits.com/products/player`). In order to make use of network streaming, you must also download Pocket Player's UPnP plug-in at `www.conduits.com/products/player/plugins.asp`.

Accessing Your Server Remotely

We've discussed the remote access feature of Windows Home Server, and shown how you can access your shared folders and files remotely over the Web. As useful as that capability is, there are times when you may not have access to a computer with Internet Explorer or Remote Desktop. Fortunately, if you have a Windows Mobile-based smart phone or PDA, there are other ways to access your shared files and connect to your server. Among them is Home Base, a simple add-in that allows you to retrieve shared files over the Internet.

For remote maintenance of your server, you can use the Terminal Services client included with Windows Mobile PDAs, or VNC (Virtual Network Computing), a system for remotely accessing computers from all sorts of devices.

Using HomeBase

The standard remote access Web site hosted by Windows Home Server cannot be accessed by the Internet Explorer Mobile, the Web browser on Windows Mobile devices. If you attempt to access it, you will be unable to log in.

In order to get around this, an add-in called HomeBase (shown in Figure 30.5) was developed as a part of the Windows Home Server Code4Fame challenge. This add-in consists of a server component that is installed on the Windows Home Server box, and a client component that is installed on the Windows Mobile device. When linked together, the client allows access to shared folders and files on the server.

In addition to the remote file access, HomeBase is used to host a blog on the Windows Home Server's Web site. Entries for the blog can be entered using either the Windows Mobile client, or a desktop client.

FIGURE 30.5

HomeBase is a Windows Home Server add-in that lets you access shared folders on Windows Mobile devices.

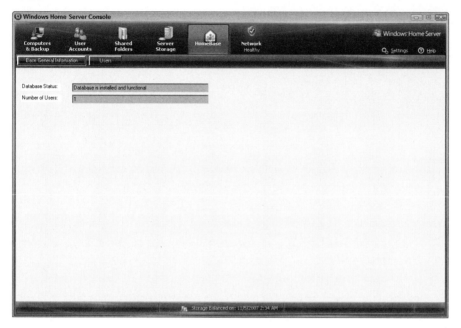

HomeBase is installed like most add-ins. Follow these steps:

1. Download the HomeBase.msi add-in from www.alekseibytecode.com/ homebase, and copy it to the /Software/Add-ins shared folder.

2. In the Console, access the Settings dialog and choose the Add-ins tab.

3. Click the Available tab, and click the Install button on the HomeBase entry.

4. After the installation, the console must be restarted. When it does, a new HomeBase tab is available in the Console.

5. If you only want to take advantage of the remote file access, you don't have to install the database as described on the HomeBase tab. The database is only used if you intend to make use of HomeBase's blogging capabilities.

After the server component is installed, you can download the client from a new Web site that has been created on your Windows Home Server. Point your browser to http://server. homeserver.com/HomeBase, replacing server.homeserver.com with the remote access URL for your server. You will access the HomeBase Web page, with two links. Select the Mobile Client link to download the client to your device, as shown in Figure 30.6.

FIGURE 30.6

Download the Mobile Client application directly from the HomeBase Web page on your server.

Set the server parameters necessary to find your server. If you are inside your network, you can simply use the IP address of the server. If external, enter your remote access domain, as shown in Figure 30.7.

FIGURE 30.7

Enter server parameters so that HomeBase can find it.

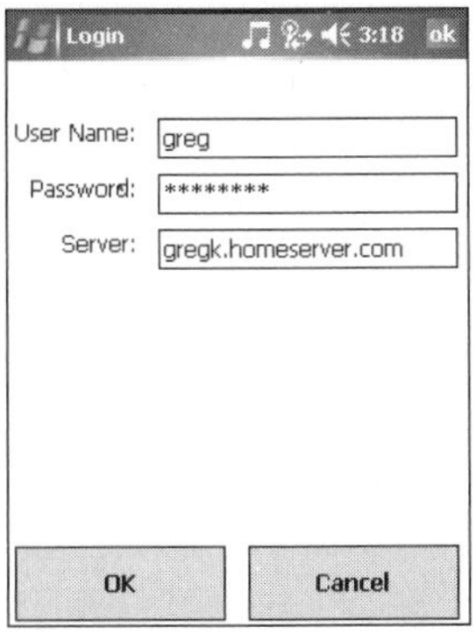

After you set the server parameters in the client, you can view the folders and files on your server, as shown in Figure 30.8.

 Learn more about HomeBase at www.alekseibytecode.com/homebase.

FIGURE 30.8

The HomeBase client interface mimics the look of the Windows Home Folder shared folders.

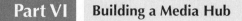

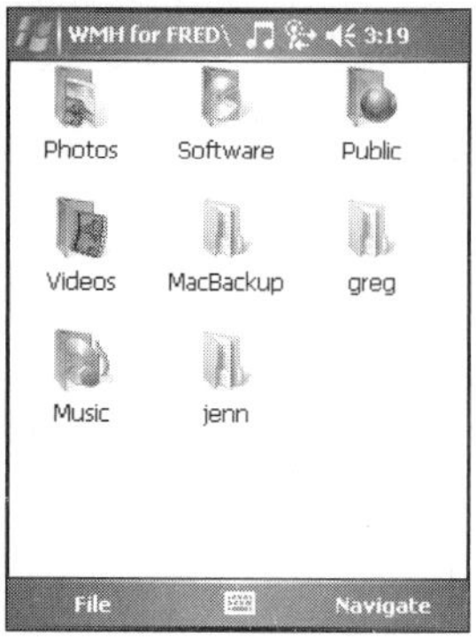

Using the Terminal Services client

As we discuss in Chapter 10, you can log on to the server's desktop remotely using the Remote Desktop client on Windows or Mac computers. As it turns out, there is a client for Windows Mobile clients for the Pocket PC platform. The client, called the Terminal Services client (named after the alternate name for Remote Desktop).

NOTE The Terminal Services client requires a touch screen, so it is not included with smartphone versions of Windows Mobile that don't include touch screens.

To connect to the server, do the following:

1. On your mobile device, navigate to the Programs folder.

2. Tap the Terminal Services client icon to launch it.

3. **Enter the name of your server.** If the server cannot be located by name, you can use its IP address instead.

4. **Make sure to uncheck the Limit size of server desktop to fit on this screen check box.**

5. **Click Connect.** If the client is able to connect to the server, you will see the authentication dialog. (You may have to scroll around the screen to see it.) This is shown in Figure 30.9. You should now be able to access the server's desktop.

NOTE Depending on the size of your Windows Mobile device's screen, the Terminal Services client may be limited to a resolution of 640 x 480, even with scrolling. At that resolution, you will be somewhat limited in what you can do on the server, especially when using the Windows Home Server Console.

FIGURE 30.9

You can use the Terminal Services client for remote server maintenance. Scrolling is required.

Summary

Mobile devices running Microsoft's Windows Mobile operating system include smart phones and PDAs that are capable of connecting wirelessly to the Internet as well as to other devices on a home network. With the addition of some software, you can turn your Windows Mobile device into a portable streaming music player or a terminal that is capable of accessing your streaming music files.

LobsterTunes is the first Windows Mobile media player that has support specifically for Windows Home Server. While the LobsterTunes client application allows the Windows Mobile device to access UPnP servers on the network, the Windows Home Server add-in component goes a step further by allowing the device to access media files remotely from a Wi-Fi hot spot or even a cellular wireless provider.

Other streaming media player solutions, such as Pocket Player, exist for Windows Mobile, and can be useful if your needs extend only to streaming media from inside your home's network.

While music streaming is nice, it's not the only thing your Windows Mobile device is good for. You an also use it to gain remote access to your server, using such tools as Home Base to access your shared files from the Internet, or Windows Mobile's own Terminal Services client to gain access to the desktop of your server.

This chapter just starts to scratch the surface of what you can do with Windows Home Server and Windows Mobile smart phones and PDAs. As these devices proliferate and Windows Home Server becomes more entrenched in the home, you should expect to see more support for these sorts of devices.

Recording Media
to the Server

In the previous chapters in this section concerning media streaming, we've focused primarily on serving up audio and video media files that you've obtained from somewhere, without really discussing where they come from. While audio files are easily ripped from a CD, recording video is a little more difficult (not to mention of questionable legality).

One intriguing idea for a 24/7 server is to use it as a digital video recorder (DVR). A DVR has one or more connected television tuners that can record digital TV signals to files on the computer's hard drive. Playback is done by streaming the video files over the network to client computers or video players. You can do this without paying additional fees to your cable or satellite provider, and it can quickly fill your hard drive up with video that you can then stream to the other devices on your network.

In this chapter, we discuss options for recording television directly to your Windows Home Server from an attached TV tuner card, as well as recording from a Vista Media Center computer. We also show you some Windows Home Server add-ins that will make the whole job easier no matter how you want to use Windows Home Server as part of your household video distribution system.

Recording Television

It seems that integrated household video distribution systems are getting more popular all the time. With the advent of digital television and TV tuner devices for computers, it's become easier to record high-quality television recordings directly to a hard drive.

With TV schedule services, applications that can schedule shows to automatically be recorded have blossomed. And with the final piece of the puzzle, high-speed networking throughout the home, it's become easy to stream this content from a central storage point to televisions and computers through the house. Broadcast TV networks, meet household TV networks.

Windows Home Server has come onto the scene at the perfect time, when the convergence of all of these technologies makes it a natural choice as a key piece of a home entertainment system.

There are two approaches to turning Windows Home Server into a media hub. The first way to do it is to capture video from another computer, such as a Vista Media Center PC, shown in Figure 31.1. Video is recorded to a shared drive on the server for storage and later streaming playback. We take a look at an add-in called the Recorded TV Manager to see how you can use it to accomplish this.

FIGURE 31.1

Windows Media Center computers are capable of working with a wide range of digital media.

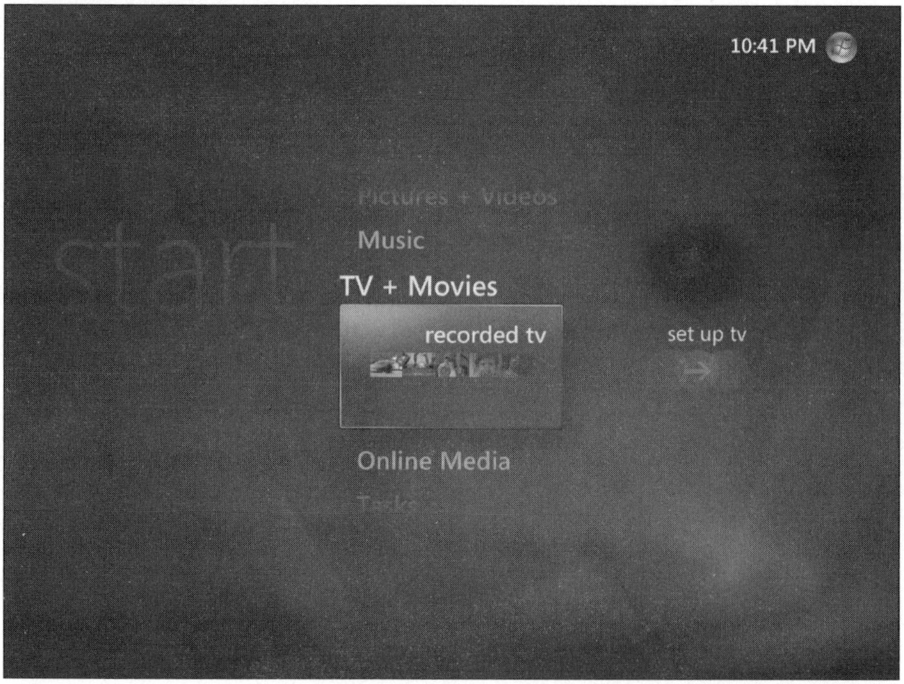

The second approach is to integrate the video recording hardware directly with the Windows Home Server computer, which is where a product such as SageTV comes in.

Getting Video from Windows Media Center

Windows Media Center is a multimedia application that was originally released as the heart of a special version of Windows XP known as Media Center Edition (MCE) that was only supplied with Original Equipment Manufacturers (OEMs). The follow-up version, Windows XP Media Center Edition 2005, was so popular that it became the de facto XP operating system included with many computers.

At the core of MCE, Windows Media Center is an application that is designed to serve just as its name implies: As a media center capable of managing all forms of digital entertainment in your home. It can record and play back television, stream music and photos, play DVDs, and much more. You can control Media Center from the computer's desktop using the mouse, or through the use of a special Media Center remote control for home theater PC use. You can use special devices called Media Center Extenders to send media from the MCE computer to displays around the house.

The MCE legacy lives on in Windows Vista, with both the Premium and Ultimate versions of the operating system, and the Xbox 360 console includes Media Center Extender functionality right from the box. Now even more people will be able to take advantage of the features offered by Windows Media Center.

ON the WEB Windows Media Center is a complex application, and entire books have been written about it alone. It is beyond the scope of this book to go into detail on how to configure and use it. To start with, however, visit Microsoft's informational page on the subject at `www.microsoft.com/windows/products/windowsvista/features/details/mediacenter.mspx`.

Installing the Recorded TV Manager add-in

The Recorded TV Manager add-in is designed to consolidate captured video files from Windows Media Center Edition and manage them. You can create rules specifying how to deal with content. All of these items are possibilities:

- For new recordings in a folder, you can have the file moved or copied to a new destination folder, such as your server's videos share.

- For new episodes of a specific series, you can have the episodes moved or copied to another folder. This allows you to treat certain TV series in a special manner — for instance, you could move a show that only one family member watches directly to their computer.

- When the last episode of a series is deleted, you can indicate to copy the next available episode to the folder when available.

ON the WEB Learn more about Recorded TV Manager and download the trial version at `www.fjdrasch.com/v2/v2_frame.htm`.

Install the add-in by following these steps:

1. Download the installation files, and copy the `.msi` file for Windows Home Server to the `\\<server>\software\add-ins` folder, with your server's name in place of `<server>`.

2. Log on to the Windows Home Server Console.

3. Click the Settings button, and click the Add-ins tab.

4. Click the Available tab.

5. Click Install to begin the installation process.

6. Recorded TV Manager must run under the administrator account on the server, because the default service account doesn't have access to network shares. When you are prompted to enter a user name, enter **.\Administrator** (with a dot-backslash in front), followed by the Windows Home Server administrator password.

After the installation is complete, the Console automatically shuts down. When you reconnect to it, you will see a new Recorded TV Manager tab on the Console, as shown in Figure 31.2.

FIGURE 31.2

The Recorded TV Manager lets you manage content from one or more Windows Media Center computers.

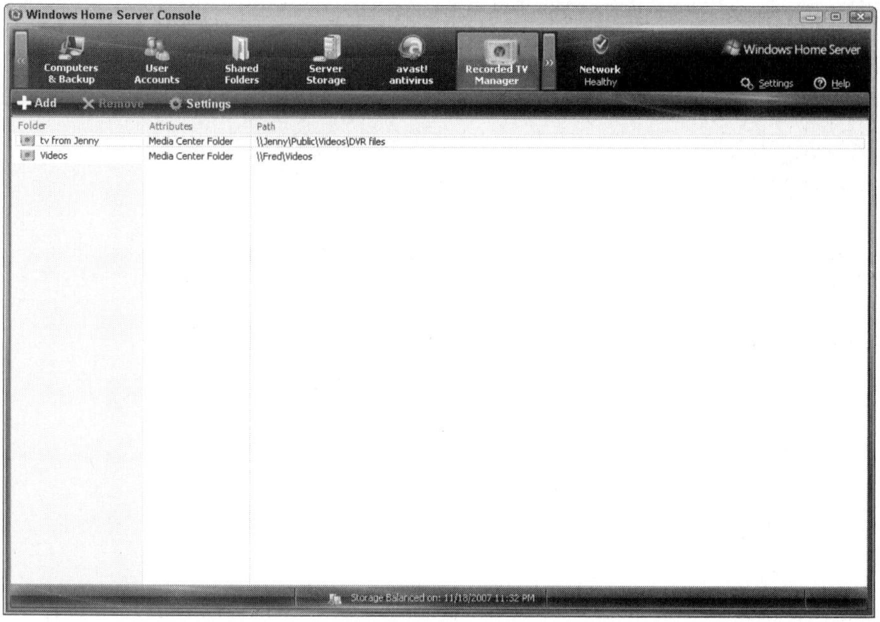

Using Recorded TV Manager

To use the Recorded TV Manager, click the Recorded TV Manager tab and click the Add button. Browse to the shared folders on the network where you have Windows Media Center content stored, and click OK.

You should also add folders that you want to use as destinations for videos. When you configure the rules, you will often be copying files from locations where Media Center creates the files to locations where it is more convenient to access them, such as from the media center computer to your Windows Home Server videos shared folder.

Once you have TV recorded, you can create rules. Rules define how Recorded TV Manager handles media files it finds in the folders you have added. Click the Settings button, and you will be sent to the Windows Home Server Settings dialog with the Recorded TV Manager section already selected, as shown in Figure 31.3.

Turn on the AutoCopy service by clicking the On button. Then, click the Rules button to configure rules.

The Recorded TV Manager includes settings to control how recordings are managed.

In the AutoCopy Rules dialog, shown in Figure 31.4, click the New button to create a new rule. Select a condition for your rule, and an action to take on the rule. In the Rule Description field, click on any underlined value to edit to refer to a series name or a source or destination folder. This is shown in Figure 31.5. If you are familiar with setting rules for mail in Outlook, you will feel right at home with this process.

FIGURE 31.4

The rules editor lets you set actions that will occur when a TV show is recorded to a MCE folder.

FIGURE 31.5

Choose conditions and actions for the rules.

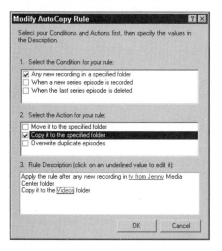

Recording Directly on the Server

It is not necessary to involve a Windows Media Center computer in the mix if you want to simply record TV to a server and access it — you can actually install a TV tuner card or USB device directly on to your Windows Home Server computer and record directly to the hard drive, which is great if you desire DVR functionality but don't like the idea of having more than one server on 24/7.

Installing a TV tuner

The first step in getting video to your server is to install a TV Tuner card or USB stick tuner. Make sure you choose one that states compatibility with Windows Server 2003, and by extension, Windows Home Server.

The typical procedure for installing a TV tuner driver is as follows:

1. **Insert the CD with the drivers into the server's CD/DVD drive.** If you don't have such a drive, you can either copy the files from the CD on to the server, or access the CD drive of another computer remotely over the network.

2. **If you are using a USB device, attach it now.** The Hardware Update Wizard should appear, as shown in Figure 31.6.

FIGURE 31.6

The Hardware Update Wizard will guide you through installing drivers for your TV tuner.

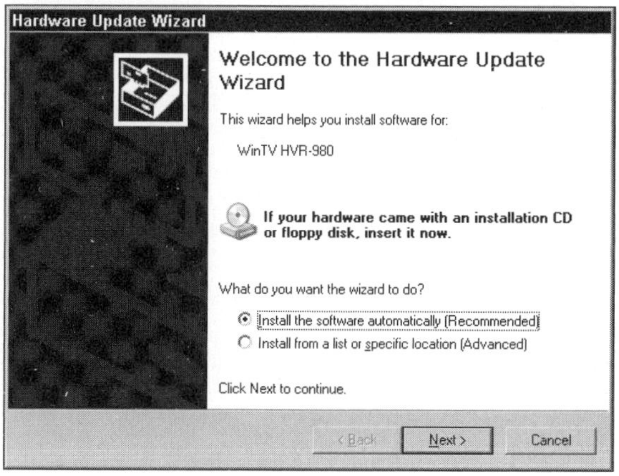

3. **Choose to install the software automatically, or browse specifically to the CD to save some time and ensure that the drivers are found.** You can install the rest of the OEM software if you like to take your TV tuner card for a spin and verify that everything works before installing SageTV.

Installing the SageTV add-in

SageTV has traditionally provided server components that work with either Windows MCE computers or with non-MCE versions of Windows. With the add-in, installation on the Windows Home Server console is a snap.

Download the installation files from www.sagetv.com, and copy the Microsoft Software Installer (MSI) file for the add-in into the \\<server>\Software\add-ins folder. Install from the Console in the usual way. After installation is complete, the Console will need to restart. When you log back in, you will see the SageTV Service tab in the Console, shown in Figure 31.7, indicating that the service is installed and operational.

FIGURE 31.7

The SageTV Service add-in tab is fairly plain: most of the action takes place on the client.

Using SageTV

Install the SageTV client application on any computer that you want to be able to use to view and manage SageTV. Run the client installation program to launch the Client Installation Wizard, shown in Figure 31.8.

FIGURE 31.8

The SageTV Client Installation Wizard will install client software to allow computers to receive recordings made by the SageTV server.

Follow these steps to install and configure the client:

1. **After launching the wizard, click Next.** Read and indicate acceptance of the license agreement, and click Next again.

2. **Enter your name and organization, and check whether SageTV should be installed for just you or for anyone who uses this computer.** Click Next.

3. **Choose the destination folder.** Select the other options on this page if they are appropriate for your installation, and then click Next.

4. **Click Next again to begin the installation.**

5. **After installation is complete, run the client by choosing Start ⇨ All Programs ⇨ SageTV ⇨ SageTVClient.** The client will first attempt to discover servers; your Windows Home Server media server should be found, as shown in Figure 31.9. Click OK.

6. **Step through the Client Configuration Wizard, and choose the preferences you like.** Choose whether to automatically load SageTV when the computer starts, adjust for overscan on your TV, or set your TV's aspect ratio, among other settings.

7. **On the SageTV client main menu, choose Setup.**

8. **Choose Setup Video Sources.**

9. **Choose Add New Source.**

10. **Choose your video capture device from the list.** If it isn't listed, there is a problem with the device on the server. Make sure it is fully connected to the computer and restart the SageTV service on the server if necessary.

SageTV searches for servers when it first starts. Choose the Windows Home Server one.

11. **Choose the type of device.**

12. **Continue to step through setup.** Choose whether to tune digital or analog, choose where to get program guide information, and finally choose your location. You should be rewarded with the Source Wizard Summary, as shown in Figure 31.10, when you are done.

Configure your TV tuner as a video source device.

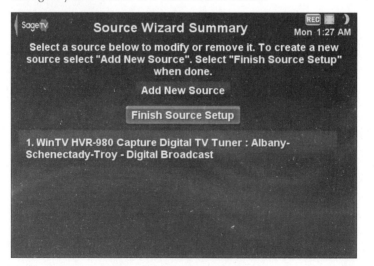

13. **Return the main menu, and choose Live TV to see if you can tune to a channel, as shown in Figure 31.11.** Now you are ready to schedule recordings, install additional clients, install more video sources, and whatever else you want to do to.

FIGURE 31.11

SageTV lets you stream live or recorded TV from your Windows Home Server.

ON the WEB Download the latest version of SageTV components and find out current pricing information and instructions at www.sagetv.com.

Summary

With distributed video systems becoming more popular all the time, Windows Home Server has a role to play as a large centralized storage device. Far more than that, however, is the ability to install add-ins to bring additional functionality to our system.

With Windows Home Server, you can manage recordings made on other computers by consolidating them in one place, such as the Videos folder for later streaming. The Recorded TV Manager add-in lets you create custom rules similar to rules for mail in Outlook that will direct recorded shows to specific destination folders.

SageTV is a popular media center application that is capable of recording video directly to the Windows Home Server's hard drive without any other computer being involved, thanks to its Media Server add-in. Video stored on the server as well as live TV can be streamed to the SageTV client to any computer on the network.

Part VII

Advanced Topics

Chapter 32

Extending Windows Home Server with Add-ins

There is no question that Windows Home Server provides a lot of functionality right out of the box, but that doesn't mean that you have to be satisfied with the status quo. In fact, many of the chapters in this book have show you how to get additional functionality from your Home Server by adding third-party software to provide such things as e-mail, enhanced media streaming with transcoding, and more.

Why not? You don't expect a desktop computer to be limited to the software that comes bundled with it. You expect to be able to install any number of software programs to enhance its usefulness. You should expect the same from a server platform, even a headless box like Windows Home Server.

The designers of Windows Home Server recognized the fact that users will want to be able to do more than the designers were able to include. At the same time, they didn't want users to have to violate the mandate that the server be manageable from the Console as much as possible. Their solution was to create the add-in capability, which allows you to install, remove, configure, and control server enhancements, all from inside the Windows Home Server Console.

In this chapter, we'll provide you with an overview of just what constitutes an add-in, and we'll show you a few of the more popular ones so that you can get a feel for the kinds of things they are suited for. We'll also point you to a few of our favorite add-in repositories on the Web.

Describing Add-ins

In reality, Windows Home Server add-ins are much like any other software package that you can install on a computer. Add-ins can install Windows services, make changes to the registry, create configuration files, register components and perform any other Windows configuration tasks that need to be done in order for it to function.

Essentially, every feature of the Windows API that is available to Windows Server 2003 developers can also be leveraged for add-ins. The difference between an add-in and a standard software package lies in how they are managed.

As we've shown previously, there is no limitation on installing standard Windows applications on the server. So why bother creating an add-in? There are a number of characteristics that make an add-in an add-in:

- Add-ins are always installable and removable from the Console.

- Add-ins can optionally extend the Console with a custom Console tab to provide a user interface for managing it.

- Add-ins can optionally extend the Console even further by creating a custom Settings tab for configuring them.

- Add-ins may provide custom Web pages as yet another alternative to extending the Console.

In essence, the goal of the add-in is to look like an integrated part of Windows Home Server. By utilizing the Console as its user interface, an add-in can automatically be managed from the server itself — whether it's from desktop computers inside your home, from the server's own desktop, or even remotely over the Internet.

CROSS-REF Are you interested in creating your own add-ins? Chapter 36 shows you what you need to do to get started, and guides you step-by-step in creating a simple add-in.

Installing add-ins

Add-ins are provided in the form of Microsoft Installer (MSI) files, with a .msi extension. You may be familiar with them already, as MSI files are standard Windows installation files, commonly used to install all sorts of programs. MSI files are archives that contain the program and data files needed by the add-in, all packaged up in a single file for convenience.

ON the WEB You can find out more information about MSI files on Microsoft's Web site. Searching for MSI can bring up a wealth of information. As a starting point, you may be interested in reading the MSI FAQ, located at www.microsoft.com/technet/community/en-us/ management/msi_faq.mspx.

Installing an add-in is a two step process. First of all, you need to put the MSI file in a place where Windows Home Server can find it. The Add-ins subfolder of the standard Software shared folder, shown in Figure 32.1, is provided for that purpose — the Console automatically shows any add-in MSI files that are copied here in the Settings console.

FIGURE 32.1

Place add-ins to be installed in the Add-ins folder. The Console knows to look for them there.

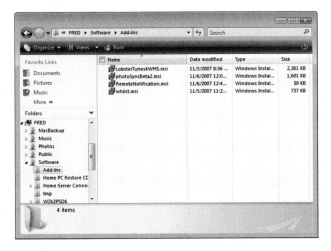

After an add-in's MSI file is copied to the Add-in folder, The Console is used to actually install it using the following steps:

1. **Log on to the Console.**

2. **Click the Settings button to access the Settings window.**

3. **Click the Add-ins tab to view the Add-ins interface.**

4. **Click the Available tab, shown in Figure 32.2, to view information about MSIs that are in the Add-ins folder but not yet installed.**

5. **Click the Install button for any add-in that you would like to install.**

Add-in installation should proceed automatically. If any settings are required as part of the installation, you may be prompted to provide them as the add-in installs. If the add-in makes any changes to the Console, such as by adding a Console or Settings tab, the Console shuts down after the installation is complete. You should see the customizations when you log back in.

FIGURE 32.2

Add-ins should be able to be installed and removed completely from the Console.

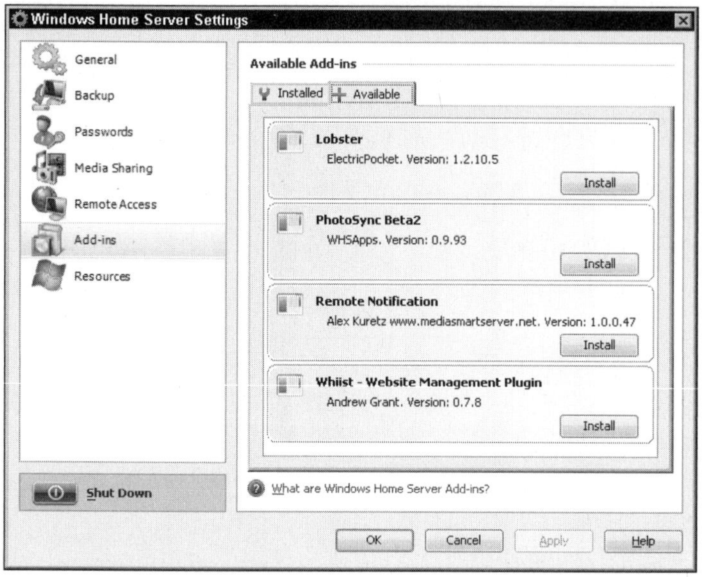

Uninstalling add-ins

Add-in removal is just the opposite of installation. Select the Installed tab in the Add-ins section of the Settings window. Click the Uninstall button for the add-in you wish to remove.

It is the responsibility of the add-in to remove any components that were installed with it. Again, if the add-in must remove any Console extensions such as custom Console tabs or Settings tabs, the Console will shut down when the uninstall is complete. You will simply need to log on to the Console again to continue using it.

Exploring Add-in Examples

As the Windows Home Server is being rolled out, the add-in scene seems to be growing at an exponential rate. Some add-ins are created by hardware manufacturers in order to differentiate their products from those of the competition. Hewlett-Packard's WebShare add-in that is provided with the MediaSmart Windows Home Server machines is a case in point. Other add-ins are created by professional software vendors to provide enhanced functionality for their products when used with Windows Home Server. In fact, we describe such an add-in, LobsterTunes, in Chapter 29.

While those are promising add-ins, the real action when it comes to developing Windows Home Server add-ins is in the hobbyist development community. The collective mindshare of the development community has been inspired by Windows Home Server's add-in capability to create a huge variety of different add-ins for a variety of purposes.

CROSS-REF   Chapter 29 provides a glimpse at two other add-ins oriented towards Windows Mobile devices such as smart phones and PDAs: LobsterTunes, a music streaming application, and HomeBase, a remote shared folder access (and blog updating) utility.

Whiist for Web site creation

No, not the card game Whist. Whiist (for Windows Home Internet Information Services Toolkit) is an add-in developed by Andrew Grant for managing Web sites on your Home Server. While still in beta at the time of this writing, Whiist (shown in Figure 32.3) is already an impressive solution to the sometimes intimidating task of managing Web sites hosted by your Windows Home Server.

FIGURE 32.3

Use Whiist to create and set properties for Web sites on your Home Server.

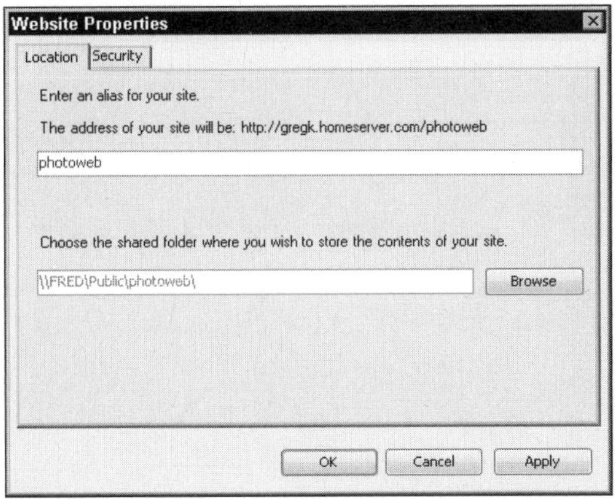

Whiist makes it easy to add new Web pages to your Windows Home Server, and gives you the following features:

- Create and manage separate Web sites. You can create sites for each member of the family, or subdivide sites for each of your hobbies.

- Create photo albums that you can use to share your family photos (shown in Figure 32.4).

- Manage properties for your Web sites, including security to limit access to users on your network.

- Create links on your public or private Windows Home Server home pages.

Whiist is a good example of how add-ins can be integrated into the Console's user interface.

ON the WEB   Download the latest version of Whiist from the developer's site at `www.andrewgrant.org/whiist`.

Whiist was the winner of the first Code2Fame challenge, a contest created to inspire interest in building Windows Home Server add-ins. See this and other contest add-ins at `www.microsoft.com/windows/products/winfamily/windowshomeserver/partners/challenge.mspx`.

FIGURE 32.4

Whiist photo albums let you easily share photos on the Web.

PhotoSync for photo uploading

Photo sharing Web sites are an increasingly popular way for people to share photos on the Web without the hassle of creating and maintaining their own Web sites. The PhotoSync add-in, shown in Figure 32.5, is designed to interface with the popular Flickr service. PhotoSync offers the following features:

- Automatically sync your photos between Windows Home Server and Flickr.
- Share all of the pictures in your Photos share, or select the folders to sync.
- Customize the length of time between automatic synchronizations.
- Set permissions for photos to public, friend, or family.

FIGURE 32.5

The PhotoSync add-in will help you manage uploads to Flickr.

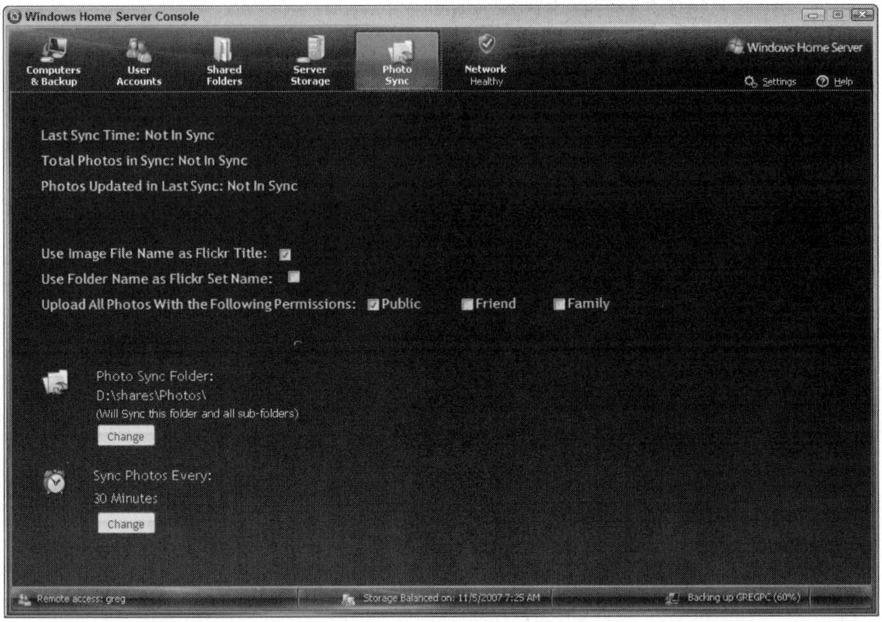

ON the WEB Download the latest version of PhotoSync from `www.edholloway.com/default.aspx`.

Remote Notification Manager

Windows Home Server's ability to monitor your network's health is great, but what if you're not around to see the notification on the Console or on the tray icon? Remote Notification Manager, shown in Figure 32.6, is an add-in that you can use to send an e-mail to any address that you choose in response to health notification messages. Send them to your work e-mail address, your Blackberry, an SMS text message to your cell phone — whatever you choose.

Remote Notification Manager sends e-mail through the Simple Mail Transport Protocol (SMTP) e-mail server that you use for your own e-mail — you can use your Internet Service Provider's (ISPs) mail server, a corporate server, or even a commercial SMTP server.

ON the WEB Though there is no Web site home for Remote Notification, you can find information and download it from `www.mediasmartserver.net/forums/viewtopic.php?t=19`.

FIGURE 32.6

Remote Notification can alert you to server notifications by e-mail.

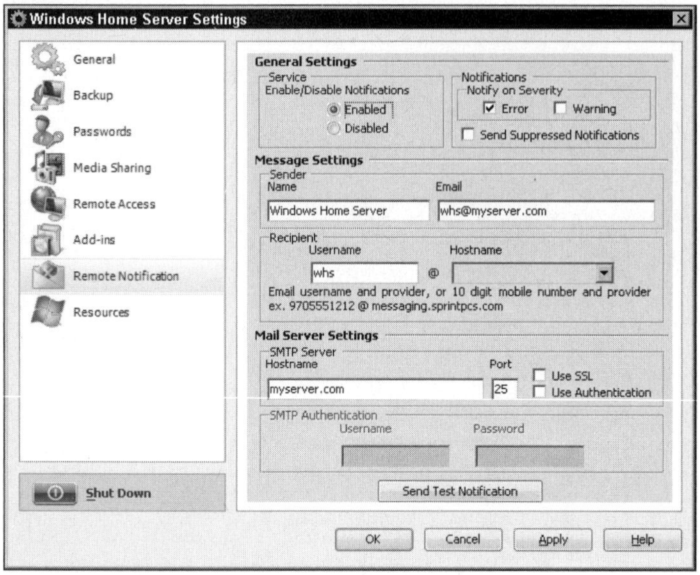

Finding More Add-ins

No Windows Home Server oriented Web site is complete without a collection or at least a link to add-in collections. In fact, we'll go a step farther and say that this book would be incomplete without pointing out a few of our favorite Windows Home Server add-in resources. This site is a must visit for any Windows Home Server owner.

We Got Served

We Got Served, located at www.wegotserved.co.uk, is a Web site located in the United Kingdom that provides Windows Home Server news in the form of a blog and an RSS feed. The home page is shown in Figure 32.7.

You can access their add-in library by clicking the Windows Home Server Add-ins button at the top of the home page. If you like, you can access the add-in library directly by going to www.wegotserved.co.uk/windows-home-server-add-ins. New add-ins as well as updates to existing ones are provided as part of the site's news stream, making it easy to keep up with developments.

We Got Served is a popular Windows Home Server news Web site.

Microsoft Communities Forums

Microsoft's Communities forum for Windows Home Server, shown in Figure 32.8, is located at `http://forums.microsoft.com/windowshomeserver/default.aspx?siteid=50`, is where the Windows Home Server development community hangs out to discuss upcoming add-ins and add-in development in general.

FIGURE 32.8

The Windows Home Server development community forum covers all things related to add-ins.

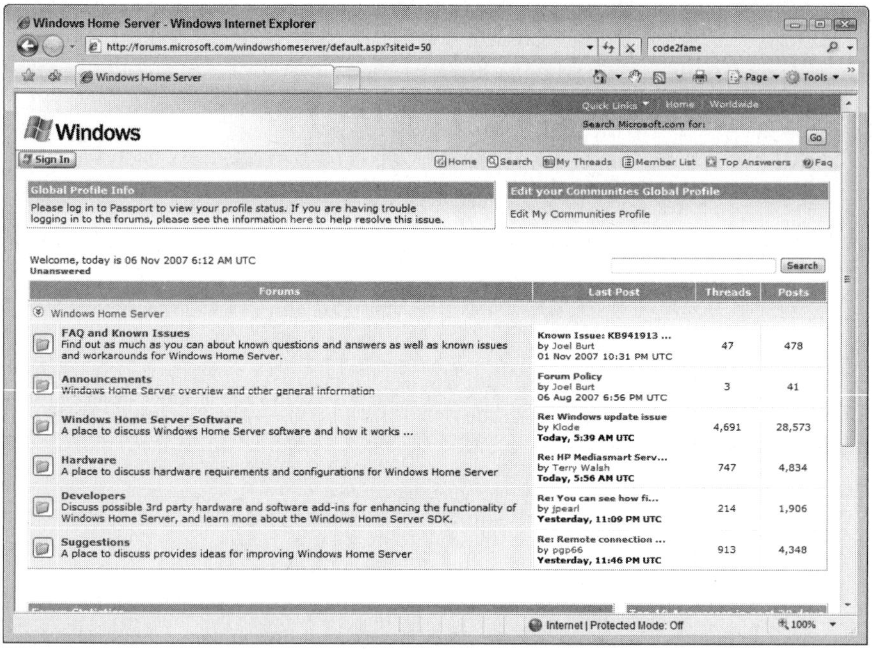

Summary

When we started writing this book, there were dozens of add-ins already available for Windows Home Server, and the OS had not even been released yet. At the time of this writing, there are already hundreds of add-ins in development from a number of sources.

Hardware vendors such as Hewlett-Packard are creating add-ins to differentiate their systems from the competition. Software vendors are creating add-ins that allow their server apps to work better with Windows Home Server.

Last, but certainly not least, is the Windows Home Server hobbyist developer community. These intrepid developers are blazing the trail in creating new add-ins driven by necessity. They use Windows Home Server, and when they see a function that they think the server could do, they simply go ahead and build it.

Chapter 33

Automating Your Home

A dmit it — you've always wanted a house like the one on the Jetsons, where a robot maid cleans house for you and automatic machines make every aspect of your life leisurely. Okay, so the technology available today still isn't anywhere close to that. However, smart home technology is here today — and it's surprisingly affordable.

Home automation is not new — the most widely used system, the X10 control protocol, has been around since the late 1970s. However, this simple system for controlling lights and other electrical devices through the power lines has been taken to the limit by marrying it to the advanced computer technology available today. Today, many people are computerizing every possible aspect of their houses, and for a variety of reasons, ranging from enhanced security, convenience, energy savings, and, yes, often just for the coolness factor.

It didn't take long for Windows Home Server to get in the home automation act. If you're going to have a server powered on 24/7, doesn't it make sense to also use it as the control center for your home automation? You can even take advantage of Windows Home Server's built-in Web server and remote access features to monitor and control your components from anywhere you happen to be.

In this chapter, we'll give you an overview of the various automation systems and components that are available, and then show you how you can make better use of them by integrating and controlling everything with software running on Windows Home Server.

Exploring Home Automation

You may be wondering exactly what you can do with home automation systems. The answer is: quite a bit. With modern automation software, coupled with devices to control lights and other electric and electronic components, you can add some or all of the following:

- Control lights on a timer at night or when you are away
- Provide images from security cameras and sensors
- Use sensors to indicate when doors are open
- Distribute audio and video
- Set the thermostat and climate control
- Set *scenes*, which consist of combinations of different lighting and other effects to set different moods

While it's possible to add all of these things individually, using simple timers and remote controls to operate them, you can easily integrate everything into a system with a central control system, such as your Windows Home Server.

Choosing Home Automation Hardware

Over the years, more and more people have become interested in home automation technology, which has led to an increase in the number of hardware options that are available. These systems all have their pros and cons, so it's a good idea to do some research before you decide how to proceed.

Should you go with ubiquitous (and cheap) X10 modules, or one of the newer systems? Next, we'll take a look at some of the pros and cons of each option.

The X10 protocol

The granddaddy of all home automation systems is X10, which was developed in 1975 by a company named Pico Electronics in Scotland. X10 is an open standard, which means that many manufacturers can (and do) build X10-compatible devices. X10 works by piggybacking control signals onto your normal household electrical wiring. At the point where AC voltage crosses the 0 volt threshold, twice every 60th of a second, a 120 kHz pulse is inserted. The sequence of pulses and lack of pulses are decoded into a bit stream, which contains addressing information for each device as well as the command the device should perform. The system is quite slow, with delays between pushing a button and the action typically between ¾ to 1 second.

In addition to the electrical signals, an radio frequency (RF) protocol is defined that allows devices to be controlled by wireless controls such as remotes.

The following types of devices are available for the X10 system.

X10 device modules

Device modules are located where the device to be controlled plugs in. For normal incandescent lights, these can consist of the following:

- **Socket modules:** These modules screw into a light socket between the lamp and the bulb, allowing direct control.

- **Wall sockets:** X10 wall sockets can either replace built-in sockets or plug directly into them.

- **Light switches:** Wall switches can be replaced with X10 devices that offer the ability to either be controlled remotely, or locally. Some wall switches include local dimmer controls as well.

For heavier duty loads such as fluorescent lights or appliances, special appliance modules are available that can control higher ampere loads.

Transceiver modules

Transceiver modules plug into an electrical outlet, and receive signals from X10 RF controllers such as remote controls. The RF signal is converted into the electrical signaling necessary to control device modules.

X10 controllers

Controllers for X10 devices range from simple controllers that can control up to four devices at a time (simple switches) up to powerful computer-controlled devices that include timers and other sundry features. Of course, to integrate X10 with Windows Home Server, you are going to need a computer controlled controller. Two popular options for computer-controlled X10 controllers are

- **CM11A:** This module, from ActiveHome, is controlled by a computer's RS232 serial port. CM11A modules can store macros and timers. The device's memory is backed up by batteries so that it will retain programmed settings even in the event of a power outage.

- **CM15A:** ActiveHome's Universal Serial Bus (USB) controller, which can be used on newer computers that don't offer RS232 ports.

- **PowerLinc 1132cu:** This controller from SmartHome is USB-based and is similar to the CM15A in capabilities.

Limitations of X10

X10 was developed in the 1970s and so was designed with the less precise digital devices of the day in mind. By modern standards, the protocol is limited, allowing only 16 devices per 16 home regions. The slow speed of the protocol limits X10 to simple commands such as on, off, or dimmer.

In addition to the speed limitations, X10 can suffer from interference on the electrical lines. Power transformers can filter the signals out from nearby devices, requiring the use of filters in outlets where they are used. A bridge device is often needed on a 220V outlet to pass signals from one phase of the household circuit to the other in order to get a strong signal to all devices.

Should these problems prevent you from using X10? Probably not. The devices are relatively inexpensive, and, therefore, are a good way to get started with home automation. You can always upgrade to a different system later, particularly one that is backward compatible such as Insteon.

ON the WEB   Information about X10 devices, software, and information can be found at www.smarthome.com/about_x10.html.

Insteon

Insteon is a newer home automation technology developed by SmartLabs, Inc., that is designed to improve upon X10 in a number of ways. It can control the same types of devices as X10, but provides the following benefits:

- All devices act as a repeater, which means that they will relay signals from one device to another until they reach the intended device. This means that you will have better propagation of signals through the house. The more devices you have, the more reliable your network will be.

- It's dual mode, which means devices can communicate over power lines or RF, or both.

- It has faster speed compared to X10. While X10 is limited to 20 bits/second, Insteon can transmit at almost 3000 bits/second.

- Devices are addressed via a permanent 24-bit unique address.

- There is no limitation on the number of devices (versus 256 maximum with X10).

- Error correction is built in.

Insteon is backwards-compatible with X10 as well. X10 devices can continue to function on the network as you upgrade other components to Insteon.

Insteon device modules

The same types of devices that are available for X10 are also available for Insteon, including socket modules, appliance modules, wall switches, and outlets. Because devices have a permanent 24-bit unique address assigned to them, you only need to link a device to an existing device in the network by pressing the on button of the first device for ten seconds, followed by the on button of the new device.

Insteon controllers

For computer control, Insteon SmartHome makes two units that are comparable to the X10 computer devices. They are as follows:

- **PowerLinc 2414S:** This serial port controller can be used with older computers without USB ports, or with software that cannot recognize them.

- **PowerLinc 2414U:** This is the USB version of the previous device listed.

Both devices contain internal memory to allow them to function even when the computer they are attached to is turned off.

> **ON the WEB** You can learn more about Insteon protocol and devices at their Web site located at www.insteon.net.

Z-Wave

Last but not least, Z-Wave is a joint specification from more than 100 home automation companies that provides a completely wireless solution to home automation. Unlike X10 and Insteon, Z-Wave is not dependent on transmission over power lines. Instead, it is strictly an RF-based wireless protocol.

Z-Wave shares many of the same benefits of Insteon, such as an ad-hoc mesh network and signals can be routed from one device to another until they reach the intended destination. As with Insteon, devices have their own permanent unique address code. A single Z-Wave network is limited to 232 devices; however, multiple networks can be bridged using a gateway.

> **ON the WEB** Learn more about Z-Wave at the Z-Wave Alliance Web site located at www.z-wavealliance.org/modules/start.

Using mControl with Windows Home Server

Windows Home Server is a natural platform for home automation. The fact that it is intended to stay on 24/7, coupled with its built-in Web server and remote access features, means that a home control application can instantly take advantage of it; even this early in the product's life, we are starting to see products aimed at home automation.

At the time of this writing, Embedded Automation's mControl is the most integrated home automation solution for Windows Home Server, as they have developed an add-in that makes it easy to set up their service and their Web-based administration console. In addition, the add-in provides a custom Windows Home Server Console tab that can be used to monitor the mControl service.

> **ON the WEB** You can read about mControl and download the 30-day trial at www.embedded automation.com/EAHAmControl.htm. The latest version, 2.0 at the time of this writing, includes the Windows Home Server add-in.

Installing the add-in

Once you've downloaded the ZIP file containing the mControl installation files, you will need to extract the contents using your favorite unzipping tool or Windows Explorer. Follow these steps to install the add-in.

1. Locate the add-in MSI file, named mControl_WHS_Setup.msi, and copy it to your \\<server>\Software\Add-Ins shared folder, with <server> replaced by your server's name.

2. Log on to the Console, and open the Settings window.

3. Click the Add-ins tab, and then choose the Available tab.

4. Locate the mControl item, and click the Install button.

5. **When the installation is complete, the Console will be closed.** Log on again to verify that the mControl Home Console tab has been added, as shown in Figure 33.1.

Monitoring the mControl service

When you select the mControl Console tab, you will see information regarding your mControl configuration, such as the number of zones, devices, macros, triggers, and so on (these terms are explained later in this chapter). You will also see version information for both mControl and your server's OS.

The heart of mControl is a standard Windows service named *mHome Automation Server*, which can be started and stopped in the Services control panel or from the command line. However, the mControl Console tab provides a toolbar that makes it easier to check the status of the service and to stop, start, or restart it if necessary.

FIGURE 33.1

The home automation program mControl includes a Windows Home Server add-in with a custom Console tab.

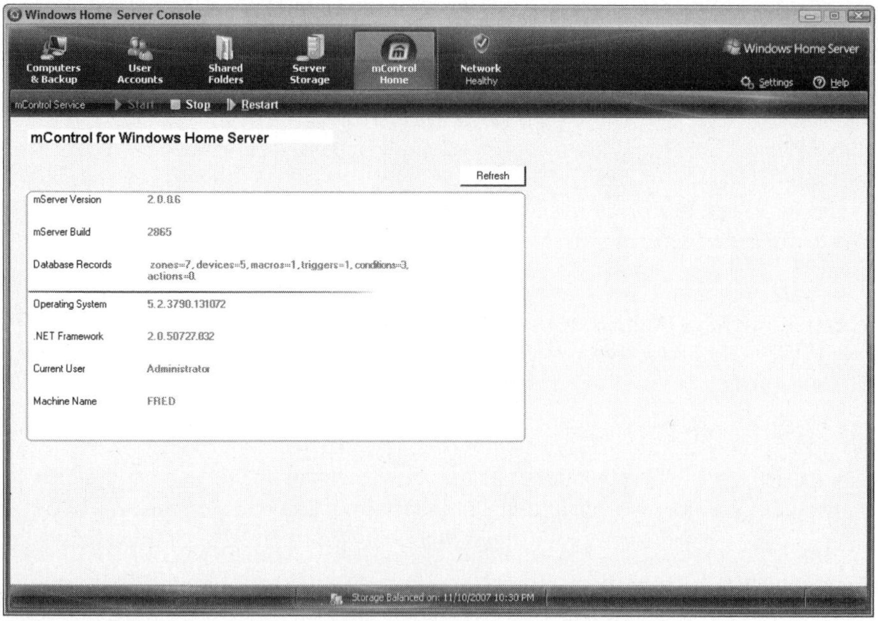

Accessing the Web interface

While the Console tab is useful for monitoring or restarting the mControl service, that's not where you will spend most of your time. All of the home automation configuration you will do will be through the Web interface that is added to your server's Web server.

When you log on to your remote access Web site, your Home tab contains a section for Web sites that you can link to, which now includes a link to your mControl installation, as shown in Figure 33.2. Click this link to access your mControl installation.

> **TIP**
> If you are on your home network, you can access mControl without having to sign on to Remote Access. Enter the URL as `http://<server>/mControl`, with `<server>` replaced by your server's system name.

> **CAUTION**
> mControl is designed to work exclusively with Internet Explorer. Other browsers, such as Firefox and Safari, will be unable to access the site.

FIGURE 33.2

A link to mControl has been added to your Remote Access Web Sites list.

Click the mControl for WHS link to navigate to the Web site. The first page you will see when you access mControl is the Zone View, shown in Figure 33.3, where you will see a list of all of the zones currently defined for your home. Zones are areas of your house that you want to be able to control as a unit. You can set up zones for each floor of your home, or even for each room individually. The choice is entirely up to you.

FIGURE 33.3

The Zone view is the master control panel for your home automation.

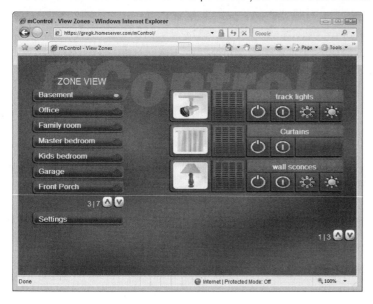

Configuring settings

If you haven't configured any zones, as will be the case when you first install mControl, you will need to do so by clicking the Settings button. The Settings page, shown in Figure 33.4, lets you manage zones, set up automation macros to script complex actions, configure infrared controls for mControl, and configure any networked cameras that you may have. In addition, you can set up the overall configuration settings for mControl. The following is a description of what you can do at each button.

Configuration

The Configuration button allows you to set parameters specific to mControl. Select either Main or Location. The Main tab lets you choose a style for mControl, which will alter the look and feel and colors of the application. Use the Location tab to set up your latitude and longitude so that mControl can calculate your dawn and dusk settings for automatic light control at night. Click Save after making any changes on this page to apply them.

Manage Zones

Use the Manage Zones page, shown in Figure 33.5, to add new zones to your system. Click the Add Zone button to do this.

You can also reorganize your zone list with the up and down arrows to the right of the zones. This will affect the order in which zones are displayed on the main page.

FIGURE 33.4

The Settings page is where you set up zones and automation configuration.

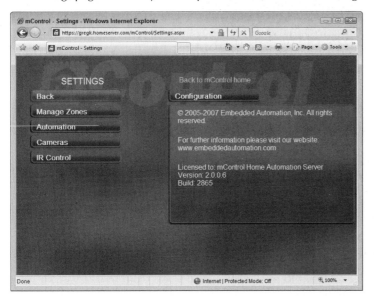

Automation

You can use automation to configure macros that can perform multiple steps, such as dimming all lights in response to a remote command, or turning on a pool pump in response to a timer. See the section on automation later in this chapter.

Cameras

If you have networked home automation cameras that you would like to configure, you can do so on the Cameras page. Choose a camera type as well as information on how to access it by providing its IP address and other access information. Cameras can take single snapshots or record small stretches of video for monitoring from the Zones page.

IR control

The IR control page is used to configure infrared remote (IR) control of mControl. If your Windows Home Server is within view of a media center, for example, you may wish to use this feature. Otherwise, this is mostly a vestigial setting for those people who install mControl on their media center PCs.

FIGURE 33.5

Add zones for each area of the house you wish to be able to control as a unit.

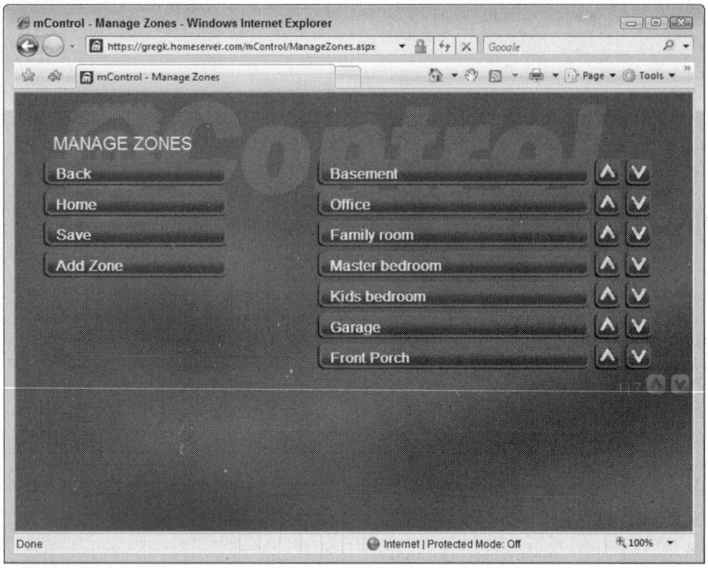

Editing zones

Automation devices are configured per zone. To configure devices for a particular zone, go to the Manage Zones page as described in the previous section, and select the zone to go to the Edit Zone page, shown in Figure 33.6. From here, you can add devices or change the order in which they are listed on the Zones page. You can also delete a zone from this page.

Click the Add Device button to access the Edit Device page, shown in Figure 33.7.

Adding devices

The Edit Device page is where you configure each of the controllable automation devices in your home. You have the following options:

- **Name:** Enter a name for the device. This will be used in the display on the main Zones page.
- **Adapter:** Choose the automation adapter that you are controlling this device with. This will be the name of the controller you have connected to your server's serial or USB port, such as a CM15A X10 module or PowerLinc 2414U Insteon device.
- **Module:** Select the device module to be controlled. The choices here will be limited to those that are compatible with the adapter you choose.

- **Address:** Module addressing will be dependent on the type of adapter you are using as well. For instance, X10 devices use Home/Unit addressing, while Insteon and Z-Wave devices have a unique identifier.
- **Image:** You can choose the image that best matches the device. This will be shown on the main Zones page.

Once you have configured a device, click Save to add it to the device list.

FIGURE 33.6

The Edit Zone page is used to configure a zone's automation devices.

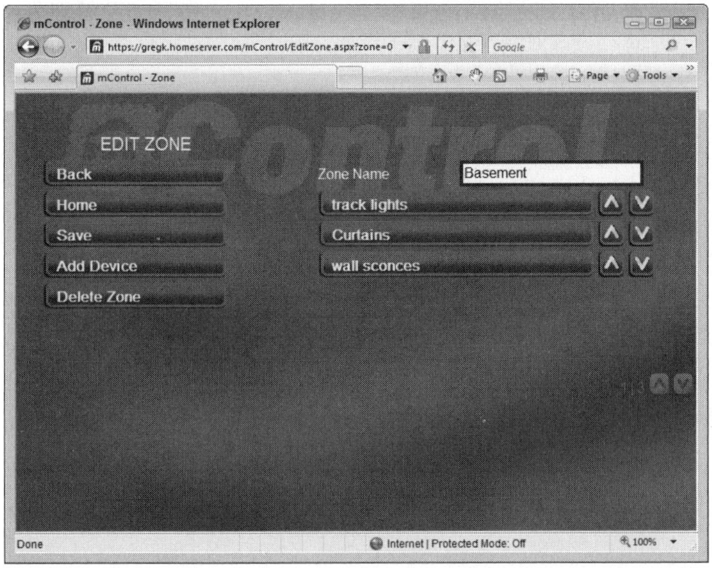

Enabling automation

In order to be able to do more than just control your devices from the Zone page, you need to set up automation macros. Macros can be configured to control one or more devices in response to a trigger. From the Automation page, you can add macros by simply clicking the Add Macro button and giving it a name. Once you have done this, you can specify the macro's actions and trigger settings by clicking it. This will bring you to the Macro Details page, shown in Figure 33.8.

Enter macro details

The Macro Details page is used to configure both the triggers and actions for a macro. As you've probably guessed, triggers specify the event that will cause the macro to be run. Actions specify exactly what the macro should do.

FIGURE 33.7

Add information for each device to be controlled.

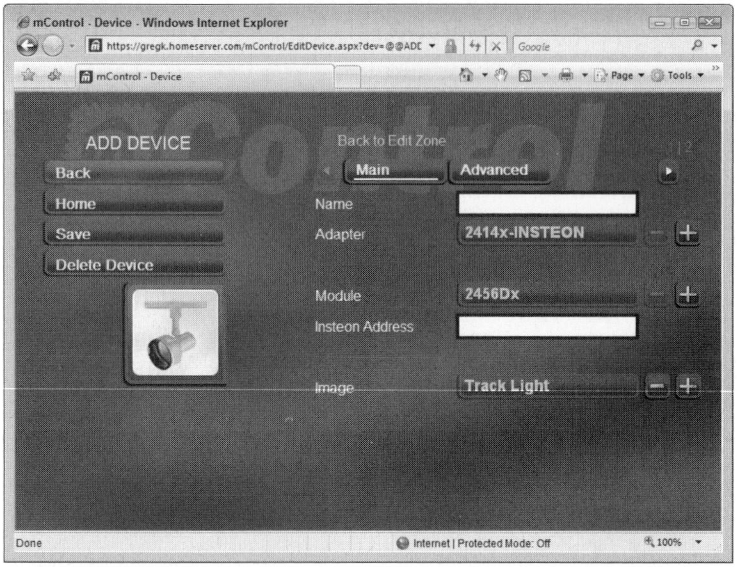

FIGURE 33.8

Macros can perform complex actions automatically.

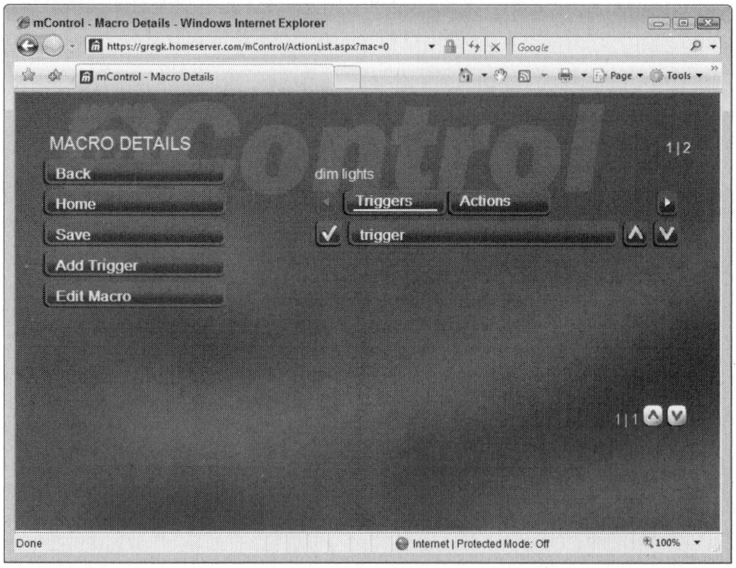

Editing triggers

Click the Add Trigger button to create a new trigger, and then click on it to open the Edit Trigger page. The only real option on this page is to name the trigger. Make it fairly descriptive, so that if your macro has more than one trigger you can find it again easily. To choose the event that will fire the trigger, click the Add Condition button.

Editing conditions

We need to choose an event that will cause the macro to be run on the Edit Conditions page, shown in Figure 33.9. Conditions can be any of the following:

- **Device Change:** Choose a device module to monitor and a device property and value. When the device reaches this state, the macro will run. You could use this to, say, turn on a camera when a motion sensor detects movement.

- **Device Status:** This is similar to Device Change, but instead of firing the trigger when the device status changes, it stays active all the time the device is in the chosen state. You should use this in conjunction with other conditions.

- **IR Event:** Fires the trigger when a defined IR event occurs. This can be useful for setting up remote controlled scenes, where lights are activated and deactivated all at once at the press of a remote button.

- **MCE Event:** If running in conjunction with a Media Center PC, it will fire the trigger when a specified even occurs. For example, you could have the lights come on automatically whenever you pause or stop a DVD.

- **Time Range:** Specify a time period during the day a trigger can fire. You can use this to only enable some triggers during the days and times that you will be home. You can specify sunrise and sunset as start times. This condition should be used in conjunction with conditions.

- **Recurring:** Fires the trigger at a regular interval on specified days, starting at a specific time of day.

- **One time:** Choose one specific date and time to fire the trigger.

- **Time of day, Sunrise, Sunset:** These options can be used to set triggers to fire at a specific time during the day. You can choose days of the week to not perform this action, and even add a randomness factor.

You can add several conditions for each trigger if you like; however in order for the trigger to fire, all conditions must be true. So if you want your automatic mood lighting with your media center DVD player to only function between 6 PM and 6 AM, you can do so.

FIGURE 33.9

Triggers can be used to specify conditions for automatic macro invocation.

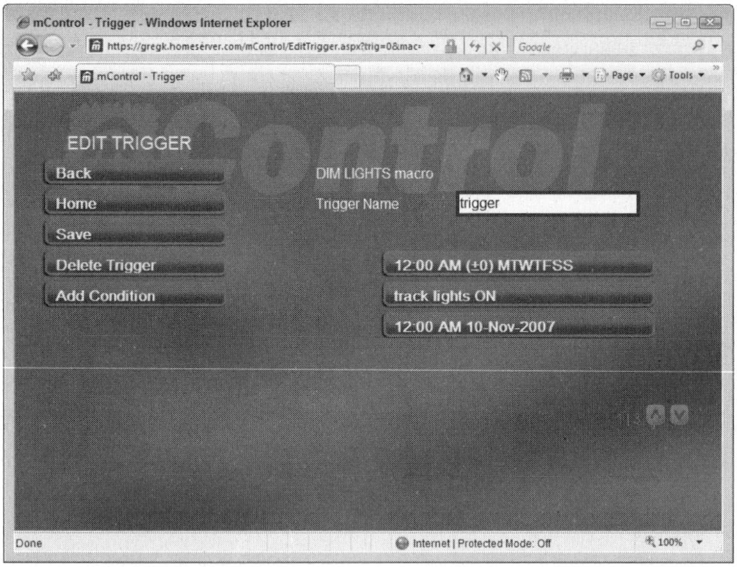

Summary

Home automation technology isn't just for Bill Gates. With relatively inexpensive options such as the Insteon, Z-Wave, and X10 solutions, you too can automate your home to provide the security, energy efficiency, convenience, and the geeky coolness factor that you desire.

Windows Home Server can act as the brain of your home automation system, with add-ins such as the mControl program that you can use to take control over all of your home automation devices, no matter what brand they are.

The mControl add-in provides a Web-based user interface that you can use from either in your home or via Windows Home Server's Remote Access feature, giving you access to all of your devices no matter where you are. Even when you are across the country, you can check in on your server and see which devices are on and even change their status. You can also monitor your security cameras over the Web.

Chapter 34

Advanced Home Server Management

As we've mentioned several times by now, Windows Home Server was designed to be operated as a headless platform, with all of the necessary server management and control performed through the Console.

For many people, this will be fine — they bought a simple home server solution in a box, and expect it to work in the way that it was advertised to with little muss or fuss. And for the most part, this will be true. For those who want to get the most out of their server, however, there is no substitute for being able to log directly onto the server's desktop and work with the standard Windows server tools and utilities.

While using the console alone is ideal, it may not always be feasible to stick with, especially this early in Windows Home Server's life when, let's face it, the operating system may have some quirks. That goes doubly if you install software that isn't explicitly designed to run on Windows Home Server.

Creating Windows Home Server from Windows 2003 Small Business Server (SBS) is a double-edged sword. The operating system is probably more complicated than it needs to be, as there are features in 2003 SBS that will likely never be used by Windows Home Server users. The benefit, however, comes from the large number of tools available on the server itself to assist you, the home server administrator.

In this chapter, we dig behind the scenes on the server, where we show you how to get to and use some of the server maintenance tools that aren't mentioned in the Windows Home Server help files.

Exploring Administrative Tools

All Windows computers contain a collection of utilities grouped together under the Administrative Tools folder. These utilities manage most of the server's configurable settings.

There are several ways that the server administrative tools can be accessed in Windows Home Server, and in fact there are two ways to access it directly from the Start menu.

- **From the All Programs menu:** Choose Start ⇨ All Programs ⇨ Administrative Tools.
- **From the Control Panel:** Choose Start ⇨ Control Panel ⇨ Administrative Tools.

It doesn't matter which one you choose. To open them in a Window instead of just as a popup menu, right-click on either one of the Administrative Tools folders and choose Explore or Explore All Users. The menu of administrative utilities is shown in Figure 34.1.

FIGURE 34.1

The Administrative Tools menu contains utilities for managing your server.

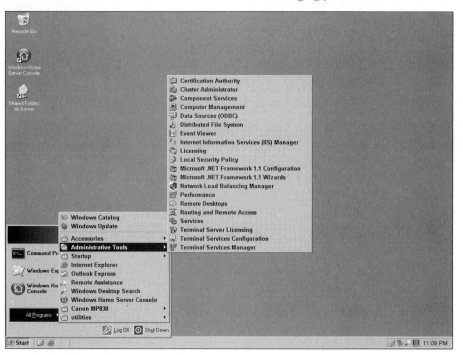

It should be noted that not all of the utilities shown in the Administrative Tools are suitable for use with Windows Home Server. Some have been carried over from previous versions of Windows Server and haven't been removed for the Windows Home Server release.

Take a look at the utilities available under Administrative Tools that are actually beneficial for Windows Home Server use. Items we discuss are Computer Management, Services, and Event Viewer. We also cover the Performance monitoring application later in the chapter.

Exploring the Computer Management MMC

The Computer Management MMC (Microsoft Management Console), shown in Figure 34.2, is really more of a collection of other tools, some of which can be accessed from elsewhere. While some of the items in the Computer MMC are also in the Administrative Tools menu, others can only be accessed from here. Let's take a look at a few of them.

FIGURE 34.2

The Computer MMC is a collection of useful server management tools.

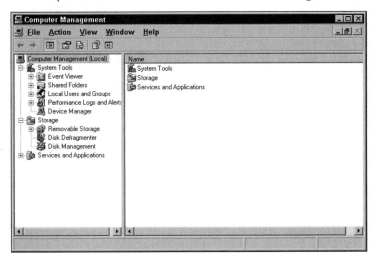

Viewing local users and groups

If you need to work with user accounts and group access, such as to add custom settings for a user account for a software package that requires it, you can do so on the Local Users and Groups section of the Computer MMC, shown in Figure 34.3.

In most cases, you are better off letting Windows Home Server manage user accounts; however, if you install an application that needs a new user account to run under, you can do so here.

FIGURE 34.3

You can edit existing users and add new ones under Local Users and Groups.

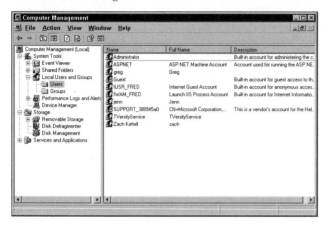

To add a new user account, open the Computer MMC, and do the following:

1. **Navigate to the Users section.**

2. **Choose Action ⇨ New User.**

3. **Enter a user name, and if you like, the user's full name and description as well.** The last two items are optional.

4. **Enter a password and then again to confirm it.**

5. **If this is an account that is not going to be used by a person to log on to the Windows Home Server box directly, but instead will be used to run a service, uncheck the User must change password at next logon box.**

6. **If you uncheck the box in Step 5, you need to decide whether the user can change this password and whether or not it expires.** Leave these at the default settings.

7. **Click Create.**

On Windows, user accounts need to have permissions assigned to them in order to be able to access the file system, perform administrative tasks, log on to Remote Desktop, and more. Rather than have the permissions applied to each user account individually, Windows allows for groups to be created that permissions can be granted to instead. User accounts are then joined to the appropriate group and those accounts "inherit" the security/permission settings defined for the group. Figure 34.4 shows the Groups panel.

FIGURE 34.4

Groups are used to grant access to server resources for multiple accounts at once.

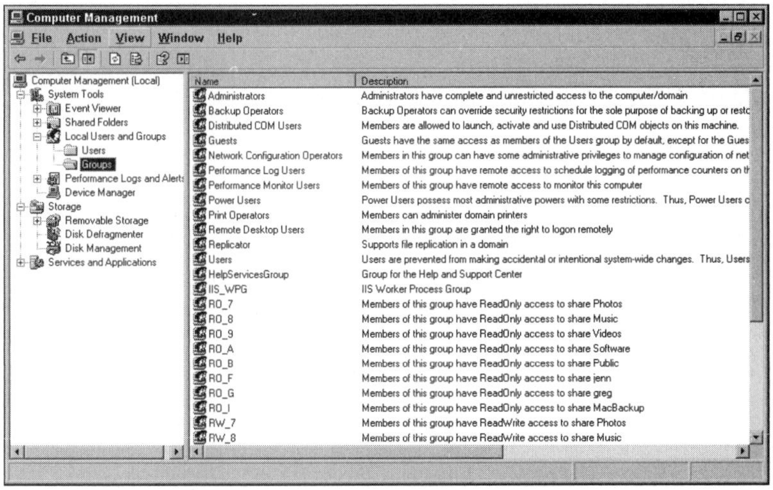

As you can see, there are a lot of groups, many of which are not going to be applicable to use with Windows Home Server. There are a few key groups that we should point out, however.

- **Administrators:** The Administrators group assigns the highest level of account access. Users with administrator access can do just about anything on the server. The administrator account is assigned to this group by default. For security purposes, user accounts that belong to Administrators will not be able to use the Remote Access feature of Windows Home Server.

- **Power Users:** The Power Users group exists mainly to provide backwards compatibility with legacy applications designed for NT 4.0. You will not likely need to grant users access to this group.

- **Users:** All user accounts get assigned to this group by default. These set the basic restrictions and permissions for an account.

- **Remote Desktop Users:** Users must be assigned to this group if they need to be able to log on via Remote Desktop.

- **Windows Home Server Users:** Windows Home Server uses this group to determine which user accounts are under its control. User accounts in this group will be visible in the Windows Home Server Console's User Accounts tab.

- **RW_0, RO_1, RW_2, RO_2, and so on:** Windows Home Server creates two groups for each shared folder you create. Users assigned to the RO_x groups are granted read-only access to the shared folders. Users assigned to the RW_x groups are granted read and write access. You can see which groups belong to each shared folder by looking at the description of the group. For the most part, though, it's best to let Windows Home Server manage these permissions.

User accounts can belong to more than one group, as shown in Figure 34.5. Access will be granted based on the group with the highest level of access. To assign a user to a group, do the following:

FIGURE 34.5

Users can be assigned to multiple groups.

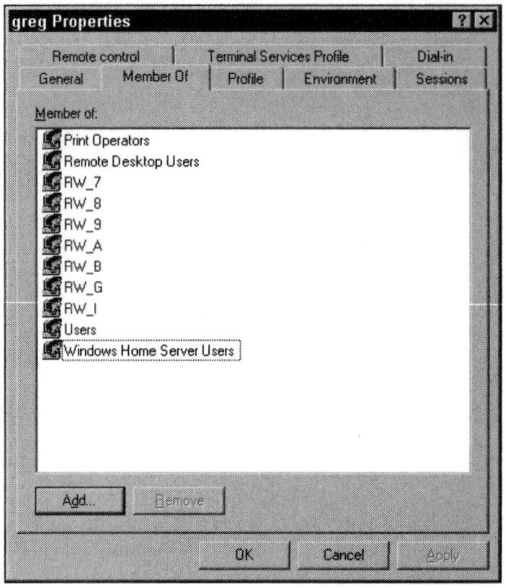

1. **Double-click on a user account in the Users pane to open its Properties window.**

2. **Click the Member Of tab.** You will see the groups that the user already belongs to, shown in Figure 34.5.

3. **Click the Add button.**

4. **Enter the group name.** If you would rather choose from a list, click Advanced followed by Find Now, and choose from the list.

5. **Click OK.** The group that you've assigned should appear on the user's Member Of list.

6. **Click OK again to save the change**s.

Defragmenting disks

Aside from managing user accounts, the Computer MMC is useful for monitoring and optimizing disk performance. To this end, it provides access to the Disk Defragmenter and Disk Management utilities. The Disk Defragmenter utility is shown in Figure 34.6.

FIGURE 34.6

Defragmenting your disks can help you to maintain top file system performance.

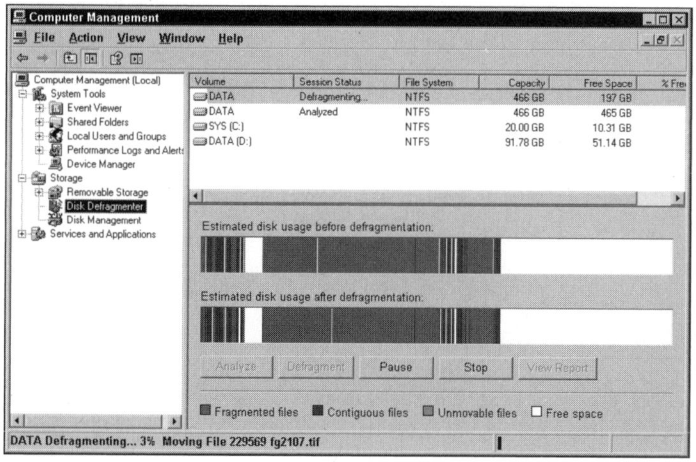

As you use your computers and files are created and deleted, the file system tends to become fragmented because new files are allocated out of space freed up by deleted files. Large files must often be split into fragments in order to fit into smaller allocation blocks. Over time, performance can suffer if you have a large number of fragmented files.

This is where disk defragmentation comes into play. You can analyze each of your disk volumes to see if defragmentation is required and if so, go ahead and defragment it. You should ideally perform this task every couple of months to keep your server running at top performance.

Disk management

For other Windows Server work, the Disk Management utility, shown in Figure 34.7, is worth its weight in gold. For Windows Home Server, with its automatic disk management, it isn't quite as useful. In fact, you should avoid using Disk Management for any drive that Windows Home Server manages as part of the storage pool, as it is possible to render the system unusable with this utility.

CAUTION The Disk Management utility can completely destroy your Windows Home Server file system. Be extremely cautious when using it.

FIGURE 34.7

Disk Management will let you explore your Windows Home Server disk configuration.

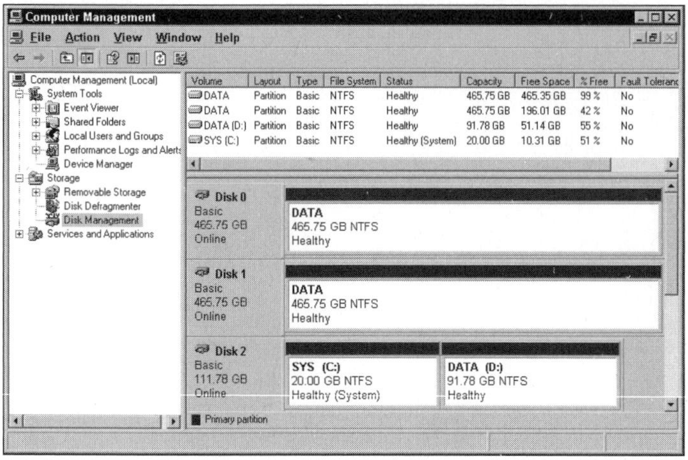

If you add a drive to use outside of the Windows Home Server storage pool, Disk Management can be used to partition and format the drive, and to assign drive letters to the partitions. To partition a new drive that isn't going to be added to the storage pool, do the following:

1. **Right-click on the drive in the Disk Management tool and select New Partition.** This opens the New Partition Wizard.

2. **Click Next.**

3. **Choose the type of partition you want.** Your choices are Primary partition, Extended partition and Logical drive. Click Next. Extended partitions are used to hold one or more logical drives.

4. **Specify the size of the partition.** Click Next.

5. **Choose whether to assign a drive letter yourself or to let Windows do it automatically.** You can choose not to assign a drive letter.

6. **Choose to format the partition.** Enter a name for the volume (optional) and a file system type to use (NTFS is recommended in most cases).

7. **Choose the disk allocation size.** For NTFS, choose whether you want the files and folder compression to be enabled. Click Next.

8. **Verify that the settings that you chose are correct, and then click Finish.**

Controlling services

We've discussed services in previous chapters. Services are Windows programs that typically do not have a user interface, but run in the background. An example of a service would be Window's Web service, Internet Information Services (IIS). IIS runs automatically when the server is started, and listens for incoming HTTP requests on the ports assigned to it. It processes the request and then returns a Web page to the sender.

Most of the Windows Home Server functionality is built on services, and knowing about them can help you to diagnose problems that your system may be experiencing.

You can access the Services console either from the Computer Management console (where it is located under Services and Applications in the tree), or from the same Administrator Tools menu you use to launch the Computer Management console.

The Services console has two different views: Extended and the Standard. Figure 34.8 shows the extended view, which is useful when trying to determine what a particular service does — it'll show the description of the service and give you ability to start, stop, or restart the service in the upper-left portion of the screen. The standard view requires you to double-click on the service to view it to see these options.

Services can either be set to start automatically or manually. Automatic services will be started when the computer restarts; manual services require a person or another program to start them.

FIGURE 34.8

Windows services can be managed from the Services console.

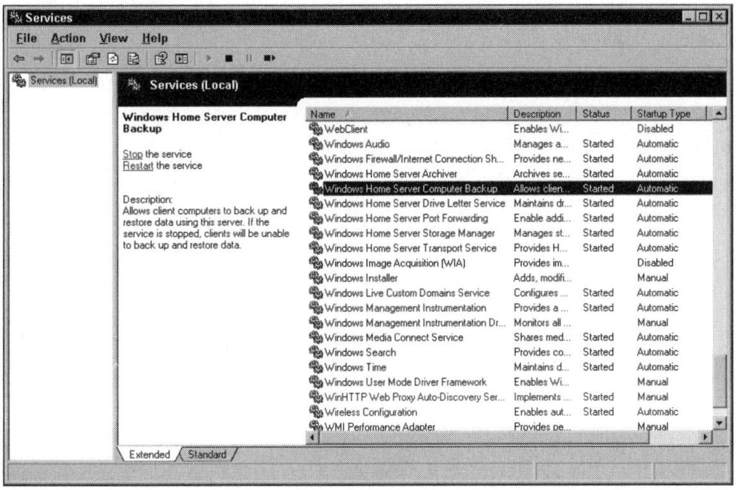

Windows Home Server includes a number of services that manage its features. Here is a list of them with a brief description of what they (and a few other important services) do:

- **Windows Home Server Archiver:** Archives the server configuration.
- **Windows Home Server Computer Backup:** Provides backup services for client computers.
- **Windows Home Server Drive Letter Service:** Maintains drive letters for folders managed by the Storage Manager.
- **Windows Home Server Port Forwarding:** Manages port forwarding for a Universal Plug and Play (UPnP) router.
- **Windows Home Server Storage Manager:** Manages storage allocation, in particular folder duplication functions.
- **Windows Home Server Transport Service:** Provides for communication with client computers running the Connector software.
- **Windows Media Connect Service:** Provides UPnP streaming media services to external devices.
- **World Wide Web Publishing Service:** IIS, your server's Web server.
- **Windows Live Custom Domain Service:** Keeps your custom domain for remote access up to date with your current IP address.

As you can see, services play a vital role for all of Windows Home Server's functions. If you receive a network health notification that one of these services has stopped, you may be able to restart it from the Services console. If a service continually fails or has problems, further diagnostic tests will be required.

Using the Event Viewer

The Event Viewer, shown in Figure 34.9, can give you important information for diagnosing problems with your server or just be used to verify that everything is functioning properly. As a part of their normal operation, Windows programs and services can log status messages to the event log, giving administrators a look at the server's health.

Events in the Event Viewer are grouped into categories depending on which aspect of the system they affect. There are three standard Windows categories, as well as a custom one unique to Windows Home Server. Other applications can add their own. The event log categories for Windows Home Server are

- **Application:** Most application programs will log information and errors to this log.
- **Security:** Information regarding access and attempted access to the server from users and other computers. Viewing this log will tell you who has logged on to the server and when.
- **System:** Windows system services will log information to this log.
- **HomeServer:** Custom log for Windows Home Server specific services.

FIGURE 34.9

The Event Viewer lets you see errors as well as normal informational messages from services and other applications.

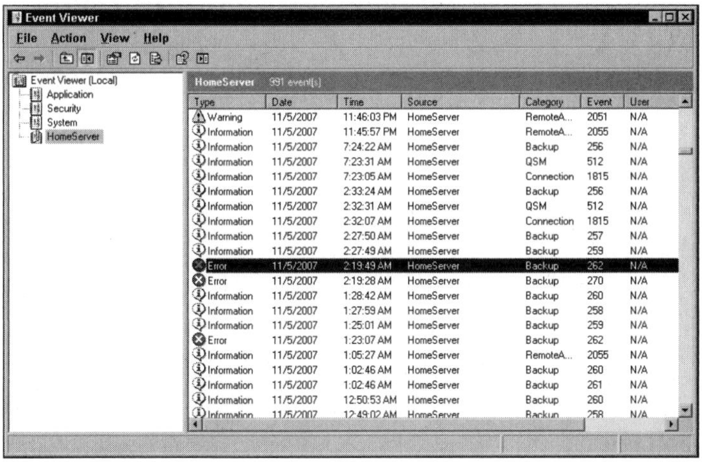

Events are can be one of three types: Information, Warning, and Error. Information events are normal and can provide with some data as to what a server or user is doing. Warning messages are logged when something non-critical but unexpected occurs. Error messages generally mean that something failed.

If you double-click on an event, the Event Properties dialog box gives you more information on the error, including a description, as shown in Figure 34.10.

When you right-click on an event log category, you will see options for saving, loading, and clearing the log file. You can use this to save the current state of the log file in case you are asked to send it to Microsoft for help in tracking down a problem, or to compare the events between server restarts. You can clear the event log to make it easier to find any subsequent events.

From the right-click menu, you can also choose properties for an event log, and set the maximum size to use for the log, as shown in Figure 34.11. The larger the log, the farther back you can maintain events. The standard Windows logs (Applications, System, and Security) have a 16 MB maximum size by default. The HomeServer log has a 512 KB maximum size by default.

FIGURE 34.10

Looking at an event gives you information as to why it was logged. In this case, an error event was logged by the backup service because a client aborted a backup that was in progress.

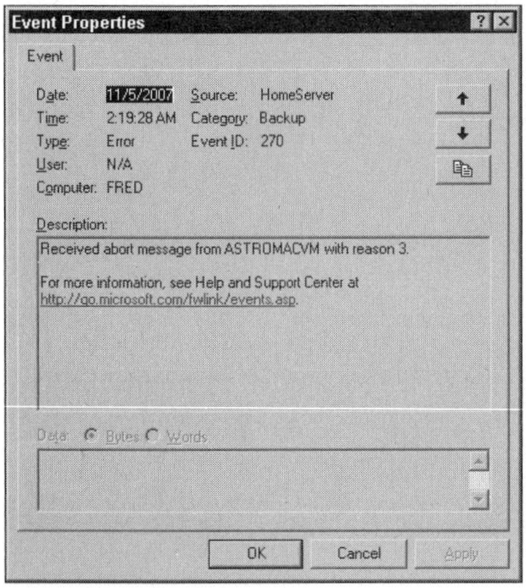

FIGURE 34.11

Event log properties let you change the maximum log size.

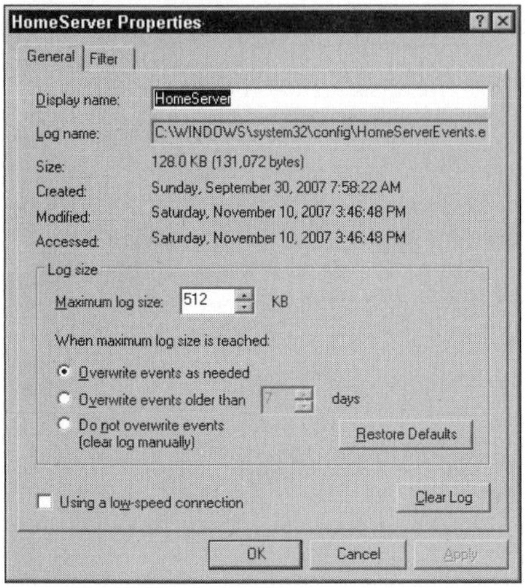

Monitoring System Performance

There are several tools that you can use to track the performance of your server and its applications. The one you may already be familiar with, Task Manager, allows you to see the status of all running processes and their memory and CPU (Central Processing Unit) utilization. You can also see overall CPU and memory use. You can use another tool, Performance, to get more detailed information tracked over time. Let's take a look at them.

Using Task Manager

There are several ways to launch the task manager, but the simplest is to use Ctrl+Alt+Delete to bring up the Windows Security dialog, and then click the Task Manager button. If you are on the desktop, you can press Ctrl+Alt+Esc to go directly to the Task Manager. You can also right-click on the task bar and choose Task Manager from the popup menu.

> **NOTE** If you are accessing the server through Remote Desktop, you need to use Ctrl+Alt+End, as Ctrl+Alt+Delete is not passed on to Remote Desktop.

The Task Manager screen, shown in Figure 34.12, has a number of tabs that you can use to access various pieces of information. They are the Applications, Processes, Performance, Networking and Users tabs.

FIGURE 34.12

You can view process information in the Task Manager.

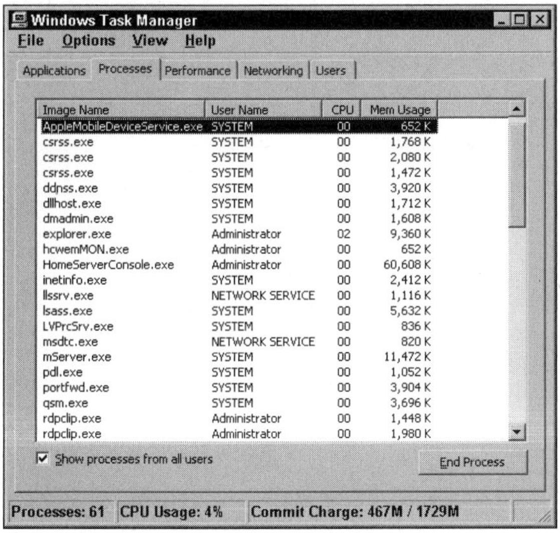

Applications tab

The Applications tab of the Task Manager shows applications windows that are running on the desktop. It doesn't include services running in the background. You can use buttons on this tab to end a task, switch the focus to it, or even launch a new task. Applications are shown by their window title rather than their process name.

Processes tab

The Processes tab shows a list of all running processes, along with the user name it is running under, and current CPU and memory utilization.

You can change the sort order of processes by clicking on the column headings. In particular, clicking on the CPU heading to sort by usage will make it easy to find a process using the majority of the CPU resource.

A whole host of additional columns can be added to the display. Choose View ⇨ Select Columns and check the ones you would like.

Performance tab

The Performance tab, shown in Figure 34.13, includes information about the total system's CPU and memory utilization. It shows the instantaneous, as well as a history, display, although the history only starts accumulating when the Task Manager is run.

FIGURE 34.13

You can find system performance information on the Performance tab.

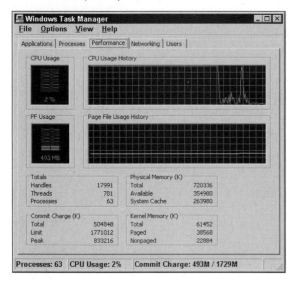

Other useful information on the Performance tab includes totals for handles, threads, and processes that are running, as well as physical (the total amount of memory on your server), kernel (memory used by the operating system), and commit charge memory (memory allocated to all programs and the system, including virtual memory) usage.

TIP If your commit charge memory regularly exceeds your physical memory, your system is doing a lot of swapping to virtual memory, which can impact performance. In this situation, you should consider upgrading your system's RAM to improve performance.

Networking tab

The Networking tab, shown in Figure 34.14, shows you the percent utilization for your server's network connection. If your server has multiple network connections, you will see multiple graphs on this tab. Use this to determine overall utilization of the network.

FIGURE 34.14

Network performance can be traced on the Networking tab.

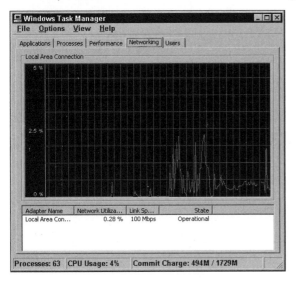

By default, the networking history graph automatically scales so that the top of the scale only shows enough to fit the maximum network peak on the graph. You can see in the graph in Figure 34.14 that there is relatively low utilization, so the graph goes from 0% to 5%. You can disable the automatic scaling on the Options menu; simply uncheck Auto Scale. Use Reset to clear the existing graphed data and start over.

Users tab

The Users tab shows you all users who are currently connected to the computer. It won't show you users connected by mapping drives, only those who are logged in via the Console, Remote Desktop, or directly onto the server's desktop.

Right-clicking on a user name gives you options for sending a message to the user (that will pop up on their screen), logging them off or disconnecting them from the server, and remote control to take control of their session. Disconnect, Log Off, and Send Message buttons are also conveniently on the main window.

Using the Performance tool

Another tool that is widely used by Windows system administrators to track performance is the Performance tool, which is known affectionately as Perfmon. Performance, shown in Figure 34.15, uses counters that are updated by various parts of the system to track usage of resources such as memory, disk throughput, network usage, application resource utilization, and much, much more. On top of all that, it can track this information over time and store it to a file to be reviewed later. You can launch Performance from the Administrative Tools menu.

Follow these steps to add counters to the graph:

1. **Right-click anywhere in the graph window and choose Add Counters.** This activates the Add Counters window shown in Figure 34.16.

2. **Make sure Use local computer counters is selected, or that the name of the server is in the box for the computer.** As you may have guessed, this setting means Performance can gather performance statistics from other computers on network. You could run Performance from a client computer on your network and point it to your server.

3. **Choose a performance object.** These cover all aspects of the system, including network, operating system resources, memory, CPU, disk performance, and utilization. If you would like to see performance stats for a particular process, you can choose Process as your performance object.

4. **Choose the counters to add to the graph.** Counters will vary depending on the performance object that you choose. You can choose one, or many, or all. Hold down the Control key while selecting in order to choose more than one. You can click the Explain button to get more information on a particular counter.

5. **Choose an instance.** This will also vary depending on the performance object you choose. For instance, if you are monitoring a process, you will choose that process here. If you are monitoring physical disk performance, you will choose the disk or disks.

6. **Click the Add button to add the counters to the graph.**

FIGURE 34.15

You can use Performance to track many aspects of system performance.

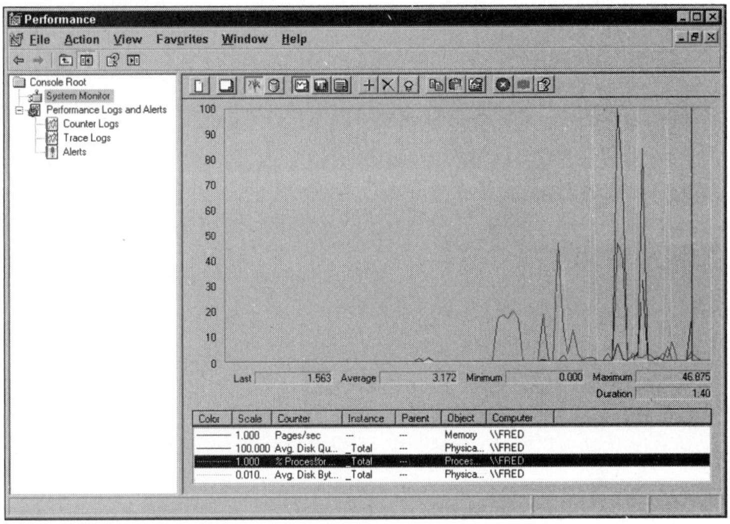

FIGURE 34.16

You can add counters to monitor all aspects of system performance.

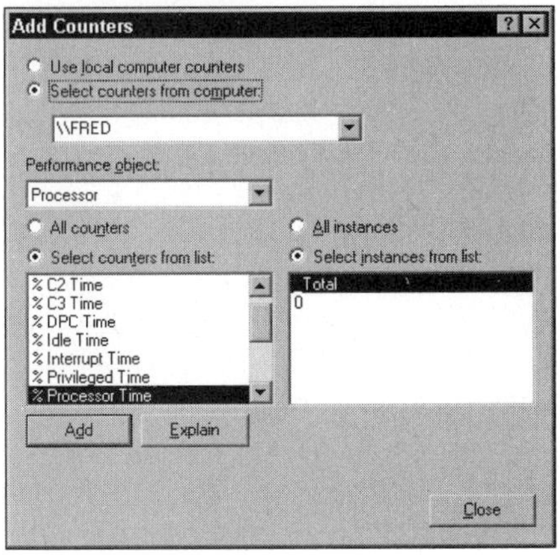

You can change the properties of the performance monitor by right-clicking on the graph and choosing Properties. This lets you edit various settings for the graphing element of the counter, including colors, titles, whether to display a graph or a histogram and several other features. You can choose whether to display the graph from real-time data or from a captured log file.

Speaking of capturing to a log file, you can do that with the Counter Logs item on the left side of the performance monitor screen. Click the Counter Logs item. Any existing counter logs will be displayed in the pane on the right. Create a new log by following these steps:

1. Choose Action ⇨ New Log Settings.

2. Give your log a descriptive name.

3. **Choose objects and counters to be logged.** These are the same items that you can log in real time in the graph display.

4. **Choose an interval to sample the counters.** The default is once every 15 seconds.

5. Click the Log Files tab.

6. **Click a file type.** The default is a binary file, but you can choose from various text formats (which can be imported into Excel or a database to be manipulated).

7. **Choose a prefix to use for the filenames.** The default is a simple numeric counter, but you can choose date/time options as well.

8. Enter a comment if you like.

9. Click the Schedule tab.

10. Choose a start date and time for the logging, or choose manual start.

11. Choose an end date and time, or choose manual stop.

12. **If you like, specify a command to be executed when a log file is closed.** This could be a batch file or a script that copies the log file somewhere.

13. Click OK to complete the log.

You can load log files into the graph view later using the Properties window, on the Source tab.

ON the WEB Are you confused by all of the Performance settings and options? Microsoft has a Performance Monitor Wizard that can simplify setting up log capturing for commonly used counters. You can download it here: `www.microsoft.com/downloads/details.aspx?familyid=31fccd98-c3a1-4644-9622-faa046d69214` or search Microsoft.com for "Performance Monitor Wizard".

Optimizing Performance

Being able to view performance information is one thing, but in order to make the system perform better, you may need to make some adjustments to server settings. Some simple things that you can change are related to memory usage. You can change how virtual memory is utilized as well as how memory is optimized depending on the expected primary usage for the computer.

Adjusting performance options

There are several performance options that you can adjust in the System Properties dialog, which you access as follows:

1. **Right-click on the My Computer icon (you can find it in Windows Explorer or on the Start menu).** Choose Properties from the popup menu.

2. **Select the Advanced tab.**

3. **Click the Settings button in the Performance section to open the Performance Options dialog.**

There are three tabs on the Performance Options dialog — Visual Effects, Advanced, and Data Execution Prevention settings.

Visual Effects

The Visual Effects settings tab lets you choose from various visual effects for the server's desktop. For top performance on the desktop, you should disable most of these — indeed, Windows Home Server has most of them disabled by default.

Because the primary means for accessing Windows Home Server is via the Console, these settings are going to be irrelevant for the most part.

Advanced

The Advanced settings tab, shown in Figure 34.17, is where the meat of the performance option settings is. You can adjust processor scheduling and system memory usage depending on the usage of the server; the choices are for best performance of programs, or best performance of background options and the system cache. As you will not be running many programs other than background services on Windows Home Server, you should leave these settings at the default values of background services (for processor scheduling) and system cache (for memory usage).

To change Virtual Memory settings, click the Change button in that section. We describe Virtual Memory settings in the next section.

Data Execution Prevention

Data Execution Prevention (DEP) is a feature designed to prevent malicious code, such as viruses, from executing code from memory that has been designated as non-executable, a common tactic. The default setting for Windows Home Server is to utilize DEP for all programs and services, and we suggest that you leave that setting enabled. However, if an application is causing problems, you may want to try disabling DEP for it to see if it is resolved. On the Data Execution Prevention tab, click the Add button and browse for your program's executable file to block it.

FIGURE 34.17

The Administrative Tools menu contains utilities for managing your server.

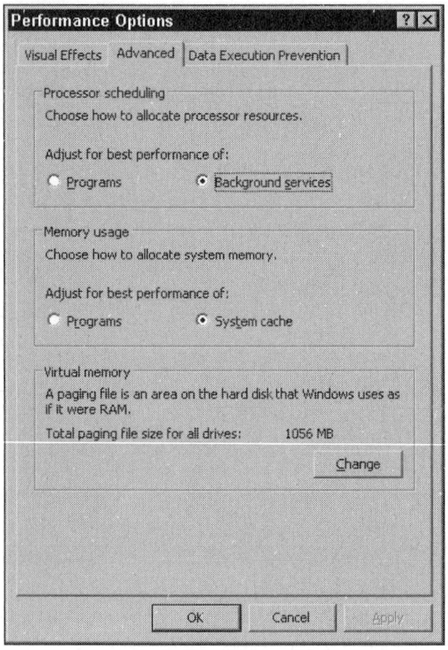

Modifying Virtual Memory settings

Tweaking Virtual Memory settings, shown in Figure 34.18, accessible by clicking the Change button on the Advanced tab of the Performance Options dialog, can be a simple way to boost performance.

Windows Home Server only includes a paging file (swap file) for the system partition, and the minimum size is set to 1.5 times the size of your system memory by default.

In general, you can leave the paging file at the recommended size — however, if your server has a limited amount of memory and you want to install additional server applications, you may wish to increase this value closer to the maximum size.

If you would like the system to automatically grow the paging file as memory usage overtakes it, you can select the system-managed size. It is not recommended to disable the cache for the system drive unless you also create one on a different drive, and as long as it's not a drive that's included in your Windows Home Server storage pool.

FIGURE 34.18

You can tweak Virtual Memory settings to improve performance.

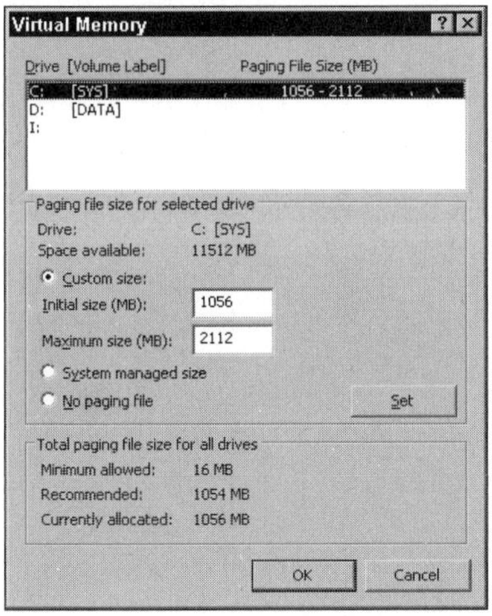

Optimizing network memory usage

You can configure memory usage by the networking components of Windows Home Server. This allows you to optimize your server for the usage profile that fits it best, either as a file server or an application server. To choose a setting, follow these steps:

1. **Open the Network settings dialog, by choosing Start ⇨ Control Panel ⇨ Network. Connections.** You may have to right-click on Network Connections and choose Open.

2. **Right-click on the Local Area Connection icon and choose Properties.**

3. **Select the File and Printer Sharing for Microsoft Networks item and choose Properties.** This opens the window with the Server Optimization settings, shown in Figure 34.19.

The default setting is to Maximize data throughput for file sharing, which you might expect for Windows Home Server's main function of acting as a file server. If you intend for your server to act more as a server for network applications, such as IIS Web, media streaming, or perhaps as a Sharepoint or mail server, you may want to choose the Maximize data throughput for network applications item.

The Minimize memory used setting is another one you can try. This setting is intended for use by servers that have less than ten clients attached to them, and usage of Windows Home Server generally falls into this category.

You can adjust memory usage based on anticipated network utilization of the server.

All in all, you may want to simply experiment with these settings to make the most of server performance for your particular usage. Trial settings followed by monitoring with performance counters for a day or so can tell you if the setting changes are having any effect on performance.

Summary

Even though Windows Home Server is designed and intended to be managed from the Console, there are a number of occasions in which it pays to log on to the server's desktop and dig into the Windows settings behind the scenes. You can use the administrative tools to do a number of server maintenance tasks and performance tweaks to get the most out of your system. Many of these items are available in the Administrative Tools menu available in the Control Panel.

The Computer MMC is a collection of tools for managing your computer. You can manage users and groups, defragment disks, and even manage disks that are to be used outside of the Windows Home Server storage pool, among other things.

You use the Services console to start and stop Windows services, those programs that run in the background performing services for your system. If a Windows Home Service stops unexpectedly, you can try restarting it in this console, or investigating why it failed in the event log.

You can use an event log to investigate the cause of errors from both the system and from applications. Windows Home Server adds a custom event log for its own applications to use, making it easy to view any errors or other unexpected actions that may occur with these programs.

You have two choices for performance monitoring built in to Windows Home Server. The performance monitoring available on the Task Manager will give you basic information on memory, processor, and network usage. If you want to go beyond this, however, you can use the Performance Monitor utility to gather all sorts of statistics on all aspects of the server's functionality.

Finally, if you are willing to experiment a bit, you may be able to gain some performance increases on your system by tweaking memory settings, including the virtual memory page file size and the network memory usage settings.

This is a lot to cover in a single chapter; however we hope that you now have at least some idea of the types of tools that are available on the server to maximize system potential.

Chapter 35

Building a Home Web Site

Do you sometimes feel that you're the last person in the world to have a presence on the World Wide Web? It does seem that just about everybody who is remotely tech savvy has a Web site or a blog to share with the world. You may or may not feel the need for all that, but maybe you just want to be able to share family photos with friends and relatives on a modest Web site that you control.

Or, maybe you do have a Web site or blog already, but you want to set up a secondary site to try new things out. Maybe you just want a private site for the family to be able to share information, sort of like a virtual refrigerator door.

Whatever your reason, you don't have to want it any longer, because your Windows Home Server has a built in Web server (Internet Information Services, or IIS) that is a powerful engine for hosting sites ranging from simple single page sites to full-blown ASP.NET Web applications.

With a little bit of work, and perhaps with a Web site builder software package, to assist you, you too can host a Web site on your own Windows Home Server.

In this chapter, we'll give you a tour of the IIS management console, and show you how the default Web sites provided with Windows Home Server (Home and Remote Access) are configured. We'll also show you how to make changes to these sites, and how to go about adding your own sites.

> **NOTE** Not every Internet Service Provider (ISP) supports or allows Web site hosting from your residential Internet account. Consult with your ISP's terms of service to see what their rules are before you decide to host a site.

Exploring the Default Web Sites

If you've played around with Remote Access, you already know that Windows Home Server has a default Web site that is accessed whenever you enter your remote access URL. In fact, Windows Home Server includes two Web sites — your Home Web site (shown in Figure 35.1) and the Remote Access Web site, which allows you to access your shared folders, the Console, and many of the client computers connected to the network. You can configure which one is accessed by default in the Remote Access settings in the Console, but no matter which you choose, you can always access each Web site by specifying their folder names in the URL:

- `http://server.homeserver.com/Home` will always access the Home folder.
- `https://server.homeserver.com/Remote` will always access the Remote folder.

> **NOTE** The Remote direct URL must always be entered as a secure URL (https). Remote access is not permitted over an unsecured (http) connection.

FIGURE 35.1

Windows Home Server's default home Web site is little more than a placeholder.

> **CROSS-REF** For information on setting up Remote Access, along with necessary router configuration, see Chapter 17.

In order to provide any sort of meaningful Web site services as a default for your URL, you'll have to add it as a third Web site option, and configure things so that the third site is the one that is accessed by default. To do that, you'll have to understand a little more about how the existing Web sites are configured in IIS. You can do this by taking a look at the settings in the IIS Manager.

Using the IIS Manager

The IIS Manager is a MMC snap-in component that is used to manage IIS Web sites. You can access it from the Administrative Tools menu, which is available from either the Start ⇨ All Programs ⇨ Administrative Tools, as shown in Figure 35.2, or via the Control Panel.

FIGURE 35.2

The IIS Manager is available from the Administrative Tools menu.

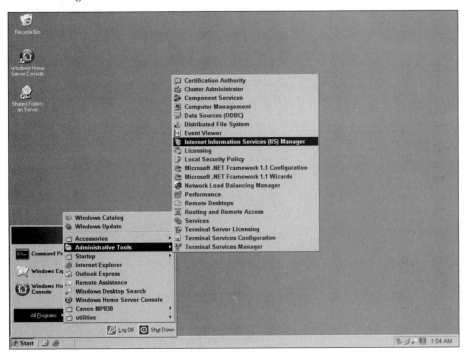

IIS Manager, shown in Figure 35.3, presents the structure of the IIS configuration as a tree view, with the local computer at the root of the tree, and three folders underneath it. The three folders are

- **Application Pools:** These provide a way to configure ASP.NET component parameters. Web sites can use the default application pool, or provide their own custom one. Windows Home Server uses custom application pools for some of the Web application components it needs.

- **Web Sites:** The Web Sites section contains all of the stand-alone Web sites on the server. All HTTP requests to the server will be directed to one of these sites. Windows Home Server includes a Default Web Site, which redirects to either the Home or Remote folders depending on the default setting, and a site called WHS (Windows Home Server) site, which is used by the client Connector software for its own needs.

- **Web Service Extensions:** This folder shows a list of Web Service extensions, which provide different ways of executing server-side code for Web applications. You can use this section to enable or disable specific extensions.

FIGURE 35.3

IIS Manager presents the structure of the server's Web and sits in a tree view.

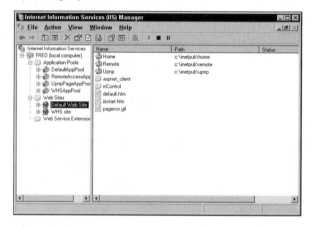

You may be wondering how IIS knows which Web site to open when you make a request. As we just pointed out, there are two Web sites, a Default site and the WHS site used by the Connectors. The answer lies in the propeties for each of the sites.

Right-click on the Default Web Site, and choose Properties to bring up the Web Site Properties dialog, shown in Figure 35.4. The default site is configured to use port 80 as its TCP listening port, and port 443 for the SSL (secure socket layer) port. These are the standard ports used for Web server requests, so any call using your server's remote access URL (that is, `http://server.homesever.com`) without specifying a port will go to this site.

If you look at the WHS Site, you will see that it is configured to use port 55000 as its Transmission Control Protocol (TCP) port and port 56000 for SSL. The Connector software that needs access to this application is hard-coded to know these port numbers. The Connector's requests specify that port number (that is, `http://server:55000`), and IIS will have that site handle the request. In this way, IIS can host multiple true Web sites all at once.

Web sites are configured to answer on a specific port. This one is using the standard ports 80 and 443.

Viewing the Home and Remote Access sites

Looking under the Default Web Site entry in IIS Manager, you can see folders for the Home and Remote sites. These are not actually stand-alone sites of their own, but instead are *virtual directories*. Virtual directories are so-called this because their actual physical presence on the disk is not necessarily in the same hierarchy that they appear to be in IIS. There is a third virtual directory, named Upnp, that doesn't appear to be a site of its own. In fact, it directs you to the Remote Access login page.

Virtual directories are used to host the Home and Remote sites so that they may be accessed from the same base URL — the only change necessary to access each site is to add /Home or /Remote to the end of your fully qualified domain name, because, as we pointed out, they make up the URLs that you can always use to reach the respective sites.

How does IIS know which site to direct you to when you just enter the base URL for your site? In the home directory for the Default Web Site, the file `default.htm`, shown in Figure 35.5, tells the story. This page is loaded by default when you access your home URL. If it deems your browser worthy (it must support JavaScript), it will forward the user automatically to the home/default.aspx page instead. It passes a parameter, *gotodefault=true*, to tell the Home Web application that the user came from the default URL rather than by entering the Home prefix themselves. This is used to determine whether or not to forward the user again to the Remote Access site if it is defined as the default in the Console.

FIGURE 35.5

The `default.htm` file in the Default Web Site is loaded when you enter your remote access URL.

```
<html>

<head>
<meta HTTP-EQUIV="Content-Type" Content="text/html; charset=utf-8">
<script language="javascript">
        document.location = 'home/default.aspx?gotodefault=true';
</script>

<title ID="titletext">Navigate to public landing page...</title>
</head>

<body>
<noscript>
    <p id="JSWarningTitle"><b>JavaScript is Required.</b><br/></p>
    <p id="JSWarningText">
        JavaScript is required to use the Windows Home Server Remote Access web site.<br />
        Please enable JavaScript in your web browser and refresh this page to proceed.
    </p>
</noscript>
</body>
</html>
```

Modifying the Home Web Site

With this knowledge of the way the existing Web sites are configured in ISS, you can see that there are two ways that you can create a new personal Web site on the server. The first way is to add a new virtual directory to store the site, just as Home and Remote have their own sites. This is your best option if you wish to maintain the integrity of the existing Web sites.

The second way is to replace the Default Web site's default.htm page with your new Web pages so that all access to your remote access domain will go to your own pages.

Although both options are feasible, the best way to go is the first approach. The integrity of the existing Web sites is maintained, and any add-ins that create their own virtual directories will still function as intended.

The Home page is not really intended to be added to, but there are a few things you can do with it to customize it a bit. There are things that immediately come to mind that could be customized, beyond the Web Site Headline you can set in the Windows Home Server Console. You can change the background image, you can add links to other Web sites, and you can remove the Logon button if you like.

Replacing the Home page image

The image on the Home page is actually a composite picture used as a background — it includes the photo along with the border around it and a large section of nearly empty space to the right to reserve space for Web site links, as you can see in Figure 35.6.

If you are planning to keep the Home Web site as your launching pad, one of the things you may want to change is the background picture. You could replace the picture with a photo of your own family, or with some other photo or artwork that you like.

In order to maintain the integrity of the page, you really just want to replace the photo insert while leaving the rest of the image intact, as shown in Figure 35.7.

FIGURE 35.6

You can edit the background picture of the Home Web site to customize it.

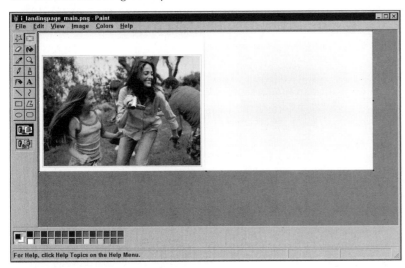

FIGURE 35.7

Paste in an appropriately sized replacement photo and drag it into place.

We show you how to do it, using nothing more than Windows Paint that is included on the server. (You can, of course, use a more advanced image-editing tool if you happen to have one.) Follow these instructions:

1. Navigate to the images folder for the Home Web site, located in `C:\inetpub\home\images`.

2. Make a backup copy of the `i_landingpage_main.png` image by copying it to `i_landingpage_main_orig.png`. This is the image you need to modify, and you want to be able to revert back to it in case you mess up.

3. Load the `i_landingpage_main.png` image into MS Paint by right-clicking on the file and choosing Edit.

4. **The photo portion of the background image is 360 x 250 pixels.** You need to locate a suitable image to replace it that is the same size. We'll cheat a bit here and assume that you have a photo ready to go at that size; however, if necessary, you can resize photos in MS Paint using the Stretch/Skew command in the Image menu.

5. Copy the new image to the clipboard (in Paint, choose Edit ⇨ Select All, followed by Edit ⇨ Copy).

6. Paste the new image into the existing background composite image, using Edit ⇨ Paste. Then, drag the new picture to the correct location.

7. **Save the background image.** You will be able to immediately see your new background image when you navigate to your home page.

Adding links

The Home page has the capability to include links to other Web sites. They can be links to other sites on your Windows Home Server, or to sites on the Internet. There is a file in the Home folder in `c:\Inetpub\home`, called `WebSites.xml`. We'll need to add links to this XML file.

Use notepad.exe to edit the WebSites.xml page, by right-clicking on it and choosing Open With, followed by Notepad. For each entry, add an XML tag similar to the following, between the <WebSites></WebSites> tags.

For sites hosted elsewhere, enter the following (with your site's information):

```
<WebSite name="Jenn's Home Page" uri="http://www.gilajenn.com"
    absolute="True" imageUrl="images/spacer.gif" />
```

For sites hosted on your Windows Home Server, enter them like this:

```
<WebSite name="Greg's WHS Page" uri="/remote" absolute="False"
    imageUrl="/home/images/spacer.gif" />
```

The key items are the Web Site name, the uri (which is either a complete URL to an external site, or a relative path from the root of the Web site.) Absolute should be set to `"True"` for external Web sites, and `"False"` for Windows Home Server hosted ones.

The spacer image listed here was only chosen because you need to specify an image, and no default image is really appropriate. You can certainly create your own icon image and place it in either the images or icon folders, and reference it here. The image you choose for an icon should be 16 x 16 pixels.

Another `WebSites.xml` file exists in the remote folder. This one works exactly the same way: if you want links to show on your Remote Access site, add them to this file.

CROSS-REF   In Chapter 32, we introduced you to a Windows Home Server add-in called Whiist. This add-in includes the ability to easily add links on both the home and remote pages, including the ability to upload icon images or use a default one. We highly recommend that you use it rather than edit the `WebSites.xml` file directly.

Removing the Logon button

If you're like us, you dislike the fact that a Logon button to gain access to the private section of your Web site is located on your public facing home page. We feel that its presence is just a little too tempting for someone to try to gain access to your server, and it would be best if it wasn't there at all. After all, we know how to get to the Remote Access page directly.

The simplest way to hide the logon button is to alter the home page's style sheet. Follow these steps to do this:

1. Navigate to your `C:\inetpub\home` **folder in Windows Explorer.**
2. **Edit the file css.css by right-clicking on it and choosing Open With, followed by Notepad.**
3. **Search for the style named .buttonLogon.**
4. **Add another line to this style, stating** visibility: hidden, **as shown in Figure 35.8.** Don't forget to add a semicolon to the end of the previous line.
5. **Save the file.**

FIGURE 35.8

You can hide the logon button just by changing its style.

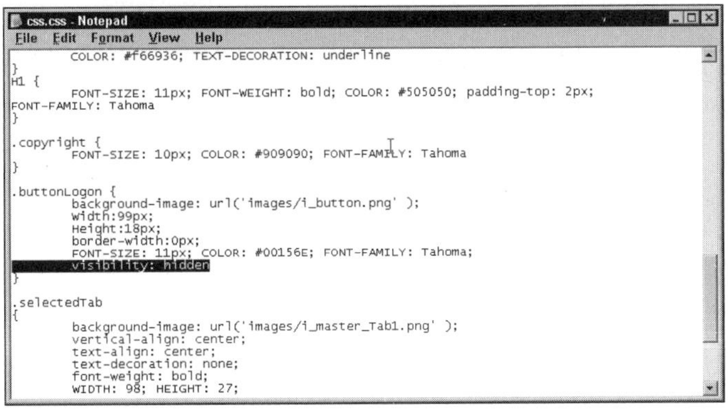

Now that you've made several changes to your home page, take a look at it in the browser. Figure 35.9 shows the changes to the default picture, the addition of the links, and the removal of the logon button. This only scratches the surface as to what modifications are possible to the home page. You can make many more changes by altering the `Default.aspx` and `css.css` files. If you go much beyond this, be sure to save the original files so that you can revert back to them as necessary.

FIGURE 35.9

The home page has been updated with our alterations.

Creating a New Web Site

Modifying the included home page is great way to quickly add some customization to your Windows Home Server Web site, but in the long run you are probably going to want to create your own Web sites with all of their content created by you. You can accomplish this simply by creating a new virtual directory to store your content.

Creating a Virtual Directory

In IIS, you can create a virtual directory virtually anywhere. Given Windows Home Server includes shared folders, we'll show you how to put your new Web site in the public share so that you can update the content from any computer you choose on the network, using virtually any Web site building tool that you can think of. Do the following to create your virtual directory:

1. **Create a folder under the public share to hold the Web site; for example,** \\server\public\mywebhome.

2. **Load the IIS Manager.**

3. **Expand the tree view, and right-click the Default Web Site.** Choose the New ⇨ Virtual Directory menu option, as shown in Figure 35.10.

FIGURE 35.10

You can create a virtual directory that points to one of your shared folders.

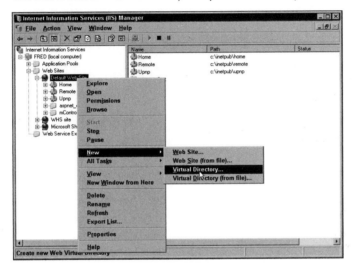

---

4. **In the Virtual Directory Creation Wizard, choose Next.**

5. **Enter an alias to use for the virtual directory, such as** my_home. This name will be used to access the directory in IIS Manager and in the site's URL. Click Next.

6. **Enter the path to the virtual directory you created in** Step 1. Click Next.

7. **Leave the security settings alone for now.** Click Next.

8. **Set access permissions for the Web site.** If you would like to use ASP scripts or execute Common Gateway Interface (CGI) on the site, check those options. We don't recommend that you check the Write or Browse options. Click Next.

9. **Click Finish.** Your new virtual directory is now visible in IIS Manager, as shown in Figure 35.11, and is accessible using your domain name followed by your site's alias; that is, http://myserver.homeserver.com/my_home.

FIGURE 35.11

Your new virtual directory is now ready for content.

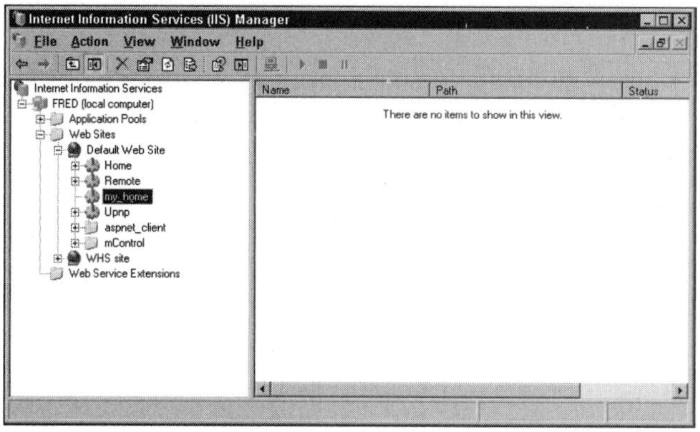

Configuring Web Site Settings

Now that you've created a new virtual directory, we'll show you some of the settings that you can apply to it. Right-click on the virtual directory name and choose Properties to open the Properties dialog box, shown in Figure 35.12.

The Properties dialog box has six tabs that are used to set various site parameters. Next, we'll take a look at them.

FIGURE 35.12

The virtual directory Properties dialog box is used to configure your site.

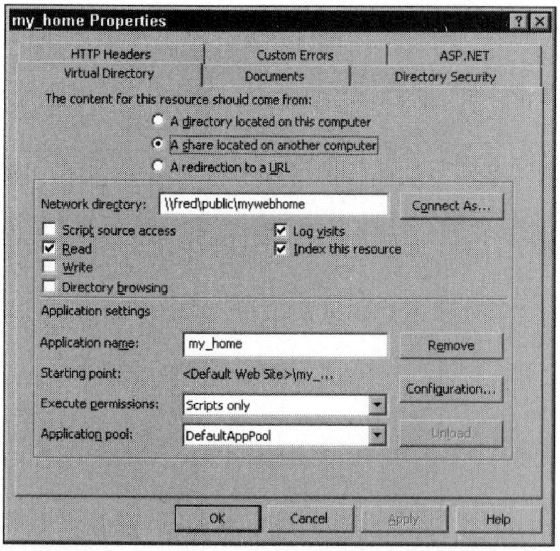

Virtual Directory tab

The Virtual Directory tab is used to set the basic parameters for your site, including the folder or URL that it points to, and the access rights.

You can set application settings here as well, which apply to this folder and any folders you create underneath it. The application name is simply the name of the virtual directory alias that you specified when creating it.

Documents tab

The Documents tab is used to specify filenames that can be used for your site's default page, which is the page that is loaded when only the folder path is entered with no filename specified.

By default, any of the following filenames can be used: `Default.htm`, `Default.asp`, `index.htm`, `iistart.htm`, and `Default.aspx`.

Filenames with an ASP extension tell the server that they should be processed by the Active Server Page engine for server side scripting. ASPX files use the ASP.NET engine.

You can specify a footer file on this tab. The footer file should contain Hyper Text Transfer Protocol (HTML) tags necessary to create the footer, not an entire HTML document.

Directory Security tab

The Directory Security tab, shown in Figure 35.13, is used to specify security settings for the Web site. If you don't want this Web site to be publicly accessible, you can use this tab to control who has access to the page.

FIGURE 35.13

The virtual directory Properties dialog box is used to configure your site.

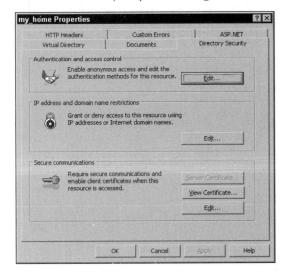

You can set the following items:

- **Authentication and Access control:** Click the Edit button to set the authentication method for the site. The default is anonymous access; however, you can disable this and set a different option. Integrated Windows Authentication is your best bet, followed by Basic Authentication. Either of these options will require the user to enter a valid Windows Home Server user ID and password in order to access the site.

- **IP address and domain name restrictions:** You can use this setting to restrict access to a single computer or to a group of computers. Use this if you would like the site to only be accessible from inside your home network by selecting the Denied access radio button and entering your network's base Internet Protocol (IP) address and subnet mask.

- **Secure communications:** You can use this option to require the use of a secure (HTTPS, or Hyper Text Transfer Protocol Secure) connection in order to access the site. This setting is used by the Remote virtual directory to restrict access to Remote Access to the HTTPS channel, and you can require the same for your site if you like.

HTTP Headers tab

You use the HTTP Headers tab to set advanced options for Web page headers. Headers are sent as part of the HTTP response, and contain information used to specify expiration settings for Web pages, content ratings, custom headers, and MIME types for files that you may allow to be downloaded.

Custom Errors tab

This tab lets you specify the pages that are displayed in response to an error. You can use this to customize the response to a 404 error (page not found) or other HTTP errors.

ASP.NET tab

You specify ASP.NET features on this tab. You can choose the ASP.NET framework version to use and the default locations for the site. These will not need to be changed for the most part, unless you install an ASP.NET application that requires a specific version of the .NET framework.

Modifying the default.htm page

If you would like your new Web site to be used as the default that people see when they visit your site, you will need to modify the default.htm page located in the `C:\Inetpub\wwwroot` folder. Navigate there using Windows Explorer, and open the file using Notepad.

This page uses JavaScript to redirect users to the site's home page. Normally, it is directed to the home/default.aspx page, but you can change it to any other page on your site that you like. Comment out the line where `document.location` is set, by putting double slashes at the beginning of the line. Then, create a new `document.location` line pointing to your site's main page relative to the site root, as shown in Figure 35.14.

FIGURE 35.14

You can modify the default.htm page in order to automatically direct viewers to your new site.

Using Web Site Building Tools

Some people like to create Web pages by hand, using nothing but Notepad, but we don't recommend that you do this for anything but the simplest of Web sites. There are a number of applications on the market that can lend a helping hand in Web site creation, by providing page templates, WYSIWYG (What You See Is What You Get) editing, and support for features such as CSS (Cascading Style Sheets). These tools are available at a wide range of price points as well. A few that you may want to look at are

- **Microsoft FrontPage:** Although this has been discontinued, it is still pretty easy to find and can be a good way to get a site up fast.

- **Microsoft Expression Web:** The replacement for FrontPage, this package harnesses the power of the .NET Framework to generate advanced content.

- **Visual Web Developer Express Edition:** Visual Studio is Microsoft's development platform and Integrated Development Environment (IDE) for all types of application development, including for the Web. The Express editions are free to download and use. Visual Studio 2008 is expected to make use of the Expression Web engine to improve its abilities in creating client-side content.

- **Adobe Dreamweaver:** This venerable utility has an easy-to-use HTML editor, and can create content with a wide range of backend technologies. This package is a professional Web site builder tool and probably overkill for the type of site you may create for Windows Home Server.

If you are on a tight budget, there are some good freeware tools available that can help build a Web site:

- **CoffeeCup Free HTML Editor:** Although their newest HTML editor is modestly priced, you can download a free version that has some of the more advanced features removed. You can download a trial version of the full editor to see if the additional features are worth the money for you. Download the free version from `www.coffeecup.com/free-editor`.

- **SeaMonkey (Mozilla Composer):** SeaMonkey is a Web browser suite from Mozilla that includes a mail and newsgroup client, a Web browser, and a WYSIWYG HTML editor. The HTML editor includes Get more information about SeaMonkey at `www.seamonkey-project.org`.

- **Nvu:** Pronounced N-view, this package is a standalone WYSIWYG editor based on Mozilla Composer, with even more features. Learn more at `http://nvudev.com/index.php`.

Creating a Web site in Expression Web

Web site creation processes will differ somewhat depending on which Web building application you choose, but many of the concepts will be the same. We'll show you how to get started creating a Web site using Microsoft's Expression Web program.

Expression Web is Microsoft's new Web designer application, replacing the old FrontPage program. Rather than rely on extensions, as FrontPage did, Expression is integrated with Microsoft's .NET Framework, although it is focused on building client-side pages rather than server-side ones as Visual Web Developer is designed to do.

To create a new Web site in Expression Web, all you have to do is open the folder that you created when you built your virtual directory, add new HTML files, and add your content to them, as shown in Figure 35.15.

Building the Web site

To create your site, use the File ⇨ Open Site menu item and browse to or enter the folder name that you created in the previous section. Recall that you added this to a shared folder, so you'll specify the complete server path name that you set up, `\\server\Public\mywebhome`.

Expression Web now knows about your Web site, and now you can begin adding pages. You'll start with a single home page based on a template, and see how it looks in the browser. Follow these steps to add a default page:

FIGURE 35.15

Creating a new Web site in Expression Web is as easy as opening the folder in which it is located.

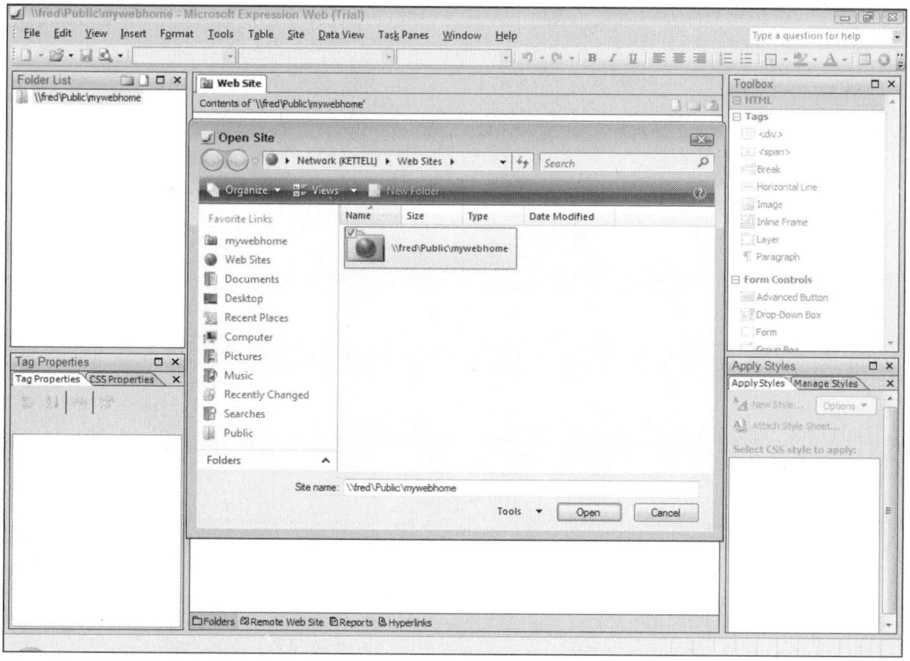

1. **Right-click on the Folder List window, and choose New followed by HTML.** Accept the default page name of default.htm.

2. **Double-click on `default.htm` in the folder list to open the page in the editor.**

3. **Enter some HTML content.** In order to test the Web site, you don't need to add much — just some text is fine.

4. **Save the page.**

You are ready to view your first Web page created for Windows Home Server. If all went well, you should be able to enter your custom domain URL in the browser and see the page, assuming you changed the main site's `default.htm` file to point to your virtual directory. Otherwise, append your virtual directory's alias to the end of the URL. Figure 35.16 shows our simple page being displayed.

FIGURE 35.16

A view of our first Web page in Windows Home Server.

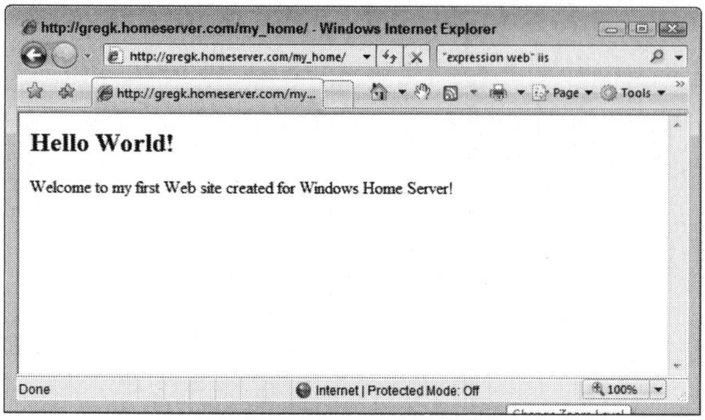

Summary

Whether you are a veteran Web developer with an established presence on the Web, a neophyte just looking to get started in learning Web development, or just someone who wants to share her family photos to friends and relatives on the Internet, Windows Home Server's built-in Web server and dynamic domain abilities mean that you can use it for your own modest Web sites hosted from your home. Although you don't want to use it to host massive Web communities with thousands of users, due to bandwidth restrictions that your ISP likely has, small sites limited to a few users are ideal.

Windows Home Server uses Microsoft's venerable IIS Web server, and can be configured using standard IIS tools, including the IIS Manager. With the IIS Manager, you can create new Web sites, create virtual directories, and configure settings for all of them to tailor your site for your own needs.

You don't have to create a Web site from scratch, because Windows Home Server provides two — a Home landing page, which you can customize somewhat to look exactly the way you want, and a Remote Access site, the more secure pages used for accessing your shared content from the Internet. Both of these sites are hosted in their own virtual directories underneath the server's default Web site.

To create a new site, you simply create a new virtual directory pointing to a folder on one of your shared folders, say Public. This will make it easy for you to add Web pages to your site from just about any Web development tool that can save files to a network share.

Chapter 36

Programming Windows Home Server Add-ins

Throughout the course of this book, we've introduced you to a wide variety of Windows Home Server add-ins. They do everything from managing streaming media to helping you create a Web site. They manage your home automation system and they upload your pictures to online photo sharing sites. It seems that the sky's the limit when it comes to extending Windows Home Server with add-ins.

Now, do you want to know a secret? Many, if not most, of the add-ins that we've described in this book weren't created by teams of programmers working for a corporation. They were created by hobbyists and entrepreneurial programmers who were inspired by the power and extensibility of Windows Home Server and decided that they wanted to be a part of extending it.

Cost is no barrier to entry when it comes to creating add-ins, either. You can use Microsoft's Visual Studio Express Edition, a free-to-use version of their venerable professional Visual Studio development package along with some libraries to provide Windows Home Server application program interface (API) functions.

While add-ins are not difficult to create, you will find that a knowledge of programming, and Windows programming, in particular, will be very helpful. That goes for when you're reading this chapter and, especially, when you decide to try your hand at creating your own add-ins.

Introducing Visual Studio Express Edition

Starting with Visual Studio 2005, Microsoft decided that they should release free versions of their full-blown Visual Studio development tools in order to encourage hobbyist development and learning, and this has continued with Visual Studio 2008. The Express editions are available as individual language installations — you can choose to download C#, Visual Basic, J#, C++ — whichever languages that interest you. You can, however, download and install them all if you prefer.

Choosing a language

The beauty of Microsoft's .NET framework is that it is language agnostic. Whether you prefer to develop in C++, J#, Visual Basic, or C# doesn't matter much when it comes to developing .NET applications, as they all utilize the same underlying framework and compile into the same intermediate language. This makes choosing a language a matter of choice more than anything.

The two most popular languages for .NET development have been C# and Visual Basic, because programmers have migrated to the platform from two different directions. Java and C++ developers tend to prefer the syntax of C#, as it more closely matches those other languages. Old Visual Basic hands feel more comfortable with VB.NET. Because they are all interoperable for the most part, everybody wins.

For this chapter, we present the example using C#.

Installing Visual C#

The first thing you are going to want to do is download and install the Visual Studio 2008 Express version of the language that you feel most comfortable with. The Web installation consists of a small initiator file that performs the installation, downloading files from the Web as necessary. If you prefer, you can also download a stand-alone installation of any of the Express languages and burn them to a CD. Each language installation is all-inclusive, with all of the framework code necessary for development in that language. If you'd like to play around with all of the languages, there is even an all-inclusive DVD image with all of the languages on it. Choose your desired method, download it, and install it. Figure 36.1 shows the Visual C# 2008 Express Edition setup in progress. For our example, we don't need any of the extras, such as SQL Server or the MSDN library, but you can choose to install them for your own perusal if you like.

 You can download the Visual Studio 2008 Express Editions from `http://msdn2.microsoft.com/en-us/express/aa974184.aspx`.

NOTE   In case it isn't clear, download Visual Studio to one of your home computers, not to your Windows Home Server machine.

Obtaining the Windows Home Server SDK DLLs

In addition to the basic development tools, you need to obtain copies of the Dynamic-Link Libraries (DLLs) necessary to enable you to develop for Windows Home Server. The two files are

- `HomeServerExt.dll`

- `Microsoft.HomeServer.SDK.Interop.v1.dll`

We don't have to look far to find these two files — they're right on your Windows Home Server computer, in the `C:\Program Files\Windows Home Server` folder. Copy them to the computer that you've installed Visual Studio on. You can create a folder for them if you like, just don't lose track as we'll point Visual C# to it soon.

FIGURE 36.1

All necessary files are downloaded from the Web during installation.

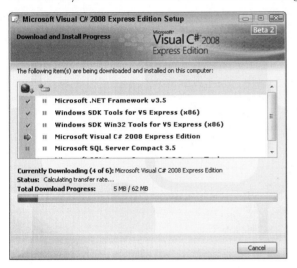

Creating an Add-in

Now that you have Visual C# installed, and your SDK DLLs in a safe place, it's time to create a sample add-in. This add-in will create a Console tab that does nothing but display information about your Windows Home Server installation. It will, however, give you an idea of what it takes to create a minimal add-in.

NOTE In essence, add-ins are simply normal Windows programs, services, and components, and can basically do anything other programs can do by interacting with the Windows API. The characteristics that make them add-ins, however, are management from the Console and installation as an add-in Microsoft Software Installer (MSI).

Building an add-in solution

In Visual Studio parlance, a *solution* refers to the overall software application that you are building. A solution can contain one or more *projects*. A Visual Studio project is a collection of code and support files necessary to build a single component, whether a DLL or an executable. In your case, given you are creating a Console tab, you need to create a DLL.

Follow these steps to create an add-in project, and a new solution at the same time:

1. **Start Visual C# Express.**
2. **Choose File ⇨ New Project.**
3. **Select Class Library, and enter a name for the project.** Call it WHSBExample, as shown in Figure 36.2. (If you prefer, you can name it something else, just be consistent throughout this example.)

Create a new project to build your Windows Home Server add-in.

4. **Click OK.** A new solution, project, and class file is created.
5. **Choose File ⇨ Save WHSBExample.** Accept the default location for the save in your Documents folder, as shown in Figure 36.3. Click Save.

FIGURE 36.3

Save the project to create the initial files.

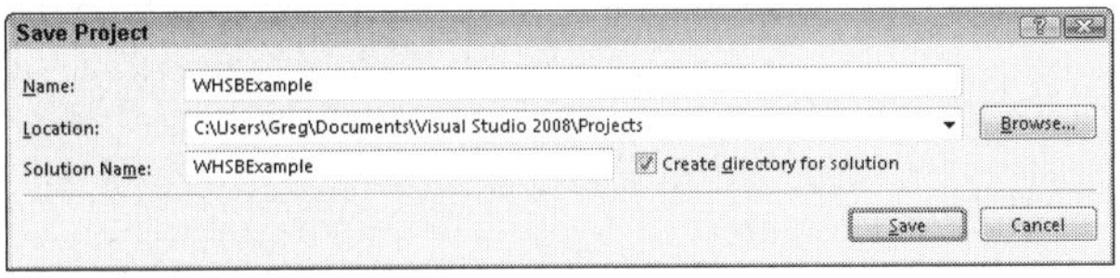

6. **Next, you need to change some properties of your project so that Windows Home Server will accept it as a Console tab add-in.** Right-click on the project name WHSBExample in the Solution Explorer, and choose Properties.

7. **Make sure the Application tab is selected.**

8. **In the Assembly name field, enter** HomeServerConsoleTab.WHSBExample.

9. **In the Default Namespace field, enter** Microsoft.HomeServer.HomeServerConsoleTab.WHSBExample. This namespace is required so that the Console will recognize your DLL as a Console tab.

10. **Change the Target Framework to .NET Framework 2.0, as that is what you have on the Windows Home Server box.** Visual Studio will need to save the project at this point; when you come back to it, the Application properties page should like Figure 36.4.

FIGURE 36.4

You must change the project properties in order for Windows Home Server to recognize your DLL.

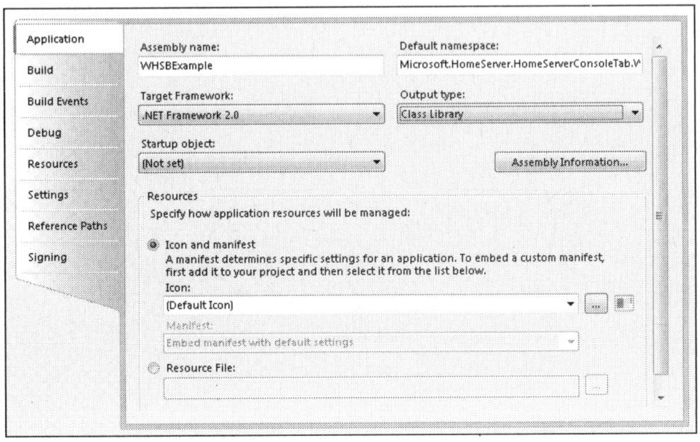

11. **While you're in the properties, add an icon to use for the Console tab.** This can be any bitmap image as long as it is 32 x 32 pixels. In a nod to vanity, we've used an image of the cover of this book, not that you can read it. Select the Resources tab.

12. **Click the link to create a default resources file.**

13. **Click the drop-down arrow to the right of Add Resource, and choose New Image ➪ BMP Image.** Name it **WHSBExampleBmp**, and click Add. Edit the image as you see fit, or copy and paste an image into it.

14. **Choose File ➪ Save All.**

Next, you'll add references to the SDK DLLs (remember them?) that you copied off of the server. This is so that when you reference them in the code, you won't get errors. Follow these steps to add the references:

1. **Right-click on the References item under the WHSBExmple project, and choose Add Reference, as shown in Figure 36.5.**

2. **Click the Browse tab.**

3. **Navigate to the location that you saved the SDK DLLs.**

4. **Select both of them, as shown in Figure 36.6, and click OK.**

5. **Add references to the** `System.Drawing` **and** `System.Windows.Forms` **objects as well.** You can find them on the .NET tab of the Add Reference window.

6. **You have one class file so far in your project.** You will need a class named `HomeServerTabExtender` for the Console's benefit, so rename it to that. Right-click on the filename and choose Rename.

7. **Save the solution by choosing File ➪ Save All.**

That's the basic solution and project. You have your basic solution, project, references, and resources defined. It's not quite a Console tab yet, but you're getting closer.

Creating a Console tab

In the previous section, you created a solution and a project for your simple add-in project, and now it's time to fill in all the pieces to make it functional.

You'll create the body of the Console window that is displayed underneath the tab from a User Control, which is essentially a container that can hold other controls. To create the user control, right-click on the project in the Solution Explorer (WHSBExample), and choose Add ➪ User Control. Name the control **WHSBConsolePanel** in the Add New Item dialog, as shown in Figure 36.7.

FIGURE 36.5

Use the Solution Explorer to add references to necessary SDK DLLs.

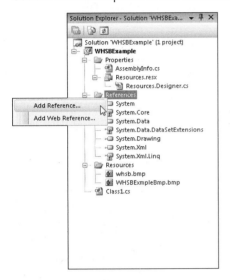

FIGURE 36.6

Add references to the two key Windows Home Server DLLs.

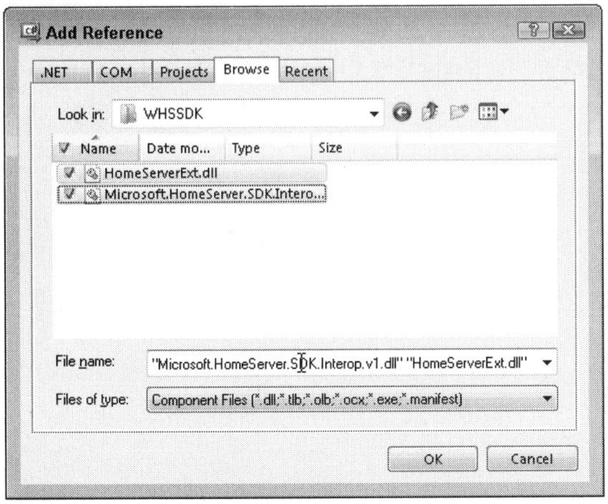

FIGURE 36.7

Create a user control to serve as the body of your add-in's Console tab.

Now, you'd like to have your Console tab actually do something. As this is a short example, we've just added a rich text box and used it to fill in some information gleaned from Windows Home Server objects. Follow these steps:

1. **Expand the user control using the resize handles on the right and bottom.**

2. **Add a rich textbox control by expanding the Toolbox icon on the left of the screen, and double-clicking the RichTextBox item.**

3. **If the Properties windows is not open, press Alt+Enter to open it.**

4. **Set the following properties: Modifiers = Internal; ScrollBars = Vertical; ReadOnly = true; Size = 400 by 300.**

5. **Also in the Properties window, set the (Name) property to rtInfoBox.**

6. **Choose File ➪ Save All.** Figure 36.8 shows the current status of your Console tab.

FIGURE 36.8

You've created a user control with a rich text box to use as the body of your Console tab.

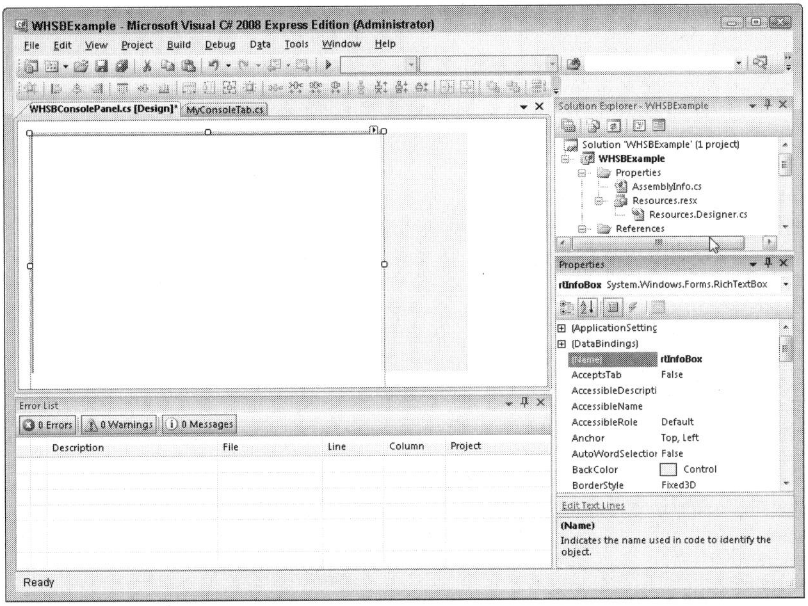

Now that you've added a user control and a rich text box, you need to add some code to populate it with data. Right-click on the `HomeServerTabExtender.cs` and choose View Code to open the source code editor.

Implementing HomeServerTabExtender

In order for your Console tab to work properly, your class for your `HomeServerTabExtender` class must implement the IConsoleTab interface, which means all of the methods defined by that interface need to be defined in the code for the class. Here are the steps involved in building your `HomeServerTabExtender` class.

Add new using directives

The first step is to add the using directives for the packages you added as references. These are added to the listing right after the existing directives, and are shown in Listing 36.1.

LISTING 36.1

Add the new using directives

```
using System;
using System.Collections.Generic;
using System.Text;
using System.Drawing;
using System.Windows.Forms;
using Microsoft.HomeServer.Extensibility;
using Microsoft.HomeServer.SDK.Interop.v1;
```

Set the namespace

The Console expects this class to be in the
`Microsoft.HomeServer.HomeServerConsoleTab` namespace in order for it to be recognized as a Console tab. You need to append the name of your own Console tab, WHSBExample, to the end of that. Listing 36.2 shows the new namespace name. Use this in place of the existing default namespace.

LISTING 36.2

Set the namespace

```
namespace Microsoft.HomeServer.HomeServerConsoleTab.WHSBExample
{
```

Add the HomeServerTabExtender class

Replace the existing class definition with one for a class named `HomeServerTabExtender` that implements the IConsoleTab interface. The name must be exact for the Console to recognize it.

You'll also define some of your class private variables here:

- **IConsoleServices services:** This will be used to hold the `IConsoleServices` object that is passed in to the constructor. You aren't going to do anything with it in this example, but you could use it to do such things as open the Settings dialog to a particular page, launch help, or open the default browser to a specific URL.

- **WHSBConsolePanel panel:** This panel is the object that implements your Console interface; that is the rich text control you added earlier.

- **WHSInfoClass whsInfo:** The `WHSInfo` class is used to return information reported and tracked in the Console, including computers, users, and storage information.

Listing 36.3 contains the new class and variable definition.

LISTING 36.3

Define the new class name and class private variables.

```
public class HomeServerTabExtender : IConsoleTab
{
    private IConsoleServices services;
    private WHSBConsolePanel panel;
    private WHSInfoClass whsInfo;
```

Add the constructor

The *constructor* is a special method that is called when the object is being initialized. A constructor always has the same name as its class. The constructor is typically used to allocate and initialize class member variables.

Given you are going to be displaying a list of client computers and their statuses, you'll populate the panel in this method for lack of a better place at this time. Listing 36.4 shows the complete constructor.

LISTING 36.4

Create a constructor

```
    public HomeServerTabExtender(int width, int height,
                            IConsoleServices consoleServices)
    {
        // Initialize data
        panel = new WHSBConsolePanel();
        panel.Size = new Size(width, height);
        services = consoleServices;
        whsInfo = new WHSInfoClass();

        // populate the panel
        string sPanelText = "Windows Home Server Bible\n";
        sPanelText +=      "------------------------\n";
        sPanelText +=      "Client computer info:\n";
        Array arComputerInfo = whsInfo.GetClientComputerInfo();
        foreach (IComputerInfo info in arComputerInfo)
        {
            sPanelText += "Name:" + info.ComputerName + "; Desc:" +
                    info.Description + "; Online:" + info.IsOnline + "\n";
        }
        panel.rtInfoBox.Text = sPanelText;
    }
```

Add properties

In C#, *properties* are special class members with publicly accessible get (and sometimes put) methods. These properties must be implemented by any class that implements IConsoleTab (see Listing 36.5). The classes include

- `string TabText`: Returns the text that will be displayed on the Console tab itself.
- `Bitmap TabImage`: Returns the icon that is displayed on the tab.
- `Control TabControl`: Returns the user control that holds your tab panel implementation.

LISTING 36.5

Add the new using directives

```
// Returns the text used for the console tab.
public string TabText
{
    get
    {
        return "WHSB Example";
    }
}

// Returns the image used for the tab icon
public Bitmap TabImage
{
    get
    {
        return Properties.Resources.WHSBExmpleBmp;
    }
}

// Implement tab control property. Returns the control used for the tab.
public Control TabControl
{
    get
    {
        return panel;
    }
}
```

Add additional methods and properties

There are a couple additional methods and properties that you need to implement for IConsoleTab, but you aren't going to make use of them for this project:

- bool GetHelp: This method is used to indicate whether your tab has custom help content to display when the F1 key is pressed. You don't need it for this project, so you'll just return false.

- Guid SettingsGuid: If you were implementing a Settings tab, you'd return a Guid (Globally Unique Identifier) to associate this tab with it. Because you are not, you'll just return an empty Guid.

Listing 36.6 shows the implementations for these two items.

LISTING 36.6

GetHelp and SettingsGuid

```
// Implement GetHelp
public bool GetHelp()
{
    return false;
}

// Implement SettingsGuid
public Guid SettingsGuid
{
    get
    {
        return Guid.Empty;
    }
}
```

When you put it all together, you get the listing in 36.7 — the complete implementation of your HomeServerTabExtender.

LISTING 36.7

Code listing for HomeServerTabExtender.cs

```
using System;
using System.Collections.Generic;
using System.Text;
using System.Drawing;
using System.Windows.Forms;
using Microsoft.HomeServer.Extensibility;
using Microsoft.HomeServer.SDK.Interop.v1;

namespace Microsoft.HomeServer.HomeServerConsoleTab.WHSBExample
```

continued

LISTING 36.7   *(continued)*

```
{
    public class HomeServerTabExtender : IConsoleTab
    {
        private IConsoleServices services;
        private WHSBConsolePanel panel;
        private WHSInfoClass whsInfo;

        public HomeServerTabExtender(int width, int height,
                                     IConsoleServices consoleServices)
        {
            // Initialize data
            panel = new WHSBConsolePanel();
            panel.Size = new Size(width, height);
            services = consoleServices;
            whsInfo = new WHSInfoClass();

            // populate the panel
            string sPanelText = "Windows Home Server Bible\n";
            sPanelText +=       "------------------------\n";
            sPanelText +=       "Client computer info:\n";
            Array arComputerInfo = whsInfo.GetClientComputerInfo();
            foreach (IComputerInfo info in arComputerInfo)
            {
                sPanelText += "Name:" + info.ComputerName + "; Desc:" +
                        info.Description + "; Online:" + info.IsOnline + "\n";
            }
            panel.rtInfoBox.Text = sPanelText;
        }

        // Returns the text used for the console tab.
        public string TabText
        {
            get
            {
                return "WHSB Example";
            }
        }

        // Returns the image used for the tab icon
        public Bitmap TabImage
        {
            get
            {
                return Properties.Resources.WHSBExmpleBmp;
            }
        }

        // Implement tab control property. Returns the control used for the tab.
        public Control TabControl
```

```
    {
        get
        {
            return panel;
        }
    }

    // Implement GetHelp
    public bool GetHelp()
    {
        return false;
    }

    // Implement SettingsGuid
    public Guid SettingsGuid
    {
        get
        {
            return Guid.Empty;
        }
    }
    }
}
```

Building the DLL

Now that you have the code in place for your sample add-in, you need to build it to generate the DLL file that will ultimately wind up installed on Windows Home Server. Choose Build ➪ Build Solution (shown in Figure 36.9) to compile your source files and generate the DLL. The Error List window shown at the bottom of the screen lets you know of any syntax or other errors that you may need to correct.

Creating a deployment package

Congratulations, you have created a Windows Home Server add-in, although a fairly trivial one. The only thing left to do is to package up the DLL into a MSI file that can be installed like any other add-in.

Unfortunately, where the free developer tools fall apart is in their capability to create installer packages. You're going to have to resort to doing things manually from here on out.

FIGURE 36.9

Use the Build menu to compile your code into a DLL.

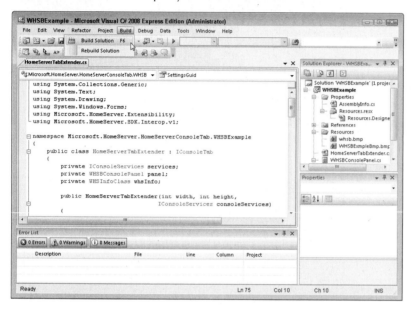

Download WiX

WiX, for Windows Installer XML, is a free MSI generator program that can integrate well with Visual Studio, with the exception of the Express editions.

Download the WiX core toolkit from http://wix.sourceforge.net/downloadv2.html. You only need to download the binaries, unless you are interested in looking at the source as well. The Votive application will not work with the Express versions of Windows Studio, so you won't be able to take advantage of them.

Once you've downloaded, unzip to a safe location, and add the folder to your path. To add to the path, follow these steps:

1. Choose Start, right-click on Computer (Vista) or My Computer (XP), and choose Properties.

2. In the Properties windows, click the Advanced tab.

3. Click the Environment Variables button.

4. Scroll down the list of system variables, and select the Path item.

5. Click Edit. Append the path where WiX is now located, as shown in Figure 36.10.

Create a WXS file

WiX uses XML as the basis for creating its MSIs. While the syntax of the overall XML is well beyond the scope of this chapter, the documentation that comes with WiX explains the attributes and tags adequately. Listing 36.8 contains our `WHSBExample.xsw` file.

FIGURE 36.10

Enter WiX to your path to ensure that it will work everywhere.

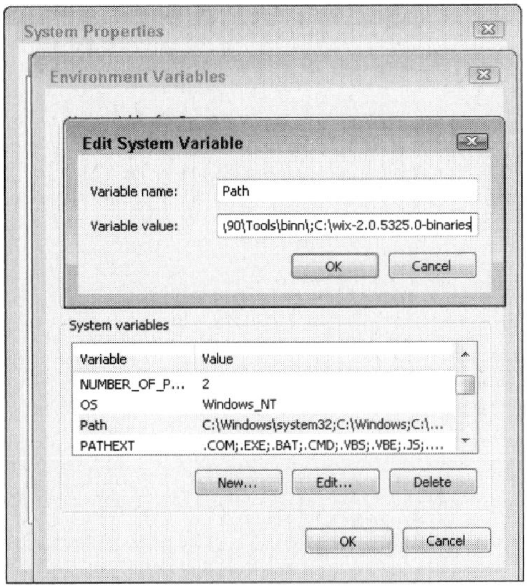

ON the WEB Need a quick GUID or two? Visit www.guidgenerator.com and you can generate up to a hundred at a time!

LISTING 36.8

Our WHSBExample XSW file

```xml
<?xml version="1.0" encoding="utf-8"?>
<Wix xmlns="http://schemas.microsoft.com/wix/2003/wi">
  <Product
    Name="My Windows Home Server SDK Sample"
    Id="d382dae4-5b69-4309-9431-e9aae527cd08"
    UpgradeCode="de8aebab-630d-4d72-9f5b-07a807d33c85"
    Manufacturer="Windows Home Server Bible"
    Version="1.0.0"
    Language="1033"
```

continued

LISTING 36.8   *(continued)*

```
      Codepage="1252">
      <Package
        Id="69a58be8-002f-4ce3-ad83-3f4b6a0d45c8"
        Manufacturer="Your Company"
        InstallerVersion="200"
        Platforms="Intel"
        Languages="1033"
        Compressed="yes"
        SummaryCodepage="1252" />
      <Media Id="1" EmbedCab="yes" Cabinet="WHSBExmple_cab" />

      <Property Id="WHSLogo">1</Property>

      <Condition Message="[ProductName] requires Windows Home Server. For more
   information, please refer to the User Guide.">VersionNT = 502</Condition>

      <Directory Id="TARGETDIR" Name="SourceDir">
        <Directory Id="ProgramFilesFolder" Name="PFiles">
          <Directory Id="WHS" Name="WHSgrp" LongName="Windows Home Server">
            <Component Id="HomeServerConsoleTab.WHSBExample.dll"
   Guid="5780814f-2308-4ba9-a897-aa6b47e992ee">
              <File Id="HomeServerConsoleTab.WHSBExample.dll" Name="Example.dll"
   LongName="HomeServerConsoleTab.WHSBExample.dll"
   Source="..\WHSBExample\bin\release\HomeServerConsoleTab.WHSBExample.dll"
   Vital="yes" KeyPath="yes" DiskId="1"/>
            </Component>
          </Directory>
        </Directory>
      </Directory>

      <Feature Id="DefaultFeature" Level="1">
        <ComponentRef Id="HomeServerConsoleTab.WHSBExample.dll" />
      </Feature>
    </Product>
  </Wix>
```

To use the WXS file, copy it to the project directory (typically under your `Documents\Visual Studio 2008\Projects` folder. Then, do the following:

1. **Open a command prompt.** Click Start and enter **cmd** and press Enter. (In XP, enter **cmd** after choosing Run.)

2. **Change to the directory that your project is located in.** In Vista, it will typically be under `c:\users\<USER>\Documents\Visual Studio 2008\Projects\WHSBExample\WHSBExample`.

3. **Run the following command:** `candle WHSBExample.wsx`.

4. **Follow it up with the command** `light WHSBExample.wsx`, **as shown in Figure 36.11.**

FIGURE 36.11

Use WiX on the command line to generate an MSI file.

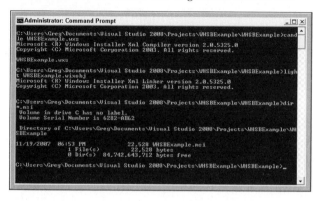

If the MSI file was generated, you may now copy it over to your `\\server\software\add-ins` folder, and then install the add-in via the Console. As a parting shot, Figure 36.12 shows the add-in that we just created running in the Console.

FIGURE 36.12

Our add-in running in the Windows Home Server Console

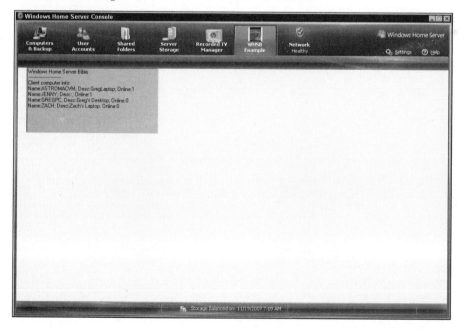

Summary

Microsoft Visual Studio 2008 Express is a great way to begin programming Windows applications of all types. The interchangeability of the core .NET languages makes it safe to choose just about any one of them for your programming as it will be able to interoperate with code written in C#, Managed C++, J#, and more.

Writing Windows Home Server add-ins is not altogether difficult — well, the code for the add-in specific code isn't difficult, in any case. It's all based on the .NET Framework, and as long as you name things properly, it's hard to go wrong. The example given in this chapter may not do a whole lot, but it can form the basis for a real add-in that can display information about a running service or a collection of objects in a database. The Console simply provides a common interface that all programs that call themselves Windows Home Server add-ins should make use of.

Index

Symbols and numerics

A